Shakespeare AND THE LAW

Shakespeare AND THE LAW

A CONVERSATION AMONG DISCIPLINES AND PROFESSIONS

Edited by BRADIN CORMACK, MARTHA C. NUSSBAUM, and RICHARD STRIER

THE UNIVERSITY OF CHICAGO PRESS

Chicago and London

The University of Chicago Press, Chicago 60637

The University of Chicago Press, Ltd., London

© 2013 by The University of Chicago

All rights reserved. Published 2013.

Paperback edition 2016

Printed in the United States of America

25 24 23 22 21 20 19 18 17 16   2 3 4 5 6

ISBN-13: 978-0-226-92493-9 (cloth)

ISBN-13: 978-0-226-37856-5 (paper)

ISBN-13: 978-0-226-92494-6 (e-book)

DOI: 10.7208/chicago/9780226924946.001.0001

Library of Congress Cataloging-in-Publication Data

Shakespeare and the law : a conversation among disciplines and professions / edited by Bradin Cormack, Martha C. Nussbaum, and Richard Strier.

    pages   cm

    "This collection emerges out of a conference on 'Shakespeare and the law' held at the University of Chicago in spring 2009"—introduction.

    Includes bibliographical references and index.

    ISBN 978-0-226-92493-9 (cloth : alkaline paper) —

    ISBN 978-0-226-92494-6 (e-book)—

    ISBN 0-226-92493-9 (cloth : alkaline paper) —

    ISBN 0-226-92494-7 (e-book)   1. Shakespeare, William, 1564–1616—Knowledge—Law—Congresses.   2. Law in literature—Congresses.   3. Shakespeare, William, 1564–1616—Criticism and interpretation.   I. Cormack, Bradin, editor.   II. Nussbaum, Martha Craveh, 1947– editor.   III. Strier, Richard, editor.

    PR3028.S533 2013

    822.3'3—dc23

2012029394

♾ This paper meets the requirements of
ANSI/NISO Z39.48-1992 (Permanence of Paper).

CONTENTS

BRADIN CORMACK, MARTHA C. NUSSBAUM,
and RICHARD STRIER

INTRODUCTION

SHAKESPEARE AND THE LAW

Shakespeare's Law

Shakespeare's most famous character offers us a striking entry into the question of how Shakespeare responded to the law and legal systems he lived under. Standing at the edge of a grave whose tenants are being evicted to make room for a new owner,[1] the prince picks up a skull (not the famous one) and, supposing it to belong to a lawyer, meditates on the law and its limitations:

> There's another [skull]. Why may not that be the skull of a lawyer? Where
> be his quiddities now, his quillities, his cases, his tenures and his tricks?
> Why does he suffer this mad knave now to knock him about the sconce
> with a dirty shovel, and will not tell him of his action of battery? Hum!
> This fellow might be in 's time a great buyer of land, with his statutes, his
> recognizances, his fines, his double vouchers, his recoveries. Is this the
> fine of his fines, and the recovery of his recoveries to have his fine pate
> full of fine dirt! Will his vouchers vouch him no more of his purchases,
> and double ones too, than the length and breadth of a pair of indentures?
> (Hamlet 5.1.93–103)[2]

Hamlet's punning questions about the law's means and ends pull the audience in two directions at once, away from the law but also, in complex ways, toward it. The satire strikes first—the spate of legal terms and Hamlet's articulation of the gap between the knowledge and practices that make the lawyer what he is and the place (literally) where that fancy technical knowledge ends up. The lawyer is satirized for his schemes to get, presumably, as much land as possible and also, more directly, for forgetting how fleeting the world and its rewards are. This is a common forgetfulness, but the lawyer's work puts him in a special relation to it. His *voucher*—a voucher is a guarantee to title in land transactions—emblematizes untrustworthiness generally because, as a legal document, it embodies the whole process of substituting formal instruments for the "real" bonds between persons that would make such things unnecessary.[3] In this register, legal agreements are the mark of a fallen world. But the

1

more technical and amusing reason that the lawyer's voucher can stand for the instability of worldly promises is that the voucher was familiar in Elizabethan common law chiefly as a legal fiction used "collusively by a vendor and purchaser" in the conveyance of land that could otherwise not be sold; and according to the fiction, it was precisely the *failure* of the vouchee (standing for the vendor) that allowed the purchaser to take possession.[4] The voucher was useful in a common-law case because everyone involved recognized that it was not going to be a guarantee at all. In this sense, Hamlet's insistence that the legal voucher is empty (because it must ultimately betray the lawyer) responds to the fact that the voucher was *already* emptied out in contemporary law—and its emptiness is precisely what made it useful.

If Shakespeare's exposure of the law's guarantee as differently fictive thickens the satire, it also has the contrary effect of pulling the engaged audience toward the law's ingenuity in achieving its ends, with the law absorbing some of Hamlet's scintillating capacity to make words do extraordinary things, sometimes against themselves. The prince's jab at his imaginary lawyer shows Shakespeare inviting the audience to judge the law's turns and tricks but also to linger in the inventiveness of its forms.

The technical playfulness in Hamlet's take on lawyers identifies a first point about Shakespeare's dramatic representation of English law. As the essays in this volume variously demonstrate, a gesture in the plays that may at first look like a simple allusion to a legal concept or practice often points to a deeper engagement with how legal professionals organized the world, whether in relation to the law's technical workings or its underlying premises or its social effects. Even when Shakespeare seems merely to be decorating his dialogue with some legal word he has picked up (no specialist he!), Shakespeare is capable of great precision in his understanding of how law works and what it is for.

Hamlet's mockery also helps us think about Shakespeare's legal thinking in a second way. The speech compactly indexes the various registers or modes in which the law existed. First and foremost, the law was a *practice* or activity, a set of actions undertaken by various institutional actors (e.g., common lawyers, canon lawyers, common-law judges, ecclesiastical judges, sheriffs, bailiffs, jurors, jailers, clerks, scriveners) for the ordering of society. Hamlet's bookish lawyer acts in the law's way, a point emphasized through the satirical comparison of the gravedigger's battery as one kind of action (primary, direct) and the law's battery as another kind (secondary, indirect). Second, the law was a body of *doctrine*, rules and norms that shifted over time as lawyers and judges, in different venues, worked either to fit the law to changes in society or to manage more efficiently (and ever more ingeniously) the problems confronting them. Third, the law functioned as an *idea* or, better, a cluster of ideas: if in one respect law was the very image of justice, it could also be seen, in Hamlet's way, as an imperfect vehicle in an imperfect world, at best a workable substitute for the unreachable ideal and at worst a machine to cover unethical behavior. Fourth, the law was recognizably a *profession*, by Shakespeare's time a main route to social and political advancement. As such, the law was a site both for nationalist pride (with the common lawyer taking the role of protector of English liberties) and for intense resentment (with the lawyer taking the role, as in Hamlet's portrait, of self-interested and mercenary scoundrel). Finally, as a *discipline*, the law was one of the learned disciplines, a kind of knowledge, along with theology and medicine, whose textual method and transmission were essential to its identity as knowledge. When Hamlet lists the instruments that allow the lawyer to become a "great buyer of land," he is pointing to one of the law's most distinctive characteristics: the law that interests Shakespeare was made on paper and on parchment, and it was transmitted, like his own plays before and after their performance, in writing and in books.

Across his work, Shakespeare responds to the law in each of these registers—as a practice, a body of rules, an idea, a profession, and a discipline.[5] As attested to by a number of recent collections on Shakespeare and law, and on law in early modern literature generally, the law is everywhere in Shakespeare's plays. This is because, most simply, it was everywhere in his culture.[6] It was there in the common-law courts and at the Inns of Court (from which the early modern stage drew an important part of its audience and some of its authors);[7] in the church courts and the municipal courts;[8] in the schools and the traditions of forensic rhetoric transmitted there;[9] on the streets and in the home; on summons and writs and in contracts;[10] in the all-important documents for conveying property or, alternatively, limiting its alienation in the future;[11] in books and the emerging notions of property in them;[12] in current ideas of the state;[13] in the consolidation of England's interests on the ocean and vis-à-vis its international neighbors;[14] and in the sense of self and of relation that people carried into their conversations and within themselves.[15]

The passion of Elizabethans for law was impressive compared even to present-day American litigiousness, one estimate suggesting that toward the end of Queen Elizabeth's reign an English population of around 4 million persons was involved in 1 million actions per year.[16] One plausible cause of this extraordinary litigiousness in the culture (and certainly an ongoing effect of it) was that, especially in the wake of the Reformation and the ascent of the common law in the polity, English law was becoming the dominant institution for the production and regulation of social relations. In Elizabethan and

Jacobean England, there was no way around law, and if Shakespeare's contemporaries were burdened by the law's constraints, they also found exciting the law's distinctly modern way of organizing their society. (We may note here that it is no accident that, apart from Shakespeare's plays and poems, most of what makes up his "documentary life" consists of legal documents or their equivalents—in fact, on the basis of the records, Shakespeare's legal transactions *are* his life.)[17]

The law gets into the plays in many ways—as a theme, as an element of characterization, as a structure in the plots. In relation to each of these, we are likely to remember, first, the great trials and quasi-trials that take place on Shakespeare's stage—in *Leontes v. Hermione* (*The Winter's Tale*), in *Shylock v. Bassanio* (*The Merchant of Venice*), in *Rex v. Catherine* (*Henry VIII*), and in *Rex? v. Daughters* (quarto *King Lear*). The law is no less memorably present in the harsh judgments that sometimes get Shakespeare's plots going—as when, in *The Comedy of Errors*, a stranger is condemned to death for traveling to the wrong city and for not having money on hand to avoid the penalty, or when, in *Measure for Measure*, a man is condemned to die for sleeping with his (at least) betrothed. And of course the law is present in Shakespeare's representation of its subordination to political interests, as at the beginning of *Henry V*, where legal interpretation is called on to rationalize Henry's military designs on France. As these different examples suggest, and as several essays in this volume attest, a crucial aspect of Shakespeare's representation of legal process and legal thinking is his emphasis on the legal system's rigid and sometimes foolish formalisms. The effect of this emphasis is that the plays concerned with law can seem not just to try legal questions (whether in the stage courtroom or, more generally, in the special forum that the play itself is) but also to try the law itself.

Law and Literature

While the essays collected in this volume are contributions most immediately to an area of Shakespeare studies, they may also be seen as contributions to a branch of legal scholarship known as the law-and-literature movement. This movement, which was initially closely associated with the University of Chicago Law School, started in the early 1970s, when courses in law and literature began to be offered at a few U.S. law schools. A founding contribution was James Boyd White's *The Legal Imagination*, first published in 1973, when White was on the faculty of the University of Chicago Law School, teaching courses like the one out of which this book emerged.[18] At a later date, Richard A. Posner's *Law and Literature*, first published in 1988 when he was regularly teaching law and literature courses at the University of Chicago Law

School, became one of the movement's most widely influential works.[19] A third Chicago connection to the law-and-literature movement was Martha C. Nussbaum's *Poetic Justice: The Literary Imagination and Public Life*, a book published in 1995, shortly after she joined the University of Chicago Law School faculty.[20]

The number of law-and-literature courses being taught in the United States has increased exponentially since the 1970s. "Law and Literature" is now, in one form or another, a recognized part of the American legal curriculum. The law-and-literature movement is less a monolith than a cluster of approaches—at times inconsistent with one another, at times mutually reinforcing. It includes scholars who differ in methodology and point of view and, perhaps most importantly, in their reasons for bringing literature into the study of law. One may (roughly) discern four groups. The first consists of legally informed lovers of literature, scholars (Posner, for example, and Robert Ferguson)[21] who, noting that legal studies have become increasingly interdisciplinary over the years, with influences from economics, philosophy, psychology, history, and sociology, seek to add literature to the conversation. These scholars have no specific viewpoint to propose and no specific discontent with existing legal scholarship. Posner's approach, for example, stresses chiefly the differences between literary and legal interpretation, differences that for him limit quite strictly what literature and law can bring to each other. In a similar vein, the literary and legal scholar Stanley Fish has emphasized that law, as a formal textual system, involves rhetorical ends that are specific to itself and justified by the exigencies of practice.[22] A second group of scholars (Nussbaum, for example, and White, and Robin West),[23] noting the dominance of economic approaches to legal analysis, argue that important elements are missing from such analyses and that engagement with literary works may supply some of those missing elements—for example, an attention to the affective dimensions of the process and rhetoric of adjudication. These writers challenge the hegemony of economic approaches to law. Scholars such as Richard Weisberg and Peter Brooks are similarly interested in reminding lawyers of the importance to legal thought of the kind of qualitative analysis that literary works exemplify.[24] A third group of scholars, working primarily within literary studies, have noted the close historical relation between literary production and legal culture and education, and they have argued that the study of literary texts can be enriched by attention to their legal and legal-rhetorical contexts, just as our understanding of law can be enriched by attention to moments in legal culture when literary texts were not so far removed from legal ones as they are now.[25] A fourth group of scholars, working in both literature and law, feel that the present legal conversation lacks a set of radical challenges to the political status quo and that attention to literary texts, especially through the lens of postmodern interpretive methods, can help legal academics and professionals construct a more radical mode of analysis. (This last approach, closely associated with the "critical legal studies" movement in legal scholarship, is not represented, except indirectly, in the present collection.)[26]

Among the Disciplines

This collection emerges out of a conference on "Shakespeare and the Law" held at the University of Chicago in spring 2009. While it is not a volume of proceedings, most of the essays included here originated at the conference; the roundtable with which the volume concludes is an edited version of an event that took place there. The conference was organized by three scholars connected to the university but who have quite different professional profiles: Martha C. Nussbaum, a philosopher who teaches in the Philosophy Department as well as at the Law School; Richard Posner, a sitting U.S. appellate judge (Seventh Circuit) who was a full-time faculty member at the Law School from 1969 until 1981 and remains a lecturer there; and Richard Strier, a professor in the English Department. The aim of the conference was to extend work the three of them had been doing in a cotaught seminar on Shakespeare by bringing together literary scholars who work on Shakespeare and law, literary scholars who work on Shakespeare generally and could be induced to think about law, philosophers with an interest in law, law professors, and practicing judges. We were fortunate in the final category to welcome a sitting member of the U.S. Supreme Court, Justice Stephen G. Breyer, and a colleague of Judge Posner's on the Seventh Circuit, Judge Diane Wood. We were eager to be as inclusive as possible in our disciplinary and professional reach.

Of course, as every scholar in the field discovers, the breadth and intensity of Shakespeare's engagement with law makes comprehensiveness of treatment impossible. What our volume aims to do is to present a series of studies that together suggest, in relation to Shakespeare but with a view to work in law and literature generally and sometimes to current political thinking and jurisprudence, a partial map of a highly generative and multivalent field of inquiry. It should be noted up front that while the volume is interdisciplinary and interprofessional in orientation, the essays proceed from particular and distinct disciplinary and professional perspectives rather than from a shared hybrid perspective. The philosophers talk like philosophers, and the three different kinds of philosophers talk like different kinds of philosophers; the judges talk like (and as) judges; the legal scholar talks like a legal scholar doing literary criticism; and the literary critics talk like (different kinds of) literary critics.

The result is a series of encounters or conversations around some quite general questions pertinent to the study of law in Shakespeare. In the spirit of the roundtable that concludes the volume, these conversations are intended to be collegial and good-humored but not necessarily harmonious or even harmonizable. In matters both of method and of particular interpretations, we have left our disagreements in place, including those that may reflect disciplinary protocols and those that are, in fact, just disagreements, unrelatable to institutional or disciplinary considerations. Our aim in leaving our disagreements in place is to engage the reader in something like the way the conversations engaged us. Consequently, some conversations are explicit, while others are waiting, we hope, to be constructed by the engaged reader. If the volume ends up raising more questions than it answers about Shakespeare's highly productive relation to law, we cannot imagine that to be a problem.

Part 1 introduces the volume by offering some useful frameworks for approaching our topic. It begins with a challenge posed by Daniel Brudney, an analytic philosopher working in the fields of both moral philosophy and aesthetics. Brudney draws a sharp contrast between the ways in which literary works establish their authority and solicit interpretation and the ways in which legal writing, including statutes and judicial decisions, does these things. Brudney claims that a literary work takes much of its authority simply from how it is written, from its specific words and their arrangement, while a legal text derives its authority from something outside itself, its "style" being irrelevant to its authority. In other words, a literary text's authority derives from its aesthetic quality while a legal text's authority derives from its role in a particular social and political system. Brudney points his readers to *Macbeth*, a play in which Shakespeare offers an unusually clear picture of the difference between morally legitimate authority and effective power. If a reader pays attention to what the play says on these matters, that is testimony for Brudney to how powerful the drama and writing is. In line with his account of the literary text as essentially an aesthetic object, Brudney argues that the role of the literary critic is to induce in the reader a powerful and consistent awareness of an aspect of a text, whereas the role of the judge, especially the appellate judge, is to come to what seems, on balance, to be the best decision without diminishing awareness of considerations to the contrary. So the practices of legal interpretation and of literary interpretation are, for Brudney, quite different.

The next essays in part 1 are by literary scholars who have worked extensively on law and Shakespeare. Each offers a perspective on law and literature that brings the fields closer together than they are for Brudney. Bradin Cormack's essay, one of several in the collection to focus on literary and legal forms, suggests that legal and literary texts are connected through their attention to linguistic differentiation, the sometimes small shifts in terms and in syntax that make both legal and literary texts effective (and even efficacious). Although literature and law remain quite distinct in their ends, Cormack argues that a poem or a play may directly meet the law by making the sometimes invisible analytical work of the law's language more apparent. Addressing *The Winter's Tale*, Cormack shows Shakespeare exploring the legal distinction between process and decision in relation to time. Turning to a different temporal category and a different genre, Cormack shows how Shakespeare's sonnets manipulate a submerged metaphysics in the concept of the legal "heir" to explore paradoxes in human emotional experience, and do so in ways that would have been recognizable to contemporary lawyers. In treating both the play and the poems, Cormack argues that moments in which Shakespeare's texts seem to be at their most "literary" or aesthetic—moments of spectacular punning, for example—may simultaneously be doing analytic work on and for the law, exposing the conceptual mechanisms, in all their weirdness, that allow the law to do its work.

For Lorna Hutson, legal and literary thinking are similarly intertwined. But where Cormack tracks these connections in relation to key words, Hutson's essay focuses on plot to ask how Shakespeare's narrative and dramatic strategies were shaped by contemporary legal developments. Placing Shakespeare's writing in the double context of rhetorical theory and sixteenth-century jurisprudence, Hutson shows how Shakespeare's plotting depends on processes of conjectural thinking that require the audience to imagine for itself aspects of the story being shown them. Hutson identifies this as a new kind of theatrical realism and associates it with rhetoric's interest in "the narrative virtue of imaginative visualization, a quality known as *enargeia* or *evidentia*." Analogous to this rhetorical effect, Hutson argues, were the inferential habits of legal inquiry demanded of justices of the peace and trial jurors. Hutson sees *Othello* as a work that explores both the costs and the gains of this conjectural culture. The play shows how rhetorical technique makes Iago's stories of Desdemona's supposed infidelity vivid and convincing to Othello. But Hutson also shows that the very same rhetorical strategies that Iago uses against Othello also foster the capacity of ordinary people to pursue justice through forensic inquiry. From the perspective of the expansion of the jury system in the sixteenth century, Shakespearean drama emerges as deeply communal in its structure and ends.

The essays in part 2 of the volume step back to ask, in relation respectively to law's forms and law's content, a more straightforward question: how much did Shakespeare know about the common law in his period? Each of them illuminates a play by recourse to developments in contemporary law. Constance Jordan addresses *Measure for Measure*, one of the plays that, naturally, is treated often in this volume. Jordan's analysis focuses on the formal and technical matter of statutory interpretation. She shows that the play, which dates to around 1604, engages not only with principles of statutory interpretation developed in the legal writings of Henry of Bracton, Edmund Plowden, Thomas Egerton, William Lambarde, and Edward Coke but also with the question of equitable interpretation. This was a question that became caught up in the broader constitutional issue of the relation between law and monarchy—a hot topic in England after James VI of Scotland's accession to the English throne in 1603. Jordan notes the striking absence of any institutional check on princely judgment in the play and sees the lack of obvious success at the end of the play as a lesson for the prince. In her reading, Shakespeare advocates rule by law or council rather than by princely discretion, and he warns the new king that some sort of interpretive guidance—other than his own conscience—will be needed to sustain a working polity.

Complementing Jordan's essay on the formal question of legal interpretation, the essay by Richard McAdams, a law professor and expert in criminal law, explores how Shakespeare exploits substantive legal doctrine in one area of the developing common law, that of criminal complicity. McAdams's essay returns us to *Othello*, a play he reads, like Hutson, in terms of the forensic character of its plot. He makes two claims for the play as a critical engagement with early modern legal culture. The first is that the play expresses the virtues of formal legal channels over private revenge as a way to deal with injury. For this argument, McAdams contrasts act 1, scene 3, which shows Othello cleared by a deliberative body of the false charge leveled against him, with act 5, which shows Othello murderously refusing Desdemona the same procedural rights that had been accorded him. McAdams's second claim concerns the peculiar weakness of Elizabethan law on the matter of accomplice liability. The audience McAdams imagines is invited to speculate, as a law student (or, as Hutson would say, a juror) might, on the legal implications of the unfolding story. In a highly illuminating section of the argument, McAdams shows how particular details in Iago's criminal behavior become legible as preemptive protection against prosecution. Like Jordan's, McAdams's essay shows how intensely Shakespeare was in dialogue with his immediate legal world. Like Hutson's essay, it shows how effectively Shakespeare could employ technical knowledge in the fashioning of a plot (in both senses) and in the fashioning of a certain kind of audience.

Part 3 of the volume inquires into Shakespeare's attitudes toward the legal systems he so often refers to and uses in his work. Two essays bring the tools of the sitting judge to bear on the trial scene in *The Merchant of Venice*. The first is by Richard Posner, a founder of both the law-and-economics and the law-and-literature movements and, as already mentioned, a sitting federal appellate judge. He takes as his assignment to rule on an imagined appeal by Shylock from the decisions dramatized in the play. Judge Posner (in the fiction and in life) thinks that Shakespeare was overly willing to allow legal maneuvering to produce an intended result while also being unwilling to present his trial as merely a triumph of legal maneuvering. Posner has little respect—much less than Shakespeare apparently does—for Portia as a lawyer. He sees her as, partly like Shylock, driven by monetary considerations. Law in Posner's Venice is seen as very much part of the commercial society it orders and serves.

In our volume, however, as in real-life appellate situations, we have more than one judge. Charles Fried, a professor at Harvard Law School who served both as solicitor-general of the United States and as a justice of the Supreme Court of Massachusetts, has written a concurring opinion to that of Judge Posner. Like Posner's, Fried's contribution views the play in a deliberately technical register. Although Fried, J., concurs with the decision of Posner, J., that Shylock did not violate the statute in using the courts to stake his legal claim, he reaches this conclusion differently. If Posner finds the law depicted in the play interesting as a commercially oriented system, Fried is interested in it strictly as a formal system. Invoking the conventions of jurisdictional accommodation, or what the early moderns called comity, Fried notes that the appellate judges are bound to follow the norms of Venice's "foreign jurisdiction" and so accept as a given the "strictness" that appears to be the defining characteristic of that "local law." According to this reading, Portia is not so much a legal trickster as an extraordinarily talented lawyer, adept at working a system in its own terms. Shylock loses not because he is outsmarted but because he doesn't have a sufficiently literalist advocate to answer back (Fried, delightfully, provides an answer). Fried follows Posner's major finding that Shylock cannot be found guilty for seeking what the law granted him, but Fried sees this conclusion as merely the logical consequence of a strictly formalist and legalistic system. At the heart of his witty essay on the technical life of Shakespeare's law is an insight into the illogic of a system that, in the world of the play, loudly proclaims the consistency of its literalisms.

Adopting a less technical approach to the question of Shakespeare's legal thought, the third and fourth essays in this section approach the plays in terms of categories and concepts that the law shapes but does not wholly control.

Like Jordan's, David Bevington's essay on *Measure for Measure* is interested in the concepts of mercy and equity. In treating these, Bevington takes a very positive view of Shakespeare's representation of law. He argues that *Measure for Measure* offers a workable and humane conception of law, a mean between the over-strictness of Angelo and the over-leniency of the Duke before his departure. For Bevington, this middle position is represented in the play by Escalus, who judges the case of Pompey carefully and wisely while simultaneously trying to help out the effective but self-undermining constable, Elbow. In Bevington's account, the middle position reflects the social virtues of a legal system grounded in equity. In that sense his essay follows Jordan's more technical analysis of equitable interpretation in relation to absolutist constructions of executive power.

In contrast to Bevington's account, Richard Strier's essay finds Shakespeare offering a much more negative view of law. Strier asks whether Shakespeare supported, in the world of the plays, even those features of a legal system that would seem most attractive and, on the surface, least controversial. Strier takes as his focus two such features of a legal system: its aspiration to impartiality and its investment in punishment. In an extended reading of *Henry IV*, part 2, Strier shows that impartiality—most clearly represented by the Lord Chief Justice and most powerfully enacted in the new king's rejection of Falstaff—is explicitly, if sometimes comically, questioned in the play, especially when it is measured against the commitment to personal allegiance and sociality for which Falstaff, among others, stands. Strier tries to show this with regard to punishment as well, focusing, in this case, on *Measure for Measure*. Strier denies that the play provides a sensible legal model and a happy legal resolution. The essay ends with some remarks on *The Merchant of Venice*. Strier sees the legal system there much as Fried does, but less approvingly; and he agrees with Posner that the system is economically and politically motivated. Unlike Posner, however, Strier (and Shakespeare as interpreted by Strier) does not consider the system so described very attractive.

The fourth part extends the essays on Shakespeare by asking how law enters into conversation with a wider politics of community, both in the plays and, for some contributors, in our own contemporary world. Kathy Eden's essay on the linguistic texture of *King Lear* adopts a topic related to Strier's and an approach similar to Cormack's. Eden shows how Ciceronian and especially Stoic ideas of community underlie the pervasive language of offices, bonds, and duties in the play. Her linguistic approach allows us to feel the presence of *munera* (gifts) within *communitas* and to notice how, in the play, that relation becomes an important standard against which the law's degeneration into legalism may be measured. Extending this observation into a philological register, Eden shows that the same concern is played out in the punning tension between *loyal* and *royal*, two terms that, etymologically and conceptually, are firmly associated with law. In her analysis of the words' relation to their own increasingly submerged histories, Eden shows how, in the course of the play, "loyalty" becomes associated with mere legality, while, almost as an effect of that word's drift from its root, "royalty" in turn detaches from legality in favor of nature. Two words that share an origin in law react to law's corruption by splitting apart as, respectively, an unnatural legalism and an extralegal nature. In this light, the play can be understood as yearning for a society in which law and nature support each other.

Stanley Cavell's essay concerns the way in which any human community, as such, is constituted by speakers, that is, by persons with the gift of linguistic expression who can exercise the gift only through recognition that other persons have it, a relation that, in Cavell's account, effectively makes us "the law for one another." He sees in *The Merchant of Venice* a play that thematizes this basic dynamic. Cavell examines two moments of legal process in the trial scene; both are moments of extreme and puzzling capitulation on Shylock's part. The first is when Shylock accedes, apparently without argument, to Portia/Balthazar's noncontextual and unlikely reading of the word *flesh* in the contract as excluding blood; the second is when Shylock agrees to the terms imposed on him in return for his not being executed. Cavell sees the first moment as one in which Shylock is brought to recognize that he did and did not mean what he said: he is forced to confront the content of his own language and to see the fantasy that his own language disguised. The second moment, as interpreted by Cavell, is one in which an exhausted Shylock essentially gives up membership in the Venetian and the human community (ironically, although Cavell does not exactly say this, through the pressure exerted upon him, nonnegotiably, to join the Christian community).

Marie Theresa O'Connor's essay, like Lorna Hutson's, concerns community in a specific historical sense. It works to connect Shakespeare's legal thinking to its immediate historical moment—in this instance to an important case at law that led to and implied a general political debate about the English or the British polity. O'Connor agrees with a number of historicist literary critics in connecting *Cymbeline* to King James's project for the union of England and Scotland and to the 1607 case of the "*post nati*" (Calvin's Case), which issued in a decision to allow persons born in Scotland after the accession of James to the English throne to hold land in England. But O'Connor reads the meaning of the Union debate and of Calvin's Case in a new way. She shows that the debate was not between pro- and anti- imperialist ideologies; rather it was between two conceptions of equality and community *within* an empire: one that saw the home or center (England) as dominant and one that saw the empire in question as fully cosmopolitan, a true Great Britain. She argues that the play favors the pro-Union vision of empire, even though this was already (by 1608) the losing side. Like Jordan, O'Connor sees Shakespeare issuing a complex message to King James, supporting James's vision of the Union but not his understanding of the basis for it in his absolute power.

If for O'Connor and McAdams Shakespeare's law is of the moment, Martha C. Nussbaum's essay reveals, with Eden's and Hutson's, the much longer historical dimension that also shapes Shakespeare's legal thinking. Because she writes not only as a historically aware philosopher but also as a public intellectual, Nussbaum's consideration of Shakespeare's engagement with law extends into the present as well as the past. Like Strier, Nussbaum focuses on a legal concept that is at once general and absolutely central. Nussbaum focuses on the very idea of the rule of law as it figures in *Julius Caesar*, where it is contrasted with the idea of rule by an absolute monarch (and here Nussbaum's philosophical essay connects with O'Connor's and Jordan's historical ones). What interests Nussbaum particularly is Shakespeare's analysis of emotion's role in the polity and in republican theory. She sees Shakespeare as presenting Brutus, committed impersonally to the rule of law rather than personally to his fellow citizens, as too purely intellectual and as surrendering the domain of emotion to Mark Antony and for that reason, inevitably, failing to move the crowd. This means that Shakespeare, in Nussbaums's view, did not allow for the possibility that emotion might bolster rather than undermine the claims of intellectual argument in republican discourse. She takes the play's representation of Brutus to be a deliberate departure from Shakespeare's sources (and a departure from historical reality). She argues that the play is, in consequence, "a misleading, even dangerous work" for suggesting that republican values will necessarily fail because they cannot tap into the world of emotion and affective loyalty. In this reading, the play reminds us, through its limitations, that the rule of law must find some way of engaging the powerful emotions that are perhaps more easily engaged by a paternalistic monarch. Calling for a "passionate republicanism," Nussbaum finds herself deeply in dialogue with Shakespeare but refusing, on philosophical and political grounds, to let him have the last word.

Our final contributor, Diane Wood, is another sitting appellate judge, a colleague of Posner on the Seventh Circuit. Wood surveys the representation of law in Shakespeare's comedies in order to ask what a contemporary judge can learn from this. Noting that the law almost always appears in these plays as overly rigorous, Wood is interested in the resources within the law for mitigating such rigor. Like Bevington and Jordan, Wood thus places the relationship between strict justice and equity, together with the role of mercy in criminal sentencing, at the center of Shakespeare's conception of legal justice. As a practicing judge, she offers a contemporary picture of equity's expression—in, for example, prosecutorial discretion, nonenforcement, and executive clemency. Wood sees the plays as offering scenarios useful to contemporary judges, sometimes in surprising ways. In her discussion of *Two Gentleman of Verona*, for example, a play that only rarely enters into discussions of Shakespeare and law, Wood posits the play's relevance to the question of immigration rights, an area of contemporary law in which "the statutes confer great discretion on the executive authorities." This is a reading of the play at which possibly only a practicing judge with a flexible literary and legal imagination could have arrived.

Wood's essay leads naturally into part 5, the concluding roundtable discussion, a feature of this book that requires special comment. Most contributors to the law-and-literature scholarship, within Shakespeare studies and beyond, have been academics, whether in law schools or in departments of literature or philosophy. A distinctive feature of the present volume is the participation of five high-ranking judges or former judges. As already noted, the contributions of Wood, Posner, and Fried offer the perspective of American judges in the twenty-first century, showing the relevance of judicial experience to the understanding of the plays and the relevance of the plays to the deliberative processes that constitute judgment. This aspect of our volume finds further expression in the roundtable, in which Justice Stephen Breyer of the U.S. Supreme Court enters into conversation with Richard Posner, Martha C. Nussbaum, and Richard Strier. Justice Breyer offers a variety of comments on the interest of Shakespeare for judges, in addition to provoking a lively exchange of views among the other participants. A fifth contributor to the discussion, who was not present during the original panel discussion, is Robert Henry, former head of the U.S. Court of Appeals for the Tenth Circuit, who is currently serving as president of Oklahoma City University.

As one might expect from a conversation among a Supreme Court justice, an appellate judge who is author of an important book on law and literature, a second appellate judge, a philosopher who has worked widely on questions of public interest, and a literary critic with deep commitments to history and theory, the conversation ranges widely. Its topics include the ghost in *Hamlet*, the place of ideas in literature, the role of disgust in legal regulation, and the nature of judicial discretion. Like the volume as a whole, the conversation is not easily summarized. Readers are invited to enjoy the conversation and to enter it in the spirit of finding their own harmonies and disharmonies among the positions and approaches represented. Readers who do so will be participating in the spirit of inquiry that this volume offers both as its organizational principle and as the source of Shakespeare's own dazzling engagement with the norms, structures, intricacies, limitations, tricks, and promise of the law.

NOTES

1. On property law in relation to *Hamlet* (and the grave), see Margreta de Grazia, *Hamlet without Hamlet* (Cambridge: Cambridge University Press, 2007), chapter 5.

2. Citations to Shakespeare in the introduction are to William Shakespeare, *The Complete Works*, ed. Stephen Orgel and A. R. Braunmuller (New York: Penguin, 2002).

3. The satire against law's formalisms for destroying the real grounds for human relation is a long-standing theme in literary encounters with the law. On the question in relation to an earlier historical moment, see Richard Firth Green, *A Crisis of Truth: Literature and Law in Ricardian England* (Philadelphia: University of Pennsylvania Press, 1999).

4. The voucher was used to break an entail. For a short account of the fiction, see B. J. Sokol and Mary Sokol, *Shakespeare's Legal Language: A Dictionary* (London: Continuum, 2004), 400–402.

5. An excellent index and guide to the legal terminology that Shakespeare uses is Sokol and Sokol, *Shakespeare's Legal Language*. For Shakespeare's voluminous response to property law, see especially Paul Clarkson and Clyde Warren, *The Law of Property in Shakespeare and Elizabethan Drama* (Baltimore: Johns Hopkins University Press, 1942).

6. Recent collections on Shakespeare include Constance Jordan and Karen Cunningham, eds., *The Law in Shakespeare* (Houndmills, UK: Palgrave Macmillan, 2007); Paul Raffield and Gary Watt, eds., *Shakespeare and the Law* (Oxford: Hart, 2008). More generally, see Lorna Hutson and Victoria Kahn, eds., *Rhetoric and Law in Early Modern Europe* (New Haven, CT: Yale University Press, 2001); Erica Sheen and Lorna Hutson, eds., *Literature, Politics, and Law in Renaissance England* (Houndmills, UK: Palgrave Macmillan, 2005); Dennis Kezar, ed., *Solon and Thespis: Law and Theater in the English Renaissance* (Notre Dame, IN: Notre Dame University Press, 2007).

7. On the Inns of Court in relation to London literary production, see Philip J. Finkelpearl, *John Marston of the Middle Temple: An Elizabethan Dramatist in His Social Setting* (Cambridge, MA: Harvard University Press, 1969). See also the essays collected in *The Intellectual and Culture World of the Inns of Court*, ed. Jayne Archer, Elizabeth Goldring, and Sarah Knight (Manchester, UK: Manchester University Press, 2011). There is a close connection between dramatic fictions and the fictive cases used in lawyers' mooting at the Inns of Court. See Karen Cunningham, *Imaginary Betrayals: Subjectivity and the Discourses of Treason in Early Modern England* (Philadelphia: University of Pennsylvania

Press, 2002), chapter 1; Karen Cunningham, "'So Many Books, So Many Rolls of Ancient Time': The Inns of Court and *Gorboduc*," in Kezar, *Solon and Thespis*, 197–217.

8. The ecclesiastical jurisdiction is not treated at length in the present volume. On Shakespeare's interest in marriage law, see B. J. Sokol and Mary Sokol, *Shakespeare, Law, and Marriage* (Cambridge: Cambridge University Press, 2003). On Shakespeare's treatment of slander and defamation, which sat between the common-law and ecclesiastical jurisdictions, see Ina Haberman, *Staging Slander and Gender in Early Modern England* (Aldershot, UK: Ashgate, 2003), esp. chapter 3 and chapters 1–2 on *Romeo and Juliet* and *Othello*; M. Lindsay Kaplan, *The Culture of Slander in Early Modern England* (Ithaca, NY: Cornell University Press, 1997), esp. chapter 4 on *Measure for Measure*.

9. On rhetoric and drama, see Joel Altman, *The Tudor Play of Mind: Rhetorical Inquiry and the Development of Elizabethan Drama* (Berkeley: University of California Press, 1976). On rhetorical circumstance in relation to equity and equitable interpretation, see Kathy Eden, *Poetic and Legal Fiction in the Aristotelian Tradition* (Princeton, NJ: Princeton University Press, 1986); Mark Fortier, *The Culture of Equity in Early Modern England* (Aldershot, UK: Ashgate, 2005), esp. chapter 4 on *Measure for Measure* and *The Merchant of Venice*. For forensic rhetoric and the literary representation of inferential thinking and proof, see Lorna Hutson, *The Invention of Suspicion: Law and Mimesis in Shakespeare and Renaissance Drama* (Oxford: Oxford University Press, 2007).

10. For Shakespeare's interest in contract law, see, for example, Andrew Zurcher, "Causes and Ends: The Fatalism of *The Comedy of Errors*," in Raffield and Watt, *Shakespeare and the Law*, 22–37. For Shakespeare's comic recasting of the fraudulent conveyance of property in *The Merry Wives of Windsor*, see Charles Ross, *Elizabethan Literature and the Law of Fraudulent Conveyance: Sidney, Spenser, and Shakespeare* (Aldershot, UK: Ashgate, 2003).

11. For property law in relation to possession and dispossession in *King Lear*, see Heather Dubrow, "'They took from me the use of mine own house': Land Law in Shakespeare's *Lear* and Shakespeare's Culture," in Kezar, *Solon and Thespis*, 81–98. On Shakespeare's treatment of uses, an early form of property trust, see Brian Jay Corrigan, *Playhouse Law in Shakespeare's World* (Madison, NJ: Fairleigh Dickinson University Press, 2004). On Shakespeare's treatment of future interests in land (such as reversions and contingent remainders), see Bradin Cormack, "Shakespeare Possessed: Legal Affect and the Time of Holding," in Raffield and Watt, *Shakespeare and the Law*, 83–100.

12. On property in relation to the institution of commercial theater and to creative labor itself, see Erica Sheen, *Shakespeare and the Institution of Theatre* (Basingstoke, UK: Palgrave Macmillan, 2009).

13. On Shakespeare's legal thinking about the state, see, for example, Constance Jordan, *Shakespeare's Monarchies: Ruler and Subject in the Romances* (Ithaca, NY: Cornell University Press, 1997); Paul Raffield, *Shakespeare's Imaginary Constitution: Late Elizabethan Politics and the Theatre of Law* (Oxford: Hart, 2010). On legal citizenship in Shakespeare, see Julia Reinhard Lupton, *Citizen Saints: Shakespeare and Political Theology* (Chicago: University of Chicago Press, 2005). For a related argument confined to *The Merchant of Venice*, see also Janet Adelman, *Blood Relations: Christian and Jew in "The Merchant of Venice"* (Chicago: University of Chicago Press, 2008).

14. On Shakespeare's *Cymbeline* and *Pericles* in relation to Scotland and international jurisdictions, see Bradin Cormack, *A Power to Do Justice: Jurisdiction, English Literature, and the Rise of Common Law, 1509–1625* (Chicago: University of Chicago Press, 2007), chapters 4 and 5; also Brian C. Lockey, *Law and Empire in English Renaissance Literature* (Cambridge: Cambridge University Press, 2006), chapter 6.

15. On Shakespeare's representation of agency and of action itself (the very stuff of drama) in relation to the law's conceptualization of intentional action in homicide and contractual promises, see Luke Wilson, *Theaters of Intention: Drama and Law in Early Modern England* (Stanford, CA: Stanford University Press, 2000), esp. chapters 1 and 4. For an extension of Wilson's argument about intentionality and action in Hamlet, see Carolyn Sale, "The 'Amending Hand': *Hales v Petit, Eyston v. Studd*, and Equitable Action in *Hamlet*," in Jordan and Cunningham, *The Law in Shakespeare*, 189–207.

16. Tim Stretton, "Women, Property, and Law," in *Early Modern Women's Writing*, ed. Anita Pacheco (Oxford: Blackwell, 2002), 40–57, at 53. Cited in Sokol and Sokol, *Shakespeare, Law, and Marriage*, 3.

17. See S. Schoenbaum, *William Shakespeare: A Documentary Life* (New York: Oxford University Press, 1975).

18. James Boyd White, *The Legal Imagination: Studies in the Nature of Legal Thought and Expression* (Boston: Little, Brown, 1973). An abridged version was published in 1985 by the University of Chicago Press.

19. Richard Posner, *Law and Literature: A Misunderstood Relation* (Cambridge, MA: Harvard University Press, 1988). The book was reissued in revised and expanded editions in 1998 and 2009.

20. Martha C. Nussbaum, *Poetic Justice: The Literary Imagination and Public Life* (Boston: Beacon Press, 1995).

21. See Robert Ferguson, *Law and Letters in American Life* (Cambridge, MA: Harvard University Press, 1984); Robert Ferguson, *The Trial in American Life* (Chicago: University of Chicago Press, 2007).

22. See, for example, Stanley Fish, "Dennis Martinez and the Uses of Theory," in Fish, *Doing What Comes Naturally* (Durham, NC: Duke University Press, 1989), 72–98.

23. See, for example, Robin West, *Narrative, Authority, and Law* (Ann Arbor: University of Michigan Press, 1994).

24. See, for example, Richard H. Weisberg, *Poethics, and other Strategies of Law and Literature* (New York: Columbia University Press, 1992); Peter Brooks, *Troubling Confessions: Speaking Guilt in Law and Literature* (Chicago: University of Chicago Press, 2000); Peter Brooks, ed., *Law's Stories: Narrative and Rhetoric in the Law* (New Haven, CT: Yale University Press, 1996).

25. On the Inns of Court in relation to London literary production, see the works listed in note 7. On law and literature in an American context, see, for example, Brook Thomas, *American Literary Realism and the Failed Promise of Contract* (Berkeley: University of California Press, 1997); Stephen Best, *The Fugitive's Properties: Law and the Poetics of Possession* (Chicago: University of Chicago Press, 2004).

26. From within critical legal studies, the work of Peter Goodrich on sixteenth-

and seventeenth-century common law has been particularly influential for law-and-literature studies in the early modern period. See, for example, Goodrich, *Languages of Law: From Logics of Memory to Nomadic Masks* (London: Weidenfeld and Nicolson, 1990); Goodrich, *Law in the Courts of Love: Literature and Other Minor Jurisprudences* (London: Routledge, 1996); Goodrich, *The Laws of Love: A Brief Historical and Practical Manual* (Houndmills, UK: Palgrave Macmillan, 2006).

PART I

How to Think
"Law and Literature"
in Shakespeare

DANIEL BRUDNEY

TWO DIFFERENCES BETWEEN
LAW AND LITERATURE

During the past thirty years, it has often been urged that there is great similarity between literary and legal texts. With both, one must understand what it is to be faithful to a text as well as what it is to engage in interpretive charity. Moreover, literary and at least some legal texts have rhetorical strategies and can be examined for their political intentions or impact. All this has led to fruitful inquiry. However, we should keep in mind that, whatever else it is, a literary text is an aesthetic object while a legal text is not. In this essay, taking my cue from that distinction, I argue for two significant ways in which literary and legal texts differ.[1]

I start with a few remarks about authority in *Macbeth*, specifically about the play's obsession with the distinction between political authority arrived at in a morally acceptable way and mere legally sanctioned and practically effective political power. These remarks will be sketchy. They are meant merely as a springboard to the theoretical issues.

§1

1. The distinction between legal and effective power and power that is morally legitimate is simple enough. The first is a condition that can be described without using normative terms and could be attained by either moral or immoral means; the second is a condition that inherently involves the attribution of a normative concept (*moral legitimacy*) and whose attainment is (usually) possible only via morally acceptable means.[2] Not surprisingly, this distinction is rife in Shakespeare's history plays. It arises every time A murders (or proposes to murder) B in order to gain the throne.[3] The distinction is there as well in *King Lear* (1604–5). Lear has yielded his power to Regan and Goneril and yet thinks he still retains something like legitimate authority; he is outraged when he is treated as if that is not the case, as if his authority has disappeared with his power.[4]

But *Macbeth* (1605) is the play where I think the distinction is thematically most interesting. The play was written at the start of the seventeenth century. A little less than a half century later, in *Leviathan* (1651), Thomas Hobbes in effect rejects the distinction. More precisely, he rejects the distinction when what is at issue is not whether one ought to try to seize power but, rather, the question of whether, if a usurper has succeeded in seizing power, the rest of us should now obey him or, instead, overthrow him on the ground that he has attained power in a morally suspect way. For that context, Hobbes's claim is that any distinction among ways of attaining effective power is, in practice, pernicious and we should obey the powers that be, however their power has been attained.[5]

This feature of Hobbes's work often goes unnoticed by philosophers who concentrate on Hobbes's discussion of the state of nature and of the covenant made there to establish a commonwealth, what Hobbes calls a "commonwealth by institution."[6] But another and more pervasive and, for Hobbes, more important way to establish a commonwealth is through a covenant with a conqueror, what Hobbes calls a "commonwealth by acquisition."[7] There, I make a covenant to obey not with my equals in the state of nature but with the conqueror himself, and moreover, with a conqueror who has me at the point of his sword. For Hobbes, this context is the source of almost all existing authority—in England, of both Stuart and Cromwellian authority, the one descending from the conquests of William of Normandy, the other from the conquests of the New Model Army. Civil peace is to be prized above all else, and this entails that effective power is self-justifying.

Perhaps Hobbes (born in 1588) knew Shakespeare's histories and tragedies. Certainly, they would not have surprised him. He had before his eyes in the 1640s the blood spilled not only by personal ambition but by religious strife. His worry was that if power was not understood to be self-justifying, there would be an endless cycle of rebellion and counterrebellion. Far better to make peace with the successful usurper.

Now, Hobbes is keenly aware that human beings can be, in fact often are, motivated by ideas more than by interests.[8] His goal is in large part to get us simply to focus on our interests, the most immediate being peace. So he would have regarded Macduff's and Banquo's concern over whether Macbeth killed Duncan as a bit of folly likely to lead to civil war—which it does.

Unfortunately for Macbeth, no one wants to make peace with him. Out of fear, Duncan's sons quickly flee. Banquo and Macduff have suspicions of Macbeth, but initially that is all. What is to be emphasized is that they assume that if Macbeth is a usurper, they have sufficient grounds and even a duty to call him to account. Moreover, Macbeth agrees. He accepts that if they believe he is a usurper, they will have good reason to resist him. That is precisely why he fears them.

2. The issue, to be clear, is between moral legitimacy and the holding of legally sanctioned and effective power. Macbeth was installed as king in the

legally proper manner. He was invested at Scone, with at least some of the Scottish nobles in attendance (2.4.31–32).[9] Legally, he is the legitimate king; legally, resistance to him is treason.[10] That said, Banquo and Macduff would not have been content to be told that Macbeth did kill Duncan but, now that he is invested, they should let bygones be bygones (Macduff, incidentally, does not attend the investment [2.4.36]). That is what Hobbes would have wanted. He would see in investment a stabilizing procedure: being invested, not deserving to be invested, is what matters. Neither Banquo nor Macduff has that attitude; nor does Macbeth. Nor, when reading or seeing the play, do we. When one of the murderers of Macduff's family and household refers to Macduff as a "traitor" (4.2.82), the word rings hollow. Whatever its legal propriety, here the term clearly has no moral force.

Hobbes would have counseled Banquo and Macduff to go about their business, and he would have counseled Macbeth to let them do so.[11] In terms of the welfare of Scotland, Hobbes would surely have been right. After all, there is little reason to think that Macbeth would have become a tyrant had he felt himself safe on the throne. What prompts his cruelty is the fear of being found not to be morally legitimate.[12] The concept of power based on some morally defensible way of acquiring the throne, on something beyond mere legality, is obviously key to the play's events. All the characters operate with this concept, and it prompts horror after horror, making life nasty, brutish (or, to alter the old joke, Scottish), and short.

3. I leave the play with a final thought. There are times when Macbeth seems unclear about his own ambition. Is it merely to have legal and effective rule over Scotland, or also to be its morally legitimate king; merely to have formally recognized power, or to have reached the throne in a proper way? Macbeth's murder of Duncan eliminates the possibility of attaining the latter. That is part of what makes Macbeth a tragic figure.

Consider Lady Macbeth's famous words, "What thou wouldst highly, / that wouldst thou holily" (1.5.20–21). This is usually taken to mean that Macbeth wants to attain the kingship, a particular end, but only by holy means. Yet, although Lady Macbeth does not see this, her words can also be taken to say that the end that Macbeth has in mind is itself a holy one, namely, to be God's *deservedly* anointed king. And to such an end, unholy means are no means at all. On this thought, a reluctance to kill Duncan is not a failure of nerve on Macbeth's part, an unwillingness to do what it takes to gain his heart's desire—an absurd idea, given his manifest martial valor. On the contrary, the point would be that regicide *cannot* gain this specific bit of Macbeth's heart's desire. Perhaps Macbeth doesn't know what to do not only because he wants power without sinning but also because he cannot separate the concept of power (of mere legally sanctioned rule) from the concept of moral legitimacy. His problem is that, at least in part, he wants to gain a specific end without committing the very sin that would necessarily thwart attaining it. A. C. Bradley remarks on "[t]hat heart-sickness which comes from Macbeth's perception of the futility of his crime."[13] This perception is said to come immediately after the murder. But why should Macbeth have an immediate perception of futility unless he cares about moral legitimacy?

Consider, too, Macbeth's frustration at not siring a line of kings. What is it that he wants for his prospective sons? Surely that they reign as and actually be the morally legitimate kings of Scotland. The desire that motivates the murder of Banquo is bound up with an understanding of royalty as power arrived at in the morally proper way—ultimately, as bound up with the thought that, as Claudius puts it (with unintended irony) in *Hamlet*, "There's such divinity doth hedge a king" (4.5.123). That's what Macbeth wants for his children.

Perhaps Macbeth hopes that the blot on the family escutcheon will fade with age. It has often been noted that time, habit, and usage can bestow moral legitimacy. However, it does take time. The first couple of generations in Macbeth's line would likely not count as morally legitimate. In at least the short term, Macbeth wants to bring about a state of affairs that his killing of Duncan makes impossible.

4. The plots of *Macbeth* and other Shakespeare plays depend on, and the texts of these plays insist on, the proposition that we take seriously the distinction between effective and even legally sanctioned power and morally legitimate political authority and that, pace Hobbes, we cannot dispense with that distinction. That prompts an obvious question. These are not actual histories but plays, bits of make-believe. Isn't it odd that we take them to be relevant to the question of whether we could really live without that distinction?

§2

1. Early in the first book of *The Republic*, Socrates and Polemarchus engage in a wrangle about the meaning of some remarks by the poet Simonides.[14] Who is right in this wrangle is less interesting than that the discussion of justice here involves arguing about what the poet said. Eventually, they leave the poet behind, but the thought remains implicit that if a thesis about justice appears in a great poem by a great poet, it has a claim on our attention. Because Socrates and Polemarchus accept that thought, they find it important to begin by interpreting the poem. As they proceed, they seem to operate with the

premise that if their interpretation leads to absurdity, the fault must be in their interpretation rather than in the poem itself.

Of course, this might be because poets are assumed to be inspired, the mouthpieces of those authoritative beings, the muses.[15] Or perhaps Socrates doesn't believe such a thing but thinks his audience does, and so, for him, re-interpreting the poem is the best debater's strategy.[16] Putting that issue aside, the point is that the authority of the poets has long been widely assumed. And despite any talk of the muses, the basis for this authority could only have been, both then and now, the power of the poet's words. As a conceptual matter, the appeal to a muse's authority must be post hoc: first someone writes what is granted to be a great poem, then the muse's inspiration is inferred. The aesthetic assessment comes first, leading to the need to find some basis for the poem's authority.

Thus we should see Socrates' eventual banning of certain poets from his ideal society as troubling not only because it curtails free speech. Certainly, Socrates' own awareness that the ban is troubling has little to do with free speech. It has to do with his awareness of the apparent authority of the poetic word, his awareness that he seems to be largely eliminating something that has authority.[17]

2. Let me dilate briefly on this thought that the aesthetically powerful word has some sort of authority. It has been a common thought, with many philosophers invoking literary texts.

First, however, I should clarify my terminology. What I will call *literary authority* obviously differs from the morally legitimate political authority that I discussed a moment ago. Most straightforwardly, the second but not the first is primarily action-guiding. Still, each is a species of a common genus. Let's say that, in general, some X has authority with respect to a proposition P (perhaps action-guiding, perhaps not) if the presence of X provides a reason to accept P or at least to take P seriously. Where we have no other reason to accept the proposition, X provides a reason; where other reasons exist, X provides an additional reason. I say nothing about the weight of the reason provided by X. (I certainly do not claim that it overrides or excludes all other reasons.) I assert merely that it has been quite common to take literary texts to have authority—that is, as providing at least some reason to accept or at least to take seriously this or that claim.

Some further clarification is in order. When I talk of literary texts, I have in mind texts of high aesthetic quality. These are not the only kind that can teach the reader, that can develop her moral understanding. *Uncle Tom's Cabin* may have changed the way many white people thought of black people. And in the early 1980s, the miniseries *Holocaust* may have newly focused many West Germans on their country's past. Such impact is far more important than, say, the development of sensibility putatively fostered by Henry James's last novels. Nevertheless, it is a common intuition that works of high aesthetic quality are morally relevant in a way that lesser works are not.[18] The intuition is not that aesthetic quality entails moral goodness. It is that such quality entails a reason to look seriously at the embedded moral propositions, including seemingly suspect ones. The thought that literary authority is at least to some degree independent of a text's moral content is why one might appeal to such authority. And that is precisely what is puzzling: how can the arrangement of words make more worthy of attention a view that, as a substantive matter, is morally suspect? How far it can do so is much debated; here, unfortunately, there is space only to register and not to address this and other puzzles about the central intuition. Note, incidentally, that the central intuition is shared by many in the law-and-literature movement: their readings of fiction focus on great works—*Bleak House*, *The Trial*, *Billy Budd*—seemingly accepting the thought that revelatory force is linked to literary quality.

I have been referring to propositions, but there is considerable dispute as to whether what we learn from literature is propositional or instead a know-how or the expansion of one's capacity for emotional and intellectual responsiveness, or perhaps other things. However, whether it would be better to take the referent of literary authority as something nonpropositional is also a topic for another day.[19]

Now, attempts to justify the *aesthetic quality intuition*, as I will call it, tend simply to restate it. The great work's "complexity" is often invoked, but bad novels can be extremely "complicated," that is, have intricate plots as well as characters with multiple traits, and to explicate the complex-complicated distinction would be, in effect, to explicate what high aesthetic quality comes to. Or one might invoke the great work's "plausibility" or "believability." It is common to say such things as that the work presents "characters not too different from you or me," or "people you might meet in real life."[20] But taken flatly, that is, as specifying certain traits, such criteria could easily be satisfied by poor-quality works. Moreover, such criteria are too narrow: who has met Don Quixote or Pantagruel? Yet taken more broadly—say, "captures the essence of a certain kind of person"—they are uninformative, empty.[21] (Incidentally, Aristotle's claim that poetry, especially tragedy, is more universal than history also doesn't help. That is a claim about genre that applies equally to good and bad instances of the genre.)[22]

Some writers assert this aesthetic-quality intuition in surprising ways. Russell Hardin, discussing the role of examples in moral philosophy, marvelously writes that "an artificial example—that is, a philosopher's hypothetical—should be especially suspect. . . . If there is a point of persuasion in using it, we should be able to find real or literary instances to illustrate our point."[23] Hardin puts literary examples, made-up examples, on the same side as real examples and opposes both to the artificial examples, the made-up examples, of philosophers. Apparently, aesthetic power can give what is made-up an authority equivalent to that of what has actually occurred.

3. Among those who write on philosophy and literature, literary authority is a relatively unexplored topic. There is much work on the cognitive status of literature, but that question concerns how we can learn anything from propositions that are, in some obvious sense, false. The proposition "One morning, Gregor Samsa woke from troubled dreams to find himself transformed into a giant cockroach" is false because Gregor Samsa never existed and so never had this rude awakening. How can a text whose propositions are false tell us anything true about the world? This is not my focus, for this question can be asked about both aesthetically impressive and aesthetically atrocious works. Of course, if one claims that the question has force only with regard to aesthetically impressive works, then one is in this essay's territory.

As I say, I take the aesthetic-quality intuition to be bedrock. I have no argument for it, yet I share it. To see its intuitive pull, imagine the following. You are a defense attorney in a capital case, and you are asking a judge to commute your client's death sentence. In your argument, you press hard that there is the possibility for redemption in even the worst offender. You consider citing a recent television adaptation of *Crime and Punishment*. But although the story line was the same as Dostoyevsky's, the script was badly written and the acting horrendous. You decide instead to cite the actual novel. Opposing counsel then gets up. She first points out that the recent television program entirely supports your view. Then she delivers a brilliant and what you concede is a very compelling reading of the novel itself, showing that, contrary to the standard view, the novel is thoroughly ironic and Raskolnikov is not the least bit redeemed. After her interpretation it will be hard to read the novel in the old way. If you feel that this new interpretation of *Crime and Punishment* at all undermines your claim with respect to the possibility of redemption—to put matters more precisely, if you wish that the great novel rather than the fourth-rate television program supported your claim—then you, too, have the intuition that something of import goes on in great works of literature and that at least part of our understanding of the moral life hangs on our interpretation of them.[24]

§3

1. I am almost ready to stake out the first difference between literary and legal texts. To do so, however, I need to introduce a distinction between two general types of authority. I will call one of them *direct authority* and the other *derivative authority*.

Some forms of authority seem to be manifest on their face, seem to derive from some intrinsic quality of the thing that has authority. Take the authority of Max Weber's charismatic leader. The idea is that such a leader's authority is not reducible to his coercive powers, his moral standing, or anything else. Rather, there is something *about* the leader that is authoritative—in Weber's words, "a certain quality of an individual personality."[25] Authority of this kind is direct and immediate.

There is also another kind of authority. Consider the scientist and the doctor. Each has authority, but it is not intrinsic to them as particular individuals. Rather, it stems from something they have acquired or developed. The scientist's authority stems from her knowledge and her reasoning capacity, the doctor's from her clinical experience and diagnostic insight. When asked, "Why do you accept as authoritative what the scientist or the doctor says?" I invoke the scientist's knowledge and the doctor's experience. The scientist's and the doctor's authority are derivative from something else, namely, their knowledge or experience.[26]

Note that with the question, "Why do you accept as authoritative the words of the charismatic leader?" I have no answer analogous to the one I give for the scientist or the doctor. Perhaps I can point to some feature of the leader—his concentrated gaze or his sonorous voice—but a noncharismatic person could have such a gaze or voice. And to register the gaze or voice in the right way—for example, to find the gaze not just "concentrated" but "penetrating"—is in fact to register the charisma, to have that perception. Here, reasons may run out rather quickly. In the end, one must simply register the leader's charisma.

2. Turning now to literature and the law, I will claim, first, that both a legal text in a sufficiently just society and a literary text of high aesthetic quality have authority. In a sufficiently just society, the fact that the law forbids parking on a certain side of the street on Tuesdays is a reason not to do so. Similarly, if the law requires certain agreed-upon arrangements, for example, contracts, to be carried out, that is an additional reason, beyond the general obligation to keep one's agreements, to keep a particular agreement.

The claim about the literary text is that the fact that certain propositions are exhibited, even if not explicitly stated, in the text is a reason to take them seriously. Shakespeare's tragedy *Macbeth* suggests that the concept of morally legitimate political authority is something human beings may not be able to dispense with. The claim is that this is a reason to take seriously that thesis about human beings.[27]

My second claim is that such authority as a literary text has is *direct authority*, while a legal text's authority is *derivative authority*. The literary text belongs with the charismatic leader, the legal text with the scientist and the doctor.

The authority of the literary text (at least qua literary text) is a function of its aesthetic power, and that is due simply to its words and their arrangement. No doubt, we could wonder whether *Macbeth* would have such authority if the play turns out not only not to have been written by Shakespeare but to have been generated by a monkey banging at a precursor of a typewriter. Perhaps—although this is puzzling and disputable—we need to see the play's words as the result of human invention and intention. However, it makes no difference whether the writer was a middle-class boy from Stratford, Christopher Marlowe, or the Earl of Oxford. The impact of this arrangement of these words is what matters. By contrast, the authority of the legal text derives not from its specific arrangement of words but from something external to the text, say, from the fact that it was duly enacted in a particular way.

3. My claims are, I think, best developed by tackling several possible objections. Let's start with an objection from the literary side. Across times and cultures, assessments of aesthetic quality have varied. Who now reads Arnold Bennett? What American agrees with the French about Jerry Lewis? Moreover, cultural prejudices influence aesthetic judgments, either directly, by not letting some texts get a fair hearing, or indirectly, by blinkering us to ways we might expand the criteria of aesthetic value. The objection from the literary side says that such variation and uncertainty in the application of criteria of aesthetic quality shows that the concept of aesthetic quality is illusory, something that can do no work and should be abandoned—but without that concept, the distinction between literary and legal authority evaporates.

In fact, to be worried about the propriety of this or that aesthetic judgment, to be worried about how we use and defend criteria of aesthetic quality, is not to reject but to rely on the concept of aesthetic quality—such worries make no sense without that concept. The thesis that English speakers have neglected a great work, X, from a certain non-English-speaking culture relies on a normative aesthetic claim: that X is a great work. The thesis implicitly accepts the validity of the concept of aesthetic quality. Similarly, the thesis that if we change our criteria of quality, we will see the greatness of a different work, Y, also accepts the concept's validity. It merely says that our current understanding of the concept is unduly narrow.

The objection from the literary side makes two mistakes. First, it assumes that the vulnerability of a concept to ideological manipulation shows that the concept is empty or somehow illegitimate. But such vulnerability obtains with many concepts and merely shows that we need to work hard to apply our concepts properly. Second, the literary objection conflates the criteria for applying a concept with the concept itself. That a concept's criteria of application vary with time and culture simply shows something about the kind of concept it is. Of course our standards of aesthetic quality change. That entails that in particular cases there is room for disagreement. It need not entail skepticism about the propriety of using the concept of aesthetic quality itself.[28]

4. Two objections might come from the legal side. To begin with, lawyers will point out that many things can be a source of law, not only constitutions, statutes, and judicial decisions. Legal casebooks can be sources of law, as can the treatises of political philosophers; so can the laws and legal writings of other cultures. There is no built-in limit. Doesn't my literature-law distinction depend on an excessively narrow, perhaps unduly positivist, conception of what can count as a legal text?

I think not. As I have drawn it, the literature-law distinction restricts the sources of law in only one way: the source of law is never a specific set of words merely qua specific set of words.[29] What gives the words their legal authority is always something else—perhaps the status of their authors, perhaps the force of the moral ideas they express. I put no limits on what this "something else" might be.

The second objection from the law side says that, properly scrutinized, law at least sometimes turns out to be a form of rhetoric. Legal writers are trying to do things with words, to make things happen; for example, a judicial opinion is trying to impose a certain reading of a statute. Legal writers do such things with the persuasiveness of their rhetorical strategies as well as with the cogency of their arguments. Doesn't that mean that, for at least some legal texts, what matters is the specific arrangement of the specific words?

Again, I think not. A legal text might have plenty of rhetorical vigor, but that is not what gives the text legal authority. Justice Holmes's pithy remarks may have been powerfully persuasive, but that is not what made them legally authoritative—if uttered by one of my professorial colleagues, they would not have been legally authoritative. Their authority came from the fact that they were (here, choose one or any combination) written by a sitting judge, written by a great sitting judge, written by Justice Oliver Wendell Holmes Jr.

Think about what will be appealed to when a practicing lawyer answers the question, "Why do you take what is said in a statute or a judicial opinion as a reason for accepting legal proposition P?" The lawyer might acknowledge that she has been influenced by the rhetorical power of the text in question, but she is highly unlikely to cite the text's rhetorical power as a reason to accept proposition P.[30] By contrast, the point of the aesthetic-quality intuition is that the aesthetic power of the literary text is a reason to take seriously a proposition one might find within it.

This is the main ground for thinking that law's possible rhetorical properties do not undermine the literary-legal distinction. There is also a second ground. To invoke rhetorical strategies as the reason to assimilate legal and literary texts is to make the highly disputable assumption that rhetorical and aesthetic goals and impacts are the same. This issue requires extended discussion, but the basic point is straightforward. Rhetoric has a practical goal: to affect agents' emotions or, more generally, their responses and so to prompt certain beliefs and perhaps certain actions. Qua works of art, at least some—perhaps many, perhaps most—literary texts have nothing resembling this sort of practical goal. Rather, a literary work aspires to an aesthetic effect, something that is often construed in terms of a particular kind of pleasure.[31] This is not to deny that literary texts have, and might be intended to have, emotional impact. But it is noteworthy that we can criticize a literary work for being "manipulative," that is, for affecting our emotions in a way that is at odds with the aspiration to aesthetic power. It would make no sense to criticize a piece of rhetoric in such terms. Similarly, we can criticize a literary work for being didactic, where we do not mean that the work fails to persuade the audience of a specific thesis (it might do that quite well) but that its didacticism makes it an aesthetic failure. By contrast, if a piece of rhetoric actually persuades, there seems no basis to criticize it qua piece of rhetoric.

§4

1. My second literature-law difference also emphasizes the difference between a text that is part of a practice involving aesthetic impact and a text that is part of a practice whose point is specific impact in the world. Here, I focus on the different models of interpretation appropriate to literature and law.

In his essay on *King Lear*, Stanley Cavell says of readings of narratives: "(1) A critical position will finally rest upon calling a claim obvious; [and]

(2) a critical discovery will present itself as the whole truth of a work, a provision of its total meaning."[32] Cavell then distinguishes between a claim to *totality* and a claim to *exhaustiveness*, and between a claim to *obviousness* and a claim to *certainty*.[33] What do these distinctions come to?

In a later book, *Pursuits of Happiness*, Cavell compares being gripped by a reading to seeing the duck or the rabbit in the famous double-image.[34] Cavell's claim is not that multiple readings are not possible—the point of the duck/rabbit image is that they are. Rather, his claim is that one can be genuinely gripped by only one reading at a time; and (a) when one is so gripped, the image seems clearly, seems obviously, to be, say, a rabbit; and (b) when one is so gripped, the image is all and only a rabbit. That last is the thought that the reading is total.

Why, then, is the reading not also certain and exhaustive? I take Cavell to be saying that certainty has to do with the claim that doubt is impossible, and exhaustiveness with the claim that one could not possibly find any unaccounted-for detail. For Cavell, such claims are not made in the moment of being gripped by the experience of seeing-as, gripped by seeing the figure *as* a rabbit. They are made from a more distant standpoint. From that standpoint, such claims might well be false, as with the claim, from such a standpoint, that the figure is solely a rabbit.

A contrast to the duck/rabbit model is the *on-balance* model. With the on-balance model, the interpreter merely says that, examining two possible interpretations, she judges that one is, on balance, superior to the other. She takes interpretation Alpha and, ideally, assesses all the considerations pro and con. Perhaps she goes down Ronald Dworkin's Herculean route and decides, overall, whether Alpha makes the text the best that it can be.[35] However, while pressing interpretation Alpha, the interpreter still keeps in mind competing interpretation Beta, with its pros and cons. It is merely that, on balance and taking everything into account—the exhaustiveness part—she finds Beta less compelling than Alpha. By contrast, with the duck/rabbit model there is no on-balance reading, because one cannot hold both readings simultaneously. One cannot stand back to balance their pros and cons. Even though one knows that two readings are possible, at a given moment one is either gripped by the duck aspect or gripped by the rabbit aspect.

As an example of the duck/rabbit model, we can take Cavell's reading of *King Lear* as about the avoidance of love. Cavell sews the text together in such a way that, under his reading's sway, the theme of avoidance of love reveals itself prominently, for example, in Lear's initial condemnation of Cordelia, and especially in Edgar's failure to reveal himself until it is too late. It is not that no moment in the play goes unaccounted for by Cavell's reading. Rather, in reading or seeing the play under Cavell's interpretation, those moments, in a sense, drop out. They are silenced. This is the force of the duck/rabbit model: one sees the play under a certain aspect and does so totally.[36] That is what it is to see the play under that aspect.[37]

2. Conceptually, the distinction between the two models is clear enough. With Cavell, the issue seems to be phenomenological, about the experience of submitting oneself to an interpretation. One might ask, then, whether there really is such a phenomenological difference between giving a reading of *King Lear* and, say, judging whether the Endangered Species Act prohibits building a particular dam because doing so would extirpate a small fish, the snail darter.[38] Is it possible to keep competing interpretations in mind when seeing *King Lear* or when interpreting the Endangered Species Act? Does interpretive decision making involve an aspect shift in either case, both, or neither?

Taking the issue as phenomenological would require working through several complications:

(1) From the legal side, one might distinguish trial from appellate court decision making. Trial court disputes often involve disputes about which factual narrative to believe. They might thus resemble interpretive disputes in literature. One could see each attorney as trying to tell a tale in which her narrative silences the other, that is, makes the jury see only the rabbit. Appellate court adjudication, by contrast, concerns the interpretation of the law, and while in some contexts there might be a narrative of previous court decisions, there will also, and fundamentally, be something more abstract: a set of reasons, of arguments (about principles and policies), that each lawyer gives to buttress her case.

(2) The phenomenological question might turn out differently depending on whether two literary interpretations are directly incompatible or merely highlight different aspects of a text. A reading of *King Lear* holding that Cordelia loves Lear is directly incompatible with one holding that she does not love Lear, but a reading that sees the play as a family drama is at most indirectly at odds with a reading that sees it as a political parable. Perhaps one could keep the latter pair of readings simultaneously in mind but not the former.

(3) There might be differences among people's interpretive experiences, especially with literary texts. Some people might find it possible, when watching *King Lear*, to keep both Cavell's and, for example, Bradley's interpretations simultaneously in mind. (Here is Bradley: in the end, "we feel . . . a consciousness of greatness in pain and of solemnity in the mystery we cannot fathom," that "the world . . . [though] convulsed by evil . . . rejects it.")[39] Others might claim that, for them, all but one interpretation disappear, that when they are

immersed in a given production, the duck/rabbit model—the aspect shift model—takes control.[40]

The phenomenological issue has considerable interest. However, it is sufficiently complex and the relevant data (people's experiences of reading texts and watching productions) are sufficiently opaque and probably sufficiently varied that here this issue is best left aside. What I want to take from the comparison of the two models is the thought that there might be an important difference between trying to impose interpretive sense on an aesthetic object, something that aspires to produce a distinctive form of meaning and pleasure via its distinctive form of coherence and consistency, and trying to impose interpretive sense on a legal text (or, often in the law, on an array of cross-cutting texts generated at different times and in different contexts), something that was not constructed with anything like such aspirations.

3. Instead of a phenomenological, we can focus on a normative question. And to keep things simple, let's limit ourselves, as far as the law goes, to appellate court adjudication. With regard to an appellate court judge, a phenomenological claim would be that the judge can in fact keep competing interpretations in mind, that she does use the on-balance rather than the duck/rabbit model. However, a more interesting claim is normative: she should use the on-balance model.

In shifting to the normative axis, I am not claiming that any interpretation fully instantiates either the duck/rabbit or the on-balance model. At issue, rather, is which model to have as one's interpretive ideal, which goal to have for interpretation in a given area.

Here, it would be useful to have an image for the on-balance interpretation. In fact, one is readily available, the model of blind justice with her scales. The impartiality of the image is obvious, but equally important is the presence of a pan on each side. The conceptual point is not that there is always something in each pan; it is that we must always take each pan into account. Even when there is nothing in one pan, the heavier pan is still outweighing the lighter—it is not that the lighter is nowhere to be found. By contrast, the conceptual point made by the duck/rabbit image is that when the duck is there the rabbit is nowhere to be seen and vice versa.

Returning now to the appellate court judge, keep in mind that in cases accepted for appellate review, there is often a prima facie basis to think that both parties have substantial reasons on their side. That may be why the case has been accepted for review. And if there are reasons, they should be addressed, not silenced: the judge's decision must itself be supported by reasons, especially by reasons to think that the losing party's reasons are not strong enough.[41] This practice fits poorly with the duck/rabbit model. When seeing the rabbit, one does not see the duck. Moreover, one does not see "reasons" to think the image is not a duck. With the duck/rabbit model, we have a moment of perception, not the recognition of reasons. That seems, and should be, foreign to the practice of appellate court adjudication. To keep in mind both sides of the case, to weigh competing considerations, seems crucial to giving each party at bar her due.

The duck/rabbit model involves silencing (at least at a given moment) all but one interpretation. On such a model, the goal is to reach an interpretive standpoint in which one party's arguments disappear. In the judicial context, that seems an unwise and disrespectful aspiration. When a judicial decision is reached, and one of the litigants must suffer some significant negative consequence—prison time, a financial penalty—respect for the losing party seems to require the judge to keep in mind both the reasons the losing party has brought to court and the refutations of those reasons. Comparing reasons (and retaining the rejected reasons) rather than shifting a perception (and eliminating the rejected perception) seems the more respectful way to acknowledge that someone's life is about to be made fundamentally worse. When a decision has severe practical impact, the decision-maker ought not to forget what can be said on behalf of the losing party. (Similar considerations suggest that the on-balance model is actually better even for a jury's deliberations in a trial court.)

For an appellate court, there is a further problem with the duck/rabbit model. That model entails that one can see only one outcome at a time, but it also entails that one knows that another, and equally compelling, outcome is possible. Judges surely know that they are fallible, but it seems problematic for a judge to believe that in a minute her decision could shift, that she could suddenly see the case in a completely different way—even in the absence of new evidence or arguments. If she now thinks the defense has the stronger argument but believes that in a few seconds she might think the plaintiff does, then she has not yet decided the case, come to a conclusion. A judicial decision, something based on reasons, must have more stability than a momentary perception. Scales are broken if they say different things at different times.

4. For an appellate court judge, the duck/rabbit model is normatively undesirable. Is this model normatively, that is, aesthetically, desirable for the reader or playgoer? Is an aesthetic experience that is obvious and total, to use Cavell's terms, superior to one that is not?

This is a question in aesthetics about which there could be dispute. Coherence and consistency might be overrated; maybe the duck/rabbit model obscures the way consciousness of contradictory moments can enhance aesthetic impact. However we decide that substantive aesthetic question, it is in fact an aesthetic question, and in resolving it the focus should be on aesthetic issues. Here, there is no analogue to the requirement to show respect for both parties before a court. Of course, one should be polite about a reading with which one disagrees. Yet no matter how personally staked to their own readings critics X and Y might be, one does neither a disservice if one finds that X's reading silences Y's. The aesthetic judgment is not about what practical consequences will obtain for one critic or the other.[42]

The distinction here is in part between argument and aesthetic perception. Arguments go into an interpretation of a novel or play, but they are in service of getting the interpreter's readers/audience to shift perspective—less to agree with an argument than to "see" the play under the interpreter's reading. The goal of getting the reader/audience to see only and utterly the rabbit is the extreme form of this aspiration (no doubt never entirely reached). This is different from the judicial goal of finding that the weight of argument falls in a certain direction and is not subject any moment to change.

The distinction here is not between advocacy and impartiality, as if the critic, in contrast to the judge, is pleading a case instead of trying to get things right. Rather, what it is to get things right is different in the different fields. A judge should seek a convincing and stable balance of argument. By contrast, one might see a novel under one compelling description today and under another tomorrow, just as different productions of King Lear could each be compelling. With the duck/rabbit, each image is, in its own way, completely right. There is nothing problematic about this; similarly, there is no imperative to decide which is "the" proper production of King Lear.[43] To say this about a judicial decision would be odd. First, serious consequences are at stake for the parties before the court, and, institutionally, one ought not to impose those consequences one way today and reverse them tomorrow. Second, and this is the conceptual point, what makes each production of King Lear compelling in its own way is its aesthetic power—and that may involve but goes beyond weighing a set of pros and cons. It is, in the end, a matter of seeing or feeling a production's aesthetic power, or not doing so.[44] This is not the familiar point that explanations come to an end, that reasons finally run out. It is a point about the specific way that reasons run out or, rather, should run out in an aesthetic context, namely, in aesthetic perception. My claim is that, in the judicial context, reasons should run out in another way, namely, by accepting that one has given all one's reasons and yet another person might—of course, to one's own mind, wrongly—weigh them differently.

Different interpretive practices involve different interpretive ideals. Given the practical role of appellate court adjudication, the duck/rabbit is a bad model; here, the on-balance model is better. Given the aesthetic role of literary interpretation, I suspect the duck/rabbit model is better, but this is, itself, an issue in literary aesthetics.[45] The point is that whether the duck/rabbit or the on-balance is the better model will not be determined by the mere fact that one is engaged in an interpretive enterprise but by the specific desiderata of the specific interpretive enterprise in which one is engaged.

§5

Literature is an aesthetic enterprise; the law is a practical one. This hardly denies that evidence and argument are relevant to both, nor that, under the guise of providing the best possible reading, both literary and legal interpretation might play political roles. Yet what there is about a text that gives it authority—something, one might say, that makes it worth interpreting—is different in literature than in law; and, in these different spheres, what makes something a proper model of interpretation is different as well.

NOTES

This essay has benefited significantly from Richard Strier's probing and judicious comments on earlier versions.

1. Several writers have noted differences between the two areas. See Richard A. Posner, *Law and Literature* (Cambridge, MA: Harvard University Press, 1998), for a recognition that literature is an aesthetic practice. Robert Cover has insisted that we keep in mind the very practical, sometimes highly punitive, role of judicial decision making. See Robert M. Cover, "Violence and the World," *Yale Law Journal* 95, no. 8 (1986): 1601–29. See also Daniel A. Farber and Suzanna Sherry, "Telling Stories out of School: An Essay on Legal Narratives," *Stanford Law Review* 45, no. 4 (1993): 807–55. Farber and Sherry note that some legal writers want legal narratives to possess aesthetic qualities and, presumably by virtue of such qualities, to have a transformative impact on the reader. In §4 I discuss the difference between the duck/rabbit model (a model of transformed perception) and the on-balance model (a model of considered judgment). My claim will be that the latter is the proper model for (at least) appellate court adjudication. This is consistent with accepting that the former could play a role in other areas of legal discourse, e.g., law review articles. Whether or how far or in what ways it should do so is a question I leave to others.

2. Here, one might see an uncertainty about what counts as the "means" of attaining morally legitimate power. Suppose I usurp the throne but then institute a stable regime of perfect justice. Some might now see my power as morally legitimate. Would

my provision of perfect justice then count as my morally acceptable "means" to power, or would my case be an exception to the claim that power is morally legitimate only if attained via morally acceptable means?

3. For an interesting discussion of the theme of political authority, see James Boyd White, "Shakespeare's *Richard II*: Imagining the Modern World," in *Acts of Hope: Creating Authority in Literature, Law, and Politics*, by White (Chicago: University of Chicago Press, 1994).

4. See, for instance, act 1, scene 4, where Kent finds in Lear's countenance that "which I would fain call master" (1.4.29–30) and goes on to designate it as "Authority" (1.4.32). That Lear thinks he still has authority is shown in his astonishment at the way Oswald treats him, namely, as merely "My lady's father" (1.4.84–86). The same thing happens in this scene in Lear's encounter with Goneril. See especially his rhetorical question "Doth any here know me?" (1.4.233). Clearly, the "me" at issue is the person who is supposed to have authority. See also act 2, scene 4 (2.4.88–91), where Lear responds to being told that Regan and Cornwall will not speak with him. He is astonished that their desires should override his command. Here is Lear:

Deny to speak with me? They are sick? They are weary?
They have travell'd all the night? Mere fetches;
The images of revolt and flying off.
Fetch me a better answer.

Lear can call these excuses images of "revolt" only if he believes he still has authority.

5. This is among the reasons why Bishop Bramhall termed *Leviathan* a "rebel's catechism." For a discussion of Bramhall's worries along these lines, see Jean Hampton, *Hobbes and the Social Contract Tradition* (Cambridge: Cambridge University Press, 1986), 197–207. On Hobbes and the Engagement Controversy, see Quentin Skinner, "Conquest and Consent: Thomas Hobbes and the Engagement Controversy," in *The Interregnum: The Quest for Settlement, 1646–1660*, ed. G. E. Aylmer (London: Macmillan, 1972). See also John M. Wallace, *Destiny His Choice: The Loyalism of Andrew Marvell* (London: Cambridge University Press, 1968), chap. 1.

6. See Thomas Hobbes, *Leviathan* (Cambridge: Cambridge University Press, 1991), chap. 17.

7. Ibid., chap. 20.

8. On this theme in Hobbes, see S. A. Lloyd, *Ideals as Interests in Hobbes's Leviathan: The Power of Mind over Matter* (Cambridge: Cambridge University Press, 1992).

9. All citations to Shakespeare's plays are to *The Works of William Shakespeare*, ed. Kenneth Muir, Arden edition (London: Methuen, 1951).

10. I thank Richard Strier for pressing me to distinguish among power, legality, and moral legitimacy.

11. See Hobbes, *Leviathan*, chap. 14, paragraph 8. The one circumstance under which Hobbes permits resistance to the sovereign is when the sovereign comes to kill you. Given that Macbeth sends murderers after Macduff, Hobbes would permit Macduff's flight and resistance. However, he would have urged both parties not to let things reach that point.

12. It may be worth noting that Holinshed's *Chronicles* say that for the first ten years

of his reign Macbeth was a good ruler, making "many wholesome laws and statutes for the public weal of his subjects." The *Chronicles* go on to say that Macbeth's eventual fear that he would be served as he had served Duncan led him to turn into a tyrant, spurred further by the desire that his own, not Banquo's, issue would succeed him. Of course, we should not get too enmeshed in interpreting the source material as distinct from Shakespeare's play. Still, it is interesting that, according to Holinshed, had Macbeth believed that others accepted the counsel to accept the powers that be, a central reason for his turning tyrant would have been removed. The citation is from Raphael Holinshed, *Chronicles of England, Scotland, and Ireland*. It is quoted in the Signet Classic edition of *Macbeth* (New York: Sylvan Barnet, 1963), 145.

13. See A. C. Bradley, *Shakespearean Tragedy* (New York: St. Martin's Press, 1981), 359.

14. Plato, *Republic* 331d–e.

15. Ibid., 331e.

16. In fact, Socrates shows the inadequacy of each account of justice attributed to Simonides. The implication would seem to be that if we want to understand justice, we should turn to philosophy rather than to poetry. Yet this section of Plato's text ends with Socrates saying that he and his interlocutor "shall fight as partners, then, against anyone who tells us that Simonides . . . said this [the inadequate claims about justice]" (335e). The statement is obviously laden with mockery. Nevertheless, Socrates seems to feel the need to assert, at least to his audience, that he is reinterpreting Simonides, not rejecting him.

17. In several places Socrates remarks upon the pleasures of poetry. At *Republic* 595b he refers to "the love and respect I've had for Homer since I was a child." It would be a large mistake to see Socrates (or Plato) as insensible to poetry in general and Homer in particular. It is because Homer's texts (like staged tragedy) do have a kind of authority—one that can corrupt—that Plato wants to ban his work.

18. See, among others, R. W. Beardsmore, "Literary Examples and Philosophical Confusion," in *Philosophy and Literature*, ed. A. Phillips Griffiths (Cambridge: Cambridge University Press, 1984).

19. It is also worth stressing that to say that a text might give us a reason to take proposition P seriously does not entail that P is "the meaning" of the text as a whole or that at which the text aims.

20. As an example of the use of such an uninformative criterion, see John Hospers's remarks, as quoted by Peter Lamarque, that good literature is "true to life," meaning that "the characters described by the novelist behave, feel, and are motivated the way people in real life behave, feel, and are motivated." Taken flatly, this is true of many bad works and untrue of many good ones. Taken less flatly, it tells us nothing. Medea's murder of her children is hardly the usual behavior of the jilted wife, yet it is, in some sense, "true to life." Such a criterion must itself be applied via an aesthetic sensibility; on its own, it is empty. For the passage from Hospers, see John Hospers, "Literature and Human Nature," *Journal of Aesthetics and Art Criticism* 17, no. 1 (1958): 46, as quoted in Peter Lamarque, *Philosophy of Literature* (Oxford: Blackwell, 2009), 225.

21. Frank Sibley makes a related point when he insists that "aesthetic concepts are not condition-governed." He says, "There are no sufficient conditions, no non-aesthetic

features such that the presence of some set or number of them will beyond question justify or warrant the application of an aesthetic term." See Frank Sibley, "Aesthetic Concepts," *Philosophical Review* 68, no. 4 (1959): 426.

22. Aristotle, *Poetics* 1451b.

23. See Russell Hardin, *Morality within the Limits of Reason* (Chicago: University of Chicago Press, 1988), 27. I have dealt elsewhere with the intuition discussed here. See my "Lord Jim and Moral Judgment: Literature and Moral Philosophy," *Journal of Aesthetics and Art Criticism* 56 (Summer 1998); and my "Styles of Self-Absorption," in *The Blackwell Companion to Philosophy of Literature*, ed. G. Hagberg and W. Jost (Oxford: Wiley-Blackwell, 2010).

24. Literary authority sometimes seems also to obtain with works of nonfiction, say, with certain historical writing. The literary brilliance of historical work A compared to the dullness of work B might seem, to some, to make A more convincing. So is literary authority disconnected from fictionality? Is it irrelevant to literary authority that a novel does not depict actual events?

We must move carefully here. First, although the stylistically brilliant historian might initially seem more convincing than the dull one, in principle she is subject to the constraint of the facts, of actual historical research. In principle, her work can be shown to be less convincing as history by something external to her text. By contrast, there is nothing external to the work of fiction. I take this to be of great importance. A novel's literary power cannot be undermined by the fact that its events and characters correspond to nothing in the historical record. No new information could undermine the novel qua novel.

Second, some historical writing attempts to present not only historical events but human nature. According to Hume, the ordinary reader finds Tacitus more compelling than Suetonius. See David Hume, *An Enquiry concerning the Principles of Morals* (Oxford: Oxford University Press, 1998), chap. 5, 112. Yet although current historians might judge that Suetonius gives a more accurate presentation of the Roman emperors, Tacitus could still be thought to reveal more about human nature. This would be to say that Tacitus should now be read as a quasi-novelist. I think that is in fact a standing possibility for great historical writing: beginning strictly as history, over time and as its particular historical claims are increasingly corrected, the text's power becomes increasingly akin to that of a novel.

25. In *The Theory of Social and Economic Organization*, Weber writes that the charismatic leader has "a certain quality of an individual personality, by virtue of which he is set apart from ordinary men and treated as endowed with supernatural, superhuman, or at least specifically exceptional powers or qualities. These are such as are not accessible to the ordinary person, but are regarded as of divine origin or as exemplary, and on the basis of them the individual concerned is treated as a leader." The idea of these powers' divine origin is analogous to the appeal to the muses: first one registers the exceptional powers, then one appeals to the divine. And as with the appeal to the muses, here the appeal to the divine explains nothing, is a mere place-holder. See Max Weber, *The Theory of Social and Economic Organization*, trans. A. M. Henderson and Talcott Parsons (New York: Free Press, 1947), 359.

26. Direct and derivative authority need not be mutually exclusive. For some people, their trust in their doctor might not be reducible to their beliefs about her training, expertise, etc.

27. As noted earlier (see note 19), that a text prompts us to take proposition P seriously does not make P the meaning or moral of the text. We could, incidentally, make a further distinction, that between *pure* and *impure* authority. This comes down to whether there is a moral-content condition for the authority of a legal or a literary text. If there is no such condition, the authority is pure; otherwise, it is impure. It has long been debated whether an immoral law is obligatory, whether moral acceptability is a condition of a law's authority. It has also been debated whether moral acceptability is a condition of aesthetic quality. I want to avoid these issues and simply claim that both law and literature have at least impure authority, meaning that, assuming that their content is minimally morally acceptable, the fact that something is duly enacted and the fact that something is enshrined in a text of high literary quality generates some sort of authority.

28. We could abandon the concept of aesthetic quality. This would not be incoherent. We could imagine (with difficulty) a world in which aesthetic judgments were never made, or if they were, no one took them seriously. However, that is very much not our world—and, I suspect, not the world even of ostensible skeptics about aesthetic judgments. Most people recommend specific books, movies, pieces of music to their friends on the ground that these works are better than other books, movies, music. Sometimes we may believe that, as with our recommendation to taste the newest flavor of ice cream, our friends will simply enjoy a book or movie. Still, in the case of many books, movies, etc. (and unlike the ice cream example), we think that they should enjoy them—because these are in fact good books, movies, etc. Like skepticism about moral judgment, skepticism about aesthetic judgment is far more easily theorized than lived.

29. One instance when the words themselves would be the source of legal authority is when my imaginary lawyer invokes the words of *Crime and Punishment*. However, that is a rather limited exception that I am happy to grant, as it confirms the acceptance of the aesthetic-quality intuition. Only if lawyers in general were to take literary works in general as sources of law, and to take them as such only qua aesthetically powerful sets of words, would there be a large enough exception to make trouble for the law-literature distinction that I am drawing.

30. A skeptic might say that sometimes a judicial opinion's rhetorical power is the lawyer's reason for accepting P, even though she will not admit it. However, I think we learn what is central to the social practice here by noting (a) that it is not among the acknowledged standards of the practice to appeal to a text's rhetorical power (compare this to a literary critic's appeal to a text's aesthetic power) and (b) that even implicitly such an appeal is likely to be extremely rare (would it ever obtain with a statute?).

At stake here may be something similar to what was observed about the writing of history (see note 24). A piece of judicial prose might be sufficiently powerful that it seems to reveal something of importance about human life. For that purpose the specific words would be key. But that would not be the source of its distinctively legal authority. That would not provide the reason that makes it legitimate for the judicial pronouncement to have practical consequences for particular individuals.

31. I thank Gabriel Lear for pressing me to note that pleasure is part of aesthetic experience but is presumably less central to legal experience.

32. Stanley Cavell, "The Avoidance of Love," in *Must We Mean What We Say?* (Cambridge: Cambridge University Press, 1976), 311.

33. Ibid., 312.

34. See Stanley Cavell, *Pursuits of Happiness* (Cambridge, MA: Harvard University Press, 1981), 36.

35. See Ronald Dworkin, "Hard Cases," in *Taking Rights Seriously* (Cambridge, MA: Harvard University Press, 1977). See also Dworkin, *Law's Empire* (Cambridge, MA: Harvard University Press, 1986). If I am Dworkin's Hercules, my reading will necessarily be exhaustive. I will have considered everything.

36. See Cavell, "The Avoidance of Love."

37. I have not "carried through" my reading of *Macbeth* (to use an idea from Cavell's *Pursuits of Happiness*; see 35–37). To do so would require making more of the text resonate with the theme of the conflation of morally legitimate with merely legal and effective power. Actually, many moments of the play could be seen through this lens. Lady Macbeth remarks, "What need we fear who knows it, when none can call our power to account?" (5.1.36–38). Coming when it does, this might be taken to allude to God's knowing it, and the account to which the Macbeths will soon be called. On my reading, the point is different and perhaps more poignant. If *they* know it, all is lost; their power is not morally legitimate. Similarly, Lady Macbeth complains, "Nought's had, all's spent, / Where our desire is got without content" (3.2.4–5). The point is that their specific desire (Macbeth's, anyway) is not had, so of course there is no content. Toward the play's end, Macbeth laments,

> that which should accompany old age,
> As honor, love, obedience, troops of friends,
> I must not look to have, but, in their stead,
> Curses, not loud but deep, mouth-honor, breath
> Which the poor heart would fain deny and dare not. (5.3.24–28)

He wishes he could have sincere protestations of honor and affection; presumably, he also wishes that he deserved these things. With such moments of the play, it might be possible to carry through my reading.

38. Dworkin uses this example in *Law's Empire*, chap. 1.

39. Bradley, *Shakespearean Tragedy*, 279 and 304.

40. Might there also be a difference between the experience of a practicing literary critic and that of the ordinary member of an audience? Or even between the experiences of the critic at work in her study and when sitting front and center as a production unrolls? Might the experience of rapt reading or watching a production be more aspect-shift-like and less on-balance-like?

41. John McDowell claims that problematic reasons do not occur to the virtuous moral agent. They are silenced. Even if I could steal without being caught, I do not need to reject the reasons in favor of stealing. If I am virtuous, those reasons do not occur

to me. I do not balance the reasons to steal against the reasons not to; rather, I directly perceive the right thing to do. See John McDowell, "Are Moral Requirements Hypothetical Imperatives?," "Virtue and Reason," and "The Role of *Eudaimonia* in Aristotle's Ethics," in his *Mind, Virtue, and Reality* (Cambridge, MA: Harvard University Press, 1998), 77–94, 50–76, 3–22. The institutional role of an appellate court makes the ideal of silencing inappropriate. Even if one party's reasons are without merit, they should not be silenced; instead, they should be judged to be without merit. The decision procedure of virtuous judging need not be the same as that of virtuous conduct in other contexts.

42. In an academic context a professor might have the obligation to let her students know of alternative interpretations, as well as to let them know of those interpretations' competing pros and cons.

43. This is not to deny that some interpretations or productions are worse than others, nor that some are flat-out wrong. It is to note that more than one can be compelling and that we need not choose one that is, at every moment, most compelling.

44. Cavell remarks, "It is essential to making an aesthetic judgment that at some point we be prepared to say in its support: don't you see, don't you hear, don't you dig?" See Stanley Cavell, "Aesthetic Problems of Modern Philosophy," in *Must We Mean What We Say?* 93.

45. It is even possible that each model is better in a different aesthetic context.

BRADIN CORMACK

DECISION, POSSESSION

THE TIME OF LAW IN *THE WINTER'S TALE* AND THE SONNETS

At the suture of the two parts of *The Winter's Tale*, Time enters and renovates a proverb: "I that please some, try all," he announces (4.1.1).[1] Try means *test* or *sift*, but here, measured against "please," it especially takes on the meaning of *afflict*. Time afflicts everyone, even those it pleases. One hears a legal quibble here, too, with Time as sovereign overseeing a court in the way Leontes has earlier overseen Hermione's "trial" (2.3.204). Shakespeare plays on that connotation later in the chorus, when, sliding "O'er sixteen years," Time, now in the role of the accused, asks the audience not to "impute" to him the "crime" of leaving "the growth untried / Of that wide gap,"

> since it is in my power
> To o'erthrow law, and in one self-born hour
> To plant and o'erwhelm custom. (4.1.4–9)

This is, of course, not quite a defense, or at least not a standard one: in answer to the content of the charge against him—namely, that he has missed part of his story—Time simply rejects the forum in which the charge makes sense, for no better reason than that he has "power" to do so. He leaves the growth of the gap *untried*, as the passage punningly has it, because trials belong to law; and Time, again like King Leontes, follows law just so far as it suits.[2]

I begin my essay with the submerged legalities of the chorus because Time's "wide gap" emblematizes in *The Winter's Tale* a mixed temporality that is at issue in the play's figuration of law and is of interest to Shakespeare elsewhere in his work.[3] In 1765, Samuel Johnson noted "the growth . . . of that wide gap" to be "somewhat irregular" for mixing its metaphors, scolding his author as one who "attends more to his ideas than to his words." Johnson resolves the irregularity in effect by circumventing it, making the "growth" that in Shakespeare's phrasing pertains to the gap refer instead to "the progression of the time that filled up the gap of the story between Perdita's birth and her sixteenth year."[4] Fair enough. But in changing the object of growth, Johnson's solution misses a doubleness in the play's conceptualization of the very category, time, that splits the play in two. On the one hand, the audience registers the gap as the *extended period* required to bring the play to its conclusion: sixteen years is a long time, enough, as it turns out, for a baby to reach marriageable age. On the other hand, the gap has the aspect not of an extended period at all, but rather of a *threshold* between two other times, each of these an extended time in which the action falls. The gap that structures the play is a temporal zone that disappears into a limit—this as a matter of art, whether the playwright's when he so distributes his plot or Time's when he "turn[s] my glass" (4.1.16) and as though by magic sends time again through its sly channel into a new volume. The growth of the gap is a paradox addressing the paradox that a limit might, in time, be constituted by extension.

This essay tracks, in two registers and in relation to two Shakespearean texts, the legal effects of this fundamental tension between a temporality of the instant and a temporality of extended time.[5] In a first section, on two scenes in *The Winter's Tale*, I look at how the play expresses these temporalities by distinguishing legal process from legal decision in order to suggest, I posit, the shape of sovereignty both at law and, indirectly, in the theater. My second section, reached by crossing an untried gap of my own, looks to Shakespeare's sonnets, specifically two of the poems addressed to the young man that deploy the language of property law. I explore here how Shakespeare's analysis of time's impingement on the idea of legal possession exposes a formal mechanics whereby, analogously to law's capacity to regulate possession, a lyric might, in time, overcome time. In both cases, law emerges as a form for organizing time in the service of establishing authority.[6]

A word on method is in order. I am most concerned here with literary texts that intensify our apprehension of the law by offering an analytical view of the formal mechanisms whereby the law itself achieves a given effect, mechanisms that might otherwise be unnoticed, even by the law itself. In line with Lorna Hutson's perceptive genealogy of Shakespeare's dramatic realism (including our "readiness to see the characters in the play as vividly realized human beings") as a function of the conjectural thinking associated with the investigative procedures of an increasingly participatory legal culture, several essays in this volume locate the interpretive force of Shakespeare's law in character, specifically the dramatic performance of imaginatively realized subject positions around some legal or constitutional issue.[7] Somewhat differently, my orientation to law and imaginative literature focuses less on emplotted character as the place from which to think about Shakespeare's legal inquiries and more on his language as such, since it is in the microanalytical force of the language—in Shakespeare's relentlessly experimental philology, that love of the word which is his insistence on turning and testing words for their potential—that his analytical work, as it were, *for* the law seems to me most apparent. Like Kathy Eden in her essay in this volume on loyalty and royalty in *King Lear*, I am more interested in the overlap between poetry's and law's attentiveness to semantic differentiation than I am in either the relations among characters as given actors in an ethical field or the a priori categories such as justice, injury, or subjecthood that often function as a starting point for a legally inflected criticism of literary texts. Relatedly, I would suggest that Shakespeare's engagement with the law is most stimulating when, in fact, it is least agonistic, when it presents itself less as a critique of, say, the law's shortcomings—even when these are at issue—than as a dramatization of the technical processes that allow the law to produce its effects in the first place.

The primacy, for my argument, of language in Shakespeare's theorization of law is reflected in my interest in Shakespeare's sonnets as an important but neglected site for his legal thinking.[8] My general point is that the productive capacity of language for testing categories and norms offers us a powerful way to think of law and literature together without supposing that they are the same, and thus to bridge the gap that is sometimes imagined to exist between an aesthetic Shakespeare and a Shakespeare of ideas. This is a false distinction. The Shakespeare of my essay is most aesthetic exactly in his analytical play, in language, with ideational categories. To that extent, I take a different position on the aesthetic, and on the possible relations between law and literature, from Daniel Brudney's in this volume. Where Brudney locates literature's specificity vis-à-vis law in a strictly formal aesthetics and concludes that literary authority and literary interpretation are for that reason quite different from legal authority and legal interpretation, I am positing that a philological approach attentive to what Shakespeare's linguistic forms are *doing* allows us to identify the aesthetic dimension of a kind of category analysis that is as central to legal thinking as it is to complex literary production.

Distributing Decision

Hermione's trial in act 3.2 of *The Winter's Tale* unfolds as a palimpsestic representation of different phenomena that go under the name of justice. As sovereign, prosecutor, and judge, Leontes offers the opening salvo:

> This sessions, to our great grief we pronounce,
> Even pushes 'gainst our heart. The party tried,
> The daughter of a king, our wife, and one
> Of us too much beloved. Let us be cleared
> Of being tyrannous, since we so openly

Proceed in justice, which shall have due course
Even to the guilt or the purgation.
Produce the prisoner. (3.2.1–8)

In this telling, justice is a procedure that openly follows to an end its due course. The scene will index that process in the language of accusation, arraignment, and indictment; in the idea of giving and hearing testimony; and in the performance of argument and counterargument: the stuff, in other words, of courtroom drama when the verdict or judgment is in question. Here, we sense, it is not. As scholars have noted, Shakespeare initially charges the scene by giving Leontes the odd statement that, contrary to appearances, he is the one on trial: "let *us* be cleared / Of being tyrannous."[9] In excess of the trial scene's dramaturgical payoff, the great interest of this *second* trial lies in the fact that its temporal character is quite different from that of the first. For whereas Hermione's trial will be, in Leontes' saying, a matter of justice's course, this other trial is already over, the judgment in the case being continuous with its articulation as a case. The one trial belongs to procedural time, the other to a present that compresses that time into the moment of judgment. If Leontes' subjunctive posits that in a quite ordinary sense the sovereign authority is always tested when the law tests those who stand accused before it, his sentence nevertheless negates the critical potential therein by asserting that sovereignty inhabits the judicial process not *as* process but as a point that instantaneously normalizes the sovereign's place in relation to law. Process, here, means that the sovereign is already innocent, all ways.

The disjunction between Leontes' two trials is refracted in the ideological order of Hermione's trial itself. Leontes refuses to admit an evidentiary paradigm into the scene of evaluation, grounding his judgment instead in the self-fulfilling "fabric of his folly, whose foundation / Is piled upon his faith," as Camillo earlier says (1.2.424–25). Accordingly, Hermione points out that the judgment that should follow from procedural form has instead preceded it, thereby containing her testimony, whatever it might be:

Mine integrity
Being counted falsehood, shall, *as I express it,*
Be so received. (3.2.25–27, my emphasis)

The temporality here is, again, noteworthy. At the very instant of expression, Hermione says, the process in which she is embedded will change what she says into its contrary. Against Leontes' self-flattering image of processual justice, Hermione poses the operation of his law as the experience of a decisive instant, which in this case she represents as tyrannical because it is out of sync, preposterous, prejudicial.[10] Leontes' courtroom is disordered because one kind of legal time intrudes upon the other, just as, at the scene's opening, the trial of Leontes' integrity has intruded upon the trial of Hermione's integrity as a decisive instant (about him) replacing an evaluative process (about her).

If Leontes' justice operates through the substitution of the instant for a process, the obverse is also true in relation to the judgment that changes what happens in a courtroom into a real-world effect. Shakespeare represents that decision as the sudden entry of knowledge into the temporal field. Most important here is the oracle delivered from Delphos: "Hermione is chaste, Polixenes blameless, Camillo a true subject, Leontes a jealous tyrant" (3.2.130–31). This is decisive language: as David Bergeron notes, the oracle "sounds much like a report of the jury at a trial's end; it systematically and concisely answers the charges made or implicit in Hermione's trial."[11] So it is notable that when Leontes rejects the decision, he does so by wresting law back into its other, extended temporality: "There is no truth at all i' th' oracle. / The sessions shall *proceed*; this is mere falsehood" (3.2.138–39, my emphasis). As Shakespeare writes the scene, Leontes thus perverts each of law's temporalities, tyrannically negating the processual through prior decision and the decisive through an appeal to endless process.

The force of the scene's temporal analysis, I want to suggest, resides not only in its mapping of tyranny but, more generally, also in its implications for law as a technical art that organizes time. Alongside the manifestly important questions of who in the courtroom decides a given question and how a question gets decided, I think that the play is posing the equally fundamental question of what a decision is. What is the structure of a decision? How does it do its work?

The critical scene in this regard is the one immediately preceding the trial, in which Cleomenes and Dion are shown returning from Delphos with the oracle in hand. In a striking recent article, Virginia Lee Strain links Apollo's oracle to the early modern "oracles of the law" such as Sir Edward Coke, thereby positioning the oracle as a figure for historical jurisprudence against Leontes' (and King James's) inappropriately personal interventions in legal-professional matters. As part of this argument, she perceptively identifies the elaborate delivery of the divine judgment as an "aesthetic achievement" analogous to the historical court performances that legitimate judgment through "the integrity of a . . . procedure that strategically conceals and reveals."[12] What interests me most in the oracle's representation along these lines is how the structure of the messengers' journey specifies the structure of decision as part of that procedure. Most obviously, act 3.1 is a scene that prepares the audience for the oracle's unsealing by displaying its mediation: although the judgment is divine, it matters that the judgment is orally delivered by an officer reading a message hand-delivered, still sealed, by two (trustworthy) servants who have it from a priest who hears it directly from Apollo. The almost exaggerated sequence of mediations functions less to undo the supposed immediacy of divine judgment (a plausible skeptical reading) than to fold the oracle's transit into the very thing the oracle is at the instant of its unsealing.[13] This temporal recalibration of the oracle is the primary force of the messenger scene.

On their way home, each of the two servants reports to the other what he found most striking at Delphos, the telling point being that Dion turns out to remember process and Cleomenes an instant. Dion says:

> I shall report,
> For most it caught me, the celestial habits—
> Methinks I so should term them—and the reverence
> Of the grave wearers. O, the sacrifice,
> How ceremonious, solemn and unearthly
> It was i' th' offering! (3.1.3–8)

Cleomenes, on the other hand, remembers, in Christopher Pye's phrasing, a violent moment of "annihilating power":[14]

> But of all, the burst
> And the ear-deaf'ning voice o' th' oracle,
> Kin to Jove's thunder, so surprised my sense
> That I was nothing. (3.1.8–11)

Now, the servants' two accounts of what mattered most are not quite in sync. But the point is not that one of the messengers (Dion, say) has misunderstood the experience and substituted style for content; nor is the whole point that each of the two parts of the oracular judgment—Dion notes the sacrifice, Cleomenes the voice—is irreducible to the other (although this is certainly the case). Rather, when taken together, the two experiences of the oracle generate a conceptual structure for the judicial event as such. The scene's dramatic effectiveness derives from the fact that it presents the audience with a message that is under way, the decision having been made but remaining unknown. This suspension of knowledge, which the audience experiences as an intensified waiting, is as conceptually disturbing as it is dramatically tantalizing. For from Cleomenes' and Dion's entry at the beginning of act 3 to the point when the seal is broken, the action can be construed as taking place, quite literally, *within* the decision, in what we might call the intensivity of the instant as this is distended into time. In the play of temporal extension against instantaneity, the effect of the dramatic suspension staged by act 3.1 is to displace onto the legal decision, and into its interior, the extended time leading up to it, such that the decision becomes legible as the event it is precisely by containing the time whose limit it is. The suspended delivery of the message emblematizes the legal decision as a dynamic form.

The dramaturgical suspension of knowledge corresponds to the play's representation of the judicial decision, which we might suppose to be instantaneous, as instead an extended event; and it is notable that in the second half of the scene, Shakespeare subjects that second word, *event*, to a slowed scrutiny. Cleomenes and Dion hope that the sealed judgment will transform the experience of their journey into something advantageous to their queen. Dion posits:

> If the event o' th' journey
> Prove as successful to the queen—O, be 't so!—
> As it hath been to us rare, pleasant, speedy
> The time is worth the use on 't. (3.1.11–14)

Dion means that the time of the journey will have been well spent if the quality of the journey's end is fitted to the quality of the journey itself. The oddity here, however, is that, although "it" in line 13 can certainly refer to "journey," the grammar more audibly refers it to "event," Dion's hope being that the "event" should prove as successful to the queen as it has been speedy to the messengers. The effect is thus to conflate the hoped-for event—which we hear initially as the journey's limit or conclusion, that is, as the upcoming judicial decision dependent upon the oracle now in transit—with the journey itself. That conflation is appropriate because the same blurring belongs to the concept of the event as such. An event is etymologically something that *comes out* (Lat. *ex* + *venire*) of something else. In a 1613 report on a homicide trial, Sir Edward Coke cites as a legal maxim a pertinent definition of the event (in this case, the victim's death): "euentus est qui ex causa sequitur, Et dicuntur euentus quia ex causis eueniunt" [the event is that which follows from the cause; and events are so called because they come out of causes].[15] This definition, which Coke incorporates into his report in order firmly to link an intentional act in the accused to a death that could plausibly be ruled as accidental, attributes cause to the very definition of event, thereby dilating the happening across the time of its own causation.[16] This structure that Coke makes internal to the word's signification is cognate with the journey that, in act 3.1, gives temporal dimension to the decisive event that the sealed judgment (already) is. Heard in this register, amusingly enough, the happy event for which Dion wishes ("the event o' th' journey") cannot but be "successful" to the queen, insofar as it is in the very nature of an event to succeed (Lat. *succedere*, "to follow") upon something else, namely its cause. The event is successful as such. (Which is not to say that it might not turn out well, too.) In a passage that, at first glance, differentiates the journey—as process, mediation, and extension—from the threshold experience of the decision that is to be the journey's outcome, Dion turns out to be wishing that the event of the journey succeed for the queen in the same way it has succeeded for the messengers, namely as a rare, pleasant, and speedy succession. The decision is the journey; Dion wants the physical journey to be a correlative for the one under the seal.

As a word for the unfolding of a consequence that cannot be understood except in relation to its origin, *event* is half-synonymous with *issue*, which relates etymologically to *exit* as something that *goes out* from something else. With that second keyword, Dion concludes the scene in a further intensification of the temporal analysis. To Cleomenes' sorrowful remark that he "little like[s]" the "proclamations / So forcing faults upon Hermione," Dion offers the following prediction:

> The violent carriage of it
> Will clear or end the business when the oracle,
> Thus by Apollo's great divine sealed up,
> Shall the contents discover; something rare
> Even then will rush to knowledge. Go—fresh horses;
> And gracious be the issue. (3.1.15–22)

The rarity and grace of the issue matches the rarity and pleasure of the eventful journey as given earlier. And here, again, Dion focuses on the moment— "*Even then* will rush to knowledge"—that compresses the journey into its end. The rush of something rare into knowledge is the rush of process into the apparently radical present of decision. But what, in this complex, is the issue? If the issue (or event) is anywhere, it is exactly in the rushing, which in its orientation toward a conclusion distends the latter, only apparently discrete, into the time of its production *as* knowledge. In bringing a process to its conclusion, rushing is not transformative, but expressive, the means by which a single temporal complex changes aspect. For this dynamic, Shakespeare invents a marvelously simple emblem in Dion's throw-away sentence "Go—fresh horses."

The horses are the materialized vehicle for judicial knowledge. Where knowledge is the temporal event that rushes across distance into arrival, process and decision are equally in the knowledge, with knowledge being an aspect of the epistemic journey.

In Shakespeare's analysis, the judicial decision is conceptualized as a temporal form that disrupts any clear distinction between extended and instantaneous time in favor of a suspended time in which the decision (as instant) becomes itself through its redistribution of processual time onto a temporal complex internal to the decision (as event). I will suggest that this account of legal time has two consequences for our understanding of the play, one political and one aesthetic or dramaturgical. We can approach the first by turning briefly to an influential account of political sovereignty in relation to the decision.

In an analysis of sovereignty that draws on the early modern theories of Machiavelli, Bodin, and Hobbes, the German jurist and political theorist Carl Schmitt notoriously defines the sovereign as the one "who decides on the exception."[17] According to a decisionist theorization of political power, the sovereign legitimates the legal order and makes politics possible, not through appeal to any norm but strictly through the sudden and quasi-metaphysical force of the decision as such, which remains heterogeneous to law even though it makes law, in the sense of a normative adjudication, possible.[18] Shakespeare's representation of Leontes' prodigiously arbitrary rejection of the oracle's judgment—"Hast thou read truth"; "There is no truth at all i' th' oracle" (3.2.136, 138)—might therefore be heard as staging the kind of radical decision that, in Schmitt's account, defines sovereignty. The problem here, as Christopher Pye suggests in an essay on the play's theorization of Absolutism, is that, whatever their content, the two decisions—the oracle's and the king's—are in fact formally aligned, not just because both issue in violence but because each depends, temporally, upon the other. The "oracle's pronouncement that the king shall live without an heir is fulfilled precisely in Leontes' refusal of it," Pye writes. "Thus, even as the reply seems to be compassed in advance by oracular law, that pronouncement is only realized—only proves law—through the response it solicits." Rather than authorizing a decisionist account of royal power, then, the king's decision in Pye's reading so disrupts "the inside and outside" of law as to put under pressure the very relation of sovereign agency to the decision that underwrites legal order.[19]

Similarly to Pye's troubling of sovereignty's relation to the decision, I would argue that, in its analysis of legal time, the play theorizes the concept of the legal decision itself, which it posits not as a threshold phenomenon but rather as an extension through time. For this response to decisionism, I find especially suggestive Samuel Weber's reading of Walter Benjamin's engagement with Schmitt in *The Origin of German Tragic Drama*. Pointing to a "methodological extremism" that Benjamin adopts from Schmitt, Weber argues that Benjamin focuses on the extremity of the exception precisely to challenge a decisionist account of sovereignty. For Benjamin, the fact that such a theory perfects itself in the image of the tyrant puts "radically into question" the "notion of sovereignty itself."[20] Against Schmitt's magisterially coherent sovereign, Benjamin represents a sovereign caught between the need to decide and the impossibility of doing so. And against a concept of sovereignty's dependence on "an absolute and absolutely definitive and ultimate decision," what Schmitt calls a "point of ascription" (*Zurechnungspunkt*) that as such "cannot be derived from a norm," Benjamin imagines an "errant" sovereign confronting the fact that there is no definitive decision, but only ongoing appeal, revision, and adjournment. In this sense, Weber punningly argues, Benjamin "takes exception to [Schmitt's] point."[21]

The point of the sovereign's decision is that it is not a point but an extension.[22] Weber's gloss on Benjamin's critique of decisionism helps us characterize, for *The Winter's Tale*, the effect of Shakespeare's distributing the legal decision onto its own time. Just as the temporal complexity of deferral and adjournment makes the decision definitively part of historical time, so too the even more radical inclusion of extended time within the legal decision moors that decision in history, thereby dismantling the kind of hermetic moment that would underwrite a purely metaphysical decisionism. Shakespeare substitutes for the punctuating instant of the sovereign's decisiveness a historical decisiveness, a deciding that is itself only by being in time. In Shakespeare's analysis, that is, decision undoes itself *as though from within* by erasing the priority of the instant. To this extent, I find that there is indeed a formal difference between the oracle's decision, as brought to Sicilia by the messengers, and the decision that the deluded king fervently desires. Leontes embraces the idea of a decision coextensive with the instantaneity of his own fantasmatic imaginings. This is an error because it misunderstands the nature of a decision as such, which is not sudden knowledge but instead a rushing of knowledge toward its fulfillment. The patient lesson the king must learn in the play's second half is literally how a sovereign decision occupies time. Returning to the oracle's statement that Leontes "shall live without an heir if that which is lost be not found" (3.2.132–34), we can usefully note that, qua judgment, this part of the oracular pronouncement is notable most for performing its own deferral, for projecting the judgment into the indeterminate future of its own fulfillment. The decision's extension toward that fulfillment mirrors what I have earlier described as the decision's extension across its own cause, as staged in 3.1. In a striking revisiting of the dramaturgical effect of that short scene, the oracle's decision does not become fully itself until the play's end, when, across the "wide gap" of sixteen years, its terms are both fully understood and finally executed.

Living in the time of a judgment distended toward its own end, Leontes is like a condemned person who, awaiting the execution of a sentence, is to that extent placed outside of time, in a substitute time of the sentence itself. The dramaturgical implication of the play's temporal analysis comes into focus here. Just as the audience feels itself suspended by act 3.1 in the decision that has been taken but is not yet known, so too the play's second half can be construed as taking place within a decision, at once the oracle's and the playwright's, that is knowable only in light of the play's conclusion. The experience of an as yet unfulfilled judicial decision finds its correlative in the experience of the artwork in orientation to its own unity. When Shakespeare distributes his story across sixteen years and daringly makes his story a story even *about* time, he gives to the play the structure of the decision he analyzes in act 3. This is to say that the play finds its authority in the same perplexing distension of time as that which sustains the law at the moment of its decisiveness. The play is an event, like the decision, that punctuates time by being in time, not out of it. In the play's last sentence, the reformed Leontes becomes spokesman for this dramaturgical position:

> Good Paulina,
> Lead us from hence, where we may leisurely
> Each one demand and answer to his part
> Performed in this wide gap of time since first
> We were dissevered. Hastily lead away. (5.3.151–55)

As J. H. P. Pafford notes in his edition, Leontes here indexes the gap that Time has produced at the beginning of act 4 by passing over a period of time: the story that has not been told will now be rehearsed offstage.[23] But one also hears in the deictic force of "*this* wide gap" a reference to the play as a whole, which Leontes' valedictory language represents as itself a gap, implicitly (and in contrast to the story that is, intimately, about to unfold) an *un*-leisurely one. Analogously to the sixteen years that have the form of a limit and to the decisive instant that has the form of history, the few hours of the play's performance gain their authority as a wide gap, an intense moment in time distended to time so as to reveal its cunning.

Locating Possession

I have been arguing that Shakespeare looks to law not only for its dramaturgical potential but also for the analytical or theoretical potential derived from probing the law's categories, even fundamental ones like judgment and decision, for the formal (and, here, temporal) mechanics upon which their operation depends. In this second part of my essay, I want to extend this claim by turning to a quite different context, to two of Shakespeare's sonnets and their treatment of legal possession, a category that, like the legal decision, is intimately structured by time. The concept of possession illuminates the sonnets, I will argue, because, like the decision that Shakespeare represents in *The Winter's Tale*, possession has the aspect not of an absolute but rather of a temporal event. For the Elizabethans, legally possessing land meant being embedded in a set of interconnecting relations: with the land, with institutions, with other persons, and with the odd quantity of time. As the sonnets reinvent the matter, the difficulties of so possessing land are effectively those of possessing another, or of possessing beauty and being possessed by it. In his encounter specifically with the time of possession, Shakespeare finds a way to imagine poetry's capacity to immortalize the beloved, this because the law offers, as what we can call a poetics of possession, a view onto the potency of form across time.[24]

Sonnet 18 ("Shall I compare thee to a summers day?") is the first of the poems addressed to the young man fully to substitute poetic for biological immortality, concluding as it does, "So long as men can breathe or eyes can see, / So long lives this, and this gives life to thee" (ll. 13–14).[25] To reach this assertion concerning the power of poetic form, Shakespeare compares human and seasonal time in terms unfavorable to the latter. Thus line 4 defines summer's decline in legal terms: "And summer's lease hath all too short a date," where, as Colin Burrow notes in his edition, "date" indicates the date of expiry on an only "temporary period of legal possession." That a human life might, in contrast, entail a different temporality depends on the friend's overcoming his own death and becoming immortal in art, a process that Shakespeare expresses by going, again, to the law:

But thy eternal summer shall not fade,
Nor lose possession of that fair thou ow'st,

Nor shall Death brag thou wand'rest in his shade,
When in eternal lines to time thou grow'st. (ll. 9–12)

The quatrain and the poem seem, then, to depend on the opposition between the temporary possession implied by the lease and the permanent possession being articulated here in relation to the ongoing cultivation of beauty.

That said, the word that most expresses that permanence also undoes it. By the contraction in "ow'st" (Q's reading), the line seems to say, paradoxically, that the friend will own (and continue to possess) the beauty he possesses by owing it. The doubleness one can hear in "ow'st" is warranted especially by the argument already made in the procreation sonnets that the young man's beauty is not his, but rather a loan from Nature (4.3), a "bounteous largess given thee to give" (4.6). But editors have proved somewhat reluctant to admit a pun between *own* and *owe* in sonnet 18. Although, for example, Burrow preserves from the 1609 Quarto the apostrophe in "ow'st," he glosses the word to mean "own absolutely and forever."[26] In this reading, owning is a stable concept, and the poem depends on two distinctions: the first between the summer's impermanent lease and the young man's ownership of his beauty, and the second between his ownership and his possession of his beauty, with "possession" now meaning an "occupancy or enjoyment of a piece of property in a manner which brings with it the right to exercise control over it" (Burrow's gloss). The concept of ownership thus articulated is complex and coherent, but it is more Roman than English. Whereas the Roman concept of possession is *usufruct*, I would argue that the one underlying the poem is *seisin*; whereas that concept of ownership is *dominion*, the one underlying the poem is the *fee* and the *estate*. The pun in "ow'st" is central to the poem because it makes present in compressed form the logic of common-law possession. According to the legal analogy, Shakespeare imagines erotic possession as a state whose temporal logic undoes the stability it pretends to, so as then to reinvent this possession in a potent lyric form.

According to the common-law system of tenure (Lat. *tenere*, "to hold"), land in England is held, not owned. This is to say that every landowner, with the exception of the king, is a tenant of some lord, holding his land either directly or indirectly from the Crown.[27] Feudal in origin, the tenurial relationship originally constituted land possession as a relationship between and among persons, a lord granting the land in exchange for a perpetual service or payment owed by a tenant, with the possibility that the tenant could then enter into another feudal relationship, this time as lord to a subsidiary tenant, and so on.[28] At no point in the resulting feudal ladder could lord or tenant be said to own the land in which he had an interest. The lord and the tenant were said, instead, to have "seisin," or to be diversely and reciprocally "seised" of the land, the lord seised "in service" and the tenant seised "in his demesne."[29] The afterlife of this feudal arrangement is the history of legal possession at common law, something that can be heard, for example, in Coke's 1628 gloss on the opening line of Littleton's *Tenures*: the tenant in fee simple, Coke writes, "hath the estate of the land, he holdeth the land of some superiour Lord, and is to perform the seruices due, and thereunto he is bounden by doome and iudgment of Law."[30]

If the first principle of English land law is that owning means holding from another, the second is that what the landowner holds is not the land at all, but rather an interest in it. The most valuable interest that can be held is an estate in the land, this being a temporal interest that is sometimes longer and sometimes shorter in duration. To follow the doctrine of estates is to follow the lawyers in a curious journey from recognizing legal possession of land as a dematerialized interest in the material thing to the rematerialization of that interest into a quantity. As the common law evolved away from its original feudal context, the tenant's interest came to be understood less as an expression of a personal relationship and more as a relationship to the land itself. This was a consequence principally of the law's coming to protect the tenant's possession (or seisin) as a heritable interest, what the lawyers referred to as a "fee." Where the law recognized the tenant's right to alienate at will, that greater-than-life interest in the land, or "fee simple," emerged as something very different from the feudal interest. As J. H. Baker writes of the fee simple: "It is not improper to call it ownership, since its continuity was no longer restrained by the claims of [the tenant's] lord or his heirs. What he owned was an estate of infinite duration. If he wished during his lifetime he could alienate it for ever. . . . If, on the other hand, he died seised, the estate did not end but descended automatically to his heir."[31]

The fee simple was the highest possible interest or estate in the land, and from it all other estates derived. So one seised in fee simple might lease the land for a term of years or grant a life interest in the land. Or he might grant land as a heritable interest, but in a diminished form, this by restricting the possible heirs to some smaller group, such as the grantee's direct line or direct male line. This is the fee tail, the "entailed" interests being of lesser duration than the fee simple, since with the failure of the designated line, the land reverted to the grantor rather than to a collateral relative of the grantee.

In summary, then, to have land in England is to hold it of another; to hold it is to be seised of it in the form of an estate or interest; and this incorporeal interest was treated, no less than the corporeal land underlying it, as a quantifiable thing that could be carved up into temporal quanta. Edmund Plowden, in his report of *Walsingham's Case* (1571), nicely summarizes the point that legal possession of a material thing is, in the end, possession of its temporal form:

> But the land itself is one thing, and the estate in the land is another thing, for an estate in the land is a time in the land, or land for a time, and there are diversities of estates, which are no more than diversities of time, for he who has a fee-simple in land has a time in the land without end, or the land for time without end . . . and he who has an estate in land for life has not time in it longer than for his own life, and so for him who has an estate in land for the life of another, or for years.[32]

In the whole hierarchy of legal interests, and even in the case of fee simple, which is the closest English law comes to ownership, time girds possession. Whatever the particular mode of tenure (whether knight-service, for example, or some form of villenage), it is technically the estate that is held, which means that a tenant's possession of the real thing is effected as possession of a time-in-the-thing, itself construed as a different thing. Taken together, the doctrine of tenure and the doctrine of estates mean that owning is provisional. In the words of one legal historian, "there is no difference in English law between absolute and temporary interest save only in their duration. We cannot separate them into two . . . species, as did the Romans; we cannot say that he who has a fee is the dominus, the owner, whereas he who has a life interest has a mere servitude. Neither has dominium. But each is seised, and for that reason their interests must be included in the same category of legal conceptions; whatever their nature, they are at least of the same inherent quality."[33]

Sonnet 18 was written from and for this legal context. The poem's comparison of the beautiful friend to a summer day depends on a hidden pun between the homonyms *season* and *seisin*, with the poem symmetrically figuring the passing season as a temporary possession and the beauty possessed by the friend as, compared to summer, a more perfect seisin. The difference between summer's lease and a form of owning that is also owing cannot be reduced to that between absolute and temporary ownership. For when one follows out the logic of common-law possession, the lease is not the category against which the friend's immortality is measured, but rather that which effectively subtends all other ways of holding, not because all land is held as in a lease from the Crown—this is entirely to miss the structure of common-law possession—but rather because the lease makes most visible the law's dematerialization of land into an interest and the rematerialization of that interest into a quantifiable duration in time.

Now Shakespeare might easily have made the poem's logic, as unfolded through the pun in "ow'st," serve a *vanitas* theme: although it may seem that there is an owning that is permanent, this argument would go, all human owning is really as by lease. Instead, after exposing the impossibility of permanently possessing something, Shakespeare turns to the terms by which poetry might nevertheless overcome that structural impossibility and make the friend's possession of his beauty permanent: "Nor shall Death brag thou wand'rest in his shade, / When in eternal lines to time thou grow'st" (ll. 11–2). The conceit here is that, through the poetry of praise, the friend will become part of time itself, consubstantial with it in the sense of being grafted (or grown) to its stock. The image is materialist in the double sense of refusing to construe immortality as a movement *beyond* time and, most impressively, of converting time itself to a material substance. As a figure for imagining the permanence of art, the figure is thus especially apposite for the common-law system on which the poem rests, a system that figures possession always as a relationship to time and in that way disrupts the idea of absolute ownership by measuring even it against time. To become identical with time is, in the only way possible, to claim ownership from within a system in which ownership is apparently impossible.

As Shakespeare deploys it, then, the metaphor comparing the possession of beauty to the possession of land is useful because it analytically amplifies the law's conversion of the possessed thing into an incorporeal form analogous to the form of beauty through which the poem intends to hold onto the beloved and make him immortal. Working through the temporal logic of the law, the poem excavates, as a lyric hypothesis, the terms under which the erotic lease might continue: not by overpowering time, but by assimilating beauty, as form, to time, now understood also in the formal sense of metrical measurement. Poetry makes the unity of form and time possible. The legal time of the lease and of common-law possession makes time in the poem audible not as a purely natural phenomenon but also as techne. As at law, time is converted here to a manipulable form that, even as it undoes the pretense to permanent possession (possession is always temporal), also makes available, in and for the poem, a version of permanence according to which a reformed thing (love as beauty as form) might indeed be aptly fitted to a reformed time (time as metrical time).

Complementing the legal effects of sonnet 18, which asks most after the temporal form of the thing possessed (land or beauty), sonnet 13 ("O that you were yourself") looks to the logic of legal inheritance as that gives shape even more intimately to the possessor or, more specifically, the possessor-across-time. The poem is of particular interest for the present argument because it conceptualizes the heir as a form at law constituted at the instantaneous threshold between one extended period of possession and another. In doing so, analogously with the formal beauty that in sonnet 18 is a poem's beauty, sonnet 13 invents the kind of person that, as it were, the beloved must become in order to live inside the poem.

Sonnet 13's opening argues that mortality makes the friend something other than himself: "O that you were your self [your selfe], but love, you are / No longer yours than you yourself [your selfe] here live" (ll. 1–2). The most audible feature of the lines is the play among the various cognates of "you," through which the poem presents a set of relations internal to self-possession: being "you" is distinct from being yourself, being yourself is dependent on your being "yours"; and being "yours" is dependent on continuing to live "here." According to this logical sequence, mortality means one does not *possess* oneself forever, which means in turn that one cannot *be* oneself. The twofold structure of the problem is reflected, chiastically, in the solution offered by the poem, which also comes in two parts. The friend is urged, "[a]gainst this coming end," to have a son, "some other" to whom he might give his "sweet semblance" and thereby perpetuate his beauty (ll. 3–4). The continuity of his beauty in another (as a possessed thing) will in turn resolve the gap expressed in lines 1–2 between the friend and his own self:

> So should that beauty which you hold in lease
> Find no determination; then you were
> Yourself [You selfe] again after your self's decease,
> When your sweet issue your sweet form should bear. (ll. 5–8)

By the doubled syllogism of the argument, aptly marked by "So" and "then," having a son will preserve the friend's beauty, which will in turn preserve himself. Making the possession of beauty permanent, the poem urges, makes possible for the friend the self-possession that is equivalent to his self-identity.

The argument concerning the efficacy of beauty thus turns back-to-front the apparent logic of the proposition that, in sonnet 1, opens the sequence as a whole: "From fairest creatures we desire increase, / That thereby beauty's rose might never die" (ll. 1–2). While there, beauty is the *reason* for courting immortality, in sonnet 13 beauty has become the mechanics of the process. This is because, behind the cliché that the son's beauty will make the father live again, there is an argument about what it means for beauty, in the terms of sonnet 13, to be a "form" that a father or son might "bear" (l. 8). Indeed, when the poem pits the "again" of line 7 against the "Against" of line 3, we can hear formal repetition as equivalent to a strike against mortality: *against the coming end,* the friend will be self-possessed by becoming himself *again*. Form is iteration; what a son offers the beloved is not so much a house in which the beloved's form will continue to exist as it is a repetition in time without which the beloved's own form will turn out itself not to have come into being. In this formal equation, no relation means no self; and it is for this reason that the poem can posit the son's bearing the father's "sweet form" as an answer to the problem of the beloved's not being himself. The iteration of form creates the possibility for self-perpetuation and self-possession because it constitutes that self-possession. To possess yourself in the sense given in lines 1–2 is always to find your form repeated elsewhere.

This is familiar as an erotic dynamic in which self-completion is never only self-fashioned. It is also, crucially, a legal structure involving the nature of legal personhood. In his edition, Stephen Booth points to a probable pun in the sonnet's second line, noting that "here" may be homonymous with "heir": "but love, you are / No longer yours than you yourself here live."[34] This is a play in language that is also found in *Henry IV, Part 1*, where Falstaff punningly says of Hal, "were it not here apparent that thou are heir apparent" (1.2.55–56).[35] In Booth's reading, the beloved is thus being told that he will be himself "only so long as you continue to be your self-heir, that is, your own heir." I think there's no doubt that the pun is operative—not just because the category of heir has been activated earlier in the procreation poems, but also because, in the legal context adduced by the poem's use of landholding as a metaphor for the possession of beauty and of oneself, Booth's suggestion indexes a legal commonplace, a fundamental principle of inheritance. At common law, you are always your own heir.

This paradox emerges in accordance with the logic of descent. When one seised of land in fee died, the fee descended to the heir, a person identifiable only according to the operation of law and the various canons of descent, including, most famously, primogeniture.[36] The particular rules aside, the important point for the present argument is that the heir came into being as heir solely according to the operation of the law. Alongside the ancestor's powerlessness to *choose* his or her heir was the striking but logical principle, in place by the middle of the fifteenth century, that the heir could not, therefore, exist until after the ancestor's death: "It is to be noted," Coke writes, "that one cannot be heire till after the death of his auncestor, he is called *haeres apparens* heire apparent." The semantic distinction between heir and heir apparent was of great importance, since it expressed the fact that the heir was less a material than a legal and formal person and, conversely, that the heir apparent, who did have material existence, precisely lacked status as a legal person. "The law does not giue the heir apparant any writ," Coke writes, "for it is not certaine whether he shall be heire, *solus deus facit haeredes*."[37] Since "no living person has an heir" (as the maxim had it), it could be said that the heir was born (as heir) only at the limit moment of the ancestor's death, before which the heir apparent was all inert matter, and the heir all active form.

The problem with this metaphysics is that the heir, too, was needed in the present, since, in the absence of ownership, it was through the person of the heir that the lawyers articulated the status of legal possession in time. Take as an example the person possessed of land in fee simple, who, according to the common-law formula, was said to "hold" the land "to him and his heires for euer."[38] It was this phrase "and his heirs" that identified the estate as unrestricted, in the sense that, even if the direct line died out, the land would still descend to a collateral heir, *some* heir, rather than reverting back to the lord from whom the holder held the land. What the phrase "to him and his heirs for ever" did not imply, however, is that these heirs had any present claim on the estate that the formula seemed also to convey to them: the land remained during her or his lifetime the possessor's to hold or to alienate at will. The common lawyers understood this by saying that where land was conveyed to A "and his heirs," the latter phrase was to be understood as "words of limitation" and not "words of purchase," *purchase* being a term that included all forms of conveyance other than descent. The heir was necessary for identifying the fullness of the grantee's interest, but it was simultaneously an impertinence to that status, not really there at all, except discursively.

So if the heir was not and could not be the heir apparent, where, before the death of the ancestor, was the heir substantially? The heir remained safely tucked into the future, as the Tudor lawyers had it, by becoming part of the ancestor. Here is Coke again, drawing on a statement by the Elizabethan justice Sir James Dyer: "for the Ancestor during his life, beareth in his bodie (in iudgment of law) all his heires, and therefore it is truly said that *Haeres ests pars antecessoris* [the heir is part of the ancestor]. And this appeareth in a common case, that if land be giuen to a man and his heires, all his heires are so totally in him, as he may give the lands to whom he will [i.e., without consideration of their interests as persons who might hold after him]."[39] One legal historian glosses the passage so: "The ancestor and the heirs are as one person and during his life the ancestor is that person."[40]

The opening lines of sonnet 13 take the common lawyers' metaphysics seriously, converting it into a dark pun around *here* and *heir*: "but love, you are / No longer yours than you yourself here live" (ll. 1–2). First, the pun allows the poem to indulge in a hyperbole: the friend will be himself if he manages to be his own heir, that is, to live on and on. More interestingly, the pun issues in a tautology, one that carries inside it, however, a nontautological analysis: the friend possesses himself while he "here" lives and "heir" lives, which is to say, twice over, that he possesses himself up to the moment when he dies, the moment at which death separates him both from the "here" and now and from the "here" or heir he has contained, as a part, totally in him.

If you are always in this sense your own heir, you are not, however, your own issue, since one's issue existed materially in natural time, and not only in the legal time that conveniently disposed the form of the heir into the future, until such time as that indefinite form should be charged by definite matter. In contradistinction to the legal person of the heir, "issue" was at law an inefficacious form: "If a man giue Lands or Tenements . . . to a man and to his Seed," Coke warns, "or to the Issues or Children of his bodie, he hath but an estate for life."[41] The heir is one thing, and the issue another, even when they turn out to identify the same body. In light of the legal distinction between issue and heir, line 8 in sonnet 13 takes on meaning as a superbly technical legal distinction:

> . . . . then you were
> Yourself again after your self's decease,
> When your sweet issue your sweet form should bear. (ll. 6–8)

The repetitions in line 8 at first seem a redundancy, the sweet issue becoming yet sweeter by bearing the father's form, which is to say his beauty. But what unfolds around the repetition is both the formal legal distinction between issue and heir and an accounting of how the one changes into the other. In one sense, line 8 turns out simply to be repeating the content of the preceding phrase, "after your self's decease," refiguring that decease as the threshold moment when the issue mysteriously becomes something else, the heir. But the line also discovers an argument about the nature of that change, since it locates the transformation at the instant in which the father's issue comes to "bear" the father's form. Taking seriously the metaphysics of the definitions whereby the common lawyers made the heir capable of doing the legal work required of the category, Shakespeare makes sense of the legal distinction as a distinction between forms. Just as the father, alive, is said to "here live" (l. 2), to live as his own heir, because he "beareth in his body . . . all his heirs," so the issue, the father dead, becomes heir by bearing the father's form and incorporating him, now as ancestor.

The poem's legal schemes are thus immensely playful, making personal immortality, the promise that Shakespeare's sonnets seem to hold out as mere hyperbole, almost a given. To put the dynamic in terms that the lawyers would have recognized but not, maybe, fully accepted, the startling point exposed by Shakespeare's verbal measurings is that in a scheme of common-law possession there can be said to be no such thing, really, as succession, but only a continuity across time in the twinned forms of possessor and possessed. Shakespeare's punning schemes are thus also very serious, because they expose, as a relation between natural personhood and formal personhood, the deep logic at law by which the law makes sense of time, compressing difference into identity and casting the formal succession to property as the continuous possession of the same—as one form's possession of another and those forms' reciprocal constitution of one another.

In this light, I would propose that the idea of the beloved's son, the strange topic of the sequence's first seventeen poems, is far more useful to the erotics of the sequence than has been recognized. In the figure of the heir as a person created at the threshold between two extended times, Shakespeare launches an idea of formal personhood capable of sustaining the sequence's broader lyric experiment to make the beloved immortal. Take, as only one example of that lyric promise, the couplet that concludes sonnet 18: "So long as men can breathe or eyes can see, / So long lives this, and this gives life to thee." The promise made here is not of continuous existence, but of a continual remaking in the irreducible instant of reading. We may think of the person whose immortality is guaranteed here as the kind of person the heir is, a particular person and a single form, but one whose material existence follows the specificity of the instant in which he is recreated—a "thee," then, to match the "this" that the poem is when it is seen and said: always different, always the same. In Shakespeare's refashioning of the energies that made the heir such an important category at common law, that legal form mobilizes for the beloved, as a lyric hypothesis, a personhood that overcomes time precisely by belonging to time as to an ongoing adjustment between the temporal limit and its extension.

A Temporal Issue

In conclusion, let me fill in a little the "wide gap" between the two parts of my essay. The heir, I have argued, is a temporal form, a formal person that coincides with a natural person only at the liminal instant that compresses the two into the same body. Heard in this light, the oracle's judgment in The Winter's Tale is odder even than we have made it in supposing that it holds the rest of the play in a kind of juridical suspension. The prediction that Leontes "shall live without an heir if that which is lost be not found" (3.2.132–34) is generally understood to be fulfilled with the discovery of Perdita, as reported in 5.2 by the gentlemen who witness the wondrous reconciliations. According to the common-law construction of the heir, however, the written oracle might well appear to be less a prophecy than a definition: the king shall *live* without an heir because that is what it means to live, which is also to say that the discovery of that which is lost must, in producing an heir, coincide with the king's death.

A strange interpretation, to be sure, even as a submerged one. But it is telling in this regard that Simon Forman, in his *Booke of Plaies*, which records a performance of *The Winter's Tale* on May 15, 1611, remembers a version of the oracle that simply erases its temporal complexity: "except the child was found again that was lost the King should die without issue."[42] Although Shakespeare has taken his oracle's wording from Robert Greene's *Pandosto*, there is evidence that the precise wording matters for the play, since in two places Shakespeare explicitly licenses the more knotted temporality that gets obscured in Forman's reductive version of the oracle. At the beginning of act 5, Paulina argues against the several counselors who are concerned about the king's "fail of issue" (5.1.27) and want him to remarry. "Care not for issue," she tells Leontes; "The crown will find an heir" (5.1.46–47). The distinction here is exactly the one at common law. Paulina means that, though the king have issue, it is time that will invent the heir, which is why in her telling the heir belongs to the Crown more than to the king. Whatever the issue might stand for in Sicilia's polity (and certainly, there is reason to desire royal issue), Paulina's "heir" emblematizes the necessary limit of this king's mortal authority.

As to the second part of the oracle's prediction, Leontes does not, of course, die when Perdita is found. Is this because she is not *yet* his heir, and the oracle not yet fully fulfilled? Or perhaps the legal context I am adducing allows us to hear anew Leontes' perplexing reaction to Hermione's statue when Paulina moves to draw the curtain against his gaze, and the king expresses the sincerity of his attachment to his dead wife, so represented there, by wishing himself to be like her:

> Let be, let be.
> Would that I were dead, but that methinks already—
> What was he that did make it? (5.3.61–63)

What interests me is the clause following Leontes' subjunctive. Already what? In what has now become the standard reading of the king's half-finished thought, Howard Staunton in 1859 argued that it is surely the statue that is already *moving*: "May I die if I do not think it moves already," Leontes means.[43] Fair enough: this makes sense contextually, in terms of what is about to unfold. But it is not quite what the line says. And what if, instead, the actor were simply to pinch himself here, as though the liveliness of the dead thing made him recognize, conversely, something creeping and foreign to his living body? Certainly the sentence's syntax supports the stranger reading, since, taken together, the adversative "but" and the adverb "already" are most easily understood as undoing the counterfactual wish with the dark intimation that it is Leontes who is already *dead*: "Would that I were dead, but that methinks already . . ." This would partly accord with a 1908 reading of 5.3.62 according to which Leontes "wishes he were dead, so stirred is his spirit with desire to join hers, but thinks he is already dead so joined with her he feels."[44] I am drawn to the syntactic reading over the simpler contextual one because, as I have noted, in a strict sense the fulfillment of the oracle through the finding of the heir *requires* this death. Perdita cannot be found in *that* way unless Leontes joins Hermione.

This legal logic means, in turn, that in the statue's awakening, which also marks Leontes' full reintegration into his life, the oracle, fulfilled, is actually undoing itself, with Perdita, the found heir, now being returned to an earlier form alongside her revivified parents. The form of the heir must disappear, I mean, at the very moment Hermione steps down into the heir's presence. As it turns out, in Shakespeare's relentless measuring of "issue" and "heir" against one another, Hermione herself posits as much, when, by way of explanation to the daughter, she rehearses the oracle but, like Forman, slightly adjusts its force:

> For thou shalt hear that I,
> Knowing by Paulina that the oracle
> Gave hope thou wast in being, have preserved
> Myself to see the issue. (5.3.125–28)

At this point of the plot's unfolding, then, it is and must be *not* the heir as promised by the oracle, but the issue: a nice distinction, in which the play finds yet another way, superbly technical and superbly legal, to say that life will go on a while longer.

Since, here as throughout this essay, I am tracing the effect of very small shifts in word choice and syntax, it can fairly be asked if, in the end, I am persuaded that this legal magic (in a scene full of magic) is actually there. Put differently, this is to ask also whether a play or poem can, really, be the kind of thing practical lawyers might go to in order imaginatively and usefully to think through their categories, their way of making the world do what's required of it. Well, I could be persuaded. In relation to the first question, the time of Shakespeare's final scene is surely strange enough; and whatever the law's logic tells us about Leontes and the happy invention of his heir, the answer must make time—decisive time, complex time—the cause. In relation to the second question, I have been arguing, for both the play and the sonnets, that Shakespeare's restless law has its origin in his acute hearing of words and their possible dispositions. His law, it seems to me, acquires its technical force chiefly as language and only secondarily as doctrine. As such, Shakespeare's stage law encounters the law of the courts and Inns as its most intimate companion, in a zone of practical thinking equally proper to those latter forums and equally recognizable to their more careful disciples.

NOTES

This essay began its life at the meeting of the Renaissance Society of America at Cambridge in 2005, where I benefited from Colin Burrow's comments and insights. It was completed with the assistance of a National Endowment for the Humanities research fellowship at the Folger Shakespeare Library. For their suggestions, I would like also to thank Kathy Eden, Julia Lupton, Stephen Orgel, and Richard Strier. I owe a special debt to Lorna Hutson, whose generous conversation has everywhere sharpened my thinking.

1. All line citations to the play are to William Shakespeare, *The Winter's Tale*, ed. Stephen Orgel (Oxford: Oxford University Press, 1996). I have also used the notes in *The Winter's Tale*, ed. Robert Kean Turner and Virginia Westling Haas, New Variorum Edition of Shakespeare (New York: MLA, 2005). For the proverb "Time tries all things," see entry T336 in R. W. Dent, *Shakespeare's Proverbial Language: An Index* (Berkeley: University of California Press, 1981), 232.

2. Peter Lindenbaum notes that in referring to "my tale" (4.1.14), Time takes on the role of yet another ruler, namely "the author of the play in which he appears." See Lindenbaum, "Time, Sexual Love, and the Uses of Pastoral in *The Winter's Tale*," *Modern Language Quarterly* 33, no. 1 (1972): 3–22, reprinted in *The Winter's Tale: Critical Essays*, ed. Maurice Hunt (New York: Garland, 1995), 200–219, at 200.

3. For an early account of the play's systematic "exploration of the meanings of time," see Inga-Stina Ewbank, "The Triumph of Time in *The Winter's Tale*," *Review of English Literature* 5 (1964): 83–100, reprinted in Hunt, *The Winter's Tale*, 139–55, at 140.

4. Samuel Johnson, ed., *The Plays of William Shakespeare* (London, 1765), 2:288–89, cited in Orgel, *The Winter's Tale*. I have regularized Johnson's italics.

5. On Shakespeare's analysis, in *Cymbeline*, of the temporal limit of the present and the spatial limit of the line, as these were theorized in legal discussions of the Anglo-Scottish Union, see Bradin Cormack, *A Power to Do Justice: Jurisdiction, English Literature, and the Rise of Common Law, 1509–1625* (Chicago: University of Chicago Press, 2007), chap. 5.

6. For Shakespeare's dramaturgical manipulation of time as a forensic circumstance, see Lorna Hutson's analysis of *Othello* and the problem of "Double Time" in her essay in this volume.

7. See Hutson's essay, p. 45. Hutson's rhetorical analysis of *narratio* as the site of legal-inferential thinking exposes the "circumstantial" mechanics of a character mi-

mesis that comes to seem natural. For some examples of character's prominence in the analysis of Shakespeare's law, see the treatments of Escalus and the Duke in *Measure for Measure* in David Bevington's, Constance Jordan's, and Richard Strier's essays in this volume.

8. For two of my earlier arguments on law in the sonnets, the first on contingent remainders and resulting uses in sonnets 74 and 87 and the second on conditional bonds in sonnets 133 and 134, see my "Shakespeare Possessed: Legal Affect and the Time of Holding," in *Shakespeare and the Law*, ed. Paul Raffield and Gary Watt (Oxford: Hart, 2008), 83–100; and "On Will: Time and Voluntary Action in *Coriolanus* and the Sonnets," *Shakespeare* 5, no. 3 (2009): 253–70.

9. Virginia Lee Strain, "*The Winter's Tale* and the Oracle of the Law," *English Literary History* 78 (2011): 557–84, at 569. I am grateful to Dr. Strain for sharing this paper with me prior to publication.

10. On the figure of the preposterous in relation to drama and broader cultural orders, see Patricia Parker, *Shakespeare from the Margins* (Chicago: University of Chicago Press, 1996), chap. 1; Patricia Parker, "Hysteron Proteron: Or the Preposterous," in *Renaissance Figures of Speech*, ed. Sylvia Adamson, Gavin Alexander and Katrin Ettenhuber (Cambridge: Cambridge University Press, 2007), 133–45; Joel Altman, "'Preposterous Conclusions': Eros, Enargeia, and the Composition of *Othello*," *Representations* 18 (1987): 129–57.

11. David M. Bergeron, "The Apollo Mission in *The Winter's Tale*," in Hunt, *The Winter's Tale*, 361–79, at 372. Bergeron's illuminating suggestion that the oracle imitates a jury verdict or report comes more sharply into focus in light of Lorna Hutson's detailed exposition of Elizabethan dramatic mimesis in relation to jury deliberation and the culture of forensic inquiry it sponsored. See Hutson, *The Invention of Suspicion: Law and Mimesis in Shakespeare and Renaissance Drama* (Oxford: Oxford University Press, 2007).

12. Strain, "*The Winter's Tale* and the Oracle of the Law," 568–73, 574.

13. On Shakespeare's theater in relation to a complex "culture of mediation" and, specifically, the reproduction of legal depositions as an instance of authority's dependence upon "multiply mediated representation," see Holger Schott Syme, *Theatre and Testimony in Shakespeare's England: A Culture of Mediation* (Cambridge: Cambridge University Press, 2012), 26, and esp. chap. 5 on *The Winter's Tale*.

14. Christopher Pye, "Against Schmitt: Law, Aesthetics, and Absolutism in Shakespeare's *Winter's Tale*," *South Atlantic Quarterly* 108, no. 1 (2009): 197–217, at 204.

15. *Agnes Gore's Case* (Mich. 9 Jac.), in *La Neuf[ies]me Part des Reports*, by Sir Edward Coke (London, 1613), sigs. 81r–82r, at 81v.

16. On the modularity of intention in early modern homicide cases, see Luke Wilson, *Theaters of Intention: Drama and Law in Early Modern England* (Stanford, CA: Stanford University Press, 2000).

17. Carl Schmitt, *Political Theology: Four Chapters on the Concept of Sovereignty*, trans. George Schwab (Cambridge, MA: MIT Press, 1985; Chicago: University of Chicago Press, 2005), 5. Given the scope of my argument, I restrict my use of Schmitt here to the core principle in his theory of the sovereign decision. More relevant for aesthetics,

however, is Schmitt's insistence on the politically constitutive force of representation (in, for example, the *figure* of the sovereign). For political representation in relation to Schmitt's account of tragic representation as the intrusion of objective political reality into a zone of aesthetic play that would otherwise not be truly political, see Schmitt, *Hamlet or Hecuba: The Intrusion of the Time into the Play*, trans. David Pan and Jennifer R. Rust (New York: Telos Press, 2009); and the essays collected in an issue of *Telos* dedicated to that work: *Telos* 153 (Winter 2010). For the argument that Schmitt's theory of sovereignty depends on his mischaracterization of early modern political representation and aesthetics, see Victoria Kahn, "Hamlet or Hecuba: Carl Schmitt's Decision," *Representations* 83 (2003): 67–96.

18. The most influential response to Schmitt's delineation of the nonnormative character of the decision is Giorgio Agamben, *Homo Sacer: Sovereign Power and Bare Life*, trans. Daniel Heller-Roazen (Stanford, CA: Stanford University Press, 1998).

19. Pye, "Against Schmitt," 203–4.

20. Samuel Weber, "Taking Exception to Decision: Walter Benjamin and Carl Schmitt," *Diacritics* 22, nos. 3–4 (1992): 5–18, at 7, 15. For Benjamin's invocation of Schmitt's core doctrine, see Walter Benjamin, *The Origin of German Tragic Drama*, trans. John Osborne (London: New Left Books, 1977), at 65, 69. On Benjamin's thesis in relation to Schmitt, especially his interpretation of *Hamlet*, see Katrin Trüstedt, "Hecuba against Hamlet: Carl Schmitt, Political Theology, and the Stake of Modern Tragedy," *Telos* 153 (Winter 2010): 94–112, esp. at 99–103; also Kahn, "Hamlet or Hecuba," 82–83 and 94n42.

21. Weber, "Taking Exception to Decision," 18.

22. In this sense, the legal temporality of the decision closely resembles the concept of time explored by Giorgio Agamben in his analysis of what Saint Paul identifies as the "time of the now" [*ho nyn kairos*], that is, the time wrought through a Messianic intrusion into history. See Agamben, *The Time That Remains: A Commentary on the Letter to the Romans*, trans. Patricia Dailey (Stanford, CA: Stanford University Press, 2005), esp. "The Fourth Day: Apostolos," 59–87. Opposing the knotted presentness of Messianic time both to prophecy, which is oriented only to the future, and Apocalypse, which attaches only to the end of time as the "instant in which time ends," Agamben understands the Messianic *kairos* ("occasion") articulated by Paul as a kind of end-oriented present, as "the time that contracts itself and begins to end" or "the time that remains between time and its end" (62). Put another way, the *kairos* that is the "time of the now" happens in time and belongs to chronological time, as both a "contracted and abridged *chronos*" (69) and as an "instant" that the Messianic event "seizes" and "brings . . . forth to fulfilment" (71). Politically speaking, the important point is that this reconfiguration of time (in the extension of the instant and contraction of *chronos*) generates a Messianic vocation, Paul's, that is itself rooted fully in a present that is neither understandable nor representable except in relation to what's coming. In Julia Reinhard Lupton's formulation, Agamben sees Paul as inaugurating a "philosophy and ethics of temporality in and for the present time." See Lupton, "Paul Shakespeare," chap. 7 in *Thinking with Shakespeare: Essays on Politics and Life* (Chicago: University of Chicago Press, 2011),

219–46, at 237. In response to Agamben's insistence on the political force of Messianic time as described by Paul, Lupton perceptively reads Hamlet's "The interim is mine" as an instance of the Pauline "time that remains for action" (238). Addressing The Winter's Tale through a similar lens, Ken Jackson looks to Paul (and Agamben) to read Leontes' unmotivated jealousy as the unsettling and unsettled "experience of messianic contracted time," whose coincidence with chronological time Leontes rejects. See Jackson, "'Grace to Boot': St. Paul, Messianic Time, and Shakespeare's The Winter's Tale," in The Return of Theory in Early Modern English Studies, ed. Paul Cefalu and Bryan Reynolds (Basingstoke, UK: Palgrave Macmillan, 2011), 192–210, at 199, 204.

23. William Shakespeare, The Winter's Tale, ed. J. H. P. Pafford, New Arden ed. (London: Methuen, 1963).

24. I use poetics here in its root sense of making, following Victoria Kahn in her analysis of the relation between the early modern political contract and the "history of poetics" as a "productive capacity . . . to create new artifacts." See Kahn, Wayward Contracts: The Crisis of Political Obligation in England, 1640–1674 (Princeton, NJ: Princeton University Press, 2004), 15.

25. William Shakespeare, Complete Sonnets and Poems, ed. Colin Burrow (Oxford: Oxford University Press, 2002). All line citations to the sonnets are to this edition. Readings from the 1609 Quarto are enclosed in square brackets and are cited from the facsimile printing in Shakespeare's Sonnets, ed. Stephen Booth (New Haven, CT: Yale University Press, 1977).

26. Alongside Burrow, Stephen Booth and Stephen Orgel avoid the pun. John Kerrigan and Katherine Duncan-Jones do note that the concept of owning is here tinged with debt. See The Sonnets, ed. Stephen Orgel (New York: Penguin, 2001); The Sonnets and A Lover's Complaint, ed. John Kerrigan (Harmondsworth, UK: Penguin, 1986); Shakespeare's Sonnets, ed. Katherine Duncan-Jones, Arden Shakespeare (London: Thomas Nelson, 1997).

27. The account of landholding in the following paragraphs draws on J. H. Baker, Introduction to English Legal History, 3rd ed. (London: Butterworths, 1990); A. D. Hargreaves, An Introduction to the Principles of Land Law, 3rd ed. (London: Sweet and Maxwell, 1952); T. H. Plucknett, A Concise History of the Common Law, 5th ed. (London: Butterworth, 1956); Frederic Pollock and F. W. Maitland, The History of English Law before the Time of Edward II, 2nd ed., with intro. by S. F. C. Milsom (London: Cambridge University Press, 1968); A. W. B. Simpson, A History of the Land Law, 2nd ed. (Oxford: Clarendon Press, 1986).

28. After passage in 1290 of the statute Quia Emptores, vendors were prevented from selling land to another by subinfeudation, that is, by creating another tenure in the ladder; instead, they were restricted to selling by substitution, the process by which the buyer took the place of the vendor in the tenurial chain.

29. Baker, Introduction to English Legal History, 296.

30. Sir Edward Coke, The First Part of the Institutes (London, 1628), sig. iv.

31. Baker, Introduction to English Legal History, 301.

32. Edmund Plowden, The Commentaries or Reports (1571, 1579; London: Brooke, 1816), 2:555. I have regularized capitalization.

33. A. D. Hargreaves, *Introduction to the Principles of Land Law*, 47.

34. For the original suggestion, Booth credits Gerald Willen and Victor Reed, *A Casebook on Shakespeare's Sonnets* (New York: Thomas Crowell, 1964), 15. On *heir* and *here* as homonyms generally, see Helge Kökeritz, *Shakespeare's Pronunciation* (New Haven, CT: Yale University Press, 1953), 111, 178–79.

35. Cited from William Shakespeare, *The Complete Works*, ed. Stanley Wells and Gary Taylor (Oxford: Clarendon Press, 1986).

36. For the canons of descent, see Baker, *Introduction to English Legal History*, 304–7; Simpson, *History of the Land Law*, 56–63.

37. Coke, *First Part of the Institutes*, sig. 8r–v.

38. Ibid., sig. 1r.

39. Ibid., sig. 22v.

40. Percy Bordwell, "Alienability and Perpetuities II," *Iowa Law Review* 23, no. 1 (1937), 1–23, at 3.

41. Coke, *First Part of the Institutes*, sig. 20v.

42. Cited from Appendix A in Orgel, *The Winter's Tale*, 233.

43. Howard Staunton's reading from his edition of the *Plays* (1856–60) is cited in the New Variorum Edition. The syntactical figure involved is *aposiopesis*, "when through some affection or interruption, . . . we cut of parte of our speach, and ende not that we haue begon." See Henry Peacham, *The Garden of Eloquence* (London, 1577), sig. E4r.

44. This is the gloss of Charlotte Porter and Helen A. Clarke from their edition of the *Works* (New York, 1903–12), as cited in the New Variorum Edition. In a different register, note also Stanley Cavell's hypothesis that in "the fate of stone" Leontes recognizes what he "has done to [Hermione], hence to him," his acknowledgment of the statue being "a projection of his own sense of numbness, of living death." See Cavell, *Disowning Knowledge: In Seven Plays of Shakespeare*, updated edition (Cambridge: Cambridge University Press, 2003), 125.

LORNA HUTSON

"LIVELY EVIDENCE"

LEGAL INQUIRY AND THE *EVIDENTIA*

OF SHAKESPEAREAN DRAMA

Chicago, 2009:
A Conference on the Legal Dimensions
of Shakespeare's Plays

A conference explicitly devoted to bringing together scholars from law, literature, and philosophy to "investigate the legal dimensions of Shakespeare's plays" necessarily assumes that the plays have legal dimensions. More than that, the assumption made by many speakers, as well as in discussions on papers, was clearly that Shakespeare's dramatis personae could be treated as fully interiorized individuals with past histories and future intentions. While it is not at all uncommon (indeed, it is normal) for discussions about meaning in Shakespeare's plays to proceed thus, the normality of the procedure itself should be an object of academic inquiry. A question, then, that ought to be explored in any conference, or volume, on Shakespeare and the law, is whether our readiness to see the characters in the play as vividly realized human beings might itself owe something to a specific synergy between the cultures of dramatic composition and legal inquiry in the late sixteenth century.

My contribution to this volume's general exploration of the legal dimension of Shakespeare's plays takes the form of trying to cast some light on this phenomenon: that is, on our readiness to work imaginatively with the hidden, causal, or motivational elements of dramatic action that are merely inferred (by us, or by characters within the play) from dialogue and narrative. I am interested in the emergence in the 1590s and 1600s of a kind of theatrical realism based not on the vividness of what is *seen* or enacted on stage, but on the exploitation, by Shakespeare and other dramatists, of the generativity of inference and conjecture. Yet my preference for focusing on what Marjorie Garber has called the "unscene"—the elements of dramatic action that Shakespeare deliberately leaves teasingly ambiguous and uncertain because unstaged—might seem to be perversely missing the obvious analogy between law and Shakespearean theater, which is usually located in the ancient affinity between trial and drama, or in the theatricality of law itself.[1] It would be pointless to deny the pervasiveness of the trope of law as theatrical performance in cultural legal studies, a trope recently analyzed with subtlety and clarity by Julie Stone Peters.[2] My reason for sidestepping it, however, has to do less with skepticism about the explanatory power of tropes of theater and performance than with a sense that their very effectiveness as figures for broader cultural processes can preempt recognition of what is innovative and enduring about English Renaissance drama in the context of world literature. For, just as critical writing on law's cultural effects has been dominated by theatrical tropes, so the professional study of English Renaissance literature has been transformed over the past thirty years by a critical vocabulary that tends to reach for theatrical metaphors to describe the cultural and political effects of the literary. Behind these metaphors—involving abstract nouns such as *power, gender, politics, masculinity,* and the like, preceded by words such as *playing, staging,* or *performing*—lie the influences of Geertzian anthropology, of Foucauldian cultural genealogy, of Greenblattian New Historicism, of Austinian speech-act theory, and of Judith Butler's influential blending of Foucault, Austin, and Derrida.[3]

While it is clear that these metaphors have actually functioned in an extremely salutary way to broaden the cultural scope and raise the political and ethical stakes of formal literary analysis rather than to carve out a new role for stage-centered criticism (a recent collection devoted to Shakespeare and performance wryly notes that New Historicism found "thick description" everywhere except in early modern stage practice), they can also, as a less important side effect, work to preclude recognition of their own metaphoricity when applied to the cultural poetics of canonical dramatic texts.[4] Thus, if one were to say that a lyric poem "stages" or "performs" a certain model or conflict of gender or politics, analysis would turn on the textual strategies and silences that enable our inferences, whereas if one says that a play by Shakespeare "stages" or "performs" such cultural work, the inferences themselves are often then simply given the names of characters and directly related to wider cultural processes.[5] Yet, when one thinks about it, the fact that one can make such rich sense of the emotional histories "behind" the speech and action in a Shakespeare play, as if the motivations for speech were to be sought less in the period's ideology and dramatic convention than in individual human complexity, is itself a remarkable achievement. It is, moreover, largely an achievement of the "unscene," understood as the innovative compositional strategies that enable us to find the whole fiction coherent and encourage us to participate in imagining the actions and words assigned to the actors as motivated not by the exigencies of historically specific semiotic conventions but by the responses of real people to one another and to the circumstances in which they find themselves.[6]

For this reason, I want to propose that the rhetorical category that offers the most to any exploration of the legal dimensions of sixteenth- and seventeenth-century dramaturgy is not that of performance, but of "narrative," or, in the Latin of Shakespeare's grammar school education, *narratio*. Although most often associated, in law-and-literature studies, with criticism of the nineteenth-century novel or with Anglo-American trial movies, the use of narrative in late-sixteenth-century theatrical performance is a technical innovation that marks the essential, if muted and understated, neoclassicism of that drama and accounts for its recognition of the power of the unscene. Significantly for the present argument, the teaching of narrative in grammar school and the analysis of the narrative elements of Latin drama had, from the early sixteenth century, a forensic cast. When reading Latin comedy, schoolboys were taught to analyze as "narratio" or narrative both "the statement of facts in a particular scene" and "any narrative passage that might occur anywhere in the five acts."[7] As early as 1532, Leonard Cox's vernacular *Arte or Crafte of Rethoryke* (based on Cicero's *De Inventione*) defined narrative or "narration" thus: "The narracion or tale is the shewynge of the dede in maner of an historye / wherein yᵉ accuser must craftly entermengle many suspicions which shall seme to make his mater prouable."[8] Narrative was also, as I will go on to show, associated with the teaching of topics of circumstance (Latin *circumstantiae*, Greek *peristaseis*), which were, in turn, considered essential to the narrative virtue of imaginative visualization, a quality known as *enargeia* or *evidentia*.[9] The purpose of this essay, then, is to show how this pedagogical theory of narrative amplification, which was germane to the rhetorical analysis of classical drama and hence to the composition of new dramatic works in English, related to another new cultural phenomenon: the rise of a vernacular literature and culture of evidential inquiry in English common law. I will argue that widely diffused techniques of rhetorical invention and vivid presentation conjoin with a no less widely diffused culture of legal inquiry to produce what one contemporary of Shakespeare called the "Lively Evidence" of dramatic dialogue that makes "Hearers" or audiences believe they are "spectators" of what they do not actually see.[10] Nineteenth-century character criticism of Shakespeare, drawing on an eighteenth-century discourse of circumstantial evidence, was thus not as wide of the mark as is often thought.

Narrative: Legal and Dramaturgical Intelligibility

The law-and-literature movement's debate over narrative is more relevant for our understanding of the legal dimension of Shakespeare's plays than its debates over the value and politics of performance, because the plays both are narrative in form and involve characters who listen to and evaluate the credibility of one another's narratives. As Peter Brooks has written (in relation to the Anglo-American legal tradition, which obviously shares a past with the English common-law culture from which Shakespeare's plays emerged), "What matters most in stories at the law is how they are evaluated and implemented by listeners: police, judges, juries."[11] When Brooks directs us to the role of the listener in the construing of narrative, in the imaginative work required to make a narrative seem coherent, intelligible, and *true*, he valuably reminds us of the extent to which forensic circumstances—the who, what, where, when elements—are corroborative or coherent only to the extent that we, as listeners or readers, recognize the cultural values and assumptions underlying the inferences we are being required to draw and from which we imaginatively reconstruct the scene. Brooks describes a seminar he taught at Yale on a rape case; first the accused was convicted, then the conviction was reversed in the first appellate court, and, finally, the original conviction was reinstated in the higher court. Four different retellings of the "same" story, he observes, depend for their radically different outcomes on differences in "the narrative 'glue' . . . the way incidents and events are made to combine in a meaningful story, one that can be called 'consensual sex' on the one hand or 'rape' on the other. In each case, the blanks (what Wolgang Iser would call the *Leerstellen*) of the story are filled according to each of the judges' general understanding of human behavior and intent." We, as listeners, bring to any narrative composition of causal and circumstantial elements "a set of unexamined cultural *doxa* (as Roland Barthes would have said) that undergird our everyday construal of narratives."[12] These cultural commonplaces inhabit everyday figures of speech— the examples Brooks gives are the epithets "bar-hopping" and "vigorous" applied to the woman in the case, as well as the judge's telling choice of verb in his expression of incredulity at the victim's being unwilling "to *participate*" in oral sex. Two levels of inference are relevant here. The lexical choice indicates, first, a doxological process underlying the judgment; as quoted by Brooks, it also invites us (as listeners to the listeners) into a further process of inferential thinking that involves the imaginative (and impassioned) re-creation of forms of subjective inwardness—forms of intention and desire—that enable us to make moral judgments even as we construe, or make sense of, a narrative.

The fact that Shakespeare's plays take a narrative form and engage in highly sophisticated ways of enabling us to feel as if events have unfolded before us as part of a longer history has been largely overlooked or taken for granted by criticism. Yet the mastery of such narrative form in drama was relatively recent and is indicative of a specific choice among a number of dramaturgical options. The box office success, in the 1580s and early 1590s, of the nonnarrative or emblematic style favored by London's premier playing company, The Queen's Men, offers a striking contrast, for example, to the Shakespearean form. Scott Mc-Millan and Sally-Beth MacLean describe the dramatic action in Robert Wilson's *Three Lords and Ladies of London* (published in 1584): "The style of performance is predominantly visual. Attention focuses on objects, costumes, the gestures of actors, and patterns of stage movement; to these elements, language tends to be subordinate."[13] "Nothing," the authors conclude, "is written with more care" in Wilson's play than the description of the stage properties, the shields and costumes that the lords carry onstage, and this "concentration on visual emblems" is maintained throughout the play. This was "a system of acting by brilliant stereotype" that crucially required the "unmistakeable sign . . . the gesture no eye can misread, the accent no ear can misunderstand."[14]

The visual and emblematic dramaturgy favored by The Queen's Men yielded to the box office success of Christopher Marlowe's *Tamburlaine* in a revolution that was, as McMillan and MacLean write, "primarily rhetorical," and Shakespeare went on to rewrite, developing this newer, rhetorical dramaturgy, no fewer than six of the Queen's Men's hit plays.[15] The fact that he did so requires us to acknowledge that his use of rhetorical techniques to pursue an illusion of narrative unfolding onstage was a conscious choice, a dramaturgical innovation. Like other innovators—Marlowe and Kyd earlier, and later Ben Jonson—Shakespeare embraced the challenge of using speech (monologue and dialogue) as the medium of this illusion of temporal continuity. He also, like Ben Jonson, was innovative in emphasizing the extent to which dramatis personae are themselves caught up in the imaginative projections that vivid narrative encourages.

Shakespeare's and Jonson's interest in the dramatic illusion of temporal continuity took different forms, but for each dramatist this technical interest was related to the question of fixity or fluidity in the representation of space on the stage. In France and Italy, humanist drama followed the practice of Roman New Comedy and Senecan tragedy in tending to adhere to a single location throughout the time of the dramatic action. This practice actually went with an encouragement of the imaginative importance of descriptive *ekphrasis* and narrative *enargeia* (a way of telling a story so vividly that it seems to take place before one's eyes), since the confinement of the dramatic action to a fixed locale required that events taking place elsewhere—at the harbor, or in one of the off-stage "interiors"—be narrated by one character to another. Both Jonson and Shakespeare loosened the specificity of place demanded by neoclassical practice—Jonson by shifting location to permit a new, critical perspective on the action (as when we move from Volpone's house to the piazza in *Volpone*, or to the outside of Lovewit's house in *The Alchemist*) and Shakespeare by disintegrating the unitary perspective of the fixed-locale stage and identifying plurality of perspective, and fluid change of location, with the play's creative engagement of the audience's imaginations.[16]

Nevertheless, Shakespeare's permissiveness with imaginative location did not cause him to reject the neoclassical recourse to narrative as a means of vividly conveying events that the characters and audience *suppose* (and the possible fictitiousness is important) to have happened elsewhere. Indeed, the rejection of the neoclassical innovation of unity of time meant, in a peculiarly Shakespearean development, that the off-stage "elsewhere" could become the suggestion of a "meantime," so that a sense of duration could become imaginable, through impressionistic narrative reconstruction, in a way that had not been possible in native emblematic and moral dramaturgical traditions. Critics—once they have dismissed the idea that Shakespeare was constrained by the neoclassical rule of unity of time—have often treated the question of time in his plays as if it were a problem or a "crux" to be solved. But such an approach misses the momentousness of Shakespeare's dramaturgical achievement, suggesting that there already existed a normal "realism" of narrative time in the theater, which Shakespeare was free to disrupt, if he chose. On the contrary, Shakespeare's achievement was to unfold a single coherent narrative for his audience that offers glimpses into the pasts—the habits, the routines, the crises—of different characters in ways that seem psychologically rich and compelling. It was important to this achievement that for Shakespeare, "time" was not a problem to be solved or a rule to be broken, but a circumstantial question to be explored in appealing to an audience's or an interlocutor's ability to *imagine for themselves* the story being told.

Time as a "Problem" in *Othello*

The most audacious, or at least the most notorious, of Shakespeare's experiments in producing the illusion of temporal continuity while simultaneously suggesting a more capacious scope of offstage action and longer individual histories occurs in *Othello*, first performed in 1604.[17] And in criticism of this aspect of *Othello*, from Thomas Rymer's acidly funny attack of 1693 through the defenses, solutions, and disavowals of the following four centuries, we discover precisely how inseparable are questions of moral or ethical liability from those of narrative coherence and intelligibility. The chief problem or crux identified by critics of *Othello* since Rymer involves the fact that the time indicators in the play are simply inconsistent on closer inspection (although the incoherence is not apparent to an audience watching the play). Thus, on the one hand, it is suggested that Othello and Desdemona are married the instant the play begins, that they leave for Cyprus that night, and that the Cyprus scenes fall within two successive days, so that we have the absurd situation of Othello murdering his wife for adultery "a thousand times committed" (5.2.212) on the first night after their marriage. On the other hand, suggestions simultaneously abound that a much longer period of time has elapsed; that Othello and Desdemona are a longtime married couple, familiar with each other's dispositions, and that Iago has repeatedly urged his wife to help him steal Desdemona's handkerchief as part of a long-term, slowly developing plot to erode Othello's confidence in his wife's fidelity. Rymer's initial exposure of this inconsistency took the form of denouncing the indecorous unfitness for tragedy of the characters in the play. Behaving in so untimely a fashion, they become absurd and undiscriminating about one another; they emerge as a bit dense—pathetic, perhaps, but certainly not tragic. So Othello, tortured by the thought of his wife's "stolne houres of Lust" is, as Rymer comments, a victim of short-term memory loss, for he "forgets he has not yet been two nights in the Matrimonial Bed with his *Desdemona*."[18]

Rymer's objections eventually generated, in their refutation, the most influential development in Shakespeare criticism in the nineteenth century: that is, the discovery of the theory of "Double Time." According to this theory, which was most famously articulated by John Wilson (who wrote in *Blackwood's Magazine* under the pseudonym Christopher North), Rymer mistook for a failure of narrative coherence what should actually have been understood as a compositional virtue.[19] Wilson's double-time-scheme solution, as Joel Altman has commented, "satisfies the need for two kinds of probability: long time is needed to convince the audience that what Othello imagines has taken place could have taken place; short time is needed to make Othello's gullibility credible."[20] Wilson's discovery also laid the foundation for numerous later developments in Shakespeare criticism, including Bradleyan character criticism and psychoanalytic criticism, the assumptions of which still govern most of our talk about Shakespeare. Thus, although the double-time theory itself has been progressively ridiculed as symptomatic of a Victorian tendency to treat Shakespeare's plays as nineteenth-century novels, it is not as easily discarded as the critics who pour scorn on it would like to suggest.[21] A humanist criticism inevitably bases its ethical readings on the timing of imagined (unstaged) events, on the unscene. So, for example, while Graham Bradshaw denounces the "factitious and distracting . . . myth" of double-time theory in *Othello*, his own criticism of the play involves a psychoanalytic reading of Othello's sexual frustration, which relies on supposing (from the indeterminate evidence of act 2, scene 3) that Othello's marriage to Desdemona was unconsummated. Bradshaw counters Stephen Greenblatt's reading of Othello's excessive sexual pleasure in Desdemona with the comment: "far from being "too familiar with his wife" by taking "excessive pleasure" in the marriage bed, Othello hasn't taken any."[22] It's clear that twentieth-century critics who most wish to reject the positivistic double-time theories of the Victorians nevertheless produce their own circumstantial "narrative glue" in imagining a sequence of events and inferring their probable psychological effects.

Rymer's criticisms in 1693 and Bradshaw's in 1993 both reveal the inseparability of humanist criticism—involving moral, ethical, or psychoanalytic interpretations of human characters as revealed by their action and speech—from narrative circumstantiality. They both also, intriguingly, reserve their greatest distaste for those moments in *Othello* when an excessive interest in narrative circumstance threatens to transform the audience's appreciation of tragic passion into the factual grubbing of the criminal lawyer. Of Shakespeare's denouement, Rymer complains, "never was old Deputy Recorder in a Country Town, with his spectacles, in summoning up the evidence, at such a puzzle" (254). Bradshaw is similarly repelled by critics whose minute investigations of where, when, and how lead "our attention away from Othello's obsession towards the kind of details that might obsess an Inspector from Scotland Yard."[23]

Bradshaw's scorn is primarily directed at the kind of pseudo-forensic investigation that constituted John Wilson's critical discovery of the double-time theory in 1850. Wilson's dialogue is, indeed, explicitly interested in linking Othello's obsession to the details that might obsess a lawyer or detective. "Christopher North" (Wilson's persona) concludes his disquisition on the longtime indicators at Cyprus by observing that Othello's language to Emilia "denotes a somewhat long attendance [in Cyprus] on Desdemona." He begins his conclusion: "Iago's 'thousand times committed' can only lengthen out the stay at Cyprus. Othello still believes that she once loved him—that she has fallen to corruption." At this point another member of the group interrupts North with a single-word suggestion, "Antenuptial?" North's response is filled with moral repulsion ("Faugh!"), insisting that had such been the disgusting inference the audience were to draw, Shakespeare would have made it explicit (505). But the investigation is by no means over. Another interlocutor, called Seward, proposes "that Shakespeare assumed the marriage to have taken place sometime before the commencement of the Play—sufficiently long to admit the possibility of a course of guilt before the play opens." A lawyer called Talboys objects: the marriage, he says, took place on the same night. Different evidence is brought forward: Seward points out, "The only evidence as to the history of the marriage is that given by Roderigo in the First Scene," noting that Roderigo, "with the most manifest anxiety to prove himself an honest witness," declares how Desdemona has eloped. Seward claims that Roderigo can only answer that he *thinks* so when interrogated by Brabantio, "Are they married, think ye?" and he answers, "Truly I think they are" (506).

Although Seward's embryonic theory of a marriage long antedating the play's action is shot down by the others, the doubts and questions it raises linger on as doubts, unanswered. Seward's point is the *uncertainty*, the less-than-total reliability, of the information on which we base our sense of when the wedding took place. Although the others dismiss Seward's conclusion from this that the marriage may have taken place some time ago, they do acknowledge that there is something odd about its being so clandestine. Talboys asks, "Why should such a private marriage have been resorted to; and if privacy was desirable at first, what change had occurred to cause the public declaration of it?" Seward acknowledges, "A private marriage is, under any circumstances, a questionable proceeding; and our great Dramatist was desirous that as little of the questionable as possible should either be or appear in the conduct of the "Divine Desdemona;" and therefore he has left the private marriage very much in the shade" (507).

Seward's theory is richer than its rejection in the dialogue might imply. For, resting as it does on the uncertainty, the "questionability," of Othello's marriage to Desdemona, both in dramatic time (*when* did it take place?) and in law (being private, or unwitnessed), the theory suggests the possibility—which emerges more clearly from Iago's handling of Othello—not only that the two forms of questionability are associated in our sense-making processes, but also that the emotional disturbance of moral questionability can make the listener or audience receptive in such a way that the questionable incoherence of a narrative, far from detracting from its credibility, somehow contributes to its positive, quasi-visual imaginative force. It is certainly striking that Shakespeare decided to present the action immediately preceding the opening of his play—the event of Othello's and Desdemona's marriage—in the form of an accusatory narrative about which questions hover unresolved, yet which nevertheless impresses us with a sense of the event's theatrical vividness and immediacy. I devote the rest of this essay to considering what, for Shakespeare's contemporaries, might be the connection between questionable narrative circumstances and the illusion, in language, of quasi-theatrical presence. First, however, in the following section, I consider the way in which Shakespeare's handling of the story of Othello's deception by Iago's manipulation of circumstance is marked, in ways that powerfully distinguish it from its Italian source, as the product of a participatory legal culture, a culture of amateur investigatory procedures and popular forensic techniques.

The Denouement of *Othello*: Popular Forensic Elements

Shakespeare took the story of Othello from Giovanni Baptista Giraldi Cinthio's *Hecatommithi*, a collection of tales mostly on love and marriage, first published in 1565.[24] Among the differences in the story's handling, critics have focused on Shakespeare's brilliant dramatic compression of the repeated actions and habitual time characteristic of intrigue as narrated in the prose fiction. Yet perhaps the most startling difference between Shakespeare's and Cinthio's treatments of the material involves less the ways in which the Iago figure's deceptions come to seem plausible to Othello than the ways in which the circumstantial intricacy of these deceptions is, or is not, exposed to all involved in the aftermath of Desdemona's murder. In Cinthio's story, that is to say, while the auditors of the narrative declare that that it is the work of providence that both the Moor and his Ensign should have died for the murder of Desdemona, they appear to be unconcerned that the intrigue that both dishonored her and brought about her death was not publicly disclosed by any kind of evidential procedure involving either her friends and neighbors in Cyprus or the Venetian signory. The story of murderous intrigue comes to light as a rather contingent and unofficial afterthought appended to the trials of the Moor and his Ensign, as if designed merely to explain how the narrator knew the facts. "And all these events," the narrator comments, "were told after his death by the Ensign's wife, who knew the facts, as I have told them to you." The Ensign dies horribly of ruptured organs as a result of being tortured on a completely different murder charge; and although the Moor had previously been tried and tortured for his part in the murder of Desdemona (following accusations brought by the Cassio figure), he resists all attempts to make him confess, and so is not convicted. Retribution finds him later when, in exile, he is vengefully slain by Desdemona's relatives. The lack of connection between the public disclosure of the truth and the deaths of the murderers, however, does not prevent the audience of Cinthio's narrative from seeing in it the work of providence: "All praised God," Cinthio comments, "because the criminals had suitable punishment."[25]

The contrast with the aftermath of Desdemona's murder in Shakespeare's play could hardly be greater. Whereas Cinthio's novella shows no concern with any suspicions the neighbors might have had about the purportedly "accidental" nature of Desdemona's sudden death, Shakespeare's play obliges us to attend to the protracted discovery and disclosure, first by Emilia, of the fatal causes and effects of Othello's erotic gullibility, and subsequently by Lodovico and Cassio, of the extent of Iago's murderous calculations. The sustainedly high emotional pitch of Shakespeare's denouement thus depends on a sense of *community participation* in the forensic disclosure of the causes of Desdemona's death, an element that is simply absent—not felt to be necessary—to the summary providentialism asserted by the audience of Cinthio's story. Most critics feel that in Shakespeare's play the victims of Iago's malignity and Othello's rashness—Desdemona, Emilia, and to some extent even Roderigo—are dignified not only in their victimhood but also in their dying attempts to accuse, bear witness, or forgive. As "Christopher North" says in Wilson's dialogue, Emilia is "raised into worth by her contact with Desdemona—into heroic worth!" and he notes especially her sublime resistance to the domestic ideology expressed in the law of coverture that would prevent her witnessing against her husband: "Perchance, Iago, I will ne're go home" (504). For Rymer, however, the moment from which Emilia cries out, "The Moor hath killed my mistress! Murder, murder!" (5.2.162–63), produces nothing but the sensationalism of Newgate narrative: "from this Scene to the end of the Play we meet with nothing but blood and butchery, described much-what to the style of *the last Speeches and Confessions of the persons executed at Tyburn*" (253).

The contrast between Rymer's late-seventeenth-century and John Wilson's Victorian response to Shakespeare's denouement is telling. Today we are more likely to agree with Wilson. For most of us, I suspect, powerful feelings are aroused by listening to Emilia's insistence on bearing witness to the truth even as she dies. Shakespearean theater's use of the emotional power of threshold moments such as these, where the utterances of the dying bear the authority of the unknown place from which they are now speaking, might now be associated with Shakespearean nostalgia for pre-Reformation spiritual forms of penitent self-disclosure. However, Rymer's scorn points intriguingly, and not unintelligently, in a different direction—to Newgate "last Speeches and Confessions," or to what Shakespeare critics and historians of the early modern period characterize as the Protestant "politicization" of penance.[26] While contemporary critics seem to prefer to think of Shakespeare's emotional power as deriving from the sacramental forms of Catholic penitential theology, it seems clear that, in *Othello*, Shakespeare is actually interested in the outward, community-oriented form of popular-forensic speech. And it is the forensic orientation of the dying speech-act—the authority granted to the words of those about to face the judgment of another—that accounts for its tonal instability when used in fiction and theater. This, in turn, explains Rymer's scorn for the protracted garrulity of the last scenes of *Othello*, which remind him of a provincial courtroom. In the play's denouement, the sublimity admired by Wilson thus comes within a hair's breadth of the otiose circumstantiality and cheap providentialism that characterizes popular crime narrative, from the seventeenth-century Newgate fiction to the nineteenth-century rise of the detective novel.[27]

Take, for example, the moment when Cassio reports that Roderigo "spake / After long seeming dead" (5.2.325) to bear witness, in corroboration of letters providentially found in a search of his corpse, to Iago as his murderer and as principal instigator of his own accessory violence against Cassio: "Iago hurt him, / Iago set him on" (5.2.326–27). Such miraculous deathbed testimony— here narrated, but the most laughable cheap trick when theatrically staged (as Bottom's playing of Pyramus reminds us), draws *Othello* close to such pamphlets of providential justice as Arthur Golding's work *A briefe discourse of the late murther of Master George Saunders* (1573), which was itself dramatized in *A Warning for Fair Women* (1599). In Golding's pamphlet, a casual victim of the murderer, a servant called John Beane, was, like Roderigo, severely wounded and left for dead, but he "did by Gods woonderfull providence reyyve againe, and creeping a great waye on all foure, was found by an old man and . . . conveyed to Woolwich, where he gave evident tokens and markes of the murtherer."[28] And even Emilia's dying testimony as to Desdemona's chastity—

> Moor, she was chaste, she loved thee, cruel Moor,
> So come my soul to bliss as I speak true!
> So speaking as I think, alas, I die (5.2.246–48)

—seems to need some editorial distancing from its dangerous proximity to the theater of the mechanicals in *A Midsummer Night's Dream*. Ernst Honigmann comments in the Arden edition that Q gives "I die, I die" for F's "alas, I die," but he says this "sounds uncomfortably like MND 5.1.306, 'Now die, die, die, die, die.'"

The tragic denouement of *Othello*, quite unlike the conclusion of Cinthio's novella, appears thus to be deeply invested in the representation of community and in the linking of tragic feeling to the participation of the community in discovering and bearing witness to the truth. In this sense, Shakespeare's play is recognizably part of a developing culture of community participation in accusatory and evidentiary procedures, a participation in which community agency is not subsumed by the "state." In the Roman law system with which Cinthio was familiar, no conviction could be had without either the full proof of a confession or the statements of two reliable witnesses, and in the absence of these, torture was used as part of the legal process, to elicit the confession that would secure conviction.[29] Reference to this is made in the English play when, in response to Iago's vow that he "never will speak word" henceforth, Gratiano responds gravely, "Torments will ope your lips" (5.2.302). But Lodovico's more impassioned exclamation, "What, not to pray?" (5.2.302), points in a different direction: we feel for a moment the profound horror of the solipsism that is Iago's existence. Not to pray means, of course, not to beg God for mercy, but prayer for mercy also means the acknowledgment of hurt to others, of the existence of others, of belonging, and of forgiveness.

Lodovico's "What, not to pray?" raises the question of how these forms of confession—accountability to God and to the state—relate to each other. A common critical account of the effects of the Reformation in England links the demise of the one to the rise of the other. "From a practice that was mandatory at Easter and woven into the penitential season of the liturgical year, confession was essentially relegated to the last dying speech of the criminal penitent in the context of punishment and execution," as Sarah Beckwith succinctly puts it.[30] She here summarizes what I take to be a broadly dominant view of the meaning of shifts in the relative jurisdictions of church and state over questions of sin, crime, and social morality in the period. Broadly, that is, it is argued that the abolition of auricular confession severed the link between the Eucharist and a form of social reconciliation adjudicated by the priest in the sacrament of penance, leaving in its place only the discourse and spectacle of ecclesiastical court penance and common-law criminal repentance, both orchestrated by the state in the interests of law and order.[31]

My reading of the last act of *Othello*, and of the role of Emilia in bringing the circumstances of Desdemona's murder to public knowledge, involves a challenge to accounts such as Beckwith's, which assume that Protestant procedures of forensic investigation in ecclesiastical and criminal courts are entirely political, entirely without moral and spiritual meaning for their participants. For the English state did not entirely control the processes of criminal justice, and although, as one social historian says, it is very difficult to establish for certain the motivation of the kin, neighbors, servants, and friends who involved themselves in the detection and disclosing of murder, the fact remains that they did so voluntarily.[32]

There are further complexities involved in generalizing, as Beckwith does, about the spiritual effects of the demise of sacerdotal jurisdiction over the forum of conscience. For the act of judging in criminal cases was, for Christians, fraught with spiritual danger. The original purpose of judicial torture, introduced in Continental Europe after the abolition of the ordeal in 1215, had been to ensure that a merely mortal judge did not condemn innocent men to death on a subjective assessment of mere *indicia*, or circumstantial proofs, where witnesses to the crime were absent.[33] Judicial torture was designed to elicit confession, the "full proof" necessary for conviction. In the English jury system, by contrast, judges protected themselves from the dangers of sin and damnation not by adding up fractions of proof and following the regulated processes leading via torture to confession, but by displacing the moral responsibility for the verdict or truth-saying onto the people supposed to know—the jurors. The English system produced no tariff of proofs, so conviction might be made purely on the basis of circumstantial *indicia*. Witness statements were only "an evidence, which the jurie should not be bound to beleue," as Christopher St. German wrote.[34] At the same time, jurors were aware that they themselves were "in *foro conscientiae* certainly guilty of . . . *Murther*" if they condemned someone to death without being persuaded in conscience of his or her guilt.[35] Thus, even as the forum of conscience is ceasing to be a separate jurisdiction presided over by the priest, the criminal justice system is itself raising the stakes of personal moral responsibility for acts of investigation and evidence evaluation.[36]

Even before a case was tried, there was scope for popular participation in the preparation of evidence; witnesses and the kin of the accused needed "to make a convincing case to men whose task it was to evaluate the evidence before taking appropriate action."[37] These men were justices of peace (who were, unlike Continental judges, untrained and unpaid), and they were obliged by legislation passed in Mary Tudor's reign to take examinations of suspects "as well concerning the facte itselfe, as the circumstances thereof" before granting bail or committing them to prison.[38] Thus, for example, four years after the first performance of *Othello*, on January 13, 1608, the Surrey justice of peace, Bostock Fuller, recorded in his notebook, "Thomas Kyllyck hathe accused . . . Edward Rogers uppon a very slyght suspicion of ffelonye of stealing of a horse which being examined on bothe sydes before me hathe noe probabylitye."[39] At the same time, the "probability" found by justices in the circumstantial narratives of witnesses could serve to convict in the absence of any confession. Thomas Cooper marveled, in 1620, at a murder trial in which, although the deaths had taken place many years previously and the victims' skeletons had been recovered from a pond, the justice of peace had nevertheless gathered, from neighbors and witnesses, "18 Evidences . . . by way of circumstance and consequence to prove the same," and the accused was accordingly convicted in spite of his denial.[40] Thus the English system encouraged popular participation in evidence evaluation, but it also encouraged a sense of the importance of this activity for the *souls* of those involved. Indeed, it might not be too much to say that the post-Reformation imbuing of English legal process with communal spiritual responsibility for conviction or acquittal was consonant with other features of the Reformation democratization of spirituality, such as the Angli-can practice of communal prayer described by Ramie Targoff, or the Lutheran emphasis on the immanence of God in ordinary material life, as described by Richard Strier.[41]

This evidentiary system helps explain why, in Shakespeare's denouement, the discourse is of the circumstance of stealing a handkerchief ("Why was not this call'd the Tragedy of the Handkerchief?"),[42] while the voices of dying victims, friends, and accessories declare, exonerate, and accuse, in a way that contrasts sharply with the abruptly punitive and decidedly less clamorous conclusion of Cinthio's story. The latter belongs to a culture of professional autopsies and closed criminal trials in which learned men worked to accumulate the frac-tions of proof and used torture to elicit the full proof of confession. In England, more haphazardly and unlearnedly, there was a high level of amateur engage-ment: ordinary people dug for bodies, searched corpses for signs of violent death, and measured skeletons.[43] A rhetorical and literary effect of this preva-lence of popular detection, moreover, was the investment of the voice of its humblest agent with spiritual authority.

"'Twill out, 'twill out!" as Emilia says, defying men and angels (5.2.218). In murder pamphlets, the sequence of events leading to discovery and convic-tion—accidents, portents, popular discoveries, the testimony of the dying or wounded—was God's providence working through legal process. Paradoxi-cally, too, those moments that seem to us so theatrically improbable (whether in printed pamphlets or in legal depositions) when victims announce their own deaths and either forgive or accuse their killers, were in fact moments of excep-tional "probability": moments, that is, of subordinating this-worldly forms of understanding to the authority of those at the threshold of the next life. "Many murder victims," writes Gaskill, "announce their impending deaths. A York-shire man deposed in 1618 that he heard gunfire and instantly a man 'cried he was slaine' . . . witnesses needed to show that the unlawfulness of the death had been communicated by the victim, either before death, or, as with ghosts and dreams—after death."[44] Although these moments could be seen as the in-trusion into the forensic scene of a kind of certainty associated with full con-fession, their real significance is that they remain fully forensic in orientation, assimilating the authority of speaking from the threshold between temporal and spiritual worlds to the community's own processes and procedures for disclosing the truth. Thus it is, too, that Shakespeare's denouement juxtaposes the rudimentary detective work of victims and community (Cassio's searching of Roderigo's corpse, Emilia's "smelling" of the handkerchief plot) with the authority claimed by the voices of the dying and takes the risk of locating the real meaning of Lodovico's "What, not to pray?" in the pathos of this community's desire to know the truth and understand.

So the sequence in which Emilia discovers her mistress's death and begins to realize how it has come about, though mocked by Rymer ("In this kind of dialogue they continue for forty lines farther, before she bethinks herself to cry Murder" [253]), is the more profoundly moving for representing Emilia's attempt to establish the cause of Desdemona's death before crying out. Here, too, the dead are witnesses, as Desdemona exclaims "O falsely, falsely murdered!" (5.2.115). Likewise, Emilia's first question is a forensic one: "O, who hath done / This deed?" (5.2.121–22). Desdemona speaks again, precisely to undo her former accusation in painfully compassionate false witness: "Nobody. I myself. Farewell" (5.2.122). If, in the absence of medical forensics, a dying person's words had such strong evidential status on spiritual grounds, Shakespeare's brilliant twist to this is to have Othello "confess" by accusing Desdemona of risking her soul's damnation to protect him; greater and more ironic proof of love would be harder to find. Emilia points this out with abrasive scorn, but as Othello's exoneration of his own proceeding "upon just grounds" (5.2.136) begins to implicate Emilia's husband, we sense her beginning to reconstruct the narrative. It is, pace Rymer, a sign of Shakespeare's perfect judgment that it is only after we sense this work of evidential reconstruction going on in her mind that we hear her defy Othello's sword and cry out, to as many witnesses as will hear, "The Moor hath killed my mistress! Murder, murder!" (5.2.163). The emotional contrast with the deathbed of Desdemona in Cinthio's narrative, in which neighbors apparently accept without demur the Moor's and the Ensign's gruesome fabrication of an accidental death by falling plaster, could not be greater.[45] This is surely why, just as we do not believe Lodovico's confident prediction that "torments" will "ope" Iago's lips, neither do we feel that any kind of justice depends on the disclosure that would result.

Questionable Circumstance and *Evidentia*

Shakespeare's denouement is strongly marked by the forms of popular evidence-gathering, departing, as we have seen, very far from the tragic plot of Cinthio's story in its apparent need to unravel all the circumstances of the handkerchief and of Iago's ruin of Cassio (disclosed by letters found in the dead Roderigo's pocket). At the same time, as Joel Altman has recently shown, the play of *Othello* as a whole is profoundly concerned with thematizing and critiquing the rhetorical techniques by which the world is made knowable and "probable" in language. Altman shows how the dramatis personae of *Othello* repeatedly "invent" themselves and each other as rhetorical topics and themes, using the technical terms of humanist dialectics and reproducing the tendency of these to confuse word with thing. When Othello refuses to hide from Venetian law, saying,

> I must be found.
> My parts, my title and my perfect soul
> Shall manifest me rightly (1.2.30–32),

he uses the language of rhetorical and topical invention (*invenire* in Latin is "to find") as if it were the language of the interior truth that Christianity insists is knowable only to God. Altman comments: "Othello speaks of himself here as the theme of a discourse, whose main topics, which he readily supplies, will reveal him truly."[46] Iago, by contrast, instead of assuming that invention will reveal people truly, treats others as discursive matter (*res*) to invent at will, to be made into impassioned arguments of suspicion and conjecture: "Cassio's a proper man: let me see now. . . . He hath a person and a smooth dispose / To be suspected, framed to make women false" (1.3.391, 396–97). From Altman's analysis, then, Shakespeare's play emerges as profoundly critical of the psychology encouraged by the predisposition to regard the world as matter for rhetorical invention. "The peculiar composition of this play," comments Altman, "whereby the audience's perception of time is progressively distorted in a manner that parallels Iago's disorientation of Othello, seems to be related to his larger attitude towards probability . . . Shakespeare is using words that seem referential but are actually referenceless."[47]

Yet *Othello* does not feel quite as vertiginously skeptical a play as this account of it would suggest. And the reason it does not, I suggest, has to do with a perceived affinity, in early modern England, between the sensuously illusory capacity of language imbued with *enargeia*—that is, with the power to make readers and hearers feel that they can see in their mind's eye what the words evoke—and the language of circumstantial forensic investigation. Such an affinity is suggested, in the first place, by the fact that the more usual word for *enargeia* in sixteenth-century rhetorics was *evidentia*, a word meaning "clearness," "visibility," or "distinctness" (from *ex*, "out of" and *video*, "I see"), a word that, for English readers, was obviously cognate with the word *evidence*, giving its legal sense a luminosity that it has since all but lost.[48] Altman glosses "a rhetoric imbued with *enargeia*" as "a rhetoric of 'thingness,'" contrasting it with a second "incantatory rhetoric" that charms the ear by leaving lacunae, "'nothingnesses'—which the audience is tempted to supplement by piecing together ambient verbal fragments."[49] This contrast, however, is belied by the extent to which *enargeia* and *evidentia* are defined, in rhetorical handbooks, as being produced by the topics of circumstance, the *circumstantiae* or *peristaseis*, that take the form of the questions of fact (motive, place, occasion, instrument, time) or person (race, country, age, sex, education, culture, desire, and so on). In other words, *energeia/evidentia* can be produced by "nothingnesses" or questionable hints, arousing inferences, just as much as it can be produced by sensuous particulars.

We have already seen that the word *circumstance* was a part of the technical vocabulary of evidential inquiry in sixteenth-century common law. Nearly a century before Michael Dalton's *Countrey Justice* was advising justices to "take due examination . . . as well concerning the facte itselfe, as the circumstances thereof," Thomas More referred to witnesses in felony trials and before "iustyces of ye peace" as offering "deposycyons with such contrarye othes and all the cyrcumstaunces therewith geuen in euydence to the iury at the barre."[50] What More and Dalton referred to was the very same mode of rhetorical inquiry and invention that made its way, by way of Cicero and Quintilian, first into the manuals of priestly confessors and then, after the English Reformation, into justicing handbooks and the rhetorics of Erasmus, Thomas Wilson, and others.[51] Thus, in the 1592 edition of William Lambarde's *Eirenarcha, or the Office of Justices of Peace*, Lambarde adapts Cicero's discussion of the *circumstantiae* in a conjectural state, or issue of fact, and represents them for the reader in the form of a Ramist diagram (maybe Bostock Fuller had a copy or memo of Lambarde's diagram as he examined Thomas Kyllyck and Edward Rogers in 1608).[52] At the same time, vernacular and Latin manuals of rhetoric were teaching students to use the *circumstantiae* to render their narratives more vivid and probable. As early as 1532, Leonard Cox had told English readers that in order to prove that the accused could have done a thing,

> ye must go to the circumstaunce of the cause
> as that he had leyser ynough thereto
> and place convenient and strength withall.[53]

At the end of the century, John Hoskins recommends that in amplifying a narrative, "you inquire in every controversy for the circumstances," which are these, "the persons who and to whom, the matter, the intent, the time, the place, the manner, the consequences."[54]

Scholars have noted the importance of the *circumstantiae* for narrative amplification and for judicial examination in the period but have not made the connection with the theatrical sense of presence that is the achievement of *enargeia/evidentia*.[55] This may be because, in the most famous of sixteenth-century treatments of *enargeia/evidentia*, Erasmus's *De duplici copia verborum ac rerum*, the section on *circumstantiae* and *evidentia* is one in which the author refrains from giving any example, because, as he says, the method works through the whole of a composition and so "cannot be illustrated by a brief example." For Erasmus, the evocative visual details of *evidentia*, given as the fifth method of amplifying a topic in the *De copia*, should anticipate, and be used in conjunction with, the probing topical questions of circumstance.[56] This becomes clear when he comes to the eighth method of amplifying, which, as he says, "is taken from circumstances, which the Greeks call περιστασεις" These *circumstantiae* are clearly the same forensic topics as are set out in the justicing manuals. Erasmus divides them into attributes of the fact ("cause, place, occasion, instrument, time mode and so on") and of the person ("race, country, sex, age, education, culture, physical appearance"). As a compositional virtue, mastery of the *circumstantiae* is absolutely fundamental to *evidentia*: "timely and appropriate use of circumstances," he says, "has many advantages . . . in *evidentia*, about which we spoke just above" (*in evidentiam, de qua paulo ante diximus*). And he concludes: "You can discern a rhetor anywhere from his skilful combining [of circumstances] commodiously in their places (*Ita ubiuis ex huiusmodi circumstantiis commode suo loco admixtis rhetorem intelligere possis*)."[57]

The "lively evidence" of Act 1, Scene 1 of *Othello*

In conclusion, I suggest that the achievement of *evidentia* by the use of topics of circumstance becomes, in Shakespeare's innovative dramaturgy, both the source of our sense of theatrical immediacy and presence (and the source, thus, of Othello's tragic susceptibility to Iago) and, by virtue of its connection with ordinary people's agency in the pursuit of justice, the reason why we still maintain, at the end of the play, faith in the capacity of knowledge to withstand the vertiginous malignancy of rhetorical modes of cognition. If we return, once more, to the question of the temporal impossibility of *Othello* and, in particular, to the question of when Othello's and Desdemona's marriage actually took place, we will find that Shakespeare produces the event's theatrical presence and immediacy by the very same means by which he produces its legal and factual questionability. In other words, Shakespeare uses the forensic rhetoric of circumstantial inquiry both to make us feel that the marriage is taking place *as we watch* and to oblige us, in retrospect, to find every circumstance of it open to doubt.

The opening of Cinthio's novella compresses into a single sentence the vague prehistory of the hostility of Desdemona's kin to her marriage, along with the apparent triumph of her current marital harmony and content: "So propitious was their mutual love that, although the Lady's relatives did all they could to make her take another husband, they [she and the Moor] were united in marriage and lived together in such concord and tranquillity while they remained in Venice, that never a word passed between them that was not loving."[58] Shakespeare brilliantly transformed this anteriority into theatrical immediacy by fusing the neoclassical device of *narratio*—for, as Erasmus comments, "the narratives of messengers in tragedies [are] remarkably rich" in *evidentia*, "because they are presented instead of the spectacle and they report the things which it is either impossible or inappropriate to present on stage"—with the participatory processes of accusation, arrest, and examination in English common law.[59] The scene is explicitly accusatory. Brabantio, Desdemona's father, is roused from sleep first by a raucous hue and cry ("Awake, what ho, Brabantio, thieves, thieves!") and then by Iago's lurid slanders. Brabantio's robust dismissal of these apparently drunken gallants and their antisocial behavior is, however, vanquished by the *evidentia* of Roderigo's narrative of Desdemona's elopement. Roderigo's speech follows various Ciceronian examples in evoking, through an appeal to the audience's competence in its own culture's circumstantial topics or commonplaces of "person" (Erasmus's "race, country, sex, age"), the listener's readiness to supply further intimate details of the sexual scene. (Just so Quintilian, commenting on an example of *evidentia* in Cicero, admires the way in which it makes the reader "imagine for himself some of the things which are not mentioned," adding that he himself seems to see the couple's "unseemly caresses" [*deformes utriusque blanditias* (8.3.65)]).[60] So, in Roderigo's skillful narrative, travel by gondola becomes transport "with a knave of common hire, a *gondolier*," omitting the vessel to suggest being borne from the hired man's arms to the "gross clasps of a lascivious Moor" (1.1.122–23). Thus, in keeping with the rhetorical use of "commonplaces" (*koinos topos* or *loci communes*), the woman herself seems to have moved from one "common" place (the place of hire) to another (the place of "an extravagant and wheeling stranger / Of here and everywhere" 1.1.134–35), while even the circumstance of the time has become sordid, indifferent in its voyeurism, neither one thing nor the other: "this odd-even and dull watch o' th' night" (1.1.121).

That this sexually charged fantasy connects with Brabantio's own fears is suggested by his sense of premonition ("This accident is not unlike my dream" [1.1.140]). His next moves—questioning Roderigo, fetching an officer, rehearsing the probable case against Othello as a necromancer, before commanding his arrest ("I therefore apprehend and do arrest thee / . . . a practiser / Of arts inhibited" [1.2.77–79])—are all shaped by English pretrial procedures and common-law habits of mind. Most astonishing, though, is the way in which Shakespeare fashions these homely processes of legal inquiry themselves—

the circumstantial questioning of the facts of the marriage and even of its legality—into our sense of the marriage's theatrical immediacy and reality. Brabantio thus questions Roderigo on discovering that Desdemona is, indeed, missing:

> Now, Roderigo,
> Where didst thou see her?—O unhappy girl!—
> With the Moor, say'st thou—Who would be a father?—
> How didst thou know 'twas she?—O, she deceives me
> Past thought!—what said she to you? Get more tapers,
> Raise all my kindred. Are they married, think you? (1.1.160–65)

The counterpointing of Brabantio's questions with his exclamations of self-pity artfully varies what would otherwise be a straightforward enumeration of the topics of circumstance (questions of where, who, and what) that were designed to put the narrator on the spot and to establish the probability or otherwise of his narrative. So Brabantio wants to know exactly *where* Roderigo saw her (skeptically interrogating Roderigo's claim to have been an eyewitness), exactly *how* he could be sure it was Desdemona and not some other Venetian girl, exactly *what* she said to him, and, finally, whether the two of them are legally married. Most artful is the way in which the questions themselves, though unanswered by Roderigo, produce the illusion of having established something, so that both we and Brabantio feel more certain of the truth of Roderigo's account. So while Brabantio at first neither recognized Roderigo's voice nor gave credit to his words on learning his name, we now register the weight Brabantio seems to give to Roderigo's solemn answer to his question about being married: "Truly" says Roderigo, "I think they are" (1.1.166). All this occurs without Iago, who is absent precisely because he does not want to be produced in court as a witness against Othello ("It seems not meet, nor wholesome to my place / To be produced as, if I stay, I shall / Against the Moor" [1.1.143–45]).

Importantly, however, the reality and legality of the marriage remain, precisely, uncertain and questionable. The next scene opens with Iago urging Othello to anticipate the challenge Brabantio is about to bring against the legality of his marriage: "But I pray you sir, / Are you fast married?" (1.2.10–11). A few lines later, to Cassio, Iago emphasizes the yet-to-be-proved nature of the marriage: "tonight" says Iago, he "hath boarded a land carrack: / if it prove lawful prize, he's made for ever" (1.2.50–51, my italics). The marriage's dramatic reality is thus entirely the product of Brabantio's first challenging of the evidence for it and Iago's then asking Othello to preempt such a challenge by being sure that his marriage is technically provable (or "probable") in law: both are *forensic* constructions that bring a situation into verbal being by defensively anticipating the need to gather evidence, to make a case.

From this we can see that the so-called double-time crux of *Othello* is the effect of Shakespeare's "skilful combining of circumstances commodiously in their places," as Erasmus instructed. Time is one of the "circumstances" that a Iago might use to bring Othello to the very door of suspicion, which he calls "truth," just as it is a circumstance that a rhetor or a dramatist may combine with others to compose a probable fiction. But circumstantial enquiry still contributes, through Emilia, to our sense that truth is recoverable and that recognition of it is possible, even in this world, and even by those most deceived.

So when Emilia uses circumstantial questions openly to challenge Othello's private slander of his wife as a "whore" ("Why should he call her whore? who keeps her company? / *What place, what time, what form, what likelihood?*" [4.2.139–40, my italics]), it is possible (as Ernst Honigmann suggests in his footnote to this line) that Shakespeare "trusted his audience not to notice" that his "short time scheme" did not allow for these forms of likelihood. But it is also possible that this moment perfectly instances the alignment of popular forensic habits of mind with the most avant-garde techniques of theatrical illusion, exemplifying the very specific synergy between the cultures of dramatic composition and moral/legal inquiry in the late sixteenth century.

NOTES

I would like to thank Martha Nussbaum and Richard Strier for their careful reading and very helpful comments on this essay. Thanks, too, to Chicago's anonymous reader, and to Bradin Cormack and Vicky Kahn for extensive criticism and much-needed encouragement in response to earlier drafts.

1. See Marjorie Garber, "'The Rest Is Silence': Ineffability and the 'Unscene' in Shakespeare's Plays," in *Ineffability: Naming the Unnameable from Dante to Beckett*, ed. Peter S. Hawkins and Anne Howland Schotter (New York: AMS Press, 1984), 35–50. For an eloquent statement of the relevance of the "theatre-as-lawcourt" metaphor to Renaissance drama, see Subha Mukherji, *Law and Representation in Early Modern Drama* (Cambridge: Cambridge University Press, 2006), 1–2.

2. Julie Stone Peters, "Legal Performance Good and Bad," *Law, Culture, and the Humanities* 4 (2008): 179–200.

3. See, for example, Stephen Greenblatt, *Renaissance Self-Fashioning* (Chicago: University of Chicago Press, 1980); Louis Montrose, "The Purpose of Playing: Reflections on a Shakespearean Anthropology," *Helios*, n.s., 7 (1980): 51–74; Steven Mullaney, *The Place of the Stage: License, Play, and Power in Renaissance England* (Chicago: University of Chicago Press, 1988); Leonard Tennenhouse, *Power on Display: The Politics of Shakespeare's Genres* (New York: Methuen, 1986). More recently, the emphasis has been on "staging"

and "performing" certain cultural conditions, so, for example, Wendy Wall, *Staging Domesticity* (Cambridge: Cambridge University Press, 2006); Kathryn M. Moncrief and Kathryn R. McPherson, eds., *Performing Maternity in Early Modern England* (Aldershot, UK: Ashgate, 2007). For an account of Judith Butler's Foucauldian transformation of Austin's conception of linguistic performatives, see James Loxley, *Performativity* (New York: Routledge, 2007).

4. For New Historicism's lack of interest in stage practice, despite its interest in "theatricality," see Barbara Hodgdon and W. B. Worthen, eds., *A Companion to Shakespeare and Performance* (Oxford: Blackwell, 2005), 3.

5. A critic who, by contrast, offers brilliantly nuanced readings of the cultural and ethical work of Shakespearean drama using Austin's and Stanley Cavell's concepts of linguistic "performativity" is Harry Berger Jr. See his *Making Trifles of Terrors: Redistributing Complicities in Shakespeare* (Stanford, CA: Stanford University Press, 1997).

6. Of course, successful forms of "theater" and "performance" by no means always involve coherent fictions. Shakespeare's plays, however, make a point of doing so.

7. Marvin T. Herrick, *Comic Theory in the Sixteenth Century* (Urbana: University of Illinois Press, 1964), 28.

8. Leonard Cox, *Arte or Crafte of Rethoryke* (London, 1532), sig. D8r.

9. See, for example, Ruth Webb, *Ekphrasis: Imagination and Persuasion in Ancient Rhetorical Theory and Practice* (Farnham, Surrey, UK: Ashgate, 2009), 88–89.

10. George Chapman, "In Seianum Ben Ionsoni," in Ben Jonson, *Sejanus his Fall* (London, 1605), sig. ¶ 4v.

11. Peter Brooks, "Narrativity of the Law," *Law and Literature* 14, no. 1 (2002): 1–10, at 3.

12. Ibid., 3–4.

13. Scott McMillan and Sally-Beth MacLean, *The Queen's Men and Their Plays* (Cambridge: Cambridge University Press, 1998), 125.

14. Ibid., 127.

15. Ibid., 161, 166.

16. Peter Womack, "The Comical Scene: Perspective and Civility on the Renaissance Stage," *Representations* 101 (2008): 32–56.

17. "Appendix 1: Date," in William Shakespeare, *Othello*, ed. E. A. J. Honigmann (London: Arden Shakespeare, Cenage Learning, 1997), 344. References to the play in the text are from this edition.

18. Thomas Rymer, "A Short View of Tragedy," in *Critical Essays of the Seventeenth Century*, 3 vols., ed. J. E. Spingarn (Oxford: Clarendon Press, 1908), 2:241. Subsequent references are parenthetical in the text.

19. John Wilson [Christopher North], "Dies Boreales, no. 6, 'Christopher under Canvas,'" *Blackwoods Edinburgh Magazine* 67 (April 1850): 481–512. Subsequent references are parenthetical in the text.

20. Joel B. Altman, "'Preposterous Conclusions': Eros, *Enargeia*, and the Composition of *Othello*," *Representations* 18 (1987): 129–57, 145.

21. On the continued relevance of "double time" to *Othello* criticism, see Honig-

mann's introduction, in *Othello*, 17; for a recent intriguing "explanation" of double time, see Steve Sohmer, "The 'Double Time' Crux in *Othello* Solved," *English Literary Renaissance* (2002): 214–38.

22. Graham Bradshaw, *Misrepresentations: Shakespeare and the Materialists* (Ithaca, NY: Cornell University Press, 1993), 198.

23. Ibid., 148.

24. *Hecatommithi, ouero cento novelle di M. Giovanbattista Giraldi Cinthio* (Venice, 1580), fols. 159r–163v.

25. Giovanni Battista Giraldi Cinthio, *Gli Hecatommithi* (1566), trans. Geoffrey Bullough, in *Narrative and Dramatic Sources of Shakespeare*, vol. 7, *Major Tragedies* (London: Routledge, 1973), 252.

26. See, for example, Sarah Beckwith, "Medieval Penance, Reformation Repentance, and *Measure for Measure*," in *Reading the Medieval in Early Modern England*, ed. Gordon McMullan and David Matthews (Cambridge: Cambridge University Press, 2007), 193–204; Peter Lake, *The Antichrist's Lewd Hat: Protestants, Papists, and Players in Post-Reformation England* (New Haven, CT: Yale University Press, 2002).

27. See, for example, Ian A. Bell, "Eighteenth Century Crime Writing," and Lyn Pykett, "The Newgate Novel and Sensation Fiction, 1830–1868," in *The Cambridge Companion to Crime Fiction*, ed. Martin Priestman (Cambridge: Cambridge University Press, 2003), 7–17, 19–40.

28. Arthur Golding, *A briefe discourse of the late murder of Master George Saunders* (London, 1573), sig. A4r.

29. Barbara Shapiro, *"Beyond Reasonable Doubt" and "Probable Cause": Historical Perspectives on the Anglo-American Law of Evidence* (Berkeley: University of California Press, 1991), 203.

30. Beckwith, "Medieval Penance," 198.

31. J. A. Sharpe, "Last Dying Speeches: Religion, Ideology, and Public Execution in Seventeenth Century England," *Past and Present* 107 (1985): 144–67; Lake, *The Antichrist's Lewd Hat*, 229–73.

32. Malcolm Gaskill, *Crime and Mentalities in Early Modern England* (Cambridge: Cambridge University Press, 2000), 250. See also Steve Hindle, *The State and Social Change in Early Modern England, 1550–1640* (Houndmills, UK: Palgrave, 2002).

33. See John H. Langbein, *Torture and the Law of Proof: Europe and England in the Ancien Regime* (Chicago: University of Chicago Press, 1976; reissued with new preface, 2006), 3–8 (page references in the 2006 edition); Lisa Silverman, *Tortured Subjects: Pain, Truth, and the Body in Early Modern France* (Chicago: University of Chicago Press, 2001), 42–44.

34. Christopher St. German, *Salem and Bizance*, in *The Yale Edition of the Complete Works of St. Thomas More*, vol. 10, ed. John Guy, Ralph Keen, Clarence H. Miller, and Ruth McGugan (New Haven, CT: Yale University Press, 1987), 361.

35. Quotation from John Hawles, *The English-mans right: A Dialogue between a barrister-at-law and a jury-man* (London, 1680), 22. See James Q. Whitman, *The Origins of Reasonable Doubt: Theological Roots of the Criminal Trial* (New Haven, CT: Yale University Press, 2008).

36. On this see Cynthia Herrup, *The Common Peace: Participation and the Criminal Law in Seventeenth-Century England* (Cambridge: Cambridge University Press, 1987).

37. Gaskill, *Crime and Mentalities*.

38. See Herrup, *Common Peace*, 67–87. On the legislation obliging justices of the peace to take written examinations, see John Langbein, *Prosecuting Crime in the Renaissance: England, Germany, France* (Cambridge, MA: Harvard University Press, 1974). The quotation is from Michael Dalton, *The Countrey Justice* (London, 1635), 22.

39. See Granville Leveson-Gower, esq., "Note Book of a Surrey Justice," in *Surrey Archaeological Collections* (London: Surrey Archaeological Society, 1888), 9:161–232.

40. Thomas Cooper, *The Cry and Revenge of Blood* (London, 1620), sigs. G3v–G4r.

41. See Ramie Targoff, *Common Prayer: The Language of Public Devotion in Early Modern England* (Chicago: University of Chicago Press, 2001); Richard Strier, "Martin Luther and the Real Presence in Nature," *Journal of Medieval and Early Modern Studies* 37, no. 2 (2007): 271–302.

42. Rymer, "A Short View of Tragedy," 2:251.

43. Gaskill, *Crime and Mentalities*, 255–59.

44. Ibid., 234.

45. In Cinthio's story, the ensign tells the Moor that as the ceiling in his house has cracks, they will be able to murder Desdemona and cause the ceiling to fall on her head, and "nobody will feel any suspicion." After the murder, they accordingly bring down the ceiling, so "the neighbours ran in and found the bed, and the Lady dead under the rafters," but none inquire about the circumstances of the death. See Bullough, *Narrative and Dramatic Sources*, 7:250–51.

46. Joel B. Altman, *The Improbability of Othello: Rhetorical Anthropology and Shakespearean Selfhood* (Chicago: University of Chicago Press, 2010), 129.

47. Ibid., 205.

48. Quintilian, *Inst.* 4.2.64; Erasmus, *De copia verborum ac rerum*, ed. Betty I. Knott, in *Desiderii Erasmi Roterodami Opera Omnia* (Amsterdam: North Holland, 1969–), vol. 1, part 6, p. 202, ll. 160–61.

49. Altman, *Improbability*, 183.

50. Dalton, *The Countrey Justice*, 22; More is quoted by J. G. Bellamy, *The Criminal Trial in Later Medieval England: Felony before the Courts from Edward I to the Sixteenth Century* (Thrupp, UK: Sutton, 1998), 107.

51. See D. W. Robertson, "A Note on the Classical Origin of the 'Circumstances' in the Medieval Confessional," *Studies in Philology* 43 (1946): 6–14.

52. William Lambarde, *Eirenarcha, or the Office of Justices of the Peace* (London, 1592), 218–19.

53. Cox, *Arte . . . of Rethoryke*, sig. E6r.

54. John Hoskins, *Directions for Speech and Style*, ed. Hoyt T. Hudson (Princeton, NJ: Princeton University Press, 1935), 28.

55. Peter Mack, *Elizabethan Rhetoric: Theory and Practice* (Cambridge: Cambridge University Press, 2002), 37, 129–30.

56. Erasmus, *De copia*, vol. 1, part 6, p. 202, l. 160; Erasmus, *On Copia of Words and Ideas*, trans. D. B. King and H. D. Rix (Milwaukee: Marquette University Press, 1999), 47.

57. Erasmus, *On Copia*, 57; *De copia*, vol. 1, part 6, p. 218, ll. 514–28.

58. Cinthio, *Gli Hecatommithi*, 242.

59. Erasmus, *On Copia*, 48; *De copia*, vol. 1, part 6, pp. 203–4, ll. 203–6.

60. See, for example, Ruth Webb's comments on Quintilian's engagement with this passage in Cicero. Webb, *Ekphrasis*, 108.

PART II

Shakespeare's Knowledge of Law

STATUTE LAW, CASE LAW

CONSTANCE JORDAN

INTERPRETING STATUTE IN *MEASURE*
FOR MEASURE

Shakespeare's dramatization of justice in *Measure for Measure* has long been recognized as problematic, representing the government of an absolute prince who is both rigorously punitive and mercifully forgiving. This thematic ambivalence is not easily or conveniently resolved; in that sense the play remains a conflicted work. Yet a look at its action in light of contemporary English legal practice can suggest how it serves obliquely to comment on and indeed criticize features of the Stuart rule that its first audiences were about to encounter.[1] This essay examines how such audiences might have reacted to the action of the play and particularly its characters and their roles: the Duke, the prince-legislator; Angelo, the deputy who interprets the Duke's "strict statutes and most biting laws" (1.3.19);[2] and Escalus, the magistrate who supports Angelo. I shall also try to determine the dramatic function of the rogue Lucio and whether his descriptions of the Duke constitute slander. Finally, this essay will assess why the play's representation of the Duke may seem—for "seeming" is the trope that informs the plot of the play as a whole—to be fashioning a portrait of James VI and I. Its features reflect passages on government in *The Trewe Lawe of Free Monarchies* (1598) and *Basilicon Doron* (1599), as well as contemporary accounts of English law.

The figure opening the play, the too-indulgent ruler who recognizes the political consequences of a lax administration, has two sources. Shakespeare's Duke of Vienna, having allowed his state to become lawless through neglect of his own duties, transfers the management of the state to his experienced magistrate Escalus and gives executive authority to his young deputy Angelo. Apparently confident of Escalus's discretion and Angelo's judgment, the Duke seems to believe that he has guaranteed not only reform but also his own exemption from public criticism. As he tells his confidant Friar Thomas:

Sith 'twas my fault to give the people scope,
'Twould be my tyranny to strike and gall them
for what I bid them do . . .
[Angelo] may, in the ambush of my name, strike home. (1.3.35–37, 41)

The plan in part alludes to James's advice to his son Prince Henry on ascending the throne, a reflection of his own experience: "For I confesse, where I thought

101

(by being gracious at the beginning) to win all mens hearts to a louing and willing obedience, I by the contrary found, the disorder of the countrie, and the losse of my thankes to be all my reward." Henry must rather pursue a tough justice that, once achieved, may be tempered by mercy: "when yee haue by the seuertie of Iustice once setled your countries, and made them know that ye can strike, then may ye thereafter all the daies of your life mixe Iustice with Mercie, punishing or sparing as ye shall find the crime to haue been wilfully or rashly committed, and according to the by-past behauiour of the committer."[3] The Duke's plan also recalls that of Machiavelli's Cesare Borgia, who not only deputizes "Remirro de Orco, a cruel and energetic man" to settle Cesare's newly conquered Romagna but subsequently orders de Orco's execution, fearing that the people would blame him, Borgia, for the excesses of de Orco's rule.[4] The Duke endorses James's reasoning and adopts Machiavelli's ruse of appointing a second to execute a dreadful law. He also engages in deception: he remains in Vienna, disguised as a "Friar Lodowick," in order to observe Angelo's conduct and the consequences of his own stratagem. However, even as he attempts to conclude his plan for the restoration of order in Vienna, the state is further jeopardized.

Neither of the Duke's deputies has proved capable. To the crimes identified in act 1, fornication and bawdry, rape and murder have been added. By act 5, Escalus has become uncharacteristically intemperate and Angelo is out of office, at last exposed as no enforcer of the law but rather a disgraced "seemer" (1.3.54; 2.4.150). The situation is clarified to a degree after a series of revelations. Most critically, when asked for help by Escalus, Lucio unmasks the Duke in his disguise as "Friar Lodowick" and makes public his deception.[5] This Lucian (or light-giving) action allows the Duke to recover his status as absolute prince-legislator. But crucial questions remain to be asked: is the Duke's stratagem worthy of a head of state? Has Angelo, however disgraced, provided the Duke with the means necessary to restore that government and social order the Duke has wished he himself had established from the beginning of his rule? And at what cost?

In a subtler and perhaps more terrifying sense, *Measure for Measure* dramatizes the terms of a government that the pending accession of James to the English throne can only have made ominous. The action throughout the play establishes that the Duke is a prince-legislator and his authority is absolute; he (or his deputy) functions as the law; he does not govern by means provided by the institution of a court of law. *The Trewe Lawe* made comparable claims for the power of the Scottish king, who is represented as "above the law, as both the author and giuer of strength thereto. . . . [Admittedly] a good king will frame all his actions to be according to the Law; yet hee is not bound thereto but of his good will."[6] James conveys the power of this monarchy by allusion to 1 Samuel 8, where the prophet describes its dangers to subjects: "For as ye could not haue obtained one without the permission and ordinance of God, so may yee no more, fro hee be once set ouer you, shake him off without the same warrant. And therefore in time arme your selues with patience and humilitie, since he that hath the only power to make him, hath the onely power to vnmake him; and ye onely to obey."[7] The king is beyond the people's judgment: their obedience ought to be "as to Gods Lieutenant in earth, obeying his commands in all things, except directly against God, as the commands of Gods Minister, acknowledging him a Iudge set by GOD ouer them, hauing power to iudge them but to be iudged onely by GOD, whom to onely hee must giue count of his iudgement."[8] This understanding of monarchic rule as a divinely created right to personal government runs counter to an important and arguably decisive understanding of English law: Henry de Bracton (d. 1268), in *De legibus et consuetudinibus Angliae*, celebrates the stability of law and the place of the king in terms that were to become the basis of what Sir Edward Coke would later call the "ancient constitution."

In Bracton's view, Parliament, representing the consent of the people, makes positive law that is confirmed by the king's assent to it: "Since [the laws] have been approved by the consent of those who use them and confirmed by the oath of kings, they cannot be changed without the common consent of all those by whose counsel and consent they were promulgated."[9] Describing the authority of the king who confirms the law, Bracton announces a near-paradox. He stands above all his subjects. Only God can punish him: "Since no writ runs against him there will be opportunity for a petition that he correct and amend his act; if he does not, it is punishment enough for him that he await God's vengeance. No one may presume to question his acts, much less contravene them." Yet he is also under the law:

The king must not be under man but under God and under the law, because law makes the king. Let him therefore bestow upon the law what the law bestows upon him, namely, rule and power. For there is no *rex* where will rules rather than *lex*. . . . [The king] can do nothing save what he can do *de iure*, despite the statement that the will of the prince has the force of law, because there follows at the end of the *lex* the words "since by the *lex regia* which was made with respect to his sovereignty"; nor is that anything rashly put forward of his own will, but what has been rightly decided with the counsel of his magnates, deliberation and consultation having been had thereon, the king giving it *auctoritas*.[10]

In short, this monarchy is subject to a kind of legislative body, a "counsel of magnates." Absent any mention of such a body in *Measure for Measure*, those in Shakespeare's audience familiar with English law can regard Vienna's prince as its only legislator, he who created the "strict statutes" that Angelo is belatedly to enforce. Angelo's decision to execute Claudio for his admitted crime of fornication, rendered as it is without a formal hearing or trial, vacates Bracton's *lex regia* and implies the office of a prince-legislator who can in fact act *supra iurem*. Yet insofar as the Duke and his deputy function as sole exponents of law without the legal constraints imposed by a court, the play constantly contests their government.

The play's "invention" or principal theme—drawing on Matthew 7:1–2, "Iudge not that ye be not iudged. For with what iudgement ye iudge, and with what measure ye mete, it shalbe measured vnto you againe," and, slightly changed, in Luke 6:37, "Iudge not and ye shall not be iudged: condemne not, and yee shall not be condemned: forgiue and yee shall be forgiuen"—describes the essentially self-reflexive role of the judge.[11] It is also represented in James's advice to Henry on monarchic conduct in *Basilicon Doron* (1598), where it suggests that the role of judge and monarch are one and the same: "censure your selfe as sharply as if ye were your owne enemie: For if ye iudge your selfe, ye shall not be iudged, as the Apostle saith."[12] Given the judge's obligation to be thus "measured," the audience will in turn judge how well the Duke exercises his authority and whether there is any equivalent in his government to Bracton's "counsel of magnates." Could his rule have benefited from such "counsel"?

The play's "invention" engages two other discourses: first, the interpretation of the words of the law as expressed in a statute in light of the intention of its maker; and second, the significance, relevance, or meaning of such an interpretation for the case to be decided and the judgment the court must render. It also suggests a corruption of the norm, the judge who judges wrongly, and his corresponding restraint. But by whom? Juvenal's "conceit"—*quis custodiet ipsos custodes?* (who shall guard the guardians)[13]—suggests how vulnerable the Duke may become. Constitutionalists insisted that the king was constrained by positive law produced by a legislative body; if not, he became de facto absolute, a prince-legislator checked only by God. Provocatively, *Measure for Measure* refuses to harmonize these two dispensations.

The "commissions" the Duke gives to his deputies Escalus and Angelo represent key elements in contemporary works on interpreting statutes and their translation in judicial decisions (1.1.13, 47).[14] The Duke orders Escalus, who in the Duke's words is as "pregnant" in the "terms for common justice. . . . As art and practice hath enriched any that we remember," to put his qualifications, his art and science, to "work" for the government of Vienna (1.1.9, 10–13); he is to be the Duke's "secondary" (1.1.46). Angelo—as the Duke's deputy (and so inexperienced that he asks for a "test" [1.1.48])—is as the Duke would have been had the Duke remained as himself in Vienna: "mortality and mercy in Vienna / Live in thy tongue and heart" (1.1.44–45). Neither deputy is clear about his duties: Escalus notes, "A power I have, but of what strength and nature / I am not yet instructed" (1.1.79–80), and Angelo suggests they consult together to determine how to proceed (1.1.81–83). In the absence of any judicial body, their uncertainty is understandable and specifically recalls Coke's insistence that the discretion of a commissioner be circumscribed by law: "Although the words of the commission give authority to the commissioners to act according to their discretion, their proceedings ought nevertheless to be limited and bound within the rule of reason and law. . . . they are not to act according to their wills and private affections."[15] The Duke insists that Escalus respect "the city's institutions," but neither Escalus nor Angelo acknowledges such "institutions" or their intervention in the life of the state whose power they must acknowledge. Angelo's naïveté represents a graver problem. James had counseled Henry: "Choose then for all these Offices, men of knowen wisedome, honestie, and good conscience; well practised in the points of the craft that yee ordaine them for,"[16] and Bracton had warned judges: "Let no one unwise and unlearned, presume to ascend the seat of judgment, which is like unto the throne of God, lest for light he bring darkness and for darkness light, and, with unskillful hand, even as a madman, he put the innocent to the sword and set free the guilty, and lest he fall from on high, as from the throne of God, in attempting to fly before he has wings."[17] But the Duke simply dismisses this possibility, telling Angelo: "no more evasion" (1.1.50). Bracton's image of the novice as a fallen angel does, however, continue to resonate throughout the play: Angelo is such a creature.

Angelo's commission, requiring him to "enforce or qualify the laws" of Vienna though mindful of "mortality" and "mercy" (1.1.65, 44), refers particularly to the control of sexual conduct—fornication and prostitution, or "bawdry." It is first realized by Angelo's order to arrest "Signor Claudio" for "getting Madam Julietta with child" (whom the audience soon will learn he has contracted to marry) and, although Angelo never confronts Claudio directly, to regard Claudio's offense as a capital crime. Led away to prison by the Provost,

Claudio admits to the rogue Lucio that his "restraint" by law has come from his exercise of "too much liberty, Lucio, liberty" (1.2.64, 72–73, 125), a particular "liberty," however, that many in *Measure for Measure*'s audience would have known that English law in practice condoned: sex with the woman to whom a man is "contracted" to marry.[18] Angelo also orders a "proclamation" closing down the "houses of resort" in the "suburbs" (1.2.95–96, 101–2); this specifically addresses the conduct of Claudio's fellow citizens the rogues Pompey and Froth, who are suspected of profiting from a trade in prostitution. Generally categorized as a "public nuisance" in English common law,[19] brothels might well have been regarded as criminal by some in Shakespeare's audience. William Lambarde's *Eirenarcha, or of the Justices of Peace* (1614), states: "if a man in the night season hant a house that is suspected for Bawdrie, or use suspicious company, then may the Constable arrest him. . . . For Bawdrie is not meerely a spiritual offence, but mixed and sounding somewhat against the Peace of the Land."[20] Yet in 1603 the site in which the play was being performed, Bankside in the Liberty of Southwark, though populated by "theeves, horsestealers, whoremongers, cozeners, coneycatchers," was exempted from the restrictions forbidding such activities in the city.[21] Prostitution was tolerated there: Bankside was home to the Bell, Barge and Cock, a triple brothel owned by Philip Henslowe of the Rose theater, and the biggest brothel there was the property of the Bishop of Winchester.[22] It therefore appears that each case Angelo judges— fornication and bawdry, when matched by a contrasting reality known to the play's audiences—forces a consideration of accepted methods of interpreting the words of the law and also of finding their meaning in relation to the case at hand. What are these methods, and does Angelo follow them?

They are made explicit in a text central to any education in the practice of law, Plowden's commentary on the interpretation of statute in *Eyston v. Studd*, in *Reports* (1599): "And in order to form a right Judgment when the Letter of a Statute is restrained, and when enlarged by Equity it is a good Way, when you peruse a Statute, to suppose that the Law-maker is present, and that you have asked him the Question you want to know touching the Equity, then you must give yourself such an Answer as you imagine he would have done, if he had been present."[23] That is, while the power of the legislator to make law is not to be questioned, *how* he would have exercised it in the case his interpreter confronts has imaginatively to be determined. In theory, the "how" the judge seeks is a position between two possibilities: the "Letter" of the statute may either be "restrained," or taken literally; or it may be "enlarged" to include apt and relevant though unspecified considerations. The Duke's instructions to Angelo embrace Plowden's alternatives. He is to "enforce" the law presumably in literal or "restrained" applications and, no less important, also to "qualify" the law again presumably in "enlarged" applications. When the Duke later describes Angelo as "precise" (1.3.50), he signals that Angelo will prove an exponent of "restrained" or literal interpretation, an insight corroborated when Lucio observes that Angelo "follows close the rigor of the statute" (1.4.67); to Angelo, fornication is simply a capital crime. But what if Angelo were to read the Duke's "strict statutes and most biting laws" as "enlarged" by "Equity"?

King James, recognizing equity in principle, had offered Prince Henry a simple instruction: "the lawe must be interpreted according to the meaning, and not to the literall sense thereof: *Nam ratio est anima legis*."[24] Lawyers faced its complexities. Lambarde, speaking of the court of Chancery in *Archaeion; or, a Discourse upon the High Courts of Justice in England*, written in the 1590s, defends its practice of equitable jurisdiction: "Considering that the *Prince* of this *Realme* is the immediate *minister of Justice* under God . . . he may both supply the want, and correct the rigour of that *Positive* or *written Law*, which of it selfe neither is nor can be made such a perfect *Rule*, as that a *Man* may thereby truly square out *Justice* in all *Cases* that may happen."[25] Yet the power of that court is limited: "*Equitie* should not bee appealed unto but only in rare and extraordinary matters, lest on the one side, if the *Iudge* in *Equitie* should take *Iurisdiction* over all, it should come to passe (as *Aristotle* saith) that a *Beast* should beare the rule: For so hee calleth man, whose *Iudgement*, if it been not restrained by the Chaine of *Law*, is commonly carried away with unruly affections." In any case, a good chancellor will not "overthrow the authoritie of the Courts of *Common Law* but permit the Common Law to hold her just honour . . . the short measure thereof extended by the true consideration of *Iustice* and *Equitie*."[26] Like Ranulf de Glanvill, who represents the king as "crushing the pride of the unbridled and ungovernable with the right hand of strength and tempering justice for the humble and meek with the rod of equity (*uirga equitatis*),"[27] Lambarde insists that equitable interpretation does not violate the ultimate authority of the common law or augment the power of the judge to that of legislator; it merely makes suitable the application of a positive law.[28] The judge must ask, however, how the letter of positive "written law" can yield an equitable interpretation.

Coke's report on *Heydon's Case* (1584), explains when the words of a statute may be "enlarged" to fashion an "extensive" interpretation, that is, an interpretation understood to apply to subjects not mentioned in the statute but implied by its terms. In such cases, the judge must consider "the common law before the Act," "the mischief and defect for which the common law did not provide," "[the] remedy the Parliament hath resolved and appointed to cure the disease of the Common wealth, and the true reason of the remedy." Thus a judge will make "such construction as shall suppress the mischief and advance the remedy . . . according to the true intent of the makers of the Act, *pro bono publico.*" Plowden's report on *Stradling v. Morgan* (1560), explains how the words of a statute could be enlarged (paradoxically) to produce a "restrictive" interpretation, that is, an interpretation understood to apply only to subjects who ought rationally to be included in it: "from which cases it appears that the sages of the law heretofore have construed statutes quite contrary to the letter in some appearance, and those statutes which comprehend all things in the letter they have expounded to extend but to some things, and those which generally prohibit all from doing such an act they have interpreted to permit some people to do it, and those which include every person in the letter they have adjudged to reach some persons only. . . . [T]hey have ever been guided by the intent of the legislature which they have always taken according to the necessity of the matter and according to that which is consonant to reason and good discretion."[29] But whether "extensive" or "restrictive," such "enlarged" interpretations test the limits of literal meaning as understood in "restrained" interpretations. They do so without disturbing the authority of "Parliament," the figure of the legislator.

In his *Discourse on the Exposition and Understanding of Statutes* (c. 1560), Sir Thomas Egerton more specifically notes how the judge may "enlarge" the words of the statute. He is to attend to its words, "parollz" and "sentences": the former is best understood through the context in which words are used; the latter in light of the "sence" the sentences have in relation to the argument of which they are a part.[30] Here the issue in question is of paramount importance: "it is commenlye said, *res consilium dabit*, which who so of himselfe is not hable to descerne doethe but lose his tyme & trauell in the lawe."[31] In short, to proceed "per Equytye" is to discover "sense & meaning" as it applies to a particular situation: "For synce that wordes were but invented to declare the meanynge of men, we muste rather frame the wordes to the meanynge then the meanynge to the wordes. Yt is therfore to be knowen that sommetyme statutes are taken by equytye more then the wordes, sommetyme contrary to the wordes, sommetyme it is taken strayctelye accordinge to the wordes, and sommetyme, where there are no wordes in the statute and yet a case happenethe upon an estatute, the commen law shall make a construction."[32] To this end, Egerton follows Plowden, asserting that the legislator's intention provides the key that unlocks the meaning of the text: "the statute shall be taken . . . *ex mente legislatorum*, for that is chiefe to be considered, which although it varie in so muche that in maner so manie heades as therewere, so many wittes; so manie statute makers, so many myndes; yet, notwithstandinge, certen notes there are by which a man maie knowe what it was. And this helpethe, not onlie to knowe where a statute shall be taken by equytie, but also where it shall be taken straight-elie accordinge to the naked & bare letter."[33] Most radically, an interpretation may be so "enlarged" that it escapes the words (is "conter les parollz") of the text, a recommendation that has special relevance to Angelo's commission. Not only are penal laws particularly required to be "enlarged" and thereby to achieve "restrictive" interpretation, "for in [such cases] it is true that Paston saiethe, *Poenas interpretatione augeri non debere* [do not augment punishments by interpretation]: for the law alwaies favoureth hym that goeth to wracke, nor it will not pulle hym on his nose that is on his knees,"[34] but they are also to be understood to limit the responsibility of the accused. As Bracton states: "It is the duty of the judge to impose a sentence no more and no less severe than the case demands. . . . Punishments are rather to be mitigated than increased."[35] Given contemporary English law, *Measure for Measure*'s audiences are invited to determine whether Angelo's decisions fairly address what "the case demands." As Sir Christopher Hatton observes, most "Transgressions" of penal laws are punished for "Example's sake: *Ut poena unius fit metus multorum*,"[36] precisely Lu-cio's claim when he gives Isabella the reason that Angelo will decide to fol-low "the rigor of the statute": that is, "To make him [Claudio] an example" (1.4.67–68).

Certainly Angelo's task is grave: he is to restore social order and decorum and restrain disruptive "liberty," which, in the Duke's words, is plucking "jus-tice by the nose" (1.3.29). As Lucio tells Isabella, Angelo intends to "give fear to use and liberty"; as the Duke confesses: "I have on Angelo impos'd the office, who may . . . strike home" (1.3.40–41). Angelo interprets the law strictly (1.2.69; 1.4.64–66); he dismisses the advice of Escalus and the Provost, who urge intro-spection and patience, and he ignores the moderation required of justice: "The king should put on the bridle of temperance and the reins of moderation lest being unbridled he be drawn toward injustice."[37] James also warns of extremes: "*Nam in medio stat virtus*. . . . For in infinities *omnia concurrunt*: and what dif-ference is betwixt extreme tyrannie, delighting to destroy all mankinde; and extreame slackenesse of punishment, permitting euery man to tyranize ouer his companion?"[38] Escalus seems mindful of such cautions: "Let us be keen, and rather cut a little, / Than fall, and bruise to death" (2.1.5–6). He asks that Angelo be self-critical: have you "not sometime in your life / Err'd in this point which now you censure him?" (2.1.14–15). The Provost, reflecting that "all ages" have been subject to Claudio's temptation (2.2.5), warns Angelo that "af-ter execution, judgement hath / Repented o'er his doom" (2.2.11–12), perhaps to imply that Angelo's sentence creates the "iniquitye" Egerton thought that the law's interpretation should absolutely avoid. Admittedly, both Escalus and the Provost reject "slacknesse." When the otherwise silent Justice states, "Lord Angelo is severe," Escalus responds: "It is but needful. Mercy is not itself that oft looks so. Pardon is still the nurse of second woe" (2.1.282–84). The scrutiny they give the case is, however, remarkable. As I have mentioned, Claudio, betrothed to Julietta, would not have been considered unequivocally a fornicator; moreover, given that his betrothed was pregnant, he had a legal remedy and a social solution. Ecclesiastical law regarded a contract of the kind Claudio and Juliet had entered—*sponsalia per verba de presenti*—as constituting a legally valid marriage, however much a liturgical context was also essential to making it "fully licit."[39] Juliet's pregnancy makes plausible Isabella's solution: "O, let him [i.e., Claudio] marry her" (1.4.49). In cases threatened with bastardy statutes, common-law courts intervened to require couples to marry so that their child did not burden the parish with its care.[40] If they did not marry (and, as a result, their child was abandoned to the parish), the offending couple could be punished, as Lambarde notes: "Two Justices of the peace (the one being of the Quorum) in or next to the limits wher the parish Church is in which a bastard child (left to the charge of the Parish) shalbe born, ought to take order by their discretion, aswel for the reliefe of the parish, and keeping of childe, as also for the punishment of the mother, and reputed father thereof."[41]

Nevertheless, by probing Angelo's motives as they do (although to no constructive end), Escalus and the Provost effectively follow Plowden's recommendation that the judge inform himself by asking questions of the law, particularly if its interpretation could admit an "Idea" not explicitly stated in statute or if the statute itself violates "the Common Usage in former times."[42] In Claudio's case the relevant "Idea" is of marriage itself, what constitutes it—a contract, that is, a "true contract" (1.2.145); a "pre-contract" (4.1.71); and what "Common Usage" would permit—sexual congress (4.1.72). Escalus and the Provost offer Angelo a chance to consider such questions, but he turns it down. What could have caused Angelo to embrace "enlargement" or (in Claudio's words), to recognize his decision as an *effect* of "the demigod, Authority" beyond contradiction before the law—"'tis just" (1.2.120, 123)—yet (somehow, paradoxically) not predicated on the law in its fullest sense? The question goes to the nature of Angelo's judicial character.

Angelo exhibits in an extreme form the willfulness against which James warns Henry: "beware ye wrest not the word to your owne appetite, as ouer many doe, making it like a bell to sound as ye please to interprete; but by the contrary frame all your affections to follow precisely the rule there set downe."[43]

Bracton categorically forbids the same: "For there is no *rex* where will rules rather than *lex*." Angelo condemns Claudio for a crime, fornication, that he himself wants to commit and, after the fact, believes he has committed. This flaw is matched to a passionate temperament. He lacks the "discretion" that, in Coke's words, allows the judge to renounce his own preferences: "Discretion is a science . . . and they [judges] are not to act according to their wills and private affections."[44] Angelo's encounter with Constable Elbow reveals his inability to summon discretion in the act of judging and interpret the law *ex mente legislatorum*. True, Elbow's mockery of language and logic would try any magistrate's patience and foil any attempt to rely on Egerton's assurance that in a perplexing situation "*res consilium dabit*." The "*res*"—the thing or case—at issue before Angelo (whether Pompey and Froth have business in Mistress Overdone's "hothouse" and if so what it is) cannot be clearly identified; Elbow's malapropisms effectively obscure it past any ordinary understanding. But the magistrate Escalus *does* pass the Elbow test nevertheless and in his own discreet and patient way, telling Elbow to wait until he understands the situation he faces. He is not to arrest Froth until he has evidence of a crime (2.1.185–88), and he needs more officers, at least six or seven, to assist him in his duties (2.1.265–73). And Escalus warns Pompey, who has just defied the Duke's statute—"If this law hold in Vienna ten year, I'll rent the fairest house in it" (2.1.240–42)—not to come before him on any "complaint whatsoever" if he wants to avoid a whipping (2.1.246). By contrast, Angelo leaves the scene before this interrogation really gets under way, stating: "This will last out a night in Russia. . . . I'll take my leave, / And leave you to the hearing of the cause" (2.1.134–35).

His intemperate departure invites a powerful comparison. Bracton, arguing for thorough investigations, insists that in the absence of ready evidence, "the judge may descend from person to person to some low and worthless fellow, one in whom no trust must in any way be reposed. Let the judge so inquire into matters of this kind that his glory and the renown of his name may increase and that it not be said 'Jesus is crucified and Barrabas delivered.'[45] For by such inquiries, if they are carefully and discreetly made, many scandalous things may be discovered."[46] To suggest that Angelo may be a Pilate frames him not only as impatient but also unwilling to suffer (*patior*) for the truth: as Bacon would later observe, Pilate was the magistrate who had asked sarcastically, "'What is Truth' . . . and would not stay for an answer."[47] More egregiously Pilatian when he responds to Isabella's plea that he show mercy to Claudio (that is, pardon him for his crime of fornication), Angelo declares, "He's sentenc'd; 'tis too late" (2.2.55), suggesting that he values his judgment and perhaps his reputation more than a man's life. Eventually he expresses the very regret of which Escalus warned. Thinking that Claudio has been executed, he confesses: "He should have lived. . . . Would yet he had liv'd" (4.4.28, 32).

I would like now to shift my focus to the Duke and to ask how his plan to deputize Angelo to enact the justice he himself had failed to institute at the inception of his own rule yields to tyrannical deception. The Duke explains to Friar Thomas that, having given authority to deputies (1.3.35–37, 41), he will not leave the city but remain there disguised as a friar—"Lodowick"—in order to "visit both prince [i.e., his deputy, Angelo] and people" (1.3.45). He also offers the Friar "one" of several "reasons" for pursuing this stratagem: it is primarily to test Angelo's juridical nature, which is "precise," prone to strict interpretation of the law. What effect, the Duke asks, will "power" have on his deputy's cold "purpose"? He then announces his own particular purpose: "hence shall we see our seemers be" (1.3.50, 53–54), without, however, acknowledging that his own disguise will stamp him as the play's most conspicuous "seemer."

The figure of executive dissimulation had wide representation on stage but also in works on government. In itself it posed a formidable problem. To dissimulate is necessarily to withdraw oneself from the societies in which one has expected roles to perform, and *Measure for Measure* suggests that the converse is also true: simply by being absent, the Duke dissimulates: he is not where he should be; in effect, he *is* not. Sir Thomas Elyot describes Emperor Severus as such a spying executive: "he lyke a scholer or seruant wolde one day haunte one parte of the citie, an other day an nother parte: And most politikely fynd occasion to se the state of the people, with the industry or negligence of them that were officers."[48] Considering dissimulation in principle, Justus Lipsius invokes Machiavelli: "The Philosopher doth note that kingdoms are subverted by subtilitie and guile. Doest thou say it is not lawfull to conserve them by the same meanes? And that the Prince may not sometimes having to deale with a foxe, play the foxe, especially if the good and publike profit, which are always conjoyned to the benefit and profit of the Prince, doe require it? Surely thou are deceived: the forsaking of the common profit is not onely against reason, but like against nature."[49] By comparison, the Duke's reasons for his disguise are self-serving: he implicitly admits to understanding the command "judge not" as an excuse to avoid the confrontation that would come with being judged. His further reflections are suppositious: as I suggested earlier, he thinks that Angelo will judge in such a way that he will be judged.

Initially, Angelo appears to fulfill the Duke's expectations: once commissioned, he quickly picks out "an act" "to give fear to use and liberty," as Lucio reports to Isabella (1.4.62–64) and as the Duke himself has intended he should. The Duke's intention is, however, retrospectively shadowed by information forthcoming in act 3. The audience will then realize that when the Duke commissions Angelo in act 1 he knows that Angelo has failed to fulfill his spousal contract with Mariana, and it will therefore conclude that the Duke deliberately rejected Angelo's self-conscious request for a "test" because he suspected that this unfulfilled contract would end in some further sort of bad faith. And indeed, proof of Angelo's "seeming" is not long in coming, as Isabella, having rejected Angelo's proposition, tells him that he has terribly betrayed his commission: "Seeming, seeming! I will proclaim thee Angelo, look for 't" (2.4.150–51), adding later that in such "mouths" the law is "curtsy" to "will" and moved by "appetite" (2.4.175–76). If the Duke did know of Angelo's bad faith, his own deceit in seeming to be what he is not, though to preserve his own status and by extension Vienna, acquires an overtly sinister character. It is enhanced when "Friar Lodowick," having learned that Angelo has decreed Claudio's execution for the crime of fornication, tells Juliet that he will "go with instruction to him [Claudio]" (2.3.37–38). In the event, this "instruction" takes no account of the Duke's knowledge of Angelo's character as a "seemer"—that is, that Angelo wants to commit the very crime for which he has condemned Claudio (2.4.142–44, 3.1.160–64). "Friar Lodowick" tells Claudio merely, "prepare yourself for death" (3.1.167). Notably, too, the Duke fails to consider Isabella's judgment, namely that fornication between contracted parties is rendered innocuous by marriage. This is a judgment he does not hear Isabella pronounce, but the audience can infer that he honors it because it justifies his own plan to realize the contract of marriage between Angelo and Mariana in act 3.

So what kind of a man is the Duke? He appears in multiple perspectives: as himself, as "Friar Lodowick," as a responsible prince, a Machiavellian strategist. He is not, however, the conniving libertine the rogue Lucio depicts in act 3, declaring to "Friar Lodowick" that the absent Duke is a lecher who would not have prosecuted Angelo for fornication (3.2.116–20). As the Duke has confessed to Friar Peter (formerly Friar Thomas) that he is innocent of such crimes (1.3.1–3), and as Escalus, responding to "Friar Lodowick," has upheld the Duke's exemplary character ("he is a gentleman of all temperance" [3.2.237]), Lucio's accusations can be regarded as baseless. Does Lucio commit scandal? Certainly he intends to harm the Duke's reputation when he disparages the Duke to "Friar Lodowick." He is, however, exempt from prosecution by what he cannot know: "Friar Lodowick" will not and cannot bring charges against him on the Duke's behalf, because a person cannot claim an action for slander unless his reputation is damaged to a third party,[50] and no one hears Lucio but the Duke. Not knowing that he speaks to a fraud, however, Lucio must know that he risks arrest. Astonishingly, he does not seem to care. Is his risk-taking a consequence of his indifference, or does it signify a political consideration?

This odd and convoluted scene has, I think, two dimensions. First, Lucio's character functions tropologically here and throughout the play to draw attention to its repeated recourse to figures of semblance and resemblance. To himself, Lucio probably *seems* to commit scandal. Later, Mariana *seems* to be like Isabella—while Angelo's intention is to commit fornication with Isabella, his action fulfills his precontract with Mariana. Thus, too, Angelo may *seem* to himself to be a fornicator, although in the strict sense of the term he is not. Similarly, Bernadine's head *seems* like Claudio's, although Ragozine's head, especially when shaved, *seems* to be a better fit. What then is the point of these exchanges, these almost miasmic "seemings"? We are, after all, looking at a play in which almost nothing is what it seems to be. To arrive at truth and justice, the Duke has attempted to mend his aberrant government with a succession of moves employing "craft against vice." The verbal pyrotechnics with which he describes his solution to Claudio's case—Angelo's licit sex with Mariana—suggests how thoroughly the action of the play exploits its own nature as illusion: "So disguise [the figure of deception] shall by th' disguised [in this case the deception realized when Mariana substitutes for Isabella] / Pay with falsehood his false exacting [the figure of deception pays Angelo in its and his own coin] and perform an old contracting" (3.2.280–83). Second, by assuming great risk in order to express little of substance (the Duke is a lecher, etc.), however ironic in context, Lucio's performance points up the extent to which comedy must represent as farce any criticism of the prince-legislator who governs above the law. What place these exchanges have in the play's representation of law remains unclear until the end of act 5, when the play's hitherto vacuous "seemings" and Lucio's engaging impudence yield to dramatic reality.

The process is subtle. By act 4, scene 2, the Duke knows that Angelo has not honored his dishonorable bargain with Isabella to commute Claudio's sentence in exchange for her prostitution: having arranged to save Claudio from execution by hiding him in prison, "Friar Lodowick" tells Isabella that Claudio is dead and that Friar Peter will denounce Angelo before the Duke. Yet when Isabella (and not Friar Peter) accuses Angelo of rape before the newly returned Duke and his retinue and asks for "justice, justice, justice, justice" (5.1.25), the Duke notes that she speaks "in th' infirmity of sense" (5.1.47) and dismisses her cogent appeal for discretion even as she begs: "Make not impossible / That which but seems unlike" (5.1.51–52). However cruel, this travesty is justified, in a sense, because, like so much of the defensive action of the play, it is predicated on a "seeming": Angelo did not rape Isabella, as painful as it is to see Isabella arrested for telling the lie "Friar Lodowick" instructed her to tell (4.6.1–4). Nor can Lucio's derisive description of her as "handled" (5.1.274–75) count as slander, as she has already confessed in court to yielding to Angelo (5.1.101)—a lie that will be corrected only at the end of the play. Angelo's self-denunciation is yet another effect of the Duke's continued deception. The Duke in his own person tells Angelo to investigate (and disprove) Isabella's charges: "Be you judge in your own cause" (5.1.166–67), a command that inverts the maxim sustaining all common law, *nemo debet iudex in propria causa*, and serves to remind the audience that Angelo, because he has functioned in the Duke's place as prince-legislator, must, in fact, be his own judge.

The veil of "seeming"—dense throughout act 5—seems at no time more impenetrable than just before it is torn open, as the Duke speaks as his own and also as his pseudo-self, "Friar Lodowick." Acting as if he is assured that Angelo is innocent of the crime Isabella has charged him with and that Mariana has been "set on," the Duke orders Escalus to fetch the "friar" responsible and to settle the case. In other words, the Duke summons his pseudo-self as if to charge him and then proceeds to leave the scene. Escalus asks "Friar Lodowick" if he plotted with "these women" to "slander" Angelo: "they have confessed you did" (5.1.288–89). The Duke in his pseudo-self denies the charge and demands to speak to the Duke: "Where is the Duke?" (5.1.294). The question implies (and must cause the audience to recall) the stratagem that governs the plot of the play as a whole. For, "Friar Lodowick" continues, for the court to question "Friar Lodowick" is to seek a "lamb" for a "fox" (5.1.297–98), an innocent man for a conniving strategist. The court must seek the Duke—by implication a "fox":

> Is the Duke gone?
> Then is your cause gone too. The Duke's unjust
> Thus to retort your manifest appeal
> And put your trial in the villain's mouth
> Which here you come to accuse. (5.1.299–303)

That is, "Friar Lodowick" accuses the Duke of neglecting to attend to the court's legitimate appeal; the Duke has unjustly allowed the court to let Angelo—the accused and now a "villain"—try himself (5.1.302–3). Here the Duke in his pseudo-self as "Friar Lodowick" not only recalls for the court his earlier and problematic charge to Angelo: "be you judge in your own cause"; he also defames the Duke, his true self, for giving such a charge. Prompted by Lucio's accusing "Friar Lodowick" of slandering the Duke as a "flesh-monger"

(5.1.333–34), Angelo and Escalus, acting as a court, call for "Friar Lodowick's" arrest in the name of the Duke (5.1.344–50). Unhooded by Lucio, "Friar Lodowick" is then recognized as in fact the Duke. Having just declared his absence "unjust," the now present Duke secures his status as prince-legislator.

The Duke's first act in his restored identity is to charge Angelo to confess what he must regard as a crime: fornication. Probably stirring the audience once again to be mindful of countervailing English custom, Angelo, true to his commission, condemns himself to death (5.1.370–74). In a sense, he here exemplifies the kind of honorable integrity that the Duke's own actions have made entirely theoretical. (While the Duke does not order the execution of his deputy, as did Cesare Borgia that of Remirro de Orco, Angelo's punishment remains a threat to the end of the play.) From this point forward, the Duke speaks pure double-talk. He declares that he forgives Lucio's "slanders" but orders him to marry a "punk," presumably Kate Keepdown, the mother of his child: "Slandering a prince deserves it" (5.1.519–20, 524). His action, to pardon and to punish, is literally contradictory but more importantly self-reflexive: it confesses the enormity of his stratagem—fraud that includes lying, deception, and false witness—and thus reempowers himself as the Duke. Exercising his prerogative, he becomes the dispenser of general pardons. They reflect the best promptings of his conscience; at this point, he is clearly not engaged in interpreting the law but rather in deploying the resources of the state so that it can again cohere as a whole. He does not, of course, need to pardon himself.

The surveyor has thus succumbed to the effects of surveillance, the spy to being espied. For audiences already focused on his actions, Lucio's description of the Duke as "fantastical . . . of dark corners" becomes newly apposite; for those already intrigued by the image of the "fox" as prince and espionage as policy, the career of Elyot's Severus and its subsequent defense in George Whetstone's A Mirrour for Magistrates of Cyties (1584), seems even more relevant: those guilty of sexual crimes especially deserve to be detected by spies, "visible Lightes in obscure Corners."[51] Precipitated by Lucio's unhooding of the "Friar Lodowick," the action of the play thus seems to fulfill the promise with which James opens the Basilicon Doron: "there is nothing so couered, that shal not be reuealed, neither so hidde, that shall not be knowen; and whatsoeuer they haue spoken in darkenesse, should be heard in the light; and that which they had spoken in the eare in secret place, should be publikely preached on the tops of the houses."[52] But what is finally uncovered? Who is known? Notably, the Duke is recognized because Lucio exposes him. Does Lucio therefore figure the essential guardian of guardians for whom the play has been looking? If so, he has also revealed that in an absolutist state comically conceived, such a guardian can never be more than an upstart rogue, a "fantastic." He is a subject in a polity in which the people lack authority and power; their protests, were they to make them, would invariably be illicit. Wild talk like Lucio's, the noise of a "bur" (4.3.179), may be their only very perilous recourse; in any case, such a "bur" risks arrest and worse. It is entirely fitting that Isabella, whom the Duke has humiliated before the court and whose solution to her brother's case the Duke has ignored, says nothing in response to his proposal: "Give me your hand and say you will be mine" (5.1.492).

In conclusion, I think, the audience must wonder whether the play's clarification of its own "invention"—the matter of judging so that the judge is not judged—does not leave a definitive aspect of that "invention" still shadowed, to cloud, as it were, James's pious assertion of clarity that may seem to describe the action in act 5. Angelo judges Claudio on the basis of a literal or "restrained" interpretation of a statute that in light of common usage and the "*res*" under consideration the audience could accept as "enlarged," thus endorsing the solution proposed by Isabella: "O, let him marry her." True. Angelo's administration of justice was patently willful and needed discipline and discretion. Also true. But the interpretation of statute is only one aspect of the play's "invention." The question expressed by its "conceit"—"who shall guard the guardians"—addresses the nature of government itself. Absent an institution of law independent of the will of a prince or a king, I think the play reveals that a government so deficient can have no sure or certain justice, no better defender than a Lucio.

NOTES

1. On dating the play, see William Shakespeare, *Measure for Measure*, ed. Brian Gibbons (Cambridge: Cambridge University Press, 1991), 22.

2. Line citations are to William Shakespeare, *Measure for Measure*, in *The Riverside Shakespeare*, ed. G. Blakemore Evans (Boston: Houghton Mifflin, 1974).

3. King James VI and I, *Basilicon Doron*, in *Political Writings*, ed. Johann P. Sommerville, (Cambridge: Cambridge University Press, 1994), 22.

4. Machiavelli, *The Prince*, trans. Russell Price, ed. Quentin Skinner (Cambridge: Cambridge University Press, 1988), 26.

5. On scandal, see M. Lindsay Kaplan, *The Culture of Slander in Early Modern England* (Cambridge: Cambridge University Press, 1997).

6. James VI and I, *The Trewe Lawe of Free Monarchies*, in Sommerville, *Political Writings*, 75.

7. Ibid., 68.

8. Ibid., 72.

9. Bracton, *On the Laws and Customs of England*, trans. Samuel E. Thorne, 4 vols. (Cam-

bridge, MA: Belknap Press of Harvard University Press, 1968), 2:21. The original Latin text of Bracton's work *De legibus & consuetudinibus Angliae* was published in London by Richard Tottel in 1569. On statute as the will of Parliament, see also Sir John Fortescue, *A Learned Commendation of the politique lawes of England*, trans. Robert Mulcaster (London, 1573), sig. 39v–40. Baker notes: "In 1406, Gascoigne CJ declared that 'the king has committed all his judicial powers to various courts,' *Cheddar v. Savage* (1406)." J. H. Baker, *An Introduction to English Legal History*, 3rd ed. (London: Butterworths, 1990), 112.

10. Bracton, *On the Laws and Customs*, 2:33, 305.

11. I refer to the Geneva Bible: *The Bible that is the holy Scriptures conteined in the Olde and New Testament* (London, 1599).

12. James VI and I, *Basilicon Doron*, 18.

13. "But who shall keep the keepers"; Satire VI, *The satires of Decimus Junius Juvenalis*, trans. John Dryden (London, 1693), 107.

14. On the role of the commissioner, see Baker, *Introduction to English Legal History*, 19–30.

15. *Rooke v. Withers* (1598), as quoted in Baker, *Introduction to English Legal History*, 165.

16. James VI and I, *Basilicon Doron*, 37.

17. Bracton, *On the Laws and Customs*, 2:21.

18. See Martin Ingram, "Spousals Litigation in the English Ecclesiastical Court c. 1350–1640," in *Marriage and Society: Studies in the Social History of Marriage*, ed. R. B. Outhwaite (New York: St. Martin's Press, 1981), 35–57. See also Ralph Houlbrooke, *Church Courts and the People during the English Reformation, 1520–1570* (Oxford: Oxford University Press, 1979). James, however, reminded Henry of Paul's warning that a fornicator "shall not inherit the Kingdome of heauen." *Basilicon Doron*, 39.

19. Baker, *Introduction to English Legal History*, 492–93.

20. William Lambarde, *Eirenarcha, or of the Office of the Justices of Peace in foure Bookes* (London, 1614), 119.

21. See Steven Mullaney, *The Place of the Stage: License, Play, and Power in Renaissance England* (Chicago: University of Chicago Press, 1988).

22. Gibbons, *Measure for Measure*, 24.

23. Edmund Plowden, *The Commentaries or Reports* (London, 1779), 467, in print in 1599. Plowden's statement is a version of Aristotle's rule in his *Ethics* 5.10. See also Christopher St. German, *Doctor and Student*, ed. T. F. T. Plucknett and J. L. Barton (London: Selden Society, 1974), 97.

24. James VI and I, *Basilicon Doron*, 43.

25. William Lambarde, *Archaeion; or, a Discourse upon the High Courts of Justice in England, London, 1635*, ed. Charles H. McIlwain and Paul L. Ward (Cambridge, MA: Harvard University Press, 1957), 42–43.

26. Ibid., 44, 45.

27. Ranulf de Glanvill, *The Treatise on the Laws and Customs of the Realm of England Commonly Called Glanvill*, ed. and trans. G. D. G. Hall (Oxford: Clarendon Press, 1993), 1.

28. Baker notes that equity was not to be subjectively constructed: "The acts of a su-

preme legislature could not be upset by recourse to conscience; statutes might be construed equitably, but they could not be disregarded in Chancery on the grounds that they were unconscionable." Baker, *Introduction to English Legal History*, 126. See also H. F. C. Milsom: "There was no common law, no body of substantive rules from which equity could be different." *Historical Foundations of the Common Law*, 2nd ed. (Oxford: Oxford University Press, 1981), 84.

29. Sir Rupert Cross, *Statutory Interpretation* (London: Butterworths, 1976), 8–9.

30. *A Discourse upon the Exposicion and Understandinge of Statutes with Sir Thomas Egerton's Additions*, ed. Samuel E. Thorne (San Marino, CA: Huntington Library, 1942), 123.

31. Ibid., 131.

32. Ibid., 140.

33. Ibid., 151.

34. Ibid., 154–55.

35. Bracton, *On the Laws and Customs*, 2:299.

36. Sir Christopher Hatton, *A treatise concerning statutes or acts of Parliament and the exposition thereof* (London, 1677), 64–66.

37. Bracton, *On the Laws and Customs*, 2:305.

38. James VI and I, *Basilicon Doron*, 43–44.

39. See Ingram, "Spousals Litigation," 40. See also "pre-contract" in B. J. Sokol and Mary Sokol, *Shakespeare's Legal Language: A Dictionary* (London: Continuum, 2004), 289–304.

40. "Justices of the Peace (either at the petition of the pregnant woman, her representatives, or local Poor Law officers) sometimes coerced men into marrying women they had made pregnant as an alternative to being dealt with under the bastardy statutes." Ingram, "Spousals Litigation," 51.

41. Lambarde, *Eirenarcha*, 357.

42. Plowden, *The Commentaries or Reports*, 467.

43. James VI and I, *Basilicon Doron*, 13. James further condemns "vnrulie private affections" and the person who "counterfaiting the Saint while he once creep in credite, will then . . . frame the common-weale euer to aduance his particular" (20).

44. *Rooke v. Withers* (1598), in Baker, *Introduction to English Legal History*, 165; see also Hatton, *A treatise*, 65–66.

45. See Matt. 27:26; Mark 15:15; Luke 23:18; John 18:40.

46. Bracton, *On the Laws and Customs*, 2:404.

47. Francis Bacon, "Of Truth," in *Francis Bacon: A Critical Edition of the Major Works*, ed. Brian Vickers (Oxford: Oxford University Press, 1996), 341.

48. Sir Thomas Elyot, *The Image of Governance*, facsimile reproduction (1541; Gainesville, FL: Scholars' Facsimiles and Reprints, 1967), sig. M4v.

49. Iustus Lipsius, *Six Bookes of Politickes or Civil Doctrine, written in Latine . . . which doe especially concerne Principalitie* (London, 1594), 113. Lipsius insists specifically on performance and on policy; see 23, 79. Cf. Machiavelli's advice in *Il Principe*: "It is to be noted that, in taking a state, the conqueror must arrange to commit all his cruelties at once, so as not to have to recur to them every day," as quoted in Lord Radcliffe of Werneth,

The Problem of Power: The Reith Memorial Lectures, 1951 (London: Secker and Warburg. 1952), 40. Ambivalent about showing himself in public, James feared misrepresentation: kings are set "upon a publike stage, in the sight of all the people; where all the beholders eyes are attentiuely bent to looke and pry in the least circumstance of their secretest drifts." *Basilicon Doron*, 4. It was a fear that, according to popular accounts, prompted him to visit the Merchant's Exchange in disguise. Ian Ward, *Shakespeare and the Legal Imagination* (London: Butterworths, 1999), 85–86.

50. "Since the basis of the action for words was the loss of credit or fame and not the insult, it was always necessary to show a publication of the words. . . . The one essential was that the words should have been understandable in a defamatory sense by the person to whom they were published." Baker, *Introduction to English Legal History*, 504–5. See also R. H. Helmholz, ed., *Select Cases on Defamation to 1600* (London: Selden Society, 1985), xxxiv.

51. Quoted in William Shakespeare, *Measure for Measure*, ed. J. W. Lever (London: Methuen; Cambridge, MA: Harvard University Press, 1965), xlv.

52. James VI and I, *Basilicon Doron*, 3, quoting Luke 12:2–3.

RICHARD H. MCADAMS

VENGEANCE, COMPLICITY, AND
CRIMINAL LAW IN OTHELLO

Criminal law offers a revealing frame for examining *Othello*, while the play offers in return some provocative thought experiments for examining law. The play encourages attention to law because, among other reasons, it favorably contrasts the deliberative elements of legal process with the more arbitrary process of private vengeance. In act 5, Othello refuses to accord Desdemona the very procedures that vindicated him of a false charge in act 1. Thus, while some emphasize Shakespeare's criticism of law and lawyers, I contend in section 1 of this essay that *Othello* shows the virtue of legal processes by the tragedy its absence produces.

For the lawyer, the play also poses a legal question: is Iago criminally liable for the murder of Desdemona? In section 2, I examine the rules of criminal complicity in place at the time Shakespeare wrote the play. *Othello* is a brilliant thought experiment for testing the limits of Elizabethan complicity law, especially for dealing with clever villains like Iago. In section 3, I use the criminal complicity rules set out in section 2 to explain two otherwise puzzling choices Iago makes: (1) his effort to dissuade Othello from using poison to kill Desdemona and (2) his lack of effort to be present at the killing. Of course, the law of England would not have literally applied to the events in *Othello*, given that they occurred outside England among non-English subjects. But the audience for whom Shakespeare wrote would have interpreted the characters' actions in the light of their English understanding of legal categories, which might have influenced how Shakespeare structured the action. At the least, a legal analysis shows us how legally trained members of the original audiences might have interpreted the play.

Section 1 justifies the legal frame that I explore in sections 2 and 3. There is some tension in my first claiming that the play reveals the virtues of legal process and my later demonstrating that Iago stood to benefit, by accident or design, from certain limits or defects in the period rules of criminal law. Yet there is nothing unusual in finding such ambivalence in Shakespeare, whose ultimate views on important matters such as law are often hard to pin down.[1] The common point is that law has more to say about *Othello* (and vice versa) than has been previously understood.

1. *Othello*'s Legal Frame:
Public Process versus Private Revenge

Various commentators assert that Shakespeare, like other educated nonlawyers of his day, knew a lot about law.[2] Besides having his own share of litigation, there is evidence that Shakespeare once lived near the Inns of Court, where he had friends and relatives and where he performed for collections of lawyers.[3] There was popular interest in law and high attendance at actual legal proceedings, so the plays of the era frequently included trials and made reference to legal concepts.[4] In addition, "lawyers made up a large part of the Bard's audiences wherever his plays were actually performed."[5] Shakespeare thus used his legal "knowledge in his plays to create dramatic situations in areas of then current controversy."[6]

When Shakespeare scholars discuss the law in his plays, however, they usually neglect *Othello*. This omission is unjustified. Even a casual reading reveals that legal themes and terms pervade the text, and not just because we observe various crimes and accusation of crimes (discussed below). For example:

- Iago complains that Othello made Cassio his lieutenant. Three men went to Othello "[i]n personal suit to make me his lieutenant" (1.1.8),[7] but Othello "Nonsuit[ed] my mediators" (1.1.15). A nonsuit is a legal judgment against a plaintiff for failing to establish a prima facie case.
- Roderigo says that if he is lying about Desdemona's having married Othello, Brabantio can "Let loose on me the justice of the state" (1.1.137).
- Desdemona promises to present Cassio's "suit" to Othello: "For thy solicitor shall rather die / Than give thy cause away" (3.3.27–28). English lawyers are either barristers or "solicitors." Brabantio and Othello speak of legal "causes," as discussed below.
- Iago tells Othello he should not be obligated to reveal all his thoughts, arguing:

  Who has a breast so pure
  But some uncleanly apprehensions
  Keep leets and law-days and in session sit
  With meditations lawful? (3.3.141–44)

  Leets were "special courts, held by some lords of the manor once or twice a year."[8]
- Speaking to Emilia, Desdemona decides there is an innocent explanation for Othello's strange mood:

  Arraigning his unkindness with my soul,
  But now I find I had suborned the witness

And he's indicted falsely. (3.4.153–55)

- When Iago recommends that Othello strangle Desdemona in "the bed she hath contaminated," Othello replies that the "justice of it pleases" (4.1.205–6). When Othello is about to kill Desdemona, he comments that her "balmy breath . . . dost almost persuade / Justice to break her sword" (5.2.16–17).

Omitted from this list are the crucial events in act 1, scene 3, where Othello answers Brabantio's charge that he has unlawfully taken Desdemona. The legal framing here deserves sustained attention. Act 1 has the distinction that its events were created entirely by Shakespeare; they have no parallel in the acknowledged source for the play, Giovanni Cinthio's *Un Capitano Moro*, from *Gli Hecatommithi* (1565).[9] Samuel Johnson suggested that act 1 could be deleted without substantial loss,[10] and, indeed, Verdi's opera *Otello* omits it. Scholars have identified various purposes served by the act.[11] I wish to add an overlooked point: the opening act creates a legal baseline for evaluating subsequent events. In act 5, Othello seeks vengeance for what he believes to be Desdemona's adultery. In killing Desdemona and seeking the death of Cassio, he denies to them some of the very elements of a legal process from which he benefits in act 1 and which would have almost certainly unmasked Iago's fragile deception. Thus, the play shows the need for law by depicting the tragic horror that can result from its absence. This reading requires a close comparison of act 1, scene 3, and act 5, scene 2.

THE ELEMENTS OF LEGAL PROCESS IN ACT 1, SCENE 3

In act 1, Brabantio believes that Othello has wronged him by taking his daughter Desdemona from his possession by force or fraud, a serious crime.[12] As will be true when Othello believes in act 5 that Desdemona has wronged him, the source of the error is Iago. Directly and with Roderigo's assistance, Iago truthfully reports to Brabantio that his daughter is secretly away with Othello, but Iago adds sexual imagery to inflame Brabantio's anger (1.1). Later, Iago reports to Othello that Brabantio spoke in "provoking terms / Against your honour" (1.2.7–8), which made Iago contemplate a violent response (1.2.5). Iago also warns against relying on law, suggesting that Brabantio has so much political power that he will turn the governing council against Othello and "put upon" him "what restraint or grievance / The law" will allow (1.2.15–17). Iago thus seeks to provoke a violent confrontation when the two men meet.

The meeting occurs later in act 1, scene 2. Brabantio, Roderigo, and some officers meet Othello, Cassio, and Iago on the street, and each side draws swords. Iago tells Othello that Brabantio "comes to bad intent" (l. 56). Brabantio calls Othello a "thief" (ll. 57, 62) and accuses him of "[a]bus[ing] [Desdemona's] delicate youth with drugs or minerals / That weakens motion" (ll. 73–75). At this moment, on the cusp of violence, Brabantio could seek to avenge himself through private action or Othello might act preemptively as Iago has suggested.

Instead, Othello discourages swordplay and Brabantio invokes a legal process. Brabantio charges that Othello has acted "out of warrant" and commands his men to make an arrest: "Lay hold upon him; if he do resist / Subdue him at his peril!" (ll. 79–81). When Othello asks, "Where will you that I go / To answer this your charge?" Brabantio replies,

> To prison, till fit time
> Of law, and course of direct session
> Call thee to answer. (ll. 83–86)

As it turns out, the "fit time" for Othello to answer the charge is right away, because the Duke is in council that night attending to matters of war, and his messengers bring word that he has sent for Othello. Brabantio is satisfied to submit his "cause" (l. 95) to the Duke and the council.

In act 1, scene 3, the Duke hears Brabantio's accusation, which now also includes the serious crime of witchcraft (1.3.65). Although the Duke is not a judge, and he treats the matter informally, he takes the action to be determined by law, telling Brabantio that if they determine that an individual has used witchcraft against Desdemona, Brabantio shall read "the bitter letter" from "the bloody book of law" (ll. 68–69)—that is, be permitted to select the harshest punishment the law allows.

We observe in the scene several basic elements of legal process. The most important contrast to private revenge is that, instead of the accuser / purported victim deciding the case, the parties submit the issues to a (relatively) neutral and impartial decision maker. The Duke proclaims his impartiality, saying that should the charges prove true, the harsh punishment should be applied "though our proper son / Stood in your action" (ll. 70–71), that is, even if his own son were the party accused.

Second, the accuser Brabantio states a specific claim against Othello, providing the accused with notice of his alleged crime—that he has obtained Desdemona's consent to marry only by the use of witchcraft or drugs (ll. 60–65; 95–107). Third, the Duke makes clear that the truth of the charges will be decided by evidence. Upon hearing Brabantio's second accusatory speech, the

Duke replies: "To vouch this is no proof, / Without more certain and more overt test" (ll. 107–8).[13]

Fourth, Othello is given an opportunity to answer the charges and introduce his own evidence. He accepts the authority of the council and serves as a witness in his own defense, stating that he will "present" (l. 126) how he was able to win Desdemona's love without witchcraft or potions (ll. 129–70). He also requests permission to call the only other relevant witness, Desdemona:

> Send for the lady . . .
> And let her speak of me before her father.
> If you do find me foul in her report
> . . . let your sentence
> Even fall upon my life. (ll. 116–18, 120–21)

The Duke replies, "Fetch Desdemona hither" (l. 122); and when she arrives, Othello says: "Here comes the lady, let her witness it" (l. 171). Desdemona's statement then provides the crucial evidence that causes her father to drop his case. The result of this process is the rightful exoneration of Othello, ending Iago's first plot against him.

THE MISSING ELEMENTS OF LEGAL PROCESS IN ACT 5, SCENE 2

Act 5 offers a parallel. At this point, Othello stands in the position of Brabantio, wrongly believing himself the victim of a "crime" (5.2.26), while Desdemona and Cassio stand in the position of Othello, being falsely suspected. Adultery was an ecclesiastical crime,[14] as well as a basis for a legal separation known as a divorce *a mensa et thoro*.[15] Desdemona previously referred to the legal nature of adultery when she denied being a "strumpet" by telling Othello that she preserved her "vessel" from any "hated foul *unlawful* touch" (4.2.86; emphasis added). Again in act 5, when Othello charges her with being "used" by Cassio, she clarifies by asking, "How? unlawfully?" and Othello answers "Ay" (5.2.70).[16] Othello could have pursued the legal charge of adultery in a church court or, alternatively, could have sought an informal resolution by soliciting an arbiter such as the Duke. But Othello refuses to give Desdemona or Cassio the procedural rights that produced his deserved vindication in act 1, opting instead for private revenge.

Most prominently, Othello is a judge in his own case. In the first words of the final scene, Othello famously states, "It is the cause, it is the cause" (5.2.1). He sees himself not as merely slaying his unfaithful wife, but as performing a public service, a necessary "sacrifice" (l. 65) "else she'll betray more men" (l. 6). When he says "O balmy breath, that dost almost persuade / Justice to break her sword!" (ll. 16–17), Othello clearly thinks of himself as meting out Justice or even as the embodiment of Justice.[17] As Honigmann notes, the emblems of Justice usually include not only a sword but also a scale to weigh evidence.[18] By this time, Othello has decided what evidence to consider—only the "ocular proof" he demands from Iago (3.3.363). Thus, despite being an interested party, Othello has taken it upon himself to perform all these functions: weigh the evidence, determine guilt, set the sentence, and carry out the execution.

Consider the other missing elements from act 5. Cassio is never directly accused. Regarding Desdemona, Othello's accusations before act 5 are vague; he never specifies the man he suspects her with, much less the basis for his suspicion. Only in act 5 does Othello name Cassio, and by then there is little benefit to this procedural "notice" because Othello has just stated he is there to kill Desdemona and that there is only time for her to confess and pray for forgiveness. Even then, Othello supplies no detail to the charges and no evidence against her. He mentions no circumstances of her supposed assignations.

Of particular note, Othello denies to Desdemona the one evidentiary right she requests. Where Othello was allowed to call a witness (Desdemona) to present evidence in his defense, he refuses Desdemona's request to call Cassio. Shakespeare makes the contrast explicit. Where Othello previously says, "Send for the lady . . . let her speak" (1.3.116–17), and the Duke replies, "Fetch Desdemona hither" (l. 122), Desdemona says of Cassio, "Send for the man and ask him" (5.2.50), and "Send for him hither, / Let him confess the truth" (5.2.67–68). Where the Duke hears the witness Desdemona, Othello sends Iago to kill the witness Cassio, though Cassio has never once been confronted with the accusation for which he and Desdemona are condemned.

THE MEANING OF THE COMPARISON

If the parallel between these scenes were not already clear, note another common thread. In act 1, Brabantio remarks that the case he will present to the Duke is "not an idle cause" (1.2.95), while, in his defense, Othello refers to himself speaking poorly for "my cause" (1.3.89). Regarding Othello's suspicion of Desdemona, Iago and Desdemona both refer to it as a "cause," (3.3.414, 3.4.158), which is echoed in act 5 when Othello states, "It is the cause, it is the cause" (5.2.1).[19] We thus observe how differently the legal causes are resolved. In act 1, Othello's innocence is determined by a semipublic process that includes several basic procedural elements from legal trials. In act 5, Desdemona and Cassio's guilt is determined by an interested party who bypasses law for private vengeance. The comparison makes Othello look all the more flawed and hypocritical.

Othello does have reason to prefer private vengeance. A lawsuit would publicize his dishonor and fail to give him the deaths he seeks for Desdemona and Cassio (adultery was not a capital crime). Yet a legal process would have given Othello something of infinitely greater value. The act 1 process reaches the truth, exonerating the wrongly accused, while private vengeance tragically misfires, destroying both the innocent accused and the accuser.

The omission of legal procedures would be less significant were it not for one additional fact: the fragility of Iago's scheme.[20] The absence of law *causes* the tragedy, because we have every reason to believe that legal process would have exposed Iago's deception. Perhaps the best evidence for this point is how quickly Othello reverses course as soon as he hears Emilia assert, without corroboration, that she stole Desdemona's handkerchief at Iago's request and gave it to him (see 5.2.223–27). Iago proclaims that Emilia is lying, but her mere assertion is enough to provoke Othello to attack Iago. Ironically, Othello did not believe Emilia in act 4, when she vehemently stated that Desdemona and Cassio spent no time alone together (4.2.1–23). The difference in act 5 is that there, as in an open trial process, he reveals for the first time the grounds of his suspicion—the handkerchief and Iago—allowing Emilia to give her relevant testimony. When she presents the previously unthinkable possibility that Othello's "ancient,"[21] "Honest Iago,"[22] has deceived him, Othello realizes that all the evidence against Desdemona is linked to Iago, rendering it correlated and suspect. Just as the legal process appears to convince even Brabantio of Othello's innocence, a few lines from Emilia are sufficient to convince Othello of Desdemona's and Cassio's innocence.

A process like the one in act 1, scene 3, would have presumably included Emilia's testimony, but much more. Cassio would have been given a chance to deny Iago's charges and to explain the conversation Othello overheard (where, at Iago's prompting, he mistook Cassio's comments about Bianca to refer to Desdemona). Roderigo might have testified about Iago's scheme to induce Cassio to engage in a drunken brawl, not to mention Iago's confession of his hatred of the Moor and his initial scheme to induce Brabantio to attack Othello. With Desdemona and Cassio denying the charge, Emilia and Roderigo impugning Iago's motives, and Iago subject to rigorous questioning, there can be little doubt that any impartial fact-finder would have seen through Iago's deception.

One might object that Shakespeare could have made the contrast I am advocating more explicit, had he intended the play to praise legal process by showing the consequences of its absence. Yet the contrast is clear enough, given all the references to law. And there are more specific references to the legal alternative. When Othello first considers the possibility of Desdemona's infidelity, he contemplates what he might do if his suspicions prove true and states: "I'd whistle her off and let her down the wind / To prey at fortune" and that "my relief / Must be to loathe her" (3.3.266–71). English law, however, placed on spouses an obligation of cohabitation.[23] To "whistle her off and let her down the wind / To prey at fortune" is to repudiate this obligation, which one could lawfully do only after a divorce *a mensa et thoro*, a legal separation. Adultery was one of the grounds on which a church court would grant a separation. After Othello manifests his suspicion to Desdemona, she tells Iago that she will continue to love Othello even if "he do shake me off / To beggarly divorcement" (4.2.159–60).[24]

Shakespeare did not need to be any more explicit about Othello's legal options because they would have been obvious to his audience. We can see this option in other plays of the same era. When Shakespeare a few years later wrote *The Winter's Tale*, he had the jealous King Leontes, who suspects his wife Hermione of adultery, put her on trial for treason (although, admittedly, Leontes does not accept the resulting exoneration by an Oracle). Consider also Ben Jonson's comedy *Every Man in His Humour*, first performed a few years before Shakespeare wrote *Othello* by a troupe that included Shakespeare. The play includes a jealous character Thorello (in the original Quarto version; his name is Kitely in the revised Folio), who some critics believe is the inspiration for the name Othello.[25] Thorello believes that his wife is engaging in adultery; his response is to bring his concerns to Duke (Justice in the Folio) Clement, whose probing questions of various parties reveals Thorello's error. The magistrate concludes: "Why this is a mere trick, a device; you are gulled in this" (Q 5.1.214–15).[26] No doubt anyone investigating Iago's accusations would have said the same to Othello. Indeed, Emilia says something similar to Othello when she realizes that Iago has misled him into killing Desdemona: "O *gull*, O dolt, As ignorant as dirt!" (5.2.159–60; emphasis added).[27]

The alternative of legal process was sufficiently apparent that the play's references to the law would have alerted the audience that Othello was rejecting that option. And it is this rejection that causes the tragedy: the deaths of Desdemona, Othello, Emilia, Roderigo, and possibly even Iago. Thus, *Othello* is a play praising law or at least the virtues of the deliberative processes law employs.

2. Specific Legal Issues in *Othello*:
Was Iago Criminally Liable for the Death of Desdemona?

Given a legal frame, Iago's manipulation of Othello stands as one of literature's great thought experiments for law, specifically for evaluating the doctrine of criminal complicity (aiding and abetting or accomplice liability). The obvious question is whether Iago is, under English law of the period, guilty of some homicide offense, such as murder, for the killing of Desdemona.

THE LAW OF ACCOMPLICE LIABILITY IN ELIZABETHAN ENGLAND

Let us begin by assuming that Othello is legally guilty for the murder of Desdemona, as Emilia repeatedly suggests in act 5, scene 2 (ll. 163, 166, 181, 183), with the eventual agreement of Othello (l. 291, calling himself an "honourable murderer"). Iago's liability turns on whether he was a "principal" or an "accessory" of Othello in that murder. The common law at this time categorized principals as (1) those who commit the criminal act themselves—by their own hand—and are therefore directly guilty without need for complicity doctrine; and (2) those who do not commit the criminal act themselves but aid or encourage its commission and *are present* at its commission.[28] Later the law called these two, respectively, the principal *in the first degree* and the principal *in the second degree*. Othello would be (with caveats below) the principal in the first degree. Accessories provided aid or encouragement to a principal (before or after the fact), but unlike principals, the accessory was *not* present at the crime's commission. Presence comes to include standing as a lookout even some distance away from the actual crime.[29]

The difference between principal and accessory has important legal effects. The principal's crime stands on its own footing and is not conditioned on the conviction of some other principal. By contrast, the accessory's guilt is purely derivative from the principal's guilt, so the former can only be convicted if the latter is convicted, and only of the same crime.[30]

THE LIMITED TEXT ON WHICH IAGO IS OTHELLO'S ACCESSORY

Iago was not present at Desdemona's murder, not even outside the bedchamber door serving as a lookout, and is therefore not a principal. Is he an accessory? He did not provide physical aid in the murder, but it is a monumental understatement to say that he "encouraged" the crime. Here is a partial list of what Iago does to work Othello into a jealous rage: (1) lures Cassio into a drunken brawl so Othello will discharge him, so Cassio will seek Desdemona's help in reinstatement, and their meetings will seem to support Othello's suspicions; (2) repeatedly asserts Desdemona's infidelity and Cassio's admission to that adultery; (3) plants Desdemona's handkerchief with Cassio; and (4) stages an overheard conversation with Cassio about his sexual encounters with Bianca and manipulates it so that Othello believes Cassio is speaking of Desdemona.

Here's the surprise: Although Iago is an accessory to Desdemona's murder, none of the above behavior is necessary to make him an accessory. More astonishing, arguably none of the above behavior is *sufficient* to make Iago guilty either. For I have left out the one thing that certainly does suffice, and might be necessary, a single line Iago speaks in act 4, scene 1: "*Do it not with poison, strangle her in her bed—even the bed she hath contaminated*" (ll. 204–5).

These words may be pivotal. The standard case of complicity-by-encouragement involves an individual's *endorsing* the crime's commission (prior to its occurrence)—for example, "strangle her"—and this endorsement is absent when the individual merely suggests a motive for the crime. Or, as others have put it, in the standard case, an accomplice's encouragement is "transparent" to the principal in the first degree who understands that he is being encouraged to offend; merely creating a motive for crime lacks this transparency.[31] Whether there can be accomplice liability outside this standard case remains an open question. Real-world encouragements virtually always involve an endorsement; I haven't located a case deciding whether encouragement without endorsement is sufficient. Yet the great English criminal law commentator Sir James Fitzjames Stephen articulated the endorsement requirement in 1883, speaking *specifically about Iago*. He concluded, "Iago could not have been convicted as an accessory . . . but for one single remark—'Do it not with poison, strangle her in her bed.'"[32]

That Iago's guilt may turn on this one statement is surprising. When Emilia learns that her husband is the "insinuating rogue" (4.2.133) who drove Othello to kill Desdemona, she says to him (5.2.183): "And your reports have set the murder on." Emilia does not know that Iago ever said "strangle her" to Othello, but that seems not to be important to the truth of her conclusion.

WHAT IS IAGO'S CRIME? MANSLAUGHTER, MURDER, OR PETTY TREASON?

To this point, I have assumed that Othello *murdered* Desdemona. But there are two other legal possibilities, each showing Iago to benefit legally from being an accessory rather than a principal. First, it is possible that Othello is guilty not of murder, but of *manslaughter*. Sanford Kadish and at least one judicial opinion have noted this possibility.[33] In Shakespeare's time, murder was a killing that occurred with "malice forethought," while manslaughter was a killing that occurred upon a "sudden occasion."[34] I am skeptical of the claim that Othello killed upon a "sudden occasion," because he broods for at least several hours, considers the use of poison, and gives Desdemona time to pray. Nonetheless, a jury deciding Othello's fate might never learn all that the play's audience knows.[35] There is no one other than Othello to testify as to the final events in the bedchamber. Had Othello lived to go to (an English) trial, perhaps he would have persuaded the jury that he had suddenly become convinced of the adultery immediately before he killed Desdemona in a momentary rage. If so, Kadish notes the absurdity of Iago's benefiting from Othello's success: why should Iago get the benefit of the mitigation intended for those who kill out of a sudden occasion, when "Iago . . . coldbloodedly engineered the killing"?[36]

But if we take this scenario seriously, then the problem is even greater than the one Kadish states. If Othello committed manslaughter, the difficulty is not merely that Iago is convicted only of manslaughter, but that he is legally guilty of *no crime*. The period law Sir Edward Coke describes contains *no category of accessory before the fact for the "sudden" crime of manslaughter*.[37] The logic appears to be that if one who encourages the crime had time and inclination to leave the scene before the killing, or the principal had time to separate from the encourager before the killing, then the crime could not be sudden enough to be manslaughter. Conversely, if the crime were sudden enough to be manslaughter, there could be no encouragers of it who were no longer present at the scene. If Othello convinces the jury that he committed only manslaughter, Iago goes entirely free.

There is a parallel problem. Even if Othello and Iago were convicted of murder, the English audience might have thought Iago had committed a more serious crime—petty treason. The method of execution for petty treason was more painful than the ordinary hanging for murder.[38] In Shakespeare's day, two categories of petty treason would have been relevant: a wife killing a husband and a servant killing his master or *his master's wife*.[39] If Othello and Iago stood in a master-servant relationship, then Iago would commit petty treason if he were a principal in the killing of Desdemona. Yet because the spousal category was hierarchical, the husband, the social superior, did not himself commit petty treason by unlawfully killing his wife. As a mere accessory to Othello, Iago is guilty only of Othello's crime of murder and not the petty treason he would commit if he had himself, as a servant, done what he encouraged Othello to do. For as Coke states: "The accessory cannot be guilty of petit treason where the principal is guilty of but murder."[40]

Did Othello and Iago stand in a master-servant relationship? John MacDonnell's treatise on the law of master and servant, written two and a half centuries after the death of Shakespeare, states, "No word in legal literature is more common or more ambiguous than 'servant.'" The military context complicates matters, but it is plausible that for these purposes the ensign Iago was legally his commander's servant, given how MacDonnell states the general definition: "A servant is one who for consideration agrees to work subject to the orders of another."[41]

Certainly, Shakespeare encourages us to associate Othello and his color-bearer Iago,[42] respectively, with master and servant. First, although Iago explains to Roderigo that he is not genuinely loyal in his service to Othello, he does refer to Othello as his "master" (1.1.41–43) and speak to Othello of his "service" to him (1.2.4; 3.3.470). We see Othello treat Iago as a servant when he orders him to fetch his luggage (2.1.206–7). Second, Iago's wife Emilia is explicitly the servant of Desdemona (1.3.297), a fact that differs from Cinthio's *Un Capitano Moro*, where Desdemona and the ensign's wife are merely friends. So Shakespeare intended to introduce this master-servant relationship. We might think it a logical extension of the petty-treason rule: if it applies when a servant kills the master *or the master's wife*, then perhaps it should also apply when the servant *or the servant's husband* kills the master or the master's wife.

Thus, it is plausible that the master-servant relationship applies and therefore that the period law again misses the mark in judging Iago's crime. That Iago manipulates Othello to kill the woman he loves makes Iago's deeds *more* monstrous than if he had killed her himself. But from the law's perspective, it makes him less culpable, guilty of murder rather than petty treason, or no crime rather than manslaughter.

COULD IAGO ACTUALLY BE CONVICTED FOR THE MURDER OF DESDEMONA?

The legal problems discussed above are almost trivial, however, compared to the final issue. Period law regarded accomplice liability as purely derivative of the crime of the principal(s). If the principal(s) went unconvicted, no accessory could be convicted.[43] This is not a problem of evidence but a categorical rule. Recall that being a principal in the second degree required physical presence during the commission of the crime. Because Iago was not present at the scene of Desdemona's murder, he was merely an accessory. Thus, he stood to benefit from this peculiar limitation: because the dead could not be convicted, Othello's suicide bars Iago's conviction.[44] In sum, *Othello* illustrates a surprising set of serious deficiencies in the English criminal law of the period.

3. Using Law to Understand Iago's Scheme

Given the general interest Shakespeare and his audience had in law and the legal frame presented in *Othello*, a legal analysis might illuminate the actions in the play. Here, I claim that we can better grasp Iago's scheme by seeing how it stood to exploit deficiencies in English law identified in the previous section. Iago minimized his legal liability by preserving his status as a mere accessory. He avoided becoming a principal by two otherwise puzzling choices: (1) his decision not to be present at the scene of Desdemona's killing and (2) his effort to dissuade Othello from using poison to kill Desdemona.

TWO PUZZLES: IAGO AVOIDING POISON AND PRESENCE

In the long process by which Iago convinces Othello to kill Desdemona, there is a crucial passage in act 4, scene 1 (already partly quoted), where the two men discuss the means of her death:

> Othello: Get me some poison, Iago, this night. I'll not expostulate with her, lest her body and beauty unprovide my mind again. This night, Iago.
>
> Iago: Do it not with poison, strangle her in her bed—even the bed she hath contaminated. (ll. 201–5)

We are left with two questions that I believe are related: Why does Iago counsel against poison? And why doesn't Iago arrange for his presence at the scene of the crime he works so hard to bring about?

Iago's advice against poison is puzzling. Othello gives a strong argument for poison: he fears he will not be able to go through with a means of killing that requires direct contact with Desdemona. In act 3, scene 3, he decides to acquire "some swift means" to kill her (ll. 479–80), but when he sees her again in scene 4, he is unable to go through with it. Thus, he needs poison to kill her at a distance, "lest her body and beauty unprovide [his] mind again." Above all else, Iago does not want Othello to fail. As he says, "This is the night / That either makes me or fordoes me quite" (5.1.128–29). An abandoned attempt on Desdemona's life could lead her or others to ask questions that uncover the falsity of Othello's suspicion.[45] So why does Iago counsel against the method of killing that is most likely to succeed?[46]

The puzzle would be less acute if Iago had ensured his presence at the scene of the killing. Even if Iago had good reason to recommend strangulation, he could be confident that Othello would go through with this means of killing only if Iago were himself present to whip up Othello's fury. Of course, as act 5 unfolds, Othello kills Desdemona without Iago's contemporaneous encouragement (though by suffocation rather than strangulation). But in act 4, when Iago counsels against poison, there is no reason for him to be confident that Othello will be able to strangle her. Othello cannot maintain a consistent anger, but follows each violent statement regarding Desdemona with a forgiving or admiring one. For example, he begins "Ay, let her rot and perish and be damned tonight, for she shall not live," and ends "O, the world hath not a sweeter creature: she might lie by an emperor's side and command him tasks" (4.1.178–82). Each time his fury subsides, Iago supplies just the right words to reignite it (for example, see 4.1.189–91). Without that ongoing manipulation, Iago should worry that Othello will, as he fears, waver again when he physically encounters Desdemona.

Indeed, note that Iago arranges to be nearby on the three other occasions when he prods a person toward violence: when Othello and Brabantio meet in the streets (1.2), when Roderigo lures Cassio into a brawl (2.3), and when Roderigo tries to kill Cassio (5.1). Why not in this one case? It is not enough to say that the ambush of Cassio and the killing of Desdemona occur at the same time, because Iago could have influenced their timing.

Returning to poison, the best two arguments *against* its use are (1) the poetic justice of strangling Desdemona in the "bed she hath contaminated," as Othello recognizes in his response: "Good, good: the justice of it pleases: very good" (4.1.206); and (2) the sadistic attraction Iago may have for putting Othello onto a more active and sexualized form of killing.[47] Note that neither point will matter if Othello can't go through with the killing. One might say that the justice Othello sees in strangulation will make it more likely that he will complete the act of killing.[48] But a bedchamber strangulation is more likely to succeed only when compared to other forms of face-to-face killing. Poison would be *even more* likely to work than strangulation, because it avoids physical confrontation altogether and makes it easy for Iago to continue goading Othello up to the moment when he places the poison.

In any event, Iago and the audience should see a more powerful poetic logic in the use of poison, one more in keeping with other elements of the play. First, Iago has metaphorically referred to his jealousy (2.1.293–95) and the jealousy he inspires in Othello (3.3.328–29) as poison. He refers back to poison when Othello lapses into a trance, saying: "Work on, / My medicine, work!" (4.1.44–45; compare 3.3.335). Overflowing with toxic jealousy, Othello should now infuse Desdemona with his poison. Second, Brabantio charges that Othello has poisoned Desdemona: that he "[a]bused" her "with drugs or minerals" (1.2.74), "corrupted" her by "spells and medicines" (1.3.61–62), and won her with "mixtures powerful o'er the blood / Or with some dram" (1.3.105–6). With Iago present, the First Senator asks Othello "Did you . . . poison this young maid's affections?" (1.3.112–13). It would complete a great irony if Othello were to vindicate the false charges by poisoning Desdemona in act 5. Finally, English society then regarded murder by poison as "the most detestable of all [murders], because it is most horrible, and fearfull to the nature of man, and of all others can be least prevented," which seems the entirely apt tool for Shakespeare's greatest villain.[49]

Why would Iago advise against poison? And, having done so, why doesn't he create a plan to be near the confrontation with Desdemona to ensure that Othello goes through with strangulation? Why risk failure? These puzzles are particularly interesting because Shakespeare went out of his way to create them. In Cinthio's *Un Capitano Moro*, the Moor and the ensign are "discussing whether the Lady should perish by poison or the dagger, and not deciding on either of them,"[50] when the ensign proposes an alternative method, which they adopt: to beat Desdemona to death with a sand-filled stocking, place her in the bed, and pull the ceiling down on her, to make the death appear accidental. One might think that, in keeping a similar detail—the rejection of poison—Shakespeare was simply following his source.

Yet a careful comparison shows the opposite. First, in Cinthio's story, the plotters together consider and together reject poison. In Shakespeare's play, Othello proposes and Iago rejects the use of poison. Second, the Italian story offers no reason favoring the use of poison, whereas the play gives the powerful reason discussed above. Third, the alternative to poison in the story is a method (pulling down the ceiling) that will make the death appear accidental, whereas in the play the alternative Iago proposes (strangulation) will make the crime manifest. Nor, finally, does poison appear in the story as a metaphor for jealousy, or as a possible illicit means by which the Moor gained Desdemona's love. So the problem being discussed—why does Iago dissuade Othello from using poison?—simply does not exist in the source story. Shakespeare created it.

Shakespeare also created the puzzle about Iago's presence by removing his character from the scene of the killing. In *Un Capitano Moro*, not only is the manner of death different from that in *Othello*(!), but the ensign is free to be present at the scene with Desdemona because he has already attempted to kill the Cassio character at an earlier time. And not only is the ensign present at the scene; he is the primary actor. The Moor conceals the ensign in a bedchamber closet and, when Desdemona is nearby, the ensign jumps out and strikes her with the sand-filled stocking while the Moor watches and expresses contempt for Desdemona. Legally, if we read Cinthio's story through later English law, the Moor is there depicted as only the principal in the second degree.

Shakespeare had good dramatic reasons to make Othello the primary actor and to have him kill Desdemona with his own hands. There are also narrative advantages to narrowing the death scene to just Othello and Desdemona. But

Shakespeare does not merely reverse the roles of Iago and Othello in the killing. He also does not let Iago hang back quietly in the background of the bedchamber, ready to speak words of contempt to Desdemona (or encouragement to Othello), nor even to stand outside the door keeping watch. Shakespeare follows Cinthio's story in many details, so why does he completely remove Iago from the scene of the crime he worked so hard to bring about?

The law explains each puzzle. Iago's presence at the scene of the killing and the use of poison would both have increased Iago's legal exposure. As explained above, Iago is a mere accessory to the unlawful killing of Desdemona because he was *not present* at the scene of the crime he encouraged. As discussed, there are many reasons Iago stood to gain from staying on the accessory side of the line.

First, there is a chance that Othello could convince a jury that he had committed only manslaughter, in which case a mere accessory avoids all criminal liability. Second, as principal, Iago might be guilty of petty treason, but as accessory he cannot be. Third, anything preventing Othello's conviction will bar Iago's conviction. Many impediments might arise, some possibly with the help of Iago. I already mentioned that Othello's suicide barred Iago's conviction. Othello might also have died resisting arrest or have fled beyond the reach of Venetian authorities. There is a chance that he would have been acquitted on grounds of insanity. I am skeptical, but as with the manslaughter claim, the jury would not have learned all that the audience knows. If Othello persuaded a jury to acquit him on grounds of insanity, the law would not permit Iago's conviction as an accessory even though he is (legally) sane. Finally, there is a theoretical chance that a character in Othello's position would be pardoned by the Crown, which would also render the accessories immune from prosecution. Iago thus stood to benefit in any number of ways from maintaining his status as an accessory, which is why he avoided being present at Desdemona's death.

One might respond that, by the end, it no longer matters whether Iago evades punishment for Desdemona's death. English law would have condemned Iago to hang for his murders of Roderigo and Emilia (and Cassio if he died of the wounds Iago inflicted). But what matters here is Iago's *plan* at the time he sets up Desdemona's death. Overall, it appears that he never intended to be caught.[51] He does not appear to plan the murder of Emilia, whose untimely testimony he does not anticipate. He did plan to kill Roderigo and Cassio, but Cassio did not recognize Iago when he stabbed him in the dark and, if things had gone right for Iago, Roderigo would have died immediately from his wounds and left no letters on his person. Thus, the remaining question is how Iago could maximize his chances of evading legal responsibility for Desdemona's murder. One answer is: by avoiding presence at the scene.

Now for the second puzzle. Given that he won't be present to urge Othello on, why does Iago discourage the use of poison? There are two legal explanations. First, the law considered the use of poison sufficient to demonstrate the "malice forethought" required for murder. Poison would have eliminated the chance that Othello's killing was merely manslaughter.[52] If the killer uses poison, the law will reject the claim of sudden rage. By contrast, Iago's recommended method—strangulation—would be perfectly consistent with the kind of impulsive killing that constituted manslaughter, for which Iago could not be convicted.

In addition, there was a special complicity rule just for poisonings, an exception to the basic rule that presence is required to be a principal. Coke states the rule in the *Second Part of the Institutes of the Laws of England*, published shortly after Shakespeare's death: "In case of poysoning, albeit the delinquent be not present when the poison is received, yet is he principall, and so the principall and accessarie may be both absent."[53] Coke cites one pertinent precedent: *Vaux's Case*, decided in 1591.[54] William Vaux was convicted for giving his victim, Nicolas Ridley, a substance, "cantharides"—a preparation from the blister beetle used as a male aphrodisiac ("Spanish fly"), but highly toxic[55]—that Vaux said would help Ridley bear a child with his wife but which instead killed him. The 1604 report of that case, also written by Coke, notes: "It was agreed *per Curiam*, that Vaux was a principal murderer, although he was not present at the time of the receipt of the poison, for otherwise he would be guilty of such horrible offence, and yet should be unpunished, which would be inconvenient and mischievous."[56]

The logic is obvious: killing by poison does not require that *anyone* involved in the poisoning be present at the time and place the poison is consumed. With a rigid application of the presence requirement, there would be no principals to convict for many murders by poison. The report in *Vaux's Case* contrasts the traditional dictum, as cited by Frederic William Maitland, that "the law will suffer a mischief rather than an inconvenience" by saying that it would be *both* "inconvenient and mischievous" to let the poisoner go unpunished.[57] Requiring the principal to be present at a poisoning would be mischievous for letting a guilty party go free and inconvenient for creating a contradiction in the law.

Thus, if Othello had used poison, then the fact that Iago was not present at the scene of Desdemona's death would not guarantee that Iago was merely an accessory. If he were a principal, none of the discussed limitations on liability would apply: Iago (1) could be convicted (a) of murder even if Othello were guilty of only manslaughter and (b) of petty treason even if Othello were guilty of only murder or manslaughter; and (2) he could be convicted even if Othello were not convicted because Othello (a) committed suicide, (b) died resisting arrest, (c) fled the jurisdiction, (d) won an insanity defense, or (e) was granted a royal pardon. Thus, steering Othello away from poison was tactically brilliant, putting Iago in a far stronger legal position. As the judges feared in *Vaux's Case*, Iago "would be guilty of such horrible offense, and yet should be unpunished." In other words, he would be morally guilty of a "contrived murder" (1.2.3) but would have committed none in the eyes of the law.[58]

Of course, even with the poison exception, it is not certain that Iago would have been a principal. The exception need not make *everyone* involved in a poisoning a principal. Years later, in the *Third Part of the Institutes*, Coke describes the poison exception as applying only to one who "layeth or infuseth" the poison.[59] Iago might have remained a mere accessory if he merely brought the poison to Othello, who placed it in food or drink that Desdemona would ingest.

Yet the basic point remains. Coke's statement that, absent presence, only one who "layeth or infuseth" the poison was a principal is his subsequent gloss, published after 1628 and not available when Shakespeare wrote *Othello*. William Staunford's 1557 *Les Plees Del Coron*, the first textbook on English Criminal Law, makes no mention of the poison exception to the presence requirement, so *Vaux's Case* appears to have invented the exception.[60] As Coke's earlier report of the case does not contain the "layeth or infuseth" dictum, it would appear that at the time Shakespeare wrote *Othello* (within the period 1601–4), the only certainty the law offered was that a person could not be a principal if he was absent from the crime's commission *unless the means of killing was poison*. Thus, at the time, one planning to be absent from the commission of a murder he or she encouraged would have a strong reason to prefer any means but poison—to guarantee staying on the accessory side of the line.

In any event, even if Coke's later interpretive gloss governed, if Iago had provided poison, he could not be certain that Othello would not have involved him in placing it. Iago could not easily have refused such a request, and his participation in "laying or infusing" the poison would have certainly made him a principal.

Even though Shakespeare knew some law, we should wonder if he knew the criminal law that I have just reviewed. Did he know of *Vaux's Case*? I have located no direct evidence; I can only speculate. But the timing is interesting. The date of the decision in *Vaux's Case* is 1591, during Shakespeare's writing career but well before he began *Othello*, which was 1601 at the earliest. The first printed report of *Vaux's Case* is Coke's in 1604, while Honigmann says the play was most likely written from mid-1601 to mid-1602.[61] Others date the play as late as 1604,[62] but more salient is the fact that we know that legal knowledge of the day did not depend solely on printed reports. Lawyers orally passed on "common learning" and circulated their handwritten reports of cases.[63] So the legal community could have known of the case before Coke's report. Moreover, as noted, murder-by-poison was a terrifying news item of the period. Unless Shakespeare received his legal knowledge strictly from printed works, it is not difficult to imagine his interest in a case where a man is hanged for supplying a poison he represents to the victim as the aphrodisiac he needs to father a child.[64]

Thus, Shakespeare mostly follows Cinthio's story but removes Iago from the scene of the crime he worked so hard to bring about because Iago would otherwise be a principal, guilty of murder despite Othello's death, flight, insanity, pardon, or successful plea of manslaughter. Similarly, Shakespeare makes Iago reject the method of killing that everyone expects this villain to use—poison—to preserve his status as accessory. And it works. Given Othello's suicide, English law would have made it impossible to convict Iago of Desdemona's murder.

4. Conclusion

Othello matters to law because it brilliantly illustrates some perpetually vexing problems in the criminal doctrine of complicity. It is difficult enough to define the responsibility of one who aids or encourages crime in the typical case, where that secondary actor is less morally responsible for the crime than the principal who carries it out. Yet through Iago, the play vividly shows that an encourager of crime can be more responsible for its occurrence—more monstrous—than the one he encourages.

In turn, a legal frame matters to the interpretation of *Othello*. The tragedy occurs because Othello denies Desdemona and Cassio the legal procedures that previously vindicated him from a false charge. And law helps us understand Iago's actions. He avoids being present at the scene of Desdemona's killing and dissuades Othello from using poison in order to preserve his status as an accessory, which allows him to avoid criminal liability for Desdemona's death under a variety of scenarios, including the one that occurs—Othello's suicide. Iago's brilliant deviousness allows him to manipulate law as well as people.[65]

NOTES

I thank Jacob Corré and Dick Helmholz for generous and indispensable guidance in my historical inquiries into the English law of the period and Richard Strier for generous and indispensable conversations on *Othello*, Shakespeare, and drafts of this chapter. For insightful comments on these drafts, I also thank Bradin Cormack, Alan Dessen, Mary Anne Franks, Anna Marshall, Martha Nussbaum, an anonymous referee, the participants in the May 2009 Law and Shakespeare conference at the University of Chicago, and participants at faculty workshops at Brooklyn Law School, Emory, and the University of Chicago. Brian McLeish, Kimberly St. Clair, and Douglas Wilbur provided excellent research assistance.

1. For an argument that Shakespeare was generally uneasy with law and legal procedures, see Richard Strier's essay in this volume.

2. Daniel J. Kornstein, *Kill All the Lawyers? Shakespeare's Legal Appeal* (Princeton, NJ: Princeton University Press, 1994), 15–20; W. Nicholas Knight, *Shakespeare's Hidden Life: Shakespeare at the Law, 1585–1595* (New York: Mason and Lipscomb, 1973).

3. Kornstein, *Kill All the Lawyers*, 14–15.

4. Ibid., 15. See generally Lorna Hutson, *The Invention of Suspicion: Law and Mimesis in Shakespeare and Renaissance Drama* (Oxford: Oxford University Press, 2007).

5. Kornstein, *Kill All the Lawyers*, 15.

6. See Richard Helmholz, "Shakespeare and the *ius commune*," unpublished manuscript, May 2009, on file with the author.

7. All references to the play are to William Shakespeare, *Othello*, ed. E. A. J. Honigmann, Arden Shakespeare, 3rd ed. (Walton-on-Thames, UK: Thomas Nelson, 1996).

8. Ibid., 217n.

9. For an English translation, see Geoffrey Bullough, *Narrative and Dramatic Sources of Shakespeare* (New York: Columbia University Press, 1957–65), 7:241–52, as cited in Honigmann, *Othello*, appendix 3, 370–86.

10. See Samuel Johnson, *Johnson on Shakespeare*, ed. Walter Raleigh (Oxford: Oxford University Press, 1908), 201.

11. See, e.g., Honigmann, introduction to *Othello*, 62–64; Harold C. Goddard, *The Meaning of Shakespeare* (Chicago: University of Chicago Press, 1960), part 2, p. 81.

12. See Sir Edward Coke, *The Third Part of the Institutes of the Laws of England* (London, 1644), cap. 12, 61–62; also J. B. Post, "Ravishment of Women and the Statutes of Westminster," in *Legal Records and the Historian*, ed. J. H. Baker (London: Royal Historical Society, 1978), 150–60.

13. "Overt" invokes an element of a criminal attempt, while "test" refers to proof, trial, and evidence. See Honigmann, *Othello*, 142nn.

14. See Richard Cosin, *Apologie for Sundrie Proceedings by Jurisdiction Ecclesiastical* (London, 1593), part 1, chap. 2, p. 20.

15. See Coke, *Third Part of the Institutes*, cap. 27, 89; also B. J. Sokol and Mary Sokol, *Shakespeare, Law, and Marriage* (Cambridge: Cambridge University Press, 2003), 141–42. Divorce *a mensa et thoro* was not a complete legal severance of the marriage; the parties were not free to remarry.

16. Rodrigo also refers to his "unlawful" solicitation of Desdemona. 4.2.201.

17. See John Money, "Othello's 'It is the Cause . . .': An Analysis," *Shakespeare Survey* 6 (1953): 94.

18. See Honigmann, *Othello*, 307n17.

19. Finally, after Desdemona's death, Cassio says to Othello, "I never gave you cause" (5.2.296).

20. See M. R. Ridley, introduction to William Shakespeare, *Othello*, ed. M. R. Ridley, Arden Shakespeare, 2nd ed. (London: Methuen, 1958), lxix ("If Iago's plot does not work fast it will not work at all").

21. See, for example, 1.1.32. The "ancient" is an older term for the rank of ensign, the color bearer of the company, who must be a person of particular courage, well liked and trusted. See Paul A. Jorgensen, *Shakespeare's Military World* (Berkeley: University of California Press, 1956), 107–9.

22. See 1.3.295; 2.3.173; 5.2.71; 5.2.150. For a discussion of "honest" and "honesty" in *Othello*, see William Empson, *The Structure of Complex Words* (Cambridge, MA: Harvard University Press, 1989), 218–49.

23. See note 15 above.

24. In the final scene, when Desdemona begs for a lesser punishment—"banish me" (5.2.77)—she plausibly refers to the separation the law permits after this form of divorce.

25. See Hutson, *Invention of Suspicion*, 325.

26. Ben Jonson, *Every Man in His Humour*, ed. Henry Holland Carter (New Haven, CT: Yale University Press, 1921), 226.

27. I thank Paxson Williams for bringing this comparison to my attention.

28. Coke, *Third Part of the Institutes*, cap. 27, 89.

29. See Sir William Blackstone, *Commentaries on the Laws of England* (Philadelphia: J. B. Lippincott, 1893), book 4, chap. 3, p. 352.

30. Coke notes that "accessories sequitur naturam sui principalis." *Third Part of the Institutes*, 139.

31. See Larry Alexander and Kimberly D. Kessler, "Mens Rea and Inchoate Crimes," *Journal of Criminal Law and Criminology* 87 (1997): 1138.

32. See James Fitzjames Stephen, *A History of the Criminal Law of England* (London, 1883), 3:8, emphasis added. A second reason is that we cannot legally know Iago intends Desdemona's death until he speaks this line, because he previously (3.3.477) declared, however disingenuously, "let her live."

33. See Sanford H. Kadish, "Complicity, Cause, and Blame: A Study in the Interpretation of Doctrine," *California Law Review* 73 (1985): 323, 385; *People v. McCoy*, 25 Cal.4th 1111, 1122, 24 P.3d 1210, 1217 (2001).

34. See Coke, *Third Part of the Institutes*, cap. 8, 55.

35. See Hutson, *Invention of Suspicion*, who argues that Shakespeare and contemporary writers elicit from audiences the dual perspectives of one who knows all that the play reveals and of one who, like a jury, knows only what can be subsequently proved.

36. Kadish, "Complicity, Cause, and Blame," 386.

37. See Coke, *Third Part of the Institutes*, cap. 8, 55: "Manslaughter is a felony, and hereof there may be accessories after the fact done; but of murder, there may be accessories, as well before, as after the fact."

38. For petty treason, women were burned while men were drawn (dragged) to the gallows and hanged. See Coke, *Third Part of the Institutes*, cap. 2, 20, 21.

39. Matthew Hale, *The History of the Pleas of the Crown / Historia Placitorum Coronae* (London, 1690), chap. 29, "Concerning Petit Treason," 379.

40. See Coke, *Third Part of the Institutes*, cap. 64, 139.

41. John MacDonell, *The Law of Master and Servant* (London: Stevens, 1883), 38, 34.

42. See note 21 above.

43. On Westminster Primer, cap. 14, Coke states: "For it is the ancient and fundamentall maxime of the common law, juri non est consonum, quod aliquis accessories in curia regis convincatur, antequam aliquis de facto fuer attinctus," meaning it is not the law that any accessory can be convicted in the king's bench before someone else is attainted of doing the act. See Sir Edward Coke, *The Second Part of the Institutes of the Laws of England* (London, 1644), 183. See also 184: "[T]he charge of the jury is, that if they find the principall not guilty, they shall find the accessary not guilty also."

44. The rule was abandoned by the time of Blackstone. See Blackstone, *Commentaries*, book 4, chap. 3, p. 356.

45. Noting a parallel risk regarding Cassio, Iago says (5.1.20–22): "[T]he Moor / May unfold me to him—there stand I in much peril: / No, he must die." If he fails to kill her, the Moor might also "unfold" Iago to Desdemona.

46. Iago also shows himself to be knowledgeable of poppy and mandragora (3.3.333–36), which can be used as poisons. See Edward Tabor, "Plant Poisons in Shakespeare," *Economic Botany* 24 (1970): 81, 84–85.

47. I thank Richard Strier for pointing out this interpretation to me.

48. I thank the anonymous referee for this point.

49. Coke, *Third Part of the Institutes*, cap. 7, 47, 48. Coke is sufficiently concerned about killing by poison that "for the better finding out of this horrible offense," he lists, at 52, seven known poisons (in a legal treatise!). Coke also notes, at 48, that for some period of the early sixteenth century (before Shakespeare), murder by poison was treated as treason and punished more harshly than other murder—by boiling to death.

50. Bullough, *Narrative and Dramatic Sources*, 7:383.

51. As late as act 5, Iago is still brilliantly improvising to avoid discovery. He appears at the scene of Cassio's ambush in night attire, as if from bed (5.1.47; see Honigmann, *Othello*, 299n), and he throws suspicion onto Bianca (5.1.85–86, 104–20).

52. Coke, *Third Part of the Institutes*, cap. 7, 51.

53. Coke, *Second Part of the Institutes*, 1:183.

54. Pasch. 33 Eliz.: 76 *English Reports*, 992.

55. See A. Polettini, O. Crippa, A. Ravagli, and A. Saragoni, "A Fatal Case of Poisoning with Cantharidin," *Forensic Science International* 56 (1992): 37; L. C. Nickolls and Donald Teare, "Poisoning by Cantharidin," *British Medical Journal* 2 (1954): 1384.

56. 76 *English Reports*, 993.

57. See F. W. Maitland, ed., *Year Books of Edward II, vol. 1, 1 & 2 Edward II A.D. 1307–1309* (London: Bernard Quaritch, 1903), xviii–xix ("Our old lawyers were fond of declaring that 'the law will suffer a mischief rather than an inconvenience,' by which they meant that it will suffer a practical hardship rather than an inconsistency or logical flaw"). See the discussion in Bradin Cormack, *A Power to Do Justice: Jurisdiction, English Literature, and the Rise of Common Law, 1509–1625* (Chicago: University of Chicago Press, 2007), 174.

58. Note the parallel to Shylock in *The Merchant of Venice*, who seeks to kill Antonio by enforcing his contract rights, yet without committing a crime. See Richard A. Posner's essay in this volume, where he notes: "[Shylock] had no intention of killing Antonio unless the court ruled that he was legally entitled to do so" (p. 150).

59. Coke, *Third Part of the Institutes*, cap. 64, 138.

60. I thank Jacob Corré for his extraordinary assistance on this point.

61. See Honigmann, *Othello*, appendix 1.

62. Honigmann reviews (but rejects) scholarly work dating *Othello* as late as 1604. Ibid.

63. See J. H. Baker, *The Law's Two Bodies: Some Evidential Problems in English Legal History* (Oxford: Oxford University Press, 2001); also A. W. B. Simpson, *Legal Theory and Legal History: Essays on the Common Law* (London: Hambledon Press, 1987), 359–82.

64. News pamphlets of the period show an interest in London in murders committed elsewhere, particularly poisonings. In 1604 a news pamphlet recounted a poisoning murder in the County of Chester (today Cheshire), noting the need to correct "the rumours which ran up and down the streets of London" concerning the murder. See D. C. Collins, *A Handlist of News Pamphlets, 1590–1610* (London: South-west Essex Technical College, 1943), 67–68. The murder in *Vaux's Case* occurred in Northumberland, which is on the Scottish border, but Cheshire is the northernmost county on the Welsh border, so news could obviously travel great distances.

65. See Strier's essay in this volume.

PART III

Shakespeare's Attitudes toward Law

IDEAS OF JUSTICE

RICHARD A. POSNER

LAW AND COMMERCE IN
THE MERCHANT OF VENICE

I'll first discuss the legal issues in the play, specifically as they are presented in the trial scene of *Shylock v. Antonio*, from a rather narrow, technical standpoint, and I'll then broaden the discussion to take up more general social themes involving equity, jurisprudence, and capitalism.[1] One issue I do not discuss is whether Shylock can or should be regarded as a sympathetic figure. It seems plain that, contrary to the argument of revisionists, the play portrays him as a villain—his "merry bond" (1.3.172) a sinister trap, its character brought out by the contrast with the "friendship bond" that metaphorically secures Antonio's loan to Bassanio and by Shylock's lack of any gift or taste for merriment.[2] Shylock resented Antonio, not only because of the latter's coarse anti-Semitism but also because Antonio competed "unfairly" with Shylock (in Shylock's opinion) by making interest-free loans. And since Shylock's loan to Antonio was for only three months, Bassanio's offer to double Shylock's principal amounts to an offer of interest at an annual rate of 400 percent. Shylock's refusal of this magnificent offer, a refusal motivated in part at least by a desire to eliminate a competitor who underpriced him, confirms that the bond was a gamble, with Antonio's life the stake.

Which is not to deny that, as one critic has put it, "The seeds of sympathy are there . . . [Shakespeare] simply tried to imagine, within the confines of the plot, and within the limits that his culture set him, what it would be like to be a Jew. But dramatic imagination, when it is pitched at the Shakespearean level, becomes a moral quality, a form of humanism."[3] For "Shakespeare's greatness, his 'impersonality' . . . in his best plays, lies in the fact that, whatever univocal insights or affirmations may be expressed within any work, they are thoroughly *dramatised*—that is, set within a complex interlocutory process such that they are never the 'final vocabulary' of individual works."[4] There is a saying among actors—and Shakespeare was an actor—that no man is a villain in his own eyes. One needs to internalize this adage if one is to act a villain's role convincingly. There are self-admitted villains in Shakespeare (though Shylock is not one of them), but they tend to revel in their villainy (Edmund in *King Lear* is a good example), suggesting an inversion of values rather than a confession of evil.

So, on to the trial. And to clarify the legal issues, I'll pretend that Shylock is appealing from the decision by the judge, the Duke of Venice, and that I am the judge of the appellate tribunal to whom the writing of the opinion disposing of the appeal has been assigned. The law that I apply in my judicial opinion is the law described in the play, which is an amalgam of late-sixteenth-century English law and imaginary Venetian law. So:

POSNER, J.:

The appellant, Shylock, complains about alleged irregularities at the trial, such as that what began as a civil trial of his suit turned into a criminal trial of him. The complaint fails because it misdescribes what happened. The criminal statute that ordains the forfeiture of the assets of any alien (Shylock is not a citizen; Jews cannot be citizens in our sixteenth-century Venice) who tries to kill a Venetian citizen was used by the defendant Antonio, on advice of the supposed legal expert from Padua, as the basis of a counterclaim or defense. That is conventional and entirely proper.

Moreover, most of the procedural complaints that Shylock makes in this appeal were waived by him in the trial before the Doge. His objection to having to convert to Christianity to save himself is an example, and in any event the offer to him of that option was benign—indeed magnanimous, and thus underscores the difference between Christian mercy and Jewish vengefulness. Venice is a Christian state and we Venetian judges *know* that Christianity is the only true faith; therefore conversion gives Shylock a shot at salvation (provided he acts in good faith, and is not one of those loathsome conversos who convert to Christianity with their fingers crossed, as it were, continuing to practice the superstitious rites of Judaism in secret). Forced conversions have a long history in Christianity, and, to quote Pope Innocent III, "even if torture and intimidation had been employed in receiving the sacrament, one nevertheless does receive the impress of Christianity and may be forced to observe the Christian Faith *as one who expressed a conditional willingness though, absolutely speaking, he was unwilling.*"[5] For that Shylock should be grateful. In any event, claims waived or forfeited at trial are forfeited on appeal, except in unusual circumstances not present here.

Portia's imposture (for remember that she impersonated a legal expert summoned by the court to give disinterested advice on questions of law), though disreputable and sanctionable (and Shylock's objection to the imposture was *not* waived, because it was not discovered until after the trial), did not influence the outcome of the litigation and is therefore a harmless error. This is not because Shylock accepted her view of the law—he may have done so because he believed that she was indeed a distinguished academic lawyer. It is irrelevant because her interpretation of the contract is untenable. The contract was clear in specifying a pound of Antonio's flesh as the sanction for default, and the penalty provision would therefore be a nullity if interpreted to forbid the shedding of blood. The contract may be unenforceable, at least with respect to the penalty for breach—a question we're about to turn to—but the contract's meaning is too clear to permit the interpretation that Portia (as we now know the legal expert to have been) sought to impress upon it. We therefore reject Portia's legal advice. Shylock is correct to emphasize the importance to a commercial society of enforcing contracts in accordance with the clearly ascertainable intent of the contracting parties.

The *contract* is not illegal (the distinction to be emphasized is that between the contract and the penalty for its breach, which Shylock sought to exact). Loan agreements are enforceable, especially when they do not provide for the payment of interest, for usury remains strongly disfavored. We note that in England, under its current (1571) statute, although lending at 10 percent interest (the maximum) is not illegal, the lender has no *legally enforceable* right to insist on being paid the agreed interest, or indeed any interest at all.

The penalty provision, however, is severable from the rest of the contract. Although penalty clauses in contracts are not enforced at common law,[6] they are enforced in the civil law, which is to say the law of Continental Europe. Venice is a civil law jurisdiction, and so when Venetian and English law conflict, the former controls. But in our enlightened sixteenth century, neither civil law nor common law will enforce a penalty involving physical injury (as distinct from imprisonment for nonpayment of a debt until the debt is paid—an authorized nonmonetary remedy).[7] That is true even though enforcing such a penalty would both signal the borrower's intention to repay and increase his incentive to repay, and so could perhaps be justified in a less civilized legal culture. Moreover, there was no default in this case. It is true that the bond had come due; but that meant only that Shylock was entitled to demand payment. Bassanio always stood ready to pay back Shylock's loan. Antonio was merely a surety, as Shylock admits. Before seeking to enforce the contract against the surety, Shylock should have demanded payment from Bassanio, the primary debtor. Only if he refused to pay would Shylock be entitled to enforce the surety's bond.

This point is fundamental. The obligation of a surety or guarantor is conditional on a default by the principal obligor, who in this case is Bassanio. This is apparent from the opening lines of the scene in which the loan and bond are negotiated:

Shylock: Three thousand ducats, well.
Bassanio: Ay, sir, for three months. (1.3.1–2)

In other words, Bassanio is asking for a loan of three thousand ducats. Antonio's bond is intended as a guaranty that Shylock's three-thousand-ducat loan will be repaid in the event that Bassanio defaults. But Bassanio does not default; he is prepared to repay Shylock's entire loan with generous interest, and his financial ability to do so is, thanks to his marriage to Portia, not in doubt.

Antonio points out, perceptively anticipating an economic depression in 2008, some 413 years hence, that a nonmonetary penalty clause can disrupt the financial system because it cannot readily be valued. Had Antonio sought a new loan after signing the contract with Shylock, potential lenders would have found it impossible to determine Antonio's full liabilities, and a credit freeze might have ensued.

Anyway it is now too late for Shylock to demand repayment with or without interest. For he made clear that his objective was to kill Antonio, in part to remove him as a competitor, rather than to obtain repayment of the three thousand ducats that he had lent Bassanio. The only sanction for breach that is specified in the contract is the enforcement of the penalty bond. And from the outset of the trial, Shylock made clear that, if there were alternative remedies, nevertheless he had made a firm election to pursue enforcement of the bond. He did not say, "Give me either Antonio's life or my 3,000 ducats." This court must hold Shylock to his election.

But despite his evil intent, Shylock did not violate the attempted-murder statute. This was not because Antonio's default was unlikely; the crime of attempted murder does not require a high probability that the attempt will succeed. (Only if the means employed were wholly inefficacious might the "attempt" be deemed noncriminal.) Shylock was innocent of attempted murder for a different reason—because he sought to use legal process to bring about Antonio's death (albeit he wished to be the executioner). He had no intention of killing Antonio unless the court ruled that he was legally entitled to do so. Bad motives do not invalidate a lawful act. It is true that the statute forbids "direct or indirect attempts" (4.1.348) by an alien to kill a citizen, but "indirect" refers to the sort of scheming by which Iago procured the murder of Desdemona by the deceived Othello, rather than to lawful use of legal process; for imagine if an alien truthfully reported a crime by a Venetian citizen and as a result of the ensuing prosecution the citizen was executed.

Nor did Shylock try to subvert the legal process, by fraud or otherwise, to obtain a judgment that he knew he wasn't entitled to. Had he framed Antonio, he would have been guilty of attempted murder, even though Antonio's punishment (if the attempt succeeded) would have been administered by the state rather than by the person who had framed him. It would be as if someone had bribed the public executioner to execute an innocent person.

So because Shylock did not violate the attempted-murder statute, his property is not forfeit. But he is not entitled to the return of the three thousand ducats that he had lent Bassanio.

SO ORDERED.

So much for the trial; reclaiming my twenty-first-century identity, I turn now to some more general issues presented by the play, beginning with the distinction between "law" and "equity." Equity is the recognition, first articulated by Aristotle, that strict rules of law, however necessary to a well-ordered society, must be applied with sensitivity and tact, so that the spirit of the law is not sacrificed unnecessarily to the letter. The evolution of a legal system is from strict and simple rules to looser, more flexible standards. The former are easier to create, articulate, and enforce. This is important in a society in which the illiteracy of the population and the lack of reliable techniques of factual inquiry and complex administration make it imperative that legal rights and duties be left simple. As techniques for a more supple administration of law emerge, the price of applying simple rules to situations in which that application denies substantive justice comes to seem too high, and strict "legal" rules become overlaid with flexible "equitable" principles. Yet it is understandable that an unpopular alien would mistrust a jurisprudence that gives judges discretion to mitigate the rigors of legal rules; for he could expect any discretion to be exercised against him. A punctilious legalism is the pariah's protection. But he who lives by the letter of the law may perish by it.

The spirit of equity in *The Merchant of Venice* is just that—spirit, not legal substance. In sixteenth-century England, "equity" bore three senses. It was the spirit of the law (justice, the administration of law in accordance with conscience), a principle of loose interpretation of statutes (the Aristotelian sense), and the body of legal principles, supposedly drawn from equity in the first sense, administered by the lord chancellor, who presided over the chancery court, the court of equity or "conscience." Portia's "quality of mercy" speech is not a legal argument but an appeal to Shylock's sense of pity (he has none) and thus evokes the first sense of "equity." Her reference to mercy as proceeding from heaven and "enthroned in hearts of kings" does hint at the royal and ecclesiastical origins of the English court of equity—the power to pardon is a traditional royal (executive) prerogative—but in the world of the play, no one is empowered to trump law with equity.

That is why, when Portia's appeal to Shylock for mercy fails, she is forced to argue in legalistic terms. Within those terms her argument is stronger than may at first appear. To rebut it by pointing out in good lawyer's fashion that the bond *must* have authorized whatever action was necessary to execute it, and therefore the shedding of Antonio's blood, Shylock would have had to appeal to the spirit rather than the letter of the bond; for the bond says nothing about shedding blood. And once he had done that he would have found it hard to maintain his legal position. The spirit of the bond is to make sure that he is repaid in full, and Bassanio has offered to repay him double, or even more if Shylock insists—but Shylock suffers from the revenger's standard vice of immoderateness.

Moreover, Portia tries to minimize the damage to Venice's standing as a commercial society that would be caused by the Venetian court's refusing to enforce Shylock's contract with Antonio by basing her legal argument on the meaning of the contract, rather than asking the court to void the contract on the ground that it is inequitable; for that would be an example of the operation of discretionary justice, of which aliens doing business with Venetians would be understandably mistrustful.

Her "quality of mercy" speech is an inspiring set piece, but it is to one side of the legal issues. And it is not a window into her heart. She prefaces it by saying that since Antonio confesses the bond, "Then must the Jew be merciful" (4.1.180)—meaning that unless Shylock shows mercy, Antonio must die. She repeats this at the end of her speech:

> I have spoke thus much
> To mitigate the justice of thy plea,
> Which if thou follow, this strict court of Venice
> Must needs give sentence 'gainst the merchant there. (4.1.199–203)

In other words, Shylock, you've won. But of course he's about to lose, as she knows. By telling him that he's won, she is saving herself a packet of money. She's a trickster, as befits an impostor; it was through her trick that Bassanio, her preferred suitor, picked the right casket and so won her hand. She will pull another trick, the ring trick, at the end of the play.

Unlike Antonio and the rest of the characters in the play, Shylock and Portia understand that the law is something to be used—by Shylock to revenge himself against Antonio and by Portia to foil Shylock and save money—rather than supinely yielded to. In Shylock and Portia we see Shakespeare, as one critic says, "predicting the demise of the Belmont-Venice dichotomy"—the dichotomy between Belmont, the city of love, symbolized by Portia, and Venice, the city of self-love, symbolized by the Jewish moneylenders: "Portia's appearance in Venice in male dress tells us that she or her descendants will not willingly stay put on the pedestal in Belmont," while Shylock, by virtue of his forced conversion to Christianity, will "become a respectable businessman."[8]

Shakespeare wrote *The Merchant of Venice* at a time when nascent capitalist values were challenging the still-dominant feudal values of Renaissance England. Shylock, despite or perhaps alongside his Old Testament revenger character, personifies the capitalistic ethic. When the Duke of Venice asks him why he would rather have a pound of worthless flesh than a large sum of money, Shylock replies with a commonplace of modern economic theory—the subjectivity of value. He explains that value is determined by willingness to pay, which is a function of the preferences and resources of each individual, rather than by some external, objective, or governmental determination of merit or desert:

> I'll not answer that,
> But say it is my humor. Is it answered?
> What if my house be troubled with a rat
> And I be pleased to give ten thousand ducats
> To have it baned? What, are you answered yet?
> Some men there are love not a gaping pig,
> Some that are mad if they behold a cat. . . .
> As there is no firm reason to be rendered
> Why he cannot abide a gaping pig,
> Why he a harmless necessary cat . . .
> So can I give no reason, nor I will not. (4.1.42–48, 53–55, 59)

Shylock further defends his position by reference to freedom of contract and the rule of law and implies that the rejection of his claim for the pound of flesh would be redistributive and socialistic:

> You have among you many a purchased slave,
> Which, like your asses and your dogs and mules,
> You use in abject and in slavish parts,
> Because you bought them. Shall I say to you,
> "Let them be free, marry them to your heirs!
> Why sweat they under burdens? Let their beds
> Be made as soft as yours . . ."?
> . . . So do I answer you:

The pound of flesh which I demand of him
Is dearly bought, is mine, and I will have it.
If you deny me, fie upon your law!
There is no force in the decrees of Venice. (4.1.90–96, 98–102)

England at the end of the sixteenth century was in transition from a medieval to a protomodern society. Within a half century Cromwell would readmit the Jews to England. And a few centuries on there would indeed be women lawyers. The future would not belong to the debonair aristocrat Bassanio—the adventurer, the gambler—but to the Jewish financier and his dull gentile counterpart, Antonio.

NOTES

1. I have borrowed from my discussion of *The Merchant of Venice* in my book *Law and Literature*, 3rd ed. (Cambridge, MA: Harvard University Press, 2009), esp. 139–50. I thank Richard Strier and Stephen Greenblatt for their helpful comments on a previous draft of this essay.

2. All references to the play are to William Shakespeare, *The Complete Works of Shakespeare*, ed. David Bevington, 6th ed. (New York: Pearson Education, 2009).

3. John Gross, *Shylock: A Legend and Its Legacy* (New York: Simon and Schuster, 1992), 349.

4. David Parker, *Ethics, Theory, and the Novel* (Cambridge: Cambridge University Press, 1994), 60.

5. Innocent III, "Papal Bull on False Baptisms" (1201), in *Scattered among the Nations: Documents Affecting Jewish History, 49–1975*, ed. Alexis P. Rubin (Northvale, NJ: J. Aronson, 1995), 50–51, emphasis added. See also Solomon Grayzel, *The Church and the Jews in the Thirteenth Century: A Study of Their Relations during the Years 1198–1254*, rev. ed. (New York: Hermon Press, 1966), 103.

6. Although "penal bonds with conditional defeasance"—the promised penalty is canceled if the giver of the bond repays the loan—are enforceable, the chancery court (the English court of equity) early on began relieving some debtors against even merely pecuniary penalties in bonds. A defaulting borrower had, moreover, a right—the "equity of redemption"—to retain the property that he was about to forfeit by his default by coming up with the money that he owed, even though it was overdue, within a reasonable time. So even under English law, Antonio was properly relieved from the forfeiture, because before it took place, the money due Shylock was tendered by Bassanio—and with extravagant interest.

7. We are not surprised that Shylock and Antonio were ignorant of the law; neither of them is a lawyer and it is apparent that neither consulted a lawyer. That is always a mistake.

8. Samuel Ajzenstat, "Contract in *The Merchant of Venice*," *Philosophy and Literature* 21 (1997): 262, 273–74. Ajzenstat argues that Shylock will become a respectable business-

man because anti-Semitism in *The Merchant of Venice* is religious rather than ethnic, as shown by Lorenzo's marriage to Shylock's daughter, which the Christians accept without demur. The argument is unrealistic, given Christian suspicion that Jewish converts ("conversos") were opportunists who would continue to perform Jewish rites, in secret. See Janet Adelman, *Blood Relations: Christian and Jew in "The Merchant of Venice"* (Chicago: University of Chicago Press, 2008), 4–12. That suspicion is related to the persistent uncertainty whether to regard Jews as a religious group or as a race (in modern terms an ethnic group, like the Irish).

CHARLES FRIED

OPINION OF FRIED, J.,
CONCURRING IN THE JUDGMENT

At the outset I note, as does my brother Posner, that we sit as a court of appeal from the judgment in the first instance of the Duke (Doge) of Venice. In the city-states of late medieval and Renaissance Italy, judges were often recruited from neighboring cities to render a perhaps more impartial judgment.[1] Indeed, Portia is supposed to have come from the university city of Padua as a learned expert on the law (*jurisconsult*), who, though not a judge, gives advice to the Duke that he treats as binding. It is also clear that although we are summoned from afar—both in time and space—we are supposed to judge according to the law of Venice as we find it, our only special competences being impartiality in its application and perhaps a better, because trained, understanding of that law. As when a judge in our more familiar contexts is bound to rule as if sitting as a judge of another jurisdiction, we may not import our local sensibilities to alter the law we are bound to apply. If he is to apply the sterner law of New York, a judge in California—whether of a state court sitting in a conflicts-of-law case or as a federal judge—ought not (I do not pretend that it does not sometimes, perhaps often, happen) temper it with the looser dispositions to which that sunnier clime might have accustomed him, any more than a judge sitting in Louisiana or Texas should bring the Robin Hood dispositions of those jurisdictions[2] to a case supposed to be determined by the law of New York. Therefore I insist perhaps even more firmly than does my brother that we must judge according to the law of Venice, untinctured and unmitigated by notions and considerations drawn from juristic sensibilities of distant times and places.

It is clear to me that from the outset the merchant law of Venice is strict, unforgiving, and rigidly formalistic. Nor are Shylock, Antonio, Portia, and (perhaps reluctantly) the Duke insensible to that rigorous character of the governing law. At the very outset, an exchange demonstrating such an awareness takes place between Shylock and Antonio:

Shylock: This kindness will I show.
           Go with me to a notary, seal me there
           Your single bond; and, in a merry sport,
           If you repay me not on such a day,

> In such a place, such sum or sums as are
> Expressed in the condition, let the forfeit
> Be nominated for an equal pound
> Of your fair flesh, to be cut off and taken
> In what part of your body pleaseth me.

Antonio: Content, in faith, I'll seal to such a bond,
And say there is much kindness in the Jew.

Bassanio: You shall not seal to such a bond for me.
I'll rather dwell in my necessity.

Antonio: Why, fear not, man; I will not forfeit it.
Within these two months—that's a month before
This bond expires—I do expect return
Of thrice three times the value of this bond.

Shylock: O father Abram, what these Christians are,
Whose own hard dealings teaches them suspect
The thoughts of others! Pray you, tell me this:
If he should break his day, what should I gain
By the exaction of the forfeiture?
A pound of man's flesh taken from a man
Is not so estimable, profitable neither,
As flesh of muttons, beefs, or goats. I say,
To buy his favor I extend this friendship.
If he will take it, so; if not, adieu.
And, for my love, I pray you wrong me not.

Antonio: Yes Shylock, I will seal unto this bond.

Shylock: Then meet me forthwith at the notary's.
Give him direction for this merry bond,
And I will go and purse the ducats straight,
See to my house, left in the fearful guard
Of an unthrifty knave, and presently
I'll be with you. (1.3.142–76)[3]

Nor in the ensuing proceedings before the court below is there any doubt raised that Shylock is fully entitled, once there has been a literal default by Antonio, to insist on the literal terms of the bond: the pound of flesh closest to the heart. (Here, as an aside, it should be noted that the place from which the pound of flesh is to be cut was in the bond left to Shylock to choose: "to be cut off and taken / In what part of your body pleaseth me." This especially vindictive designation, as I shall point out later, may well have sunk Shylock.)

The talk of mercy by the Duke—the judge of first instance—Bassanio, and Portia clearly constitutes pleas to Shylock to relent from insisting on his legal due. And when Shylock rejects these pleas, it is understood by all that that is the end of all such considerations. Antonio, who hates Shylock and knows his disposition and motives, is never in doubt on this point and repeatedly urges that Shylock get on with it.

My brother Posner raises a question on this score. He states, "The obligation of a surety or guarantor is conditional on a default by the principal obligor, who in this case is Bassanio. . . . Antonio's bond is intended as a guaranty that Shylock's three-thousand-ducat loan will be repaid in the event that Bassanio defaults. But Bassanio does not default; he is prepared to repay Shylock's entire loan with generous interest, and his financial ability to do so is, thanks to his marriage to Portia, not in doubt." It is, however, agreed all around that there has been a default, and we are bound to accept this as a premise, a premise that none of the parties have put in issue. In all likelihood, whatever Bassanio's readiness and willingness to pay at the time of trial, he must have been unable—because of Antonio's misfortunes—to pay at the precise time payment was required. Any such tardiness would constitute default.[4] My brother's argument that as a matter of commercial reality, Antonio's obligation is that of a surety and that the obligation of a surety, being secondary, should be released given the certainty that the primary obligation will be discharged—albeit after a technical default—is an argument that appeals to our modern sensibilities. It would have us construe Antonio's undertaking (which I set out at the outset) as being something less and different from what it literally states. This would be to mitigate the rigors of a literal (perhaps flat-footedly literal) construal of the agreement, by a rule that says that no matter that the parties by their words and their intentions (as Antonio's avowals at trial demonstrate) agreed to a primary obligation—a kind of wager on Bassanio's prompt payment—the agreement will be construed according to its underlying commercial reality, that is, as a contract of suretyship; and further, that a surety should be released if the technical default of the primary obligor can readily be cured. This we should not do. First, because the law of Venice (though perhaps not of Belmont) lays great store by the literal enforcement of agreements; and second, because it was clear to all—and to my brother Posner—that Shylock's purpose was not just economic, and that Antonio acquiesced in the purpose. As I have said, there is some practical sense in Venetian law's unwillingness to depart from the very literal interpretation of agreements, especially when the departure would disadvantage an alien merchant. In any event, we are not free to correct Venetian law in this regard.

There is no doubt on this score in anyone's mind—and as judges bound by the law of a foreign jurisdiction, it behooves us to accept the judgment of those more acquainted with the strictness of the local law.[5] Indeed, Portia most articulately—but also the Duke—understands the reason for this law. Any departure from the strict and literal interpretation of the contract for reasons of "mercy" or "equity" will undermine the confidence of merchants trading in Venice and coming into its courts that their exact claims will be precisely respected. And once that confidence is undermined, the very considerable advantages that Venice enjoys as an international entrepôt will also be undermined. Antonio himself understood this point:

> The Duke cannot deny the course of law;
> For the commodity that strangers have
> With us in Venice, if it be denied,
> Will much impeach the justice of the state,
> Since that the trade and profit of the city
> Consisteth of all nations. (3.3.26–31)

As Judge Learned Hand, another "Daniel come to judgment" (4.1.221), put it, "in commercial transactions it does not in the end promote justice to seek strained interpretations in aid of those who do not protect themselves."[6] The wisdom of this seemingly "harsh" pronouncement by Judge Hand was soon shown when a softer judge, Roger Traynor, more given to considerations of "equity" and celebrated for his "strained interpretations," reached the opposite conclusion on the same point of contract law,[7] precipitating a legal and practical tangle from which the law has scarcely yet extricated itself.[8]

Accordingly, I concur in my brother Posner's reversal of the judgment of the court below that Shylock, considered to be an alien, was guilty of an attempt on the life of a citizen, and therefore subject to forfeiture of his goods and whatever other penalty the Duke should decree (4.1.344–61). Shylock sought no more than all agreed the law of Venice allowed him and therefore he cannot be found guilty of violating another law of Venice. Had Shylock found a way to enforce his bond in the strict sense that Portia identified, then this conflict of laws would have had to be resolved in his favor:

> Therefore prepare thee to cut off the flesh.
> Shed thou no blood, nor cut thou less nor more
> But just a pound of flesh. If thou tak'st more
> Or less than a just pound, be it but so much
> As makes it light or heavy in the substance

Or the division of the twentieth part
Of one poor scruple, nay, if the scale do turn
But in the estimation of a hair,
Thou diest and all thy goods are confiscate. (4.1.322–30)

Since Shylock could conceive of no such way—though, as we shall see, there might indeed have been one—he committed no offense if he waived his right to insist on his bond, particularly if the reason for his waiver was that he could not execute it punctiliously.

Judge Posner notes that in modern law the demand for a pound of flesh would not in any event have been enforceable, because it was stipulated not as a good faith attempt to provide a reasonable *ex ante* estimate of the possible damages (what are called "liquidated damages"), but as a penalty giving a windfall in case of default, a kind of gambling contract in which the obligee hopes for a recovery in excess of what full performance would have given. Judge Posner also notes that in modern law Bassanio's offer to pay the full amount of the debt—and then some—would have settled the matter, as a creditor is entitled to no more than his debt plus interest—just as a mortgagee is entitled to no more than his debt and not the forfeiture of the mortgaged property, the mortgagor remaining entitled to what is called the equity of redemption. But all that is quite beside the point under the law of Venice. Indeed, Judge Posner himself in another context has recognized that the distinction between a penalty and liquidated damages is quite dubious and probably inappropriate, at least in contracts between merchants, as this was.[9]

The law of Venice was more literalistic—formalistic—than is our modern law, and not irrationally so. Implicit in the whole trial scene and in Portia's speeches is the understanding that once courts begin to depart from strict adherence to the words of contracts, the door is open for all manner of subjective, unpredictable, and perhaps even corrupt considerations. This is what Judge Hand meant and what businesses working in discretionary, arbitrary, and unpredictable (or predictably hostile) legal environments have learned to their sorrow when subject to the courts of places like Russia, China, Alabama, and Louisiana.

But surely, it will be objected, such concerns do not obtain in this case, where Shylock is offered double his principal. (As this was a three-month loan, double the principal would mean interest at 400 percent.) One may argue that Shylock is unreasonable, indeed irrational, in insisting on his pound of flesh instead of taking the generous money premium offered him. But that is not what Shylock wanted; nor is it what he stipulated in act 1.3. And as Judge Posner has explained in another context:

[W]e repeat that if it appeared from the language or circumstances of the contract that the parties really intended General Motors to have the right to reject Morin's work for failure to satisfy the private aesthetic taste of General Motors' representative, the rejection would have been proper even if unreasonable. But the contract is ambiguous because of the qualifications with which the terms "artistic effect" and "decision as to acceptability" are hedged about, and the circumstances suggest that the parties probably did not intend to subject Morin's rights to aesthetic whim.[10]

It is entirely clear, of course, that the pound of flesh was Shylock's precise "whim."

Portia expresses this same thought more pithily in the principal interchange in the scene, when she rejects the argument that both mercy and reasonableness argue that Shylock be made to accept the six thousand ducats and yield in his stubborn insistence on his pound of flesh:

Bassanio: And, I beseech you,
Wrest once the law to your authority.
To do a great right, do a little wrong,
And curb this cruel devil of his will.

Portia: It must not be. There is no power in Venice
Can alter a decree establishèd:
'Twill be recorded for a precedent,
And many an error by the same example
Will rush into the state. It cannot be. (4.1.212–20, emphasis added)

Portia, as the Duke's (and Venice's) alter ego, is quite consistent. In insisting that Shylock get nothing more than the precise weight of flesh he contracted for—and flesh only, not blood—she refuses to mitigate the letter of the law in Shylock's favor, as she would not mitigate it against him. And Shylock, seeing the force of this argument—as I am not sure my brother Posner does—does not try to argue that, being entitled to the pound of flesh, he is further entitled to shed the blood that is incidental to his entitlement. Any such argument would require mitigation, and down that road lie not only Bassanio's "little wrong," but also the equity of redemption and, at the very end of the line, Judge Traynor's Belmontian justice, with all the confusion it entails. "'Twill be recorded for a precedent."

Now a greater irony yet: Shylock being hoist with his own petard.[11] There is the possibility that with as good a lawyer on his side as Antonio had on his, Shylock might have found a way out of his dilemma.

> A Somali man named Farah [speaking to Isak Dinesen] . . . felt that this was an injustice, and an avoidable one:
> "What?" said he. "Did the Jew give up his claim? He should not have done that. The flesh was due to him, it was little enough for him to get for all that money."
> "But what else could he do," I asked, "when he must not take one drop of blood?"
> "Memsahib," said Farah, "he could have used a red-hot knife. That brings out no blood."[12]

But just as Shylock was entitled to make his election between the money and the penalty, so was he entitled to forgo the penalty if he could see no way to exact it with the requisite degree of precision and thereby avoid endangering his own life. That there may have been such a way that Shylock did not see is no concern of the law, just as the "irrationality" of his election to take the penalty in the first place is no concern of the law. And it is not the office of the lawyer or judge to suggest a way to him. It's each man on his own two feet in Venice.

At least Judge Posner is forced to acknowledge, in tension with his general view of the legal system depicted in the play, that Shylock isn't even entitled to the three thousand ducats, the principal of his loan, not from Antonio, but from Bassanio. The argument there would be that Antonio was only the surety, and the release of the surety does not release the principal. After all, Bassanio's debt is still owed. But that would not do. The bargain that the three made, Bassanio, Antonio and Shylock, was that Antonio would be the obligor of the debt. And as the passage from act 1 quoted above shows, that is exactly what Shylock wanted. He wanted a chance to get at Antonio—and that chance was worth a large sum of money to him. All understood it, and Shylock said it. When the time came, then, Shylock had made his election: the pound of flesh, and there was no going back on it, just as there would be no going back on his perhaps unnecessary decision to forfeit his chance to get that pound of flesh. Venice is a world of "no takesies backsies," and that perhaps was a secret of its success.

NOTES

1. See generally Charles Fried, "The *Lex Aquilia* as a Source of Law for Bartolus and Baldus," *American Journal of Legal History* 4 (1960): 142.

2. See, e.g., *Scott v. American Tobacco Co., Inc.*, 949 So. 2d 1266 (La. Ct. App. 2007) (Louisiana); *Texaco, Inc. v. Pennzoil Co.*, 729 S.W.2d 768 (Tex. App. 1987) (Texas).

3. All references to the play are to William Shakespeare, *The Complete Works of Shakespeare*, ed. David Bevington, 6th ed. (New York: Pearson Education, 2009).

4. For a case in which such punctilio as to time of performance had dramatic effects, see *Gray v. Gardner*, 17 Mass. 188 (1821).

5. See *Morin Building Products Co. v. Baystone Construction, Inc.*, 717 F.2d 413, 416–417 (1983) (Posner, J.): "When in doubt on a difficult issue of state [Indiana] law it is only prudent to defer to the view of the district judge . . . an experienced Indiana lawyer."

6. *James Baird Co. v. Gimbel Bros.*, 64 F.2d 344, 346 (2d Cir. 1933).

7. See *Drennan v. Star Paving Co.*, 51 Cal. 2d 409, 333 P.2d 757 (1958) (Traynor, J.).

8. See John P. Dawson, William B. Harvey, Stanley D. Henderson, and Douglas G. Baird, "Comment: The Firm Offer in Context," in *Contracts: Cases and Comment*, 9th ed. (New York: Foundation Press, 2008), 274–78.

9. *Lake River Corp. v. Carborundum Co.*, 769 F.2d 1284 (7th Cir. 1985) (Posner, J.): "the refusal to enforce penalty clauses is (at best) paternalistic—and it seems odd that courts should display parental solicitude for large corporations."

10. *Morin Building Products Co.*, 717 F.2d at 417.

11. See *Hamlet* 3.4.209–16:
There's letters sealed, and my two schoolfellows,
Whom I will trust as I will adders fanged,
They bear the mandate; they must sweep my way
And marshal me to knavery. Let it work.
For 'tis the sport to have the enginer
Hoist with his own petard, and 't shall go hard
But I will delve one yard below their mines
And blow them at the moon.

12. See Daniel A. Farber, "Legal Formalism and the Red-Hot Knife," *University of Chicago Law Review* 65 (1999): 597, citing Isak Dinesen, *Out of Africa* (1937; New York: Modern Library, 1992), 267–8.

DAVID BEVINGTON

EQUITY IN *MEASURE FOR MEASURE*

I want to argue that in *Measure for Measure* Shakespeare invites special sympathy for a middle position in the legal tangle that afflicts the citizens of Vienna in that play. It is the position of taking particular circumstances into account in the process of judgment rather than settling for theoretical absolutes. As a body of legal opinion designed to enlarge, supplement, or override narrow and rigid systems of law, this is thus one to which we might apply the term *equity*, as embodied in the Elizabethan and Jacobean courts of Chancery as opposed to the common-law courts.[1] The central figure is Escalus, although we can add that he is aided in his plea for equitable justice by the Provost and, to a significant extent, by the Duke himself.[2]

Lord Angelo supports the position of absolute enforcement of the law. The law in this case demands a sentence of death for fornication and adultery (2.1.81). The law has lain dormant for years, perhaps from a general feeling that the sentence is too severe, perhaps also because the Duke's trusting nature has led him into an unduly complacent view of human carnality. The result, in any case, has been that sexual license is rampant in Vienna. This laxness has its proponents, of course, such as Mistress Overdone and Pompey, and especially Lucio, but persons of authority are worried. "We must not make a scarecrow of the law," insists Angelo (2.1.1). And the Duke agrees that vice must be kept under strict control. He tells Friar Thomas, by way of explaining why he wishes to adopt the habit of a friar in order to observe Lord Angelo and others from a vantage of anonymity, "We have strict statutes and most biting laws, / The needful bits and curbs to headstrong steeds" (1.3.19–20).[3] The Duke's purpose in testing Angelo is not to see whether Angelo can find a mild and politically popular way out of Vienna's difficulties; if Angelo were to uphold the law fairly, he would presumably win the Duke's acquiescence. In ruling Vienna in the Duke's absence, Angelo is to bear in mind that "Mortality and mercy in Vienna" are to "Live in thy tongue and heart." "Your scope is as my own," the Duke adds, "So to enforce or qualify the laws / As to your soul seems good" (1.1.45–46, 65–67). To be sure, these lines plentifully allow for the principle of equity, but they insist too on the rigor of the law. Angelo's failure in the Duke's eyes is not that he is too severe, but that he is corrupt.[4]

Angelo spells out the theory of absolute justice with precision and eloquence. When urged by Escalus to "be keen and rather cut a little" rather "Than fall and bruise to death" (2.1.5–6), by which Escalus means to spare the life of Claudio because he comes from a good family and because his lapse into fornication has been with the young woman whom he is engaged to marry as soon as dowry complications can be straightened out, Angelo has a ready answer. He concedes that Claudio's fault is of a minor kind and is indeed the sort of fleshly indiscretion that anyone, even Angelo, might find himself tempted to commit if time were to cohere with place in making the deed of copulation seem easy and virtually irresistible.[5] Yet the language of the statute makes no allowance for special circumstances, and if a judge were to take into account the socially privileged status of the offender, he might be guilty of favoritism. Angelo insists on strict interpretation.

> 'Tis one thing to be tempted, Escalus,
> Another thing to fall. I not deny
> The jury, passing on the prisoner's life,
> May in the sworn twelve have a thief or two
> Guiltier than him they try. What's open made to justice,
> That justice seizes. . . .
> You may not so extenuate his offense
> For I have had such faults; but rather tell me,
> When I that censure him do so offend,
> Let mine own judgment pattern out my death
> And nothing come in partial. (2.1.17–31)

Angelo's defense of strict interpretation thus rests on two principles. One is deterrence: punishing an offender who is in a sense only technically guilty of the statute, but nonetheless guilty, will put the fear of punishment in anyone daring to wonder if he or she could hope to escape the law by pleading that a particular violation of the law is "minor" or that the offender's superior social position might put that offender above the rigor of the law. As Angelo argues in his undertaking to persuade Isabella that her brother must die,

> I then show [pity] most of all when I show justice;
> For then I pity those I do not know,
> Which a dismissed offense would after gall,
> And do him right that, answering one foul wrong,
> Lives not to act another. (2.2.105–9)

Rigorous justice is thus paradoxically merciful by setting such an inflexible and consistent example that many potential offenders will keep away from offense and thus spare themselves the rigors of justice. Whether deterrence can work this way is not tested in the play, since we are not shown what Vienna would have been like if Claudio had been executed incorruptly to set an example, but at least the theory is clearly enunciated.

The second principle to which Angelo appeals in his defense of strict interpretation is embodied in his response to the suggestion of Escalus that Angelo should be merciful toward an act like fornication because he himself, the judge, must at some point have felt tempted to act thus and may indeed have done so. Angelo's answer is that the judge himself must then be punished if he so offends. In effect, Angelo unwittingly condemns his own act of sexual violence before he commits such an act or indeed when he assumes that he would never do such a thing. Let the law be perfectly impartial, he insists. If Angelo were to live by his creed, we would have a very different play.

What Angelo does not take into account in this play is the problem of who is to bell the cat. What subject, in an absolutist state, can bring accusation against the prince? Isabella attempts to do so, in the final scene of the play, at the instigation of the disguised Duke. Her pleading for justice from the state gets nowhere at first, of course, since the returned Duke, having put aside for the moment his disguise, turns the proceedings over to Angelo to hear his own case. The Duke is testing Angelo, knowing perfectly well what the result will be. Even Escalus is taken in, although he is pardoned for too easily assuming that Angelo must be innocent. The episode reenacts the story of Susanna and the Elders, from the Book of Daniel, in which the young, innocent Susanna brings complaint against the elders for falsely accusing her of unclean life but is shouted down by her accusers until Daniel brings heavenly deliverance. The Duke stage-manages a similar attempted travesty of justice presided over by Angelo until the Duke steps in at the last moment, having given Angelo enough rope to hang himself. The Duke thereby demonstrates how seemingly impossible it is for a subject to bring complaint against the prince who then has supreme authority to judge the case in his own favor. Angelo's theory of absolute justice thus provides no practical remedy for the phenomenon of the corrupt prince.

At the other extreme of the spectrum of justice is the model of mercy and forgiveness.[6] Its chief advocate is Isabella, who, all unwillingly, pleads to Angelo for the life of her brother, who has committed a carnal offense most repellent to her. To make matters worse, Isabella is urged to make this appeal for pardon by Lucio, the embodiment of the lustful appetite that Isabella fervently wishes to escape by committing herself to a life of religious devotion. Her plea for mercy is enveloped in ironies, then, of which she is fully aware. "There is a vice that most I do abhor," she begins, in speaking to Angelo,

> And most desire should meet the cause of justice,
> For which I would not plead, but that I must;
> For which I must not plead, but that I am
> At war twixt will and will not. (2.2.32–36)

Yet, awkward or not, her position is supported on a pragmatic basis by the Provost, who regards Claudio as

> a young man
> More fit to do another such offense
> Than die for this. (2.3.13–15)

Given these unanswered perplexities about Claudio's case for having impregnated Juliet, what is Viennese law to do about the overall problem of sexual permissiveness in Vienna, which, all the figures of authority agree, has gotten out of hand? This is where Escalus becomes an important figure, especially in the scene (2.1) in which he interrogates some purported offenders of the law, Pompey and Master Froth, who are brought before him by Constable Elbow.

Interestingly, at the start of this courtroom scene, Escalus and Angelo are jointly present as judges. Angelo, after all, has been given priority over Escalus by the absent Duke, albeit with the stipulation that "Old Escalus, / Though first in question, is thy secondary"—that is, though senior in age and first appointed, nonetheless second in command.[7] The distinction in ranking of authority becomes clear at the beginning of 2.1, as Escalus pleads for tempering the rigor of the law in Claudio's case but is overruled by Angelo. "Sir, he must die" concludes Angelo, to which Escalus obediently replies, "Be it as your wisdom will" (2.1.31–32). So much for Claudio. But what of Froth and Pompey, who are brought before the magistrates at this point by Elbow?

Angelo and Escalus begin this interrogation by sharing the task of asking questions. "How now, sir, what's your name?" Angelo asks Pompey. "And what's the matter?" When Elbow answers with fatuous malapropisms, accusing his prisoners of being "notorious benefactors" and the like, Angelo is not amused. Indeed he does not appear to have a sense of humor. Escalus, on the other hand, is at once wryly delighted to hear how Elbow "misplaces," as he observes in asides to Angelo. "This comes off well. Here's a wise officer," he says to Angelo (57–58, 88). Soon Escalus is the one who is asking the questions, engaging in a battle of wits with Pompey, whom Escalus clearly recognizes as a worthy opponent in courtroom maneuvering. Angelo says nothing more until at last, plainly bored and dismayed by the indeterminate nature of the interrogation, he announces,

> This will last out a night in Russia,
> When nights are longest there. I'll take my leave
> And leave you [Escalus] to the hearing of the cause,
> Hoping you'll find good cause to whip them all. (2.1.135–38)

Shakespeare appears to be at considerable pains, then, to depict Angelo as a magistrate thoroughly caught up in the theoretical defense of deterrent justice but without the patience or temperamental inclination to handle day-to-day petty crime in Vienna, especially when the constabulary seems inadequately selected and poorly trained in law enforcement. Escalus, on the other hand, warms to his task of making what he can of an absurdly incompetent arrest. Escalus and Pompey understand each other. They both know that Pompey is "partly a bawd" or pimp, however adroitly Pompey may "color it in being a tapster" for Mistress Overdone (219–20). They both understand that, in Pompey's vivid description, young men "will to 't" unless the authorities mean "to geld and splay the youth of the city." They both implicitly acknowledge that Constable Elbow is an officious fool, overwhelmed by his responsibilities. The question becomes What to do about it?

Pompey's knavish credo is that the law might do best to forget about trying to police something as innate as human lust. When Escalus asks him if the "trade" of being a bawd can be considered to be lawful, Pompey has his ready answer: "If the law would allow it, sir" (224–26). A witty answer, but Escalus is not deterred. "But the law will not allow it, Pompey; nor it shall not be allowed in Vienna." Lacking conclusive evidence in the present circumstance for a legal conviction, owing to inadequate police procedures, Escalus moves on to his next line of defense, which is to warn Pompey in plain terms that he will be whipped if he shows up once more in Escalus's court. Whipped, mind you, not executed, as is being planned for Claudio. Pompey is comically defiant, and he traipses off a free man with the observation, "Whip me? No, no, let carman whip his jade. / The valiant heart's not whipped out of his trade" (253–54). Master Froth is similarly given a warning, not of a whipping, since he is a gentleman, but of something undefined but no less unpleasant. Froth appears to take the point.

And so Elbow's prisoners are let go. Yet Escalus is anything but disheartened or at a loss for knowing what to do. He sees the problem for what it is: intractable human carnality, never to be entirely eradicated, and a police force inadequate to the job of keeping the problem down to manageable proportions. Escalus ends the scene by initiating another investigation, this time of the police force. How long, he asks, has Elbow been in his position as constable? "Seven years and a half," is the prompt and proud reply. "I thought, by your readiness in the office, you had continued in it for some time," says Escalus. Elbow is deaf to the sardonic tone in which this seeming praise is offered. "You say, seven years together?" continues Escalus. "And a half, sir," is the deliciously comic reply. Please, Your Honor, do not forgetfully lop off some months from the term that I have served. "Alas, it hath been great pains to you," continues Escalus, in the same sardonic tone intended for our amusement. And thus he comes to the heart of the matter. How are constables chosen? He learns that when others are selected for the burdensome duty of constable of the parish, they pay some money to Elbow to take their places. He gathers a little pocket money this way and gets to wear his constable's uniform. A perfect arrangement for him. But not for Escalus. He sees clearly that what he must do is to have Elbow bring in the name of "some six or seven, the most sufficient of your parish," so that Elbow can be replaced (2.1.256–71). Petty crime will never go away, but that is no reason to let up on the need for day-to-day enforcement. Escalus is the champion, along with the Provost, of this principle.

Arguably, the play shows how Escalus's and the Provost's patient approach to law enforcement does seem to work in reducing licentious conduct in Vienna. Pompey is set to work in the prison as an assistant to the hangman, Abhorson. For all the joking that accompanies this grisly assignment, the Provost's program of rehabilitation goes about to teach a new and necessary trade that will at least keep Pompey off the streets. We see too that Mistress Overdone is carted off to prison, not by Elbow, who has evidently been dismissed as Escalus has ordered, but by other officers under the authority of Escalus himself and the Provost (3.2.184–202). And it is through Mistress Overdone's testimonial that Escalus learns of Lucio's having fathered a child with Kate Keepdown, for which Lucio will eventually be brought to account.

To be sure, Escalus does display intemperance in the play's final scene (as observed by both Constance Jordan and Richard Strier in this present collection). Escalus is so outraged at the attempts of Isabella and the insolent Friar (i.e., the disguised Duke) to accuse Angelo of serious crimes that he energetically undertakes to prove that "this friar is a notable fellow," that is, a notorious rascal (5.1.275–76). He goes "darkly to work" in cross-examining Isabella (287), suggesting by his sexual double entendres that she is not only a liar and slanderer but a whore. He calls upon the loose-tongued Lucio to give damning evidence against her and the friar. In short, Escalus vigorously goes about to undo the cause of true justice. Structurally, this contretemps is what we might call, borrowing a term from musical analysis, the "false cadence" before the play's final resolution. Can this public official be the representative of equity at its workable best if he is so wholly misled at this point?

I believe that Escalus can easily be defended against the charge of near-perpetration of injustice. First, we note that the just-returned Duke commissions Escalus to do exactly what he does here. The Duke tells Escalus to

> Do with your injuries as seems you best,
> In any chastisement. I for a while
> Will leave you; but stir not till you have
> Well determined upon these slanderers. (5.1.264–67)

The Duke does not hesitate to call Isabella and the Friar "slanderers" and order their punishment. The Duke is testing Escalus with a ruse (a benign ruse, I would argue), just as he tests Angelo, Isabella, Claudio, Mariana, and even Lucio to see how they will respond under a misapprehension calculated to measure their respective merits. Escalus does well in that he is carrying out the Duke's orders, in circumstances that do seem to call for vigorous investigation. Escalus has had many reasons to admire Angelo as a resolute magistrate, even if Escalus differs from Angelo as to the degree of severity required to reign in carnal desire. Escalus knows nothing of what Angelo has done or has attempted to do to Isabella and Claudio and Mariana. Escalus believes with all his heart and soul that the life and welfare of a chief magistrate must be defended against slander at all costs.

To say that Escalus is nearly led into assisting in the cover-up of a crime is true enough, but this is simply to say that even the most virtuous and attentive of magistrates can be misled by malicious deception. The fallen human condition that weighs so oppressively on every moment of this tragicomic play can discover corruption in the heart of a magistrate like Angelo who considers himself incorruptible, and it can discover the potential for nearly fatal misjudgment even in a magistrate like Escalus who works day and night to improve the moral state of Vienna. The Duke's test of Escalus enables him, and us, and Angelo, to see the great truth of dangerous error lying in wait for us at every turn. The Duke has no hesitation in pardoning Escalus, of course; what he says to him is simply "What you have spoke I pardon" (5.1.369), before turning to the more serious matter of how to judge Angelo and then Lucio. The Duke knows that Escalus is a good man and that Vienna is immeasurably in his debt for his vigorous honesty, his incorruptible nature, and his judicious common sense. The Duke also knows that Escalus will learn a lesson from the error that he has tricked him into nearly enacting. As the presiding spirit and theatrical stage magician of this play, the Duke has wittily coaxed Escalus into error and then has rescued him from making that error.

When, in the play's finale, Duke Vincentio reveals himself and reestablishes himself in the seat of authority, he seems to have absorbed the lesson of his own little play-acted scenario about justice.[8] The Duke pardons Angelo after having tested him, but he requires that Angelo marry the woman, Mariana, to whom he was formerly engaged, with whom he has (unwittingly) slept, and who has pleaded for his life. He threatens Lucio with whipping and hanging but settles for forcing Lucio to marry the whore Kate Keepdown, by whom he has had a child, even though Lucio protests that "Marrying a punk, my lord, is pressing to death, whipping, and hanging" (5.1.533–34). "Slandering a prince deserves it," is the Duke's reply. Men must learn to abide by the consequences of their carnality, most of all when it results in the birth of a human being. The Duke thereby demonstrates what he meant when he said earlier to Angelo that the magistrate must "enforce or qualify the laws / As to your soul seems good" (1.1.66–67). This idea, a long-familiar commonplace about the nature of justice on earth and how it must attempt to emulate the perfect justice of the heavens, takes on here a quality of equity that the play appears to celebrate. Human justice must practice equity, if only because humans are themselves so imperfect and prone to the corruption that justice seeks to remedy or at least hold in check.

NOTES

1. On early modern debates "between the common law courts, rumored to be literalist in their adjudications, and the courts of Chancery, especially the 'equity' courts that were created primarily as a reaction to what was perceived to be an excessive rigidity in common law courts," see Karen Cunningham, "Opening Doubts upon the Law: *Measure for Measure*," in *A Companion to Shakespeare's Works*, vol. 4, *The Poems, Problem Comedies, Late Plays*, ed. Richard Dutton and Jean E. Howard (Oxford: Blackwell, 2003), 316–32, at 316. Debora Kuller Shuger explores the ways in which "the prerogative courts, civil and criminal, evolved in response to the very real defects of common law"; see her *Political Theologies in Shakespeare's England: The Sacred and the State in "Measure for Measure"* (Houndmills, UK: Palgrave, 2001), 84 and elsewhere. See also S. Cohen, "From Mistress to Master: Political Transition and Formal Conflict in *Measure for Measure*," *Criticism* 41 (1999): 431–64. Shakespeare quotations in this present essay are from *The Complete Works of Shakespeare*, ed. David Bevington, 6th ed. (New York: Pearson/Longman, 2009).

2. On Escalus as one who "urges an act of charitable empathy based on the law's assurance that, by a law of nature, all men are frail, ready to fall when the moment circumstances permit (2.1.8–16)," see Darryl J. Gless, *"Measure for Measure," the Law, and the Convent* (Princeton, NJ: Princeton University Press, 1979), 217–18, also 20, 50–52.

See also Robert B. Bennett, *Romance and Reformation: The Erasmian Spirit of Shakespeare's "Measure for Measure"* (Newark: University of Delaware Press, 2000), who argues that the play seeks to understand the need for social reform in Erasmian terms of "humility, piety, and tolerance that were central aims of humanist rhetoric, both as oratory and as drama" (18). For Ernest Schanzer, "It is Escalus who in this play illustrates the *via media* between the two excesses in the administration of justice. He possesses the proper mixture of severity and mercy which marks the ideal judge. He is 'accounted a merciful man', as Mrs. Overdone tells him, but in this very scene [3.2] he shows that he can also be severe: 'Away with her to prison. Go to; no more words.'" See Schanzer, *The Problem Plays of Shakespeare: A Study of "Julius Caesar," "Measure for Measure," "Antony and Cleopatra"* (London: Routledge and Kegan Paul, 1963), 116–17. In an essay originally published in German in 1839, Hermann Ulrici sees Escalus as "indispensable as an organic counterpoise to Angelo; and partly as a mean between him and the duke." See Ulrici, *Shakespeare's Dramatic Art*, trans. A. J. W. Morrison (London: Chapman Brothers, 1846), 312. This essay and others of historical significance are printed in George L. Geckle, ed., *Measure for Measure. Shakespeare: The Critical Tradition* (London: Athlone, 2001).

3. Josephine Waters Bennett, *"Measure for Measure" as Royal Entertainment* (New York: Columbia University Press, 1966), points out that the Duke also insists that the laws on fornication need to be enforced strictly, just like other laws; that is his reason for having deputized Angelo in his stead to "unloose" the "tied-up justice." Yet Angelo abuses his trust to such an extent that he becomes a tyrant (93–95).

4. On legal debates in the early modern English period on the "precise point at which the pursuit of sexual gratification becomes criminal," see Robert Grams Hunter, *Shakespeare and the Comedy of Forgiveness* (New York: Columbia University Press, 1965), 209–10 and 249–50n18. Mary Lascelles, *Shakespeare's "Measure for Measure"* (London: Athlone, 1953), argues the debates in *Measure for Measure* in legal terms: "The Position Occupied by *Measure for Measure*," "The Case," "The Disputants," "The Arbiter," "The Verdict."

5. This debate of Escalus and Angelo in 2.1 is ably discussed by L. C. Knights, "The Ambiguity of *Measure for Measure*," *Scrutiny* 10 (1942), reprinted in C. K. Stead, *Shakespeare: Measure for Measure: A Casebook* (London: Macmillan, 1971), 138–51.

6. J. W. Lever explores a conflict in *Measure for Measure* between the Mosaic code of the Old Testament, representing the position of strict enforcement, and a New Testament creed of forgiveness, although Lever sees more practical advice for Renaissance audiences in "the classical *via media* of equity grounded on reason" as enunciated in Cicero's *De Officiis* and Seneca's *De Clementia*. See *Measure for Measure*, ed. J. W. Lever, Arden Shakespeare (London: Methuen, 1965), lxiv. Arthur Kirsch, *Shakespeare and the Experience of Love* (Cambridge: Cambridge University Press, 1981), 71–107, especially 75–76, invokes the Sermon on the Mount, especially Matthew 7:1–5 and Luke 6:36–42, urging the faithful, "Judge not, that ye be not judged" and "Be ye therefore merciful." See also Elizabeth Marie Pope, "The Renaissance Background of *Measure for Measure*," *Shakespeare Survey* 2 (1949): 66–82; and G. Wilson Knight, "*Measure for Measure* and the Gospels," in Knight, *The Wheel of Fire* (London: Methuen, 1930 and subsequent editions). Francis Fergusson, *The Human Image in Dramatic Literature* (Garden City, NY: Doubleday,

1957), 126–43, counters with the proposal that the play is no less importantly pervaded by "the Platonic and Aristotelian philosophy of society, which is based on the analogy between the body politic and the individual"; Harriet Hawkins discusses the paradoxes of mercy and justice in *Measure for Measure*, Harvester New Critical Introductions to Shakespeare (Brighton, UK: Harvester, 1987), especially 43–88.

7. Bernard Beckerman argues that the reason "why the Duke chose Angelo over Escalus is now apparent. Escalus is too much like him" in urging lenity. See Beckerman, "A Shakespearean Experiment: The Dramaturgy of *Measure for Measure*," in *The Elizabethan Theatre II*, ed. David Galloway (Hamden, CT: Archon, 1970), 118–19.

8. Peter Corbin discusses the "wide range of interpretive potential in the presentation of the Duke." See Corbin, "Performing *Measure for Measure*," in *Measure for Measure*, ed. Nigel Wood, Theory in Practice Series (Philadelphia: Open University Press, 1996), 9–43. In the same volume, Richard Wilson discusses Michel Foucault's theories about the "Duke of Dark Corners" in an essay entitled "Prince of Darkness: Foucault's Shakespeare," 133–78. Janet Adelman writes perceptively about "our uneasiness with the final marriage proposal." See her "Marriage and the Maternal Body: On Marriage as the End of Comedy in *Measure for Measure*," in *Critical Essays on Shakespeare's "Measure for Measure*," ed. Richard Wheeler (New York: G. K. Hall, 1999), 120–44.

RICHARD STRIER

SHAKESPEARE AND LEGAL SYSTEMS
THE BETTER THE WORSE
(BUT NOT VICE VERSA)

One of the great advantages that literary texts have over others is that literary texts—unlike, for instance, legal ones—do not have to resolve the problems that they raise; they just have to raise them in interesting and provocative ways. This may be true of some philosophical texts as well, although even these sorts of philosophical texts tend to suggest some sort of resolution or accommodation of the difficulties they note. Literary texts do not even have to do that. With this in mind, the problem that I want to raise and ponder in the following essay is this: while there is no doubt that Shakespeare was able to imagine a great range of things, one of the things that he seemed consistently unable to imagine was a reasonably attractive and well-functioning legal system. What I will try to show, in fairly brief compass, is that in every instance in which Shakespeare seems to imagine such, and to give it the recognizable features of such, he also immediately raises issues that complicate, undermine, or call into question the possibility and even desirability of such a thing.

I will focus primarily on the second part of *Henry IV*, a play that has figured relatively little in the recent spate of work on Shakespeare and the law.[1] This play seems to be committed to highlighting and endorsing one central feature of a properly functioning legal system: impartiality, the application of law equally to everyone within its jurisdiction. This would seem to be an unquestionable good. The figure who embodies this in the play is, appropriately, the Lord Chief Justice of England, who has, on an occasion referred to but not dramatized by Shakespeare, ordered Prince Hal, the heir-apparent of the kingdom, to confinement for showing gross disrespect for the Chief Justice and his position (striking him, in the earlier play on this material).[2] It is significant that Shakespeare chose not to stage this scene. I do not think he omitted staging it because he did not want to show his Prince Hal behaving in that way but rather because he did not want to present his Lord Chief Justice demeaned, visibly, in that way. What he did want was to have the Lord Chief Justice explain at length the rationale for his behavior, and to do so just at the moment of Hal's elevation to the kingship. When Shakespeare has Hal, about to be formally crowned King Henry V, recall the "indignities" the Justice laid upon him, Shakespeare has the Justice reply thus:

> I then did use the person of your father;
> The image of his power lay then in me;
> And in th' administration of his law,
> Whiles I was busy for the commonwealth,
> Your highness pleased to forget my place,
> The majesty and power of law and justice,
> The image of the King whom I presented,
> And struck me in my very seat of judgment;
> Whereon as an offender to your father,
> I gave bold way to my authority
> And did commit you. (5.2.73–83)[3]

There are two major features, not entirely compatible, in this eloquent and detailed account. The first of these, and probably the dominant one, is the Chief Justice's stress on "personation."[4] He uses the term in exactly the Hobbesian sense of a "person" being an entity entitled to act publicly as an agent either of himself or of someone or something else.[5] The stress on this in the passage is very strong: "the person of your father; / The image of his power . . . The image of the King." An "image" here is thought of not as a simulacrum but as an agent, a representative, someone in whom the power of someone or something else is made present ("The image of the King whom I presented"), a "presenter" rather than (or as well as) a representation. This conception of legal entitlement culminates in a reference to "authority" (which will be Hobbes's key term) and to a merging of the representative and the represented: "struck me . . . as . . . your father." The other conception of legal "authority" in the passage is the less absolutist, more procedural one that Hutson is interested in.[6] The mention of "th' administration of his law" mediates between the two conceptions, where the impersonality of "th' administration" and potentially of "law" is qualified by the personal pronoun, "his law." The next line, however, moves fully into the alternate conception: "I was busy for the commonwealth." Suddenly the King has disappeared, and the Chief Justice acts in the name and authority of an abstract political body, the normal English translation of *res publica*.[7] The young prince is an exalted individual, "Your highness," who acted willfully ("pleased to forget"), while the Justice's authority is abstract and structural, coming from, as he says, his "place." And in the next line, the legal system becomes its own king: "The majesty . . . of law and justice." To add to this mix, the final reference to the Justice's "place" gives it a kind of biblical sacrality in the mention of "my very seat of judgment."[8]

The one thing that we can say about all the conceptions of "authority" in this passage is that all of them are impersonal. When the speech finally arrives at an "I-Thou" relation ("I did . . . commit you") and seems to involve some personal passion ("I gave bold way"), it turns out that the actual agent of punishment is "authority," and there is—and this is the key fact—nothing directly personal in it ("an offender to your father"). In all of this personation, there are no people. The new king is being asked to give the matter "cold considerance" and to speak in his "state" (98–99). He does so and commends the Chief Justice's "bold, just, and impartial spirit" (along, it should be noted, with commending his own willingness to condescend to be judged in this way). So impartiality of this sort would seem to be an unquestioned and unquestionable virtue.

Yet this interchange is embedded in another context. On both sides of the scene in which the above speech occurs are scenes at the home of a much lesser man of law, a country justice, Master Robert Shallow (interestingly, the Lord Chief Justice is not given a name; he exists entirely as a position). These scenes evoke in detail the life of a nonaristocratic country estate (like Petruchio's in *The Taming of the Shrew*). In the first of them (5.1) we see Justice Shallow arranging a supper for his visitor, Sir John Falstaff. Falstaff is amused at how concerned Shallow is with the details of his estate and how close Shallow is with his servants ("Their spirits," says Falstaff quite grandly, and in highly Latinate and semilegal terms, are "married in conjunction, with the participation of society" [5.1.65–67])—a kind of "participation" very different from that by which the Lord Chief Justice participates in the power of the king. The head of the servants seems to be one Davy. In the midst of the "business" of arranging for the supper, Davy interjects a specifically legal matter. Just as we are on an ordinary country estate here, we are made privy here (entirely in prose) to an ordinary legal dispute, one that does not involve princes and Lord Chief Justices.[9]

Suddenly and startlingly, we are in the world of specific (and perhaps actual) ordinary people.[10] Davy says to Justice Shallow, "I beseech you, sir, to countenance William Visor of Woncot against Clement Perkes a' th' Hill." Justice Shallow replies that he is familiar with the legal record concerning the defendant in this case—"There is many complaints, Davy, against that Visor"—and assures Davy that "that Visor is an arrant knave, on my knowledge." Davy's reply is worth quoting in full:

> I grant your worship that he is a knave, sir; but yet God forbid, sir, but a knave should have some countenance at his friend's request. An honest

man, sir, is able to speak for himself, when a knave is not. I have served your worship truly, sir, this eight years; and if I cannot once or twice in a quarter bear out a knave against an honest man, I have but very little credit with your worship. The knave is mine honest friend, sir, therefore I beseech your worship let, him be countenanced. (5.1.40–48)

Now, obviously this is funny, and meant to be so. But it raises some issues that the play is very interested in and that Shakespeare is very interested in. There are two key questions here: the first is the relation between justice and friendship (or other personal relations—here, service); the second, the whole matter of dealing with transgressions (since the fact of Visor's knavery is stipulated).

The first of these is an issue with which the entire span of the *Henry IV* plays has been concerned. Aristotle noted, in his immensely influential treatment of friendship in the *Ethics*, that "when people are friends, they have no need of justice."[11] What Aristotle means by this is not at all obvious. He may mean, as Christine Korsgaard argues, that friendship is the model for justice and includes it; or he may mean, as someone like Bernard Williams might argue, that there is a deep difference between the kinds of relationships that the terms denote.[12] Shakespeare's view seems to me closer to Williams's. One might be tempted—as a modern, and not at all following Aristotle—to say that friendship operates in the "private" realm, and justice in the "public" one.[13] But Shakespeare has set up the *Henry IV* plays in a way that keeps the two realms in constant juxtaposition and threatens (or promises) to allow them to mingle. Things that seem, from the point of view of the public realm, to be obvious values, are put under pressure by this juxtaposition.

The name of the figure who primarily exercises this pressure is not Davy but Sir John Falstaff. This figure, who was, as he says (I am certain with complete accuracy) "born about three of the clock in the afternoon, with a white head, and something a round belly" (2H4, 1.2.186–88) is completely Shakespeare's creation. That Prince Hal frequented the taverns of London is an inevitable part of his story; that he did so with the primary companion that Shakespeare gives him is not (in fact, as all Shakespeare scholars know, Shakespeare had to apologize for the name that he had initially used as a means of inserting this figure into the historical context, and he had to change the figure's name).[14]

The very beginning of the *Henry IV* sequence puts pressure on public and abstract values. The first line of the first play, spoken by the title character, is "so shaken as we are, so wan with care." The public world, the world of politics (and of law) is a world of "care" and of constant strife. The second scene of the play introduces us to an alternate world. On the one hand, it is a world of lawlessness; Falstaff fantasizes that when Hal is king, there will be no gallows standing in England (this could merely signify a lack of capital punishment—many thinkers and juries thought that there were too many crimes defined as capital[15]—but Falstaff clearly means it to signify no punishments whatever for crime). Yet, on the other hand, the world for which Falstaff stands seems to be a world of abundance, of enjoyment, of leisure, of companionship, and of freedom from "care."[16] The Prince has to goad him into performing an actual robbery. Falstaff's "vocation," as he wonderfully and outrageously claims, is highway robbery, but his life seems mainly to consist of sharing drink and, most of all, talk—talk of all kinds (insults, jokes, etc.)—with his longtime companions.[17] What he seems to offer, most of all, is a realm of happy and shared play. When, at the end of this hitherto all-prose scene, Hal steps out from it and gives a serious, blank-verse soliloquy explaining that he is not really engaged in the world in which he seems to manifest "the participation of society" and that his apparent engagement with this world is in fact a calculated strategy for making an impression on the political world, we cannot but feel a kind of shudder. "Cold consideration" and lack of concern for one's relationships with particular persons is already under pressure. "I know you all," Hal says chillingly.

I want to pause for a moment on this assertion and ask what exactly it means. What exactly is the knowledge that is in question here? It is impartial—one might say, judicial—knowledge, knowledge of all the faults, limits, and crimes of this group. It is the kind of knowledge that would be appropriate to a Stoic sage: "Unmoved, cold, and to temptation slow."[18] Hal here manifests exactly the characteristics that Erasmus's Dame Folly claims make Stoics incapable of true friendship and true social participation. She thinks that friendship involves not noticing faults, and she claims that in the unlikely event that "it should happen that some of these severe wisemen should become friendly with each other, their friendship is hardly stable or long-lasting, because they are so sour and sharp-sighted that they detect their friends' faults with an eagle eye."[19] Hal is not like the (Stoic) wise man who disrupts a party "by his gloomy countenance."[20] But Hal does share the wise man's attitudes and "cold eye" and does, even when he is apparently participating in the social world, keep reminding Falstaff of arrest and the gallows (1H4, 1.2.38–42). On the other hand, while Hal is, in his way, participating in Falstaff's world, he takes it upon himself to act as if he shared Davy's view ("a knave should have some countenance at his friend's request"). In part 1, Hal lies to the sheriff, the watch, and the Lord Chief Justice himself, who have come to Eastcheap in pursuit of Falstaff for the robbery at Gadshill. "The man, I do assure you, is not here," says Hal, directly lying (2.4.505), and in one of his final speeches in part 1, Hal assures Falstaff that he will lie for him again: "If a lie may do thee grace, / I'll gild it with the happiest terms I have" (5.4.156–57).

A great deal depends on what is contrasted with the world of politics and law, the world of "cold considerance" in the plays. In part 1 of *Henry IV*, two worlds contrast with the legal-political one—not just the world of Falstaff but also that of Hotspur. It is easy to think of Hotspur and Falstaff as opposites, and in relation to courage or martial heroism, they surely are so. It is therefore easy to generate a tidy "Aristotelian" scheme with Hotspur at the extreme of martial foolhardiness, Falstaff at the extreme of cowardice, and Hal as the "golden mean" between them.[21] That is certainly plausible. But the more interesting and, I believe, deeper reading of the plays sees Falstaff and Hotspur as equally divorced from the world of "cool reason" and "policy." Hotspur is consistently associated with the world of "imagination." In the first scene in which we see him, "Imagination of some high exploit / Drives him beyond the bounds of patience"; "He apprehends a world of figures" (1H4, 1.3.197–98, 207); in the battle in which he dies, he is seen as having acted "with great imagination / Proper to madmen" (2H4, 1.3.31–32). And like Falstaff, who asserts, very memorably, that "the lion will not touch the true prince" (1H4, 2.2.267), Hotspur's imagination is filled with themes from romance (his uncle, Worcester, brings him into the plot against Henry by presenting it as equivalent to walking over "a current roaring loud / On the unsteadfast footing of a spear" [1H4, 1.3.191–92]).[22] Both Hotspur and Falstaff are "lunatics," brilliantly projecting lunar mythology: "To pluck bright honor from the pale-faced moon"; "let us be Diana's foresters . . . minions of the moon" (1H4, 1.3.200; 1.2.25–26). Hotspur is the first inebriate with whom we are presented: "What, drunk with choler?" Northumberland asks him (1H4, 1.3.127). And Hotspur and Falstaff share a deep contempt for the "frosty-spirited" (see Hotspur at 1H4, 2.3.2, and Falstaff on how Hal supposedly overcomes the "cold blood he did naturally inherit from his father" [2H4, 4.3.116]) and an equally deep contempt for respectable citizens (and their wives), who do not know how to swear "a good mouth-filling oath" (see Hotspur on "in good sooth" at 1H4, 3.1.240–50 and Falstaff on "yea-forsooth" knaves at 2H4, 1.2.36).

The key fact about the second part of *Henry IV* is that Hotspur is dead.[23] There is no heroic dimension to war or to negotiation (Hotspur haggles only for fun and honor [see 1H4, 3.1.130–35]). In part 2, only two realms (not three) seem to represent value other than the Hobbesian value of political stability: the world of the Lord Chief Justice and the world of Falstaff and company (with the addition of more women and a braggart soldier, but largely without Hal).

The great military triumph in part 2 is a triumph of treachery—although understood as being legally and politically justified by being treachery to the treasonous (a practice that Paul Jorgenson long ago showed the Elizabethans had come to accept in their dealings with the Irish).[24] Moreover, the Prince in question—not Hal, but his brother, John—insists, probably correctly, that from a technical and legalistic point of view, he does not break his word with the rebels when he has them arrested and sent off to be executed after a parley and negotiated peace. He promised, "Upon [his] soul," that he would redress the "griefs" that the rebels had listed in their "articles," and he said, "If this [that is, redress of the listed complaints] may please you, / Discharge your powers" (2H4, 4.2.60–61). He fully intends, apparently, to keep his word and to redress the griefs. The rebel lords had failed to specify that they not be arrested and executed, so John is not, technically, breaking his word to them at all.[25]

Shakespeare keeps the basic contrast of the whole *Henry IV* two-play sequence in our minds by having Falstaff, in the scene following this one, give a soliloquy on the cold-bloodedness and antifestive nature of Prince John ("he drinks no wine" [4.3.87]). But the theme is present even in the "victory" scene itself. Prince John offers the rebels not only his "princely word" but also a promise of friendship and conviviality. "Let's," he says, "drink together friendly and embrace" (4.2.63). Both he and his right-hand man (Westmoreland) do actually drink to the leaders with whom they have just made a treaty. Drinking "together friendly" is, needless to say, Falstaff's world in the play. He is right that Prince John has, in fact, nothing to do with it. But perhaps this is too benign a view of what Falstaff stands for. The Lord Chief Justice sees Falstaff as standing for legal impunity, "power to do wrong," as he says (2H4, 2.1.128). The dying King Henry IV presents a tremendous vision of lawlessness as terrifying, a vision in which conviviality merges into serious criminality. He believes Hal will allow ruffians not only to "swear, drink, dance / [and] Revel the night" but also to "rob, murder, and commit / The oldest sins the newest kind of ways." And lest this latter sound oddly attractive, Shakespeare gives the dying king an image of almost biblical force to represent lawlessness: "the wild dog / Shall flesh his tooth on every innocent" (2H4, 4.5.124–32).[26]

Yet what we actually see contrasted with the world of politics and law in the play is not a world of spectacular and violent injustice but merely the world of conviviality. In his first interchange with the Lord Chief Justice, Falstaff explains that he has used the law concerning his status in the military to evade the law's claim on him as a civilian ("I was then advised by my learned council in the laws of this land-service" [2H4, 1.2.133–34]),[27] but the realm of law truly enters Falstaff's world when Mistress Quickly sends for officers to arrest him on a suit of debt (and perhaps of breach of promise, with regard to his supposedly having promised to make her "my lady thy wife" [2H4, 2.1.90]). When Falstaff physically resists the officers, the Lord Chief Justice appears again, insisting on decorum and asking Sir John, "Doth this become your place, your time, your business?" (2.1.64). But it turns out that neither law nor decorum is involved in the resolution of this suit. The resolution comes when, after a bit of unstaged private conversation, Falstaff says to Mistress Quickly (Ursula?), "Go, wash thy face" (she has been crying) "and draw [that is, withdraw] the action" (that is, the suit). Come," he says, "thou must not be in this humour with me." And then he asks her, "dost not know me?" (2.1.149–50). That settles the matter.

Again, let us think about the word *know*. Falstaff appeals to a very different kind of "knowledge" of another than that with which Hal "knows" all his companions. Hal's is detached and "moral" knowledge, connected to judgment and to (what Folly would call) relentlessly accurate assessment. The "knowledge" to which Falstaff appeals is intimate and forgiving, accepting of an entire person as such, and connected to (or a part of) love.[28] Falstaff's borrowing and Mistress Quickly's lending (and perhaps his occasional hint that she will become his "lady") are part of a long-standing and well-understood relationship between these particular persons, a relationship that has gone on for years on this basis and that includes mutual indulgence. Later on in the second act of part 2, when Falstaff and Doll Tearsheet are exchanging insults, Mistress Quickly notes that "this is the old fashion" between Falstaff and Doll, and she insists that they must "bear with another's confirmities" (2.4.57)—a wonderful malapropism that combines infirmities with settled states of character and exactly replicates Dame Folly's claim that friendship involves an ability "to wink at one another's faults."[29]

Hal enters part 2 between tavern scenes. As in part 1, he enters speaking prose (though to Poins, rather than to Falstaff), and as in part 1, he engages Poins in playing a trick on Falstaff. But, also as in part 1, he reminds his companion—in what passes for a humorous mode—of the reality of the social situation they are in; Hal says to Poins, "What a disgrace is it to me to remember thy name, or to know thy face tomorrow" (2H4, 2.2.14–15). He addresses Poins as "one it pleases me for fault of a better to call my friend" and tells Poins that he (Hal) has harmed his reputation by "keeping such vile company as thou art" (2.2.40, 47). Poins registers no offense at this, either because he is afraid to (which is unlikely) or because he is used to being addressed in such a way (which is likely), or (perhaps and) because he takes Hal to be "joking" (highly likely). But these are hardly loving jokes. Falstaff pretends to make a similar move in his part 2 escape—parallel to his appeal to the lion's "instinct" in part 1—to the trap that Hal has set for him here. Falstaff claims that in having equated Hal with Poins as another dim-witted athlete (2.4.241–52), he (Falstaff) was protecting Hal's reputation by dispraising him "before the wicked" (2.4.316). Falstaff is being moral and clear-eyed here, making proper distinctions—and no one takes him the slightest bit seriously. Doll and Mistress Quickly are not, as Hal urges them to be, offended by being referred to as "the wicked"; instead, the scene ends with both of them bidding tearful farewells to Falstaff and with Mistress Quickly reflecting on how long she has known Falstaff: "Well, fare thee well. I have known thee these twenty-nine years, come peascod-time" (2.4.379–80).[30]

I mentioned earlier that Shakespeare places the great interchange between the new king and the Lord Chief Justice between the two scenes featuring Justice Robert Shallow. The first of these scenes is that of preparation for supper, which we have examined (with Davy); the scene that follows the young king's dedication to the Lord Chief Justice is one of full-scale conviviality. Although I am sure that Colin Burrow is right that the Elizabethans would have recognized Shallow and Silence as corrupt justices of the peace, the scene is more one of holiday than of license.[31] It is filled with mottos of good fellowship, all variations on a theme: "There's a merry heart, good Master Silence," says Falstaff; "the heart's all," says Davy (consistent with himself); "a merry heart lives long-a," sings the surprisingly lively Silence. Justice Shallow commends to Bardolph Davy's loyalty: "The knave will stick by thee, I can assure you that." When Bardolph responds, "And I'll stick by him, sir," Shallow replies, interestingly and surprisingly, "Why, there spoke a king" (5.3.63–67). Moments later, Pistol arrives with the great news; Saturnalia has come to the realm—"golden times." "I speak," says Pistol, "of Africa and golden joys" (5.3.97). The scene ends on a note that does seem to move the mode from festivity to license. Falstaff says, "Let us take any man's horses—the laws of England are at my commandment" (131–33). We know from the previous scene, in which the new king took the Lord Chief Justice as his new surrogate "father" (5.2.140), that this is not at all true. But we cannot help but wonder, if we have not seen or read the play before, how the young king is going to adjudicate between friendship and impartiality in this crucial case. Before the confrontation to which the whole play—perhaps the whole two-part sequence—has been building,[32] Shakespeare interpolates a little scene in which Dame Quickly and Doll Tearsheet are arrested by a beadle, and there is suddenly, and without any preparation, talk of them being involved in a murder.[33] Yet it is still hard to root for "whipping-cheer."

The great moment arrives when Falstaff gets the king's ear and addresses him thus: "My King! My Jove! I speak to thee, my heart!" Shakespeare has carefully prepared for this line. Falstaff has been equated with Saturn (2H4, 2.4.261) and Hal with his son, Jove (2H4, 2.2.166–67). Jove notoriously dispossesses (and castrates) Saturn and ushers in, ultimately, an age of law and lead rather than one of gold, freedom, and Saturnalia. But the key term is "my heart." This is the phrase that captures much of what the alternative to law has been, and it is the phrase that, as we have seen (heard), permeated the party at Shallow's. The new king, however, has, as he has told the Lord Chief Justice, buried his "affections" (5.2.124). He addresses Falstaff with "cold considerance," saying:

> I know thee not, old man. Fall to thy prayers.
> How ill white hairs becomes a fool and jester!
> I have long dreamt of such a kind of man,
> So surfeit-swelled, so old, and so profane;
> But, being awak'd, I do despise my dream. (5.5.47–51)

Hal has moved from the coldness of "I know you all" to the coldness of "I know thee not," where the positive and the negative assertions mean the same. Here the new king recognizes and specifically rejects the kind of knowledge on which Falstaff relies. We recall "Dost thou not know me?" Hal, now Henry, treats Falstaff truly impartially, as if he had no personal relation to him; Falstaff is simply a nameless and badly behaved "old man." The acknowledgment that he does offer—Falstaff as part of a dream—renounces the whole realm of alternatives to what Sidney called the "brazen" world of ordinary history and politics (our very first description of Falstaff, by Hal, was to see him as an inhabitant of a dreamlike Land of Cockayne in which historical time was replaced by material and festive abundance: "hours were cups of sack, and minutes capons" [1H4, 1.2.7–8]).[34] Falstaff has already noted that "if to be old and merry" and fat—"surfeit-swelled"—"be a sin," then "Pharaoh's lean kine" are to be loved (1H4, 2.4.465–67). But a different biblical reference is evoked here. The new king is echoing one of the most chilling passages in the gospels. Jesus is affirmatively answering the question "Lord, are there fewe that shalbe saved?" Jesus explains that while "manie" wish to be such, only a few will be able to "entre in at the straite gate." He tells the parable of the harsh and resolute housekeeper: "When the good man of the house is risen up, and hath shut to the dore, and ye beginne to stand without . . . saying, Lord, Lord open to us; and he shal answer and say unto you, I knowe you not. . . . Then shall ye beginne to say, We have eaten and drunke in thy presence. . . . But he shal say . . . I knowe you not" (Luke 13:23–27).

So where does this leave the question? Of course Hal/Henry could not put the laws of England at Falstaff's commandment. But Shakespeare has worked hard to make us feel that the triumph of impartial justice is hardly to be celebrated. It is indeed hard to love "Pharaoh's lean kine." And it is hard not to feel that Davy, for all his outrageousness and simplicity, had a point.

Having worked in some detail on the second part of *Henry IV*, in which Shakespeare considers impartiality, I will turn more briefly to plays in which Shakespeare shows himself equally ill at ease with another fundamental feature of legal systems. We have considered only one of Davy's points, that about friendship, not his remark that "An honest man, sir, is able to speak for himself, when a knave is not."

This raises the issue of punishment. And here again, Davy is right: the issue concerns only the guilty (it is obvious that the innocent should not be punished). The play of Shakespeare's that considers this issue most sustainedly and directly is *Measure for Measure*. There it looks as if an overly lax legal system, one in which punishment has been neglected, merely needs to be supplanted by one that will attend to the matter properly. The character of Escalus in the play has been seen as the model for such a judicial position, one that occupies a sensible middle position between over-laxity and over-severity.[35] The problem with this view is not merely that Escalus—despite the opening lines of the play extolling his qualifications—turns out to be a rather minor character, and not (despite these qualifications and the fact that Escalus was "first in question" [1.1.46]) the withdrawing Duke's choice for the job of governor and chief judicial officer (these seem to be the same), but also that the issue on which the play is focused is not that of the behavior of a good judge.[36] The issue is, as the title of the play suggests, the more fundamental one of whether judgment—in the sense of assigning punishment for offenses against the law—is in itself a desirable thing. If the answer to this question is negative, then it is hard to see how there can be a legal system. I will suggest that the play leaves us in precisely that perplexity.

Shakespeare attains a number of aims by making the focus of his examination of the viability of legal systems the regulation of sexuality (he derives this issue from his source material, but that simply shifts the question to why he chose this material).[37] Within this realm, Shakespeare's focus is not laws against rape or molestation but laws against prostitution and "fornication." Prostitution is something that, as the play clearly recognizes, can be legalized. When Escalus asks the male bawd in the play, Pompey, whether his "trade" is "lawful," Pompey answers, "If the law would allow it sir" (2.1.223–24), and Pompey continues in the play as the voice for awareness of the possibility of legalizing various "illegal" practices. He points to the way in which interest-taking ("usury") has sometimes been illegal and sometimes (as in the Elizabethan-Jacobean present, within limits) not;[38] he sees usury and prostitution as equivalent and notes that "the merriest was put down, and the worser allowed by order of law" (3.2.6–8).

Pompey also raises the question of whether the existence of prostitution does not correspond to some fundamental need in human nature and society: "Does your worship mean to geld and splay all the youth of the city?" (2.1.228). The cogency of many of Pompey's retorts lends point to Constable Elbow's malapropisms (confusing benefactors with malefactors, for instance) since Shakespeare wants it to be a real question on this matter, "Which is the wiser here, Justice or Iniquity?" (3.1.174). Moreover, Pompey's final identity in the play—his punishment in being assigned to be the executioner's assistant—makes it seem as if he had been performing an equally useful service to the commonwealth in his previous role, since he is told, by an authoritative character (the virtuous Provost) that he and the executioner (pointedly named Abhorson) "weigh equally" (4.2.28). As Pompey says, with his normal sense of the way in which "legality" can be arbitrary, "I have been an unlawful bawd . . . but now I consent to be a lawful hangman" (4.2.15–16). This equation seems to raise the status of the bawd and lower that of the executioner, who is, after all, a necessary part of a legal-punitive system that includes capital punishment.[39]

The issue of the basis for prostitution in human nature and society carries on, certainly, into the issue of "fornication." The crime here is again one that makes the matter of criminalization dubious. The Elizabethans may have thought that "sodomy" (whatever that is) was abominable, and adultery legally punishable, but the matter of consensual (hetero-)sexual relations between unmarried adults was obviously in a different category.[40] And the issue is especially cloudy in a case such as the one presented in the play, where the couple is (at least) engaged, and, by some definitions, legally married.[41] For the appointed deputy to prosecute such a case (for the male offender) to the letter of the law—which apparently (it is never quoted) prescribed death for fornication—obviously raises a number of questions: first of all, does the statute itself make sense; and second, is the statute, if it does make sense, being properly applied in this case? The first issue is raised in the play—by Pompey as we have seen, and also by the rakish know-it-all and man-about-town Lucio—but, oddly, the second issue is not. When Escalus attempts to persuade Angelo not to prosecute the "fornicator" Claudio to the full extent of the law, Escalus does not offer any specific legal argument in Claudio's favor. He appeals first to a general sense of proportion ("Let us be keen, and rather cut a little, / Than fall, and bruise to death" [2.1.5–6]), and second to the fact that the condemned is from a good family (2.1.6–7)—an argument worthy of contempt, even if the Elizabethans may have only partly shared this.[42] What Escalus does not do is attempt any version of the kind of statutory interpretation that Constance Jordan has illuminated.[43] He does not raise the question of whether Claudio's actions actually constitute "fornication" even though Claudio himself has argued that he and Juliet were actually (legally) married: "Upon a true contract / I got possession of Julietta's bed" (1.2.134–45).

Rather, Escalus's main argument for clemency to Claudio is something like an appeal to human nature, and specifically to the possibility that with regard to sexuality—a presumed universal—Angelo might have "err'd" in the same way Claudio did:

> Had time coher'd with place, or place with wishing,
> Or that the resolute acting of your blood
> Could have attain'd th' effect of your own purpose. (2.1.10–13)

This is the issue on which the play focuses: should the moral status of the judge affect the judgment that he (or she) should render? Does it matter that Angelo can be imagined to have committed the crime in question, or even—to put the issue more strongly, as the play comes to—that he has in fact done so? Angelo sees the issues involved very clearly and answers them quite cogently. First of all, there is a crucial difference between intention or imagination and action: "'Tis one thing to be tempted, Escalus, / Another thing to fall" (2.1.17–18). And second, and even more important, the whole issue is irrelevant:

> The jury passing on the prisoner's life
> May in the sworn twelve have a thief or two,
> Guiltier than him they try. (2.1.18–20)

This is not a problem. The law proceeds with regard to the particular case before it: "What's open made to justice, / That justice seizes." To put the point most sharply Angelo asks, "What knows the laws / That thieves do pass on thieves?" (2.1.17–23). This is a completely coherent position. A legal system is precisely that, a system, and if the system is functioning properly, then it is functioning properly. That is what matters. This is a view that allows for the administration of justice, or, if that is too grand a way of putting it, at least for the working of a system.

This is the view that the play contests. The most riveting scene in the play (2.2) is that in which Isabella, the novice-nun sister of the condemned "fornicator" Claudio, attempts to persuade the deputy, Angelo, that he should have mercy on Claudio. Isabella's primary argument is the appeal to the human nature with regard to sexuality that Angelo is presumed to share: "You would have slipp'd like him" (2.2 65). She then adds the theological dimension to this appeal—we are all sinners in the eyes of God:

How would you be
If He, which is the top of judgement, should
But judge you as you are? (75–77)

Remarkably, Angelo is able to withstand this. He sticks to his formalist position—his own moral status is irrelevant: "It is the law, not I, condemn your brother" (80); and his own feelings are irrelevant (we are back to the issue of impartiality): "Were he my kinsman, brother, or my son, / It should be thus with him" (81–82). Angelo has some further arguments, some dubious claims about deterrence and irredentism, but he is basically sticking to his major, formalist point. What is interesting about this scene, and about the rest of the play, is that he is brought to renounce this view. Isabella presents a searing and unforgettable picture of human pleasure in abusing authority (112–24), but her central argument is the one that has been on the table since Escalus first raised it, the argument from shared human (sexual) nature:

Go to your bosom,
Knock there, and ask your heart what it doth know
That's like my brother's fault. If it confess
A natural guiltiness, such as is his,
Let it not sound a thought upon your tongue
Against my brother's life. (137–42)

When Angelo does find himself responding sexually to Isabella, manifesting "a natural guiltiness" in doing this, he completely forgets and contradicts his earlier recognition of how a legal system operates. From "What knows the laws / That thieves do pass on thieves?" he has gone over entirely to the other view: "Thieves for their robbery have authority / When judges steal themselves" (176–77).

Oddly, for the rest of the play, this view is taken to be axiomatic. The most shocking moment in the play—even more shocking than the onset of lust in Angelo—is when Angelo fails to live up to the *tu quoque* and insists on the execution of Claudio despite their new kinship in sexuality. This does not constitute a return to legal formalism ("It is the law not I"); instead, Shakespeare supplies Angelo with a self-interested motive for the execution (Claudio might take revenge for Angelo's "bargain" with Isabella [4.1.26–30]). The legal-formalist view is entirely forgotten, and with it the distinction between being tempted and falling, between a thought or feeling and an overt action (Angelo adopts the alternative view before he has actually acted upon or even attempted to act upon his newfound impulse). The play comes to oppose the legal framework that would hold that "Thought is free" (or, as the Roman maxim puts it, *Cogitationem poenam nemo patitur*).[44]

The great attack on "Thought is free" is the Sermon on the Mount. G. Wilson Knight was right about its centrality to *Measure for Measure* (though not, as we will see, in his triumphalism about this).[45] Jesus' relation to the moral teaching of the Old Testament, as embodied in the Decalogue, is not to abrogate this teaching but to "fulfill" it, which seems to mean to make it more demanding: "Yee have heard that it was sayd unto them of olde time, Thou shalt not kill. . . . But I say unto you, whosoever is angry with his brother unadvisedly, shalbe culpable. . . . Yee have heard that it was sayd unto them of olde time, Thou shalt not commit adulterie. But I say unto you, that whosoever looketh on a woman to lust after her, hath committed adulterie" (Matthew 5:21–22, 27–28). The point of recognizing one's own sinfulness in this way—"A natural guiltiness"—is to learn the most important moral lesson of all: "Judge not" (7:1). The great moral feeling is love, and the great moral action, forgiveness. This means love and forgiveness of everyone, since it is hardly an achievement to love one's friends (5:46) and—to return to Davy—the innocent do not need to be forgiven. But then, in God's eyes, as Isabella has noted, no one is innocent, and so we all need and must give such blanket forgiveness.

This view does not seem to leave a place for any sort of legal system—or rather, the only one conceivable would postulate a judge (like Christ at the Last Judgment) who does not have to be forgiven for anything. The Duke imagines such a creature—"He who the word of heaven will bear / Must be as holy as severe"; such a judge will not punish anyone for any criminal or sinful behavior toward which he can discern an impulse in himself—"More nor less to others paying / Than by self-offences weighing" (3.2.254–55, 258–59). The Duke may, to give him more credit than he probably deserves, originally have thought of Angelo as possibly being such a creature, but the Duke does not put himself forth in this theocratic and perfectionist guise. Lucio attributes the Duke's "lenity to lechery" to the Duke's having had "some feeling of the sport" (3.2.94, 115–16), but this is simply a cynical version of the appeal to universal fallen nature, of which, in this play, sexuality in general is the sign ("a natural guiltiness"). Some version of Lucio's claim is simply true; no human being can live up to the standard, with regard to bodily needs and impulses, that Angelo apparently professed (the Duke says that Angelo "scarce confesses / That his blood flows, or that his appetite / Is more to bread than stone" [1.3.51–53]) and that Lucio mocks ("a man whose blood is very snow broth," etc. [1.4.58]). So there is, as the play demonstrates through the central case of Angelo, no human being who is "holy" enough to justify being "severe." The Duke in disguise as a friar manipulates the plot to make sure that no major injustice or wrong is done (Claudio is not executed and Isabella not violated), but he does not in any way attend to legal justice.[46]

The key character for showing this is Barnardine, another purely Shakespearean invention.[47] If the legal system were working at all, and able to provide punishments as well as pardons, it would differentiate clearly between the legal situations of Claudio and Barnardine. Claudio's legal guilt as a "fornicator" is, as we have seen, questionable at best, and the "crime" at issue questionable (and questioned) as such. But Barnardine's crime is murder, a major offense in any imaginable legal system. The Provost, a model of integrity in the play, sharply distinguishes between his two prisoners condemned to execution: "Th' one has my pity; not a jot the other / Being a murderer" (4.2.59–60). Moreover, the play works quite hard to discount any legal argument (other than opposition to the death penalty itself) that would work to mitigate or prorogue Barnardine's execution: his stay in prison has not led him to be in any way reformed or penitent and there is no shadow of doubt about his guilt, which is "now apparent" as it had not been before, and "not denied by himself" (4.2.135–45). If there were ever a candidate for execution, or for the severest penalty that the law allows, it would seem to be Barnardine. In Shakespeare's source, the equivalent figure in the plot is executed.[48] A legal system that does not treat Barnardine differently from Claudio can hardly be said to be functioning.

But this is exactly what happens in the play. Both Claudio and Barnardine are spared from execution and freed from prison. And the reason for sparing Barnardine has nothing to do with law as such. The Duke claims that to execute Barnardine "in the mind he is / Were damnable" (4.3.66–67), as if this, a purely spiritual matter, were the concern of the law. At the end of the play, when the Duke has returned to put right (after a certain amount of testing) the situations that his withdrawal has created, it looks as if some semblance of actual legal thinking might be restored to the context. When Isabella passes the test, looking beyond her own situation to plead for the life of the man who intended against her (as the Duke says) "double violation / Of sacred chastity and of promise-breach," she reinstates both the distinction between intention and action and the principle underlying it: "His act did not o'ertake his bad intent. . . . *Thoughts are no subjects*" (5.1.449–51, emphasis mine). The context of this appeal strains the attractiveness of the distinction almost to the breaking point—"moral luck" is certainly involved here—but at least the legal principle is intelligible.[49] As I said, it looks as if some semblance of recognizable legal thinking is being restored. But the next major moment in the play, following shortly upon Isabella's plea, is the entrance of the two former prisoners spared from both execution and imprisonment. Barnardine is given an absolute pardon. All that matters is the state of his soul and the possible future improvement in that: "for those earthly faults, I quit them all" (481). No one, including Lucio, the "slanderer" of the Duke, is seriously punished.[50] And Barnardine is given no sign of gratitude or reformation; he is not even given the kind of ambiguous final resolution and recognition that Caliban gets.

To say that this ending shows the Duke's original leniency "to have been right" is to ignore entirely the problem that the play set out to confront: the problem of enforcement for law-breaking.[51] If anything, the situation in Vienna is worse now than it was at the beginning of the play.[52] But that does not seem to matter. Yes, we are made to feel "the sublime strangeness" of the Sermon on the Mount,[53] but we are also made to feel that, in our nonapocalyptic world, we are left with an aporia ("Judge not") where a legal system should be.[54]

Finally, I must say a few words about the play in which Shakespeare gives his fullest treatment of a legal system at work. In *The Merchant of Venice* Shakespeare really does want to give a sense of a legal system, one that is seen primarily as protecting commercial interests in a multiethnic and multinational situation. The "justice of the state" of Venice is presented as needing to be impartial because "the trade and profit of the city / Consisteth of all nations" (3.3.28–31).[55] Property rights are to be protected and, above all, contracts are to be enforced. Shylock understands the system perfectly. It allows for all sorts of absurd contracts ("If my house be troubled with a rat, / And I be pleas'd to give ten thousand ducats / To have it ban'd," that is just fine as long as Shylock has legitimately earned the money that he is using for this purpose [4.1.44–46]). But perhaps the most important feature of the legal system of Venice as presented in the play is that it allows for persons to be treated as property. Venetian society is, as Shylock points out—and no one denies—a slave-owning society, and so persons can be property, and contracts involving persons as property are, presumably, to be enforced (see 4.1.90–93).[56]

The first thing to be said about the contract that is at the center of the legal case in the play is that no one ever asserts, as certainly a contemporary (with us) judge would (and probably a Venetian judge contemporary with Shakespeare would have), that Shylock's contract with Antonio is unenforceable on the face of it.[57] The idea seems to be that in some sense, Shylock has bought Antonio as a forfeit (since we know that in this society persons can be bought).

What Shylock wants is enforcement of a contract that no one takes to be invalid. He is plied with the Gospel argument—"How shalt thou hope for mercy, rend'ring none?"; "in the course of justice, none of us / Should see salvation" (4.1.88, 195–96)—but, predictably, given the symbolic role of Judaism in the play, he is unmoved by this.[58] What he wants is not justice in general, but legal enforcement. He is relying on the system. He believes in it.[59]

Although it may seem odd to say this, it seems to me that if the legal system of Venice were shown to be working correctly—with respect to its own principles—and Shylock did not, for whatever reason (his state of mind is irrelevant), wish to take money in lieu of the specified forfeit, he should have been allowed his pound of flesh. What this means is that a system that allows for property in persons can produce monstrous results that are perfectly legal.

However, as we all know, Shakespeare does not allow the system to work in this way. The "no jot of blood" proviso brings the proceedings to a halt. This can be read in a number of ways, all of them unattractive. The first reading would be that this proviso is an obvious dodge, an extreme and absurd legalism, since if the initial contract were valid, the conditions necessary for its fulfillment would have to be acceptable as well. The second reading, that of Charles Fried, sees this proviso as consistent with the extreme formalism and literalism of the Venetian legal system as we are given it in the play. Fried argues that Shylock, given his own view of the law, "sees the force" of this argument.[60] This hardly makes the system an attractive one (despite Fried's modified defense of it). We watch Shakespeare's most famous spokesperson for mercy succeeding in out-legalizing the spokesperson for law. And unless we wish to stand with the ironically named Gratiano, we can hardly cheer for this.

But there is more to be said. Even if one takes the view that the proviso is not absurd, Portia emerges as disingenuous in her earlier statements about the validity of Shylock's contract, since the "act" to which she suddenly appeals would have invalidated the contract in the first place. And let's pause for a moment over this "act" (which, apparently, no one has ever heard of until this moment). The "act" seems to have to do not with the shedding of blood in general, but specifically with "Christian blood":

> If thou dost shed
> One drop of Christian blood, thy lands and goods
> Are (by the laws of Venice) confiscate
> Unto the state of Venice. (4.1.304–7)

Shylock is astonished ("Is that the law?" he asks) and is assured that Portia/ Balthazar can produce the text (which she never does). One might have thought that the blood in question in this case just happened to be Christian, since it was Antonio's. But that cannot be right.[61] The (unproduced) law must state that it applies only to non-Christians, since otherwise every assault on any Christian in Venice that produced bloodshed of any kind would fall under it. So now we have a system where the vaunted—and, apparently, extremely socially and economically important—impartiality of the Venetian legal system is shown to be bogus.

This becomes obvious when Portia activates her further proviso, the "other hold" (also unknown to all present) that the laws of Venice have on Shylock. Whether or not her claim that this law does apply in this case is valid, this law, now quoted, explicitly distinguishes between "aliens" and citizens, and is specifically aimed only at aliens ("If it be proved against an alien" [4.1.345]). So it turns out that the Venetian system is no more committed to impartiality than it is to honoring valid contracts. And Shylock, who seems to be a well-established resident of Venice, enjoying at least the status of an *habitator*, is suddenly simply an "alien."[62] So it turns out that "Christian blood" is quite crucial. After the second legal trick is played on Shylock, Portia succeeds, through putting pressure on the Duke, in allowing the court to feel that it has behaved in an especially merciful way in exempting Shylock from some of the provisions of this lovely (and extremely vague—"by direct or indirect attempts") anti-alien statute. To show "the difference of our spirit" between Shylock and the Duke, Shylock is spared execution and diminished in his estate and rights, if not impoverished[63]—and, oh yes, forced to change his religious identity and become a Christian.[64] So the picture of a legal system that we are given is that it either acts truly impartially and allows monstrosities as legal, or acts partially to protect a ruling elite.

What are we to conclude from all this? Shakespeare certainly did not want to "kill all the lawyers"—he made copious use of them in his own life—but he did seem to find that whenever he thought hard about legal principles or legal systems, he found himself profoundly uncomfortable.[65]

NOTES

1. There is no mention of the play in *The Law in Shakespeare*, ed. Constance Jordan and Karen Cunningham (New York: Palgrave Macmillan, 2007), and it is mentioned only in passing in the foreword to *Shakespeare and the Law*, ed. Paul Raffield and Gary Watt (Oxford: Hart, 2008), vi. Lorna Hutson comments on the play in "Not the King's Two Bodies: Reading the 'Body Politic' in Shakespeare's Henry IV, Parts 1 and 2," in *Rhetoric and Law in Early Modern Europe*, ed. Victoria Kahn and Lorna Hutson (New Haven, CT: Yale University Press, 2001), 166–98, but Hutson's essay, as its title suggests, is more

concerned with correcting the errors and countering the influence of Ernst Kantoro-wicz's *The King's Two Bodies* (Princeton, NJ: Princeton University Press, 1957) than with reading *Henry IV, part 2*. Meredith Evans's "Rumor, the Breath of Kings, and the Body of Law in *2 Henry IV*," *Shakespeare Quarterly* 60 (2004): 1–24, is concerned with legitimation rather than law. Colin Burrow, "Reading Tudor Writing Politically: The Case of *2 Henry IV*," *Yearbook of English Studies* 38 (2008): 234–50, comments in lovely detail on parts of one set of scenes in the play.

2. See the anonymous *Famous Victories of Henry the Fifth*, scene 4, in *Narrative and Dramatic Sources of Shakespeare*, ed. Geoffrey Bullough (London: Routledge and Kegan Paul, 1962), 4:309–10.

3. The play is cited from William Shakespeare, *King Henry IV Part 2*, ed. A. R. Humphreys (1966; Walton-on-Thames, Surrey, UK: Thomas Nelson, 1999), hereafter cited as 2H4.

4. There is some of this in the scene in *Famous Victories*. In committing Hal to the Fleet in response to being given a "boxe on the eare" by Hal, the Chief Justice ("Judge") says: "in striking me in this place, you greatly abuse me, and not me onely, but also your father: whose lively person here in this place I doo represent" (310).

5. See Thomas Hobbes, *Leviathan*, ed. C. B. Macpherson (New York: Penguin, 1968), chap. 16.

6. Hutson, "Not the King's Two Bodies" (see note 1 above).

7. On the title page of the sixteenth-century translation of Thomas More's *Utopia*, "De optimo reipublicae statu" is translated as "the best state of a publyqye weal," but in the body of the text, "commonweal" is regularly used. On the term in England, see, inter alia, Whitney R. D. Jones, *The Tudor Commonwealth, 1529–1559* (London: Athlone, 1970); and Markku Peltonen, *Classical Humanism and Republicanism in English Political Thought, 1570–1640* (Cambridge University Press, 1995).

8. Compare "the judgment seat of Christ" in Romans 14:10 and 2 Corinthians 5:10.

9. For these scenes as providing real historical insight into the practices of late Elizabethan justices of the peace, especially in Gloucestershire, see Burrow, "Reading Tudor Writing Politically," esp. 241–43.

10. Humphreys's note in 2H4, 159, points to some of the scholarly attempts to identify the actual families and locales involved.

11. Aristotle, *Nicomachean Ethics*, trans. Martin Ostwald (Indianapolis: Bobbs-Merrill, 1962), 215 (1155a27).

12. See Christine M. Korsgaard, *Creating the Kingdom of Ends* (Cambridge: Cambridge University Press, 1996), 191–200; for the general orientation of Bernard Williams as relevant here, see Williams, *Moral Luck* (Cambridge: Cambridge University Press, 1996), essays 1 and 5. I am not aware that Williams ever commented directly on this passage. For further relevant philosophical work and further references, see the introduction and the essays by Alan Thomas and by Theo Van Willgenburg in the collection of papers on "Reasonable Partiality" in *Ethical Theory and Moral Practice* 8 (2005): 1–10, 25–43, 45–62.

13. The term (philia) that is translated as "friendship" in the *Nicomachean Ethics*,

books 8 and 9 covers the whole range of nonantagonistic relations between persons, from commercial to familial to affective relations. See John M. Cooper, "Aristotle on Friendship," in *Essays on Aristotle's Ethics*, ed. Amélie Oksenberg Rorty (Berkeley: University of California Press, 1980), 301–40.

14. See, inter alia, Shakespeare, *Henry IV Part I*, ed. A. R. Humphreys (1960; London: Routledge, 1988), xi–xv (all references to part 1 are to this edition, cited as 1H4); David Scott Kastan, *Shakespeare after Theory* (New York: Routledge, 1999), chap. 5.

15. See, for instance, the discussion of capital punishment for robbery in the first book of *Utopia* and the notes thereon in *Utopia*, ed. Edward Surtz, S. J. Hexter, and J. H. Hexter (New Haven, CT: Yale University Press, 1965), 61–71.

16. Recall the certainty of Sir Toby (a knight not unlike Falstaff) that "care's an enemy of life." See *Twelfth Night*, ed. T. W. Craik (London: Methuen, 1975), 1.3.2–3.

17. On a major function of jokes as establishing (or solidifying) communities, see Ted Cohen, *Jokes: Philosophical Thoughts on Joking Matters* (Chicago: University of Chicago Press, 1999).

18. This is the fourth line of Shakespeare's sonnet 94, which begins, "They that have pow'r to hurt, and will do none." On the attitudinal and tonal complexities of this sonnet, see William Empson, *Some Versions of Pastoral* (1935; Norfolk, CT: New Directions, 1960), chap. 3; and Edward Hubler, *The Sense of Shakespeare's Sonnets* (Princeton, NJ: Princeton University Press, 1952), 95–109.

19. Desiderius Erasmus, *The Praise of Folly*, trans. Clarence H. Miller (New Haven, CT: Yale University Press, 1979), 32.

20. Ibid., 39.

21. For the classic statement of this view, see E. M. W. Tillyard, *Shakespeare's History Plays* (London: Chatto and Windus, 1944), 265. It has been frequently reiterated. I have put the word *Aristotelian* in quotation marks in referring to this view, since it seems to me to rely on a conception of Aristotle's doctrine of the mean as an arithmetic and substantive doctrine, a doctrine of moderation, rather than as a rhetorical one, a doctrine of appropriateness. For a clear demonstration that "the doctrine of moderation is no part of the doctrine of the mean, nor is it a consequence of the mean," see J. O. Urmson, "Aristotle's Doctrine of the Mean," in Rorty, *Essays on Aristotle's Ethics*, 162. For the complexity of understanding a particular virtue "as a mean," see David Pears, "Courage as a Mean," in the same volume, 171–87.

22. For the romance provenance of this (imagined) feat, see the note in 1H4, 30. Lancelot did it.

23. For the presence of Hotspur as "one of the play's major selling points in its own time" and as one of the major reasons why *Henry IV*, part 1, was the most reprinted of the Shakespeare quartos (with seven editions before the First Folio of 1623), see Roberta Barker, "Tragical-Comical-Historical Hotspur," *Shakespeare Quarterly* 54 (2003): 288–307.

24. Paul A. Jorgenson, "The 'Dastardly Treachery' of Prince John of Lancaster," *PMLA* 76 (1961): 488–92.

25. That Prince John sticks "precisely to the terms of the oath" is noted by John

Kerrigan in "Shakespeare, Oaths and Vows," *Proceedings of the British Academy* 167 (2010): 67.

26. Compare "I will also send wilde beastes among you, which shal spoile you, and destroy your cattel, and make you fewe in nomber: so your hye wayes shalbe desolate." Leviticus 26:22, Geneva. See *The Geneva Bible: A Facsimile of the 1560 Edition*, introduction by Lloyd E. Berry (Madison: University of Wisconsin Press, 1969). That this was Shakespeare's Bible was established long ago in Richmond Noble, *Shakespeare's Biblical Knowledge* (New York: Macmillan, 1935). All biblical citations will therefore be from this edition.

27. On this see the footnote in 2H4, 26.

28. A virtually identical moment occurs in a later Shakespeare play, in the context of tension within another couple. When Antony is berating Cleopatra after the disaster at Actium, the whole scene shifts when Cleopatra asks, "Not know me yet?" *Antony and Cleopatra*, ed. John Wilders (London: Routledge, 1995), 3.13.162. On the connections between Falstaff and Antony (and Cleopatra), see Richard Strier, *The Unrepentant Renaissance: From Petrarch to Shakespeare to Milton* (Chicago: University of Chicago Press, 2011), chap. 3.

29. Erasmus, *Praise of Folly*, 31. Folly's position, it should be noted, is stronger than this. She goes on to claim that friendship also involves an ability, with regard to one's friend "to be deceived, to be blind to his vices, to imagine them away, even to love and admire certain notorious vices as if they were virtues." I would suggest that Mistress Quickly would agree with this as well, since, with regard to Falstaff, she seems to live it.

30. There is a nice note on the precision of Mistress Quickly's recollection in 2H4, 88. In the two plays together, she is the third character (so far) whose relationship with Falstaff is given a precise duration. Bardolph, at 32 years, beats out Mistress Quickly by 3 (1H4, 3.3.45–47); and of Poins, Falstaff said, "I have forsworn his company hourly any time this two and twenty years" (1H4, 2.2.45–47). These relationships have remarkable—and very specifically marked—staying power.

31. Burrow, "Reading Tudor Writing Politically," does a rich analysis (244–49) of the economic and legal significance of what seems a throw-away line about "bullocks at Stamford fair" (2H4, 3.2.38).

32. I am not taking a position on the matter of whether the two plays were initially conceived as a sequence, but I am suggesting that the end of the second play does seem to culminate the two. This is compatible with the view put forth by G. K. Hunter in "Henry IV and the Elizabethan Two-Part Play," *Review of English Studies*, n.s., 5 (1954): 236–48. Harold Jenkins in "The Structural Problem in Shakespeare's *Henry IV*," in *Structural Problems in Shakespeare: Lectures and Essays by Harold Jenkins*, ed. Ernst Honigmann (London: Thomson Learning, 2001), 3–22, sees the issue as rather more vexed.

33. For intelligent musing on this "brief, puzzling scene," see Hugh Grady, *Shakespeare, Machiavelli, and Montaigne: Power and Subjectivity from "Richard II" to "Hamlet"* (New York: Oxford University Press, 2002), 193.

34. Sir Philip Sidney, *An Apology for Poetry*, ed. Geoffrey Shepherd (London: Thomas

Nelson, 1965), 100. Sidney saw poetry as providing an alternative to the brazen world of history and potentially acting as a transforming agent. For a Middle English Land of Cockayne poem, see "The Land of Cockaygne," in *Early Middle English Verse and Prose*, ed. J. A. W. Bennett and G. V. Smithers (Oxford: Clarendon Press, 1968), 138–44.

35. See, for instance, the essay by David Bevington, "Equity in *Measure for Measure*," in this volume. With regard to Escalus as a model, two points should be added: first, that his one clear judicial achievement in the play—sending Mistress Overdone to prison—hardly seems like a great triumph (although he may also, as Bevington suggests, try to straighten out the constabulary in Elbow's ward); and second, that, in the final act of the play, he is set up by the Duke as a complete dupe and appears, quite surprisingly, as an eager voice for harsh interrogation and torture.

36. *Measure for Measure* is cited from the edition by J. W. Lever (New York: Random House, 1967).

37. See Bullough, *Narrative and Dramatic Sources*, 2:399–530.

38. See Norman Jones, *God and the Moneylenders: Usury and Law in Early Modern England* (Oxford: Blackwell, 1989).

39. Luther explicitly affirmed the social usefulness and spiritual acceptability of the role of the executioner; he points out that no ruler "can administer the law courts alone—he must have counselors, judges, lawyers, jailors, executioners, and whatever else is necessary for the administration of justice." "Whether Soldiers, Too, Can Be Saved," in *Luther's Works*, vol. 46, *The Christian in Society III*, ed. Robert C. Schultz (Philadelphia: Fortress Press, 1967), 127. Sarah Beckwith is therefore correct in asserting that "Luther would indeed have felt that Pompey's change of trade from bawd to executioner was a great use of his skills in the service of the state." See her *Shakespeare and the Grammar of Forgiveness* (Ithaca, NY: Cornell University Press, 2011), 65.

40. On the ambiguities of "sodomy," see, inter alia, Alan Bray, *Homosexuality in Renaissance England* (1982; New York: Columbia University Press, 1995); the essays by Janet E. Halley, Donald N. Mager, and Michael Warner in *Queering the Renaissance*, ed. Jonathan Goldberg (Durham, NC: Duke University Press, 1994). On adultery, see Martin Ingram, *Church Courts, Sex, and Marriage in England, 1570–1640* (Cambridge: Cambridge University Press, 1987), 150–54; and Laura Gowring, *Domestic Dangers: Women, Words, and Sex in Early Modern London* (Oxford: Clarendon Press, 1986), chap. 6.

41. On the complexities and ambiguities of Elizabethan marriage laws and practices, see Lever's introduction to his edition of *Measure for Measure*, liii–lv; Ernest Schanzer, *The Problem Plays of Shakespeare* (New York: Schocken, 1965), chap. 2; and Lawrence Stone, *The Family, Sex, and Marriage in England, 1580–1800* (New York: Harper and Row, 1977), 30–37.

42. See Bevington's essay in this volume, 165.

43. See Constance Jordan's essay in this volume.

44. Shakespeare uses this proverbial phrase twice, once in *Twelfth Night*, ed. T. W. Craik (London: Methuen, 1975), 1.3.68; and once in *The Tempest*, ed. Frank Kermode (1958; London: Routledge, 1988), 3.2.121. For the Roman juridical maxim ("No one is punished for thinking"), see *The Digest of Justinian*, 48.19.18, ed. Theodore Mommsen

with Paul Krueger, trans. Alan Watson (Philadelphia: University of Pennsylvania Press, 1985), 4:850.

45. G. Wilson Knight, "*Measure for Measure* and the Gospels," in his *The Wheel of Fire: Interpretations of Shakespearean Tragedy* (1930, 1949; New York: Meridian Books, 1957), 73–96.

46. For a view of the Duke's assumption of the disguise of a friar as a critique of (Elizabethan-Jacobean) state power, see Beckwith, *Shakespeare and the Grammar of Forgiveness*, 75–76.

47. A character equivalent to Barnardine figures in the plot of one of Shakespeare's sources for the "unjust judge" story, Giraldi Cinthio's "Story of Epitia," but this character is never presented directly. See Bullough, *Narrative and Dramatic Sources*, 2:420–42.

48. Ibid., 2:441.

49. On "moral luck," see the essay of that title in Williams, *Moral Luck* (see note 12 above) and the essay by that title in Thomas Nagel, *Mortal Questions* (Cambridge: Cambridge University Press, 1979).

50. One can hardly take seriously Lucio's protestation that being forced to marry a woman whom he has gotten pregnant, presumably on a promise to marry her (3.2.193–94), is "pressing to death, / Whipping, and hanging" (5.1.520–21).

51. Knight, "*Measure for Measure* and the Gospels," 95.

52. Barnardine is free; Pompey is employed by the state; and even with regard to brothels, it is not entirely clear that the situation has improved—if their abolition is held to constitute an improvement. One passage early after the "proclamation" concerning fornication is made suggests that the brothels, as a business enterprise, have simply become an urban franchise. The brothels in the suburbs "must be plucked down," and those in the city "had gone down too, but that a wise burgher put in for them" (1.2.91–92).

53. Knight, "*Measure for Measure* and the Gospels," 96.

54. Debora Kuller Shuger's *Political Theologies in Shakespeare's England: The Sacred and the State in "Measure for Measure"* (New York: Palgrave, 2001) provides, with deep historical awareness, a reading of the play close to Knight's, but it seems to waver between seeing the play's conception of Christian "justice" as radical or strange, and seeing it as perhaps practicable.

55. *The Merchant of Venice* is cited from the edition by John Russell Brown (1959; London: Methuen, 1964).

56. Shylock's speech on slavery in Venice is normally either ignored or not taken to be relevant to the central issues in the trial scene. I take it to be central. And there is certainly some historical truth to Shylock's claim. Alberto Tenenti notes that "Nell' Italia del secolo XVI lo schiavo è ormai sopratutto un oggetto di lusso, riservato ai nobili ed ai ricchi mercanti" (in sixteenth-century Italy, the slave was above all a luxury item, reserved for aristocrats and rich merchants)—exactly the groups with which Shylock is concerned. Tenenti also notes that "schiavitù nel Cinquecento si fa spiccatamente domestica" (slavery in the sixteenth century was primarily domestic)—which also seems to be recognized in Shylock's speech, focusing as it does on household items and con-

cerns. See "Gli Schiavi di Venezia all Fine del Cinquecento," *Rivista Storica Italiana* 67 (1955): 52–69; the quotations are from 54. In a brief note in 1924, with the title "Law and *The Merchant of Venice*," Ezra Pound stressed Venice's history in the Mediterranean slave trade as crucial for understanding the play (which he thought that most readers have not). He intriguingly, with historical backing, connects the Venetian slave trade to the production of eunuchs—certainly a connection lurking in the underbrush of the play. *See Ezra Pound's Poetry and Prose Contributions to Periodicals*, ed. Lea Baechler, A. Walton Litz, and James Longenbach (New York: Garland, 1991), 4:343–44. I owe this reference to Jennifer Scappettone. In a recent article entitled "Shylock and the Slaves: Owing and Owning in *The Merchant of Venice*," *Shakespeare Quarterly* 62 (2011): 1–24, Amanda Bailey treats the question of property in persons in the play with regard to treatment of debtors, but (despite her title) she considers Shylock's analogy of slave and debtor as "merely sensational" (12), since slavery was more "an evocative concept" than an institution in England. She does not consider the situation in Venice.

57. This point is made by Charles Fried in his essay in this volume. For the opinion that a Venetian court of the period "would have either severely punished lender and borrower alike or deemed them both insane and treated them accordingly," see Benjamin Ravid, "The Venetian Government and the Jews," in *The Jews of Early Modern Venice*, ed. Robert C. Davis and Benjamin Ravid (Baltimore: Johns Hopkins University Press, 2001), 26.

58. For a reading of the play in terms of the Old Law versus the New, see, inter alia, Barbara K. Lewalski, "Biblical Allusion and Allegory in *The Merchant of Venice*," *Shakespeare Quarterly* 13 (1962): 121–36.

59. This, I think, is what makes Stephen Greenblatt's marveling at the fact that Shylock does not kill Antonio when he physically has the chance to do so beside the point. See "Shakespeare and Shylock," *New York Review of Books*, September 30, 2010, 91. Shylock's reliance on the legal system is what leads both Richard Posner and Charles Fried to view Portia's second "hold" on Shylock as not legally valid. Working within the law cannot be a crime. See the essays by Posner and Fried in this volume. Bradin Cormack's remarks on Shylock's relation to the law as "poignantly formalist" and on the depth of what Shylock means when he says that he "craves" the law (4.1.202) are exceptionally apt (see "Strange Love: Or, Holding Lands," *Law and Humanities* 2 [2007]: 221–22).

60. See "The Opinion of Fried, J," in this volume. For an argument that Portia's way of reading the bond would actually serve to undermine rather than support the Venetian business community, see Thomas C. Bilello, "Law, Equity, and Portia's Con," in Jordan and Cunningham, *The Law in Shakespeare*, 123. Stanley Cavell's essay in this volume makes the extraordinarily interesting suggestion that, on the conscious level at least, Shylock really was focused on Christian flesh, and not on Christian blood.

61. Janet Adelman puzzles over "why this specification" in *Blood Relations: Christian and Jew in "The Merchant of Venice"* (Chicago: University of Chicago Press, 2008), 125–27.

62. On the matter of the rights of Jews as citizens or as *habitatores*, see Julius Kirshner and Osvaldo Cavallar, "Jews as Citizens in Late Medieval and Renaissance Italy: The Case of Isacco da Pisa," *Jewish History* 25 (2011): 269–318. Julia Reinhard Lupton, *Citizen-Saints: Shakespeare and Political Theology* (Chicago: University of Chicago Press,

2008), 79, stresses the importance of Shakespeare's making Shylock "part of a world" but takes it for granted that Shylock lived in the Venetian ghetto (86–87, 98). He would have, were the play entirely true to the situation of Jews in Venice in the later sixteenth century (the ghetto was designated as a mandatorily Jewish area in 1516, before which Jews were denied permanent residence in the city). See Riccardo Calimani, *The Ghetto of Venice*, trans. Katherine Silberblatt Wolfthal (New York: M. Evans, 1987). But one of the most striking features of Shakespeare's play in relation to the historical actuality is that the play never mentions or hints at the existence of the ghetto (noted by Ravid, "The Venetian Government and the Jews," 26). Shylock wishes to close off his daughter and his "sober house" from the merriment and music of "Christian fools" who disport themselves in the "public street" (2.5.28–36)—which locates his house on such a street where such things happen. What this means is that Shakespeare presents the figure of Shylock as more integrated into Venetian society than a Jew would actually have been. Whether Shakespeare knew about the ghetto is unclear; he could have, though probably not by name. The word does not seem to appear in print in English before *Coryate's Crudities* (1611), although it was used by Fynes Morison earlier (though not in print until 1617). Laurence Aldersey, in Hakluyt's *Principal Navigations* (1589), notes that in Venice the Jews "dwell in a certaine part of the Citie" (unnamed). See "Christian Travelers in the Ghetto of Venice: Some Preliminary Observations," in Benjamin Ravid, *Studies on the Jews of Venice, 1382–1797* (Aldershot, Hampshire, UK: Ashgate, 2003), 111–24.

63. The exact financial terms of Shylock's punishment are quite unclear. First it is stated (by the authoritative legal expert and judge, "Balthazar") that half of Shylock's estate is to go to Antonio and half to "the state" (4.1.348–50); but then the Duke asserts that the state's half can be reduced to a fine, if Shylock, at some unspecified time and in some unspecified way, exhibits good behavior ("humbleness" [368]). But then Antonio seems to renounce his half of the estate in return for the Duke's willingness to allow Antonio to administer the state's half during Shylock's life as long as Shylock is willing to have this half pass on to Lorenzo (pointedly referred to as "the gentleman / That lately stole his [Shylock's] daughter") after Shylock's death (377–81). And then, after the conversion requirement, Antonio adds the proviso that the rest of Shylock's estate, including "all he dies possessed [of]," shall also go to Lorenzo (although now Shylock's daughter is also mentioned as a legatee [384–86]). Richard H. Weisberg argues that "all he dies possessed of" is a weird exacerbation of the conditions; see his "Antonio's Legalistic Cruelty: Interdisciplinarity and *The Merchant of Venice*," *College Literature* 25 (1998): 15–16. But, as I have said, none of this is crystal clear. Critics differ on what Antonio means by saying that he is prepared to "quit the fine for one half of [Shylock's] goods" and on what his request to have "the other half *in use*" (379) denotes and connotes. Holding land "in use" was, as Bradin Cormack puts it, "the dominant way to hold land" (though not "goods") in early modern England ("Shakespeare Possessed: Legal Affect and the Time of Holding," in Raffield and Watt, *Shakespeare and the Law*, 96). It meant that the land was held by someone (the feoffee) for the benefit of someone else ("cestui que use"). This is probably, as B. J. Sokol and Mary Sokol say in *Shakespeare's Legal Language: A Dictionary* (London: Continuum, 2010), 386, the denotative meaning of Antonio's proposal: "Antonio will be the feoffee, and *cestui que use* is

Shylock." But this reading of "in use" means that the phrase, as Brown in his edition (119) and Sokol and Sokol insist (385), does not imply that Antonio would give or receive interest. But these efforts to limit the scope of the phrase, while certainly legally correct, only testify to the power, in the context, of the meaning that is being so assertively excluded. The phrase cannot but ring strangely in the apparently anti-usury context of the play, especially in the mouth of Antonio, who consistently and fiercely "rated" Shylock about, as Shylock says, "my moneys and my usances" (1.3.103). Stephen Orgel and A. R. Braunmuller, in The [New] Pelican Shakespeare (New York: Penguin, 2002), 319, try to have it both ways: while glossing the phrase as "in trust," they add that "the earlier meaning, 'lend at interest,' is probably present." So it is not clear how much of his estate, if any, Shylock ends up with, nor exactly what will happen to it before his death. Three things, however, are clear: (1) that Shylock's life depends on his conversion; (2) that he will lose control of at least half of his estate; and (3) that he will lose the right to determine his heirs.

64. The conversion, it should be noted, is Shakespeare's addition to the story. It does not appear in his narrative source, Il Pecorone [The dunce], by Ser Giovanni Fiorentino, where the last that is said about the legally defeated Jew is that he tears up the bond in frustration. Bullough, Narrative and Dramatic Sources, 1:474. Posner's attempt to present the conversion demand as nonobjectionable, within the historical context, is quite forced, and the extraordinary and almost consciously sophistical ruling by Innocent III concerning stipulated "willingness" hardly helps the case, especially when the problem of the conversos is added. See Posner's essay in this volume, 148.

65. My colleague Richard McAdams claims to have located an instance in which Shakespeare portrays a legal process positively—and in Venice, no less. See the comments in his essay in this volume on act 3, scene 1, of Othello. I would reply that it is important, as McAdams notes in passing, that "the Duke is not a judge" and that the procedure in question is (as McAdams says) "informal" (p. 124)—not a set and formal legal process. My claim is that the more formal and official the legal situation, the more what is presented is a legal system or an official representative of such, the more reservations Shakespeare manifests. That is the important point. However, I would also note that the issue of impartiality, which seems to be entirely positive in the Othello scene (the Duke proclaims it), would have been put under interesting pressure, given the military situation, had the Duke and the council thought Othello guilty. I would add further that the Duke's initial asseveration of impartiality—"though our proper son / Stood in your action"—is, of course, untested and refers to a rigor that Shakespeare clearly found very dubious, as in the first scene of Titus Andronicus, where Titus thinks he is acting justly when he does indeed kill his "proper son."

PART IV

Law, Politics,

and Community

in Shakespeare

KATHY EDEN

LIQUID FORTIFICATION AND THE
LAW IN *KING LEAR*

This essay offers an argument about Shakespeare's handling of the law in *King Lear*. The crux of the argument is philological; it concerns Shakespeare's crafting of the language of the play, in particular his craftsmanship in deploying two words with complicated histories: *loyal* and *royal*. But the point of departure for the philology is philosophy, and especially the popular Renaissance reception of Stoic philosophy, with its doctrine of natural law, its narratives of the relationship between law and kingship, and its distinction between legal and extralegal forms of exchange.[1] I will begin with the last of these three—the forms of exchange—because that is where I assume Shakespeare began when he turned to the task of remaking his sources.

As is well known, Shakespeare borrowed from several literary sources, but most informing is the anonymous drama *King Leir*, written roughly a decade before Shakespeare's version and brought back to the stage shortly before the later play made its debut in 1605 or 1606. It is also well known that Shakespeare complicated the older drama by interweaving an episode from Philip Sidney's prose romance *Arcadia*, which served as model for Gloucester's family drama.[2] Both of these sources feature a father who misjudges his children, rewarding the false ones, who repay trust with treachery, while a true but rejected child perseveres in filial devotion in spite of being mistreated. As part of his remake, Shakespeare set the plot composed of these two interlocking tales within a Stoicized worldview. This Stoicized world is recognizable not only from its sparks of temper and pre-Christian divinities, as others have noted, but also from its unwavering attention to the triangulated activities of giving, receiving, and returning favor.[3]

Any account of the Stoicized world of *King Lear*, in other words, must address the dictates of Cicero's *De officiis* (*On Duties*) and Seneca's *De beneficiis* (*On Benefits*), both Roman manuals that became Renaissance best-sellers about the do's and don'ts of social exchange within the family and in the larger community.[4] In thinking about the impact of Stoic philosophy on Renaissance drama, and especially on this drama, we do well to remember that the root of *community*, both philologically and anthropologically, is the Latin *munus*, that is, something exchanged, a gift or a service. *Community*, then, is the sharing of *munera*, gifts; it is the network of relations defined by favors, in the form of gifts and services given, received, and returned.[5] So Seneca begins his treatise *On Benefits* by identifying what he calls the three favors or graces—the three *gratiae*—as the three offices of giving, receiving, and returning (1.3.2). And he observes that this exchange of benefits binds human society together (*maxime humanam societatem alligat*) (1.4.2).[6]

From beginning to end, the Shakespearean characters who populate the world of this play express their familial and social obligations in the Stoically inflected terms of benefits, offices, duties, and bonds. Cordelia, for example, claims to love her father "According to [her] *bond*" (1.1.93) and promises, in regard to the favor he has shown her, to "return those *duties* back as are right fit" (1.1.97).[7] Unlike Lear, Kent understands the sufficiency of this promise and so takes it as his "duty" in the opening scene to counsel Lear first not to disinherit his youngest daughter and then to revoke his "gift" to the other two (1.1.148, 1.1.165).[8] Skillful at deploying this same language of giving, receiving, and returning favor, Edmund answers Cornwall's acknowledgment of the "childlike *office*" he has shown to Gloucester with "It was my *duty*" (2.1.106–7). Meanwhile, Gloucester himself chooses to ignore Cornwall's express orders against helping the king and acknowledges a "duty" to Lear that overrides such "hard commands" (3.4.144–45).[9] And Lear, beginning to feel the effects of his misguided gift-giving, excuses Regan's discourtesy with the reflection that "Infirmity doth still neglect all *office*/Whereunto our health is *bound*" (2.2.295–96). He insists further that, unlike Goneril, Regan knows "The *offices* of nature, *bond* of childhood, / Effects of courtesy, dues of gratitude" (2.2.367–68). Whereas Regan insists, in turn, that her sister has not "scant[ed] her *duty*" (2.2.329), Lear has already cursed Goneril for her ingratitude by wishing on her a "child of spleen" to turn all her mother's "*benefits* / to laughter and contempt"

> that she may feel
> How sharper than a serpent's tooth it is
> To have a thankless child. (1.4.274–81)

Even Goneril's husband Albany, failing to temper his wife's unkindness, eventually recoils from such thanklessness to "A father, and a *gracious* agèd man" by those he "so *benefitted*" (4.2.42–46). One sure mark of the failure of this community is the filial ingratitude with which Lear's giving is received and returned.

For any but the most casual reader of this play, moreover, there is no need to multiply examples of its Latinate language of *ingratitude*, alongside its Germanic counterpart, *thanklessness*. Nevertheless, it may be worth remarking that the cluster of words to which *ingratitude* belongs, including *grace* and *graciousness*,[10] also belongs to the Stoic discourse of benefits, with its three Senecan graces or *gratiae*: giving, receiving, and returning. Indeed, Seneca identifies "being *gratus*" (grateful) as the most praiseworthy act (4.16.3) and ingratitude (being *ingratus*) as worse than homicide, tyranny, adultery, and sacrilege (1.10.3–4). "Not to return gratitude for benefits is a disgrace," he proclaims, "and the whole world counts it as such" (3.1.1), because, he continues, "there is nothing that so effectively disrupts and destroys the harmony of the human race" (4.18.1). "For how else," he asks,

> do we live in security if it is not that we help each other by an exchange of good offices (*mutuis officiis*)? It is only through the interchange of benefits (*beneficiorum commercio*) that life becomes in some measure equipped and fortified (*munitior*) against sudden disasters. Take us singly, and what are we? . . . For, while other creatures possess a strength that is adequate for their self-protection, and those that are born to be wanderers and to lead an isolated life have been given weapons, the covering of man is a frail skin; no might of claws or teeth makes him a terror to others, naked and weak as he is, his safety lies in fellowship (*nudum et infirmum societas munit*). (4.18.1–2)[11]

Like Lear, in other words, Seneca acknowledges man, when he is stripped to the bone and beyond the protection of society—Shakespeare's "unaccommodated" man—as no more than a "poor, bare, forked animal" (3.4.105–6) that must exchange benefits to survive.

One by one, all but the worst characters in this play are forced into exile; and most of these move out beyond the protection of society to the realm of nature. At this remove, they require and even request this same Stoic favor, or *gratia*, in another, etymologically related, form: *caritas*, related, in turn, to both the Greek for favor, *charis*, and the Stoic *caritas generis humani*, a love for the human race.[12] Whereas the earlier play sets its "perfit charity" in an exclusively Christian context, aligning it with the forgiveness that characters such as Cordella and Leir pray for in Church from the Lord (ll. 1089–92; ll. 1668–71), Shakespeare's play, without forfeiting the Pauline echoes, resonates as well with a Stoic *caritas* that, according to Cicero, enables us to extend the care and affection we routinely bestow on those closest to us to nameless strangers as members of the larger family of humankind. Stripped of his legal identity in the forms of his birthright and even his name—"Edgar I nothing am" (2.2.192)—Poor Tom is just such a nameless stranger who must learn, as he himself puts it, to "enforce . . . *charity*" (2.1.191; 3.4.59)—the same charity that Gloucester, in spite of Cornwall's express prohibition mentioned earlier, shows to Lear in his unaccommodated state. "Go you and maintain talk with the Duke," Gloucester instructs Edmund, "that my charity be not of him perceived" (3.3.14–16).[13]

Here is another mark of failed community: Gloucester's punishment, technically in keeping with what Cornwall labels "the form of justice" (3.7.25), for graciously rendering a service—in Stoic terms, doing a favor. And yet, Gloucester's punishment smacks of a double injustice insofar as the defining character of benefits as the basis of community is their extralegal status. They are outside the law. But they are not just outside the law; they are superior to its legal forms of exchange. Even though an act of ingratitude is the most injurious, the most monstrous—Seneca agrees with Lear—it is nowhere (except in Macedonia) liable to prosecution (3.6.1–2).[14] "The penalty for homicide, for poisoning, for parricide, and for the desecration of religion," Seneca observes (3.6.2), "is different in different places, but they have some penalty everywhere, whereas the crime that is the commonest of all is nowhere punished, but is everywhere denounced." Far from bemoaning this fact, however, Seneca applauds it, because, as he explains,

> the best part of a benefit is lost if it can become actionable, as is possible in the case of a fixed loan or of something rented or leased. For the most beautiful part of a benefit is that we gave it even when we were likely to lose it, that we left it wholly to the discretion of the one who received it. If I arrest him, if I summon him before a judge, it gets to be, not a benefit, but a loan.
>
> In the second place, although to repay gratitude is a most praiseworthy act, it ceases to be praiseworthy if it is made obligatory. (3.7.1–2)

There is, in short, no law against ingratitude—no positive law, that is. It does, on the other hand, infract the law of nature. "Even wild beasts," Seneca remarks (1.11.5), "are sensible of good offices, and no creature is so savage that it will not be softened by kindness (cura) and made to love the hand that gives it."[15]

As at least some recent scholarship of the play readily acknowledges, the traditional opposition between not only law and nature but also positive and natural law is fundamental to the dramatic action.[16] Forcibly removed from the legal trappings of the court, the characters rendered vulnerable to nature's "blasts" (4.1.9), and especially Lear, recognize both the strength of the natural bonds that unite them—parent to child, master to servant, human to human— and the frailties of the legal conventions that bind them to court life. Originally designed, according to Stoic philosophy, to enforce a justice consistent with natural law, positive law always runs the risk of degenerating, as it does in this play, into the forms of authority that obstruct justice. In his dialogue *On the Laws*, Cicero addresses this degeneration.

In his own voice through the interlocutor "Marcus," Cicero insists that the law "is not some piece of legislation by popular assemblies" but is rather "something eternal which rules (*regeret*) the entire universe through the wisdom of its commands and prohibitions."[17] "The most stupid thing of all," Marcus warns, "is to consider all things just which have been ratified by a people's institutions or laws," because there is only one justice "which constitutes the bond among humans (*quo devincta est hominum societas*), and which was established by one law. . . . The person who does not know it is unjust, whether the law has been written anywhere or not."[18]

From the vantage point of a community reconstituted in nature, Lear too rails against the defects of a positive law out of sync with natural law. In the Quarto's third act (3.6), for instance, during the so-called mock trial, he insists on an arraignment of his daughters that benches the "yoke-fellow of equity," long identified with natural law, beside "the robed man of justice" (3.6.36–37), while in the fourth act (4.6.156–59), he indicts both the "rascal beadle" who whips the whore and the usurer who hangs the cozener.[19] Both episodes provide obvious expressions of the very degeneration of the legal institutions dispensing justice that worried Cicero. But there is a less—much less—obvious expression of this worry, the case for which, as my title announces, requires a little "liquid fortification."

The "liquid fortification" I have in mind is not the kind unrepentantly advocated and routinely enjoyed by Alfred Doolittle in the musical *My Fair Lady*, although the phrase itself is his. The liquids of my title are linguistic rather than alcoholic—more likely to be of interest to Eliza's teacher, Henry Higgins, than to her father. They are, in other words, the letters—or rather the sounds—/l/ and /r/. These liquids, experts teach us, function in curious ways in more than one language. Japanese, for instance, registers /r/ but not /l/, Chinese /l/ but not /r/. In Hittite, /l/ is possible in word-initial position, but /r/ is not; and in Indo-Iranian, the two liquids are sometimes confused.[20] This ancient confusion in particular, I want to suggest, leaves its mark on the tragedy of *King Lear*, through what one Renaissance scholar, Bradin Cormack, has called Shakespeare's "experimental philology," whereby the playwright enlists the formation of key words as, in Cormack's phrase, a "form of invention."[21] In *King Lear*, as I hope to show, Shakespeare uses two words in a dazzlingly inventive way.

The two key words, *loyal* and *royal*, share two key features: each begins with one of the two liquids /l/ and /r/; and each not only anglicizes a corresponding French term—*loyale* and *royale*, from *loi* and *roi*—but coexists with another English term with the same meaning that corresponds to the older Latin root: *legalis* and *regalis*, from *lex* and *rex*. Alongside *loyal* and *royal*, in other words, English preserves the synonymous alternatives, *legal* and *regal*. Whereas *royal* and *regal* remain more or less lexically identical in Shakespeare's day, *loyal* and *legal* do not. Shakespeare's own usage, especially in his comedies, demonstrates the gradual decoupling of *loyal* from *legal* as the affective dimension of the term eclipses its relation to the law.[22] In *King Lear*, however, Shakespeare exploits the older meaning of *loyal* even as he enforces its pairing with *royal*, whose formation in English mirrors its own.

For the only character in the play explicitly—not to mention counterintuitively—designated *loyal* is Edmund, the natural or bastard child ruthlessly intent on securing legitimacy, that is, legal status, in the interest of securing others' property rights: first Edgar's, then Gloucester's, and finally Regan's (see 5.3.75–79).[23] This selective identification of *loyalty* with a single character—and with a singularly degenerate character—is Shakespeare's innovation. The older *King Leir*, in contrast, applies the term much more straightforwardly to the Kent-like counselor Perillus, reserving the qualification *disloyal* for the ungrateful daughters.[24]

Consequently, when Gloucester addresses his illegitimate son as "Loyal and natural boy," the *legality* of Edmund's *loyalty* is more than just suggestively invoked by the traditional pairing of law and nature. It is unambiguously affirmed by the adjoining declaration (2.1.83–85) "and of my land . . . I'll work the means / To make thee capable."[25] Edmund's so-called *loyalty*, in other words, coincides with his *legality*. Like Gloucester, moreover, Edmund himself not only echoes the opposition between law and nature, already noted as fundamental to the structure of the play, but he does so through the language of *loyalty*. Pledging allegiance to the legal over the natural bond as a cover for just the kind of gross ingratitude that the likes of Cicero and Seneca deplore, Edmund announces to Cornwall, his lawful superior, that by informing against his own father, "nature thus gives way to *loyalty*" (3.5.2–3), a "course of *loyalty*" that is, he claims, in conflict with his "blood" (3.5.22–23). In the next act, Oswald once again proclaims Edmund's course as "*loyal* service" (4.2.7).[26] Indeed, Shakespeare's tendency in the tragedies and histories to couple *loyalty* with "subjects" and their "services" reinforces its origins in legality.[27] Even Desdemona's oath (to switch tragedies for an instant), "Your wife, my lord; your true / And *loyal* wife" (*Othello*, 4.2.33–34), reaffirms the lawful union that her father called into question in the opening moments of that tragic play. *Blood*, on the other hand, to return to Edmund's disingenuous claim to feel conflicted, is just as regularly associated in Shakespeare's plays with *royalty*.[28] And this association figures prominently, albeit subtly, in *King Lear*.

If Edmund alone among the many characters in this play is counted *loyal*, Lear is *almost*, until the final moments of the play, the only character designated *royal*. Here again, Shakespeare deviates from his dramatic source, which applies the term to marriages (l. 11), thrones (l. 45), dowries (l. 319), states (l. 934), and races (l. 721), as they apply in turn to Leir, his daughters, and the King of France.[29] Throughout Shakespeare's play, in contrast, only the person of the eponymous king, with the single exception to which I will return momentarily, enjoys this title. In the opening scene, Kent calls him "Royal Lear" (1.1.140), while Burgundy addresses him as "Most royal majesty" (1.1.194), "Royal sir" (1.1.206), and "Royal King" (1.1.243). In the second act, Kent schools the superserviceable Oswald on the contrast between the vanity of his mistress and the *royalty* of Kent's own master (2.2.35–36), while in the fourth act the unnamed gentleman answers Lear's insistence that he is a king with the deferential "You are a *royal* one, and we obey you" (4.6.197). In the next scene, the returned Cordelia offers comfort to her declining father with "How does my *royal* lord?" (4.7.44).

Shakespeare, then, counterbalances Edmund's singular identification with *loyalty* against Lear's (almost) singular identification with *royalty*; and this balancing act supports a peculiarly inventive piece of "experimental philology," not only in that the two terms, as we have seen, exhibit corresponding relations to their French and Latin roots, but also in that, given the confounding of the liquids /l/ and /r/ in Latin's ancient cousin Indo-Iranian, *lex* and *rex* may share their very earliest history.

The philological evidence regarding *loyalty* and *royalty*, in other words, may attest to an even closer kinship between them than their parallel formation suggests and so to a deeper connection between law and kingship as sources of rule. For Latin *rex* derives from the same Indo-European root as Sanskrit *raj*, and so very possibly, but somewhat more surprisingly, does *lex*, according to not a few etymological dictionaries as well as experts on Indo-European linguistics, although those sources hasten to add that the etymology of *lex* remains obscure.[30] Latin *rex*, moreover, originally designated a position closer to priesthood than kingship, in that royal power entitled the *rex* to draw the boundary or make divisions between property, including between the sacred and the profane. The role of the *rex* was to *regere finem*, that is to draw boundary lines.[31]

Strangely resonant with the dramatic hypothesis of the Lear story, this kingly role of divider is reflected in the affiliation of *rex* with the family of words in English, as well as in other modern European languages, derived from *reg** or *rec**, including not only *regulate* and *rectify* in English but also *Recht*, the German word for law.[32] And this deep connection between the law and division, especially the division of property, is also reflected in the Greek word *nomos*, one of whose principal meanings is *law*, from the verb *nemein*, to divide. Like the king, the law rules—*regere*—by making divisions. While locating an alternative etymology for *lex* (which contemporary linguists dispute) in the verb *legere*, to choose, Cicero does, as we have seen in his discussion of the laws (page 207), characterize *lex* as something that rules.[33]

If the philological evidence for the deep connection between *lex* and *rex* remains speculative, the philosophical evidence—and especially the evidence from two key Stoic texts—is entirely straightforward. In *De officiis*, for instance, Cicero puts on record both the common cause of law and kingship and the historical shift from the one to the other: "The establishment of laws (*legum*) and the institution of kings (*regum*) had the same cause. For a system of justice that is fair is what has always been sought: otherwise it would not be justice. As long as they secured this from a single just and good man, with that they were content. When it ceased to be so, laws were invented, which always spoke to everyone with one and the same voice."[34] This Ciceronian account of the evolution of political institutions, featuring the historical transition from *rex* to *lex*, corresponds with Seneca's account to Lucilius (*Ep.* 90.4–6), where laws are only eventually founded by wise legislators to replace kings who have become tyrants. For the first men "followed nature, having one man as both their leader and their law" (90.4), needing no other institutions as long as their rulers considered ruling "a service (*officium*), not an exercise of royalty (*regnum*)" (90.5). "But when vice stole in and kingdoms (*regna*) were transformed into tyrannies," Seneca explains, "a need arose for laws (*legibus*); and these very laws were in turn framed by the wise" (90.6).[35] In sharp contrast to Cicero's republicanism, however, Seneca asserts in the *De beneficiis* and elsewhere that "a state reaches its best condition under the rule of a just king" (*cum optimus civitatis status sub rege iusto sit*) (2.20.2).[36]

In *King Lear*, Shakespeare rehearses a version of the Senecan rather than the Ciceronian account, shifting our attention—and arguably our attachment—from loyalty to royalty, from *lex* to *rex*, from Edmund to Lear. But he does so only after establishing the parallels between the two dramatic characters. Even as the innovative integration of the two literary sources with analogous plots invites the ready comparison between the two misguided fathers, Shakespeare's "experimental philology," linking *loyalty* and *royalty*, works alongside other commonly deployed dramatic strategies to link the father of the older drama with the son of the prose romance.

The most obvious link involves the repeated invocation of Nature. Edmund's in the second scene is predictably sophistic.[37] For he offers his oath of service to his goddess, backed by his professions against the conventions of positive law, here discredited as "the plague of custom" (1.2.3), only to secure Nature's aid in installing him in the very customary titles of legal ownership blocked by both his bastardy and his birth order: "some twelve or fourteen moonshines / Lag of a brother" (1.2.5–6).[38] Acknowledged as the "natural" son in the beginning of the action, Edmund single-mindedly in the course of the play cauterizes his natural bonds for a loyalty that the audience easily recognizes as mere legality. Indeed, Edmund dramatizes not only the perils of a legality decoupled from natural law, lamented earlier by Cicero, but also the extremes of unnaturalness in the extralegal acts of giving, receiving, and returning favor.

Lear's invocation of Nature (1.4.267–81), in contrast, calls on the goddess to exert control over just this extralegal economy—one that renders not only one grateful service for another, as we have seen, but also ingratitude for ingratitude, requiting a daughter's unnaturalness toward a father with a "disnatured torment" in the person of her child (1.4.275). Wishing on Goneril a "child of spleen" (1.4.274), in other words, Lear counts on Nature herself as the original benefactress to return one act of disfavor with another. In the second scene, moreover, Edmund's utter perversion of the acts of receiving and returning favor, in regard to not only a devoted father but a trusting brother, serves as the dramatic complement to Lear's perversion of gracious giving in the first scene. While Edmund perseveres in his unnatural loyalty, however, Lear abandons both physically and philosophically the discredited legality of the court, attaining thereby a natural royalty that Kent, Cordelia, France, and even the King himself cannot disavow.

For if one of Shakespeare's canniest readers of the second half of the twentieth century is right, and Shakespearean tragedy is not about what becomes of us but about what we become, then Lear, not only in the course of his tragedy but as a consequence of it, becomes "every inch a king" (4.6.106) despite his smell of mortality (4.6.129)—someone whom the likes of Kent, Cordelia, and Albany would fain call master (1.4.29).[39] "No, they cannot touch me for coining," Lear declares, "I am the King himself. . . . Nature's above art [and we might add law] in that respect" (4.6.83–86). If loyalty in the person of Edmund is reduced to legality, then royalty in the person of Lear is exalted to nature.[40]

Elsewhere in his histories and tragedies, as I have already mentioned in passing, Shakespeare features this exaltation by coupling *royalty* with *blood* (see note 27), the liquid (to turn to another kind of liquid for a moment) most closely identified with the workings of nature over and against those of the law. Edmund himself supports this claim when, as we have seen, he couches his treachery in a supposed conflict between *loyalty* and *blood* as an alternative formulation of the law's traditional opposition to nature (3.5.22–23). And so does his brother Edgar when, in the final moments of the play, in response to something in *his* nature, he earns from Albany the qualifier *royal*: "Methought thy very gait did prophesy / A *royal* nobleness" (5.3.173–74). Having been introduced in the opening scene of the play as Gloucester's son "by order of law" (1.1.18), having been cheated by a brother intent on defrauding him of his "legitimacy" (1.2.16–21), and even having been, as Gloucester puts it, "outlawed from my blood" (3.4.163) and so unable to inherit, Edgar far surpasses mere legality by becoming what nature bequeaths: a gracious—even beneficent—son to a gullible father. As with Lear, so with Edgar, *royalty* leaves behind a tainted *loyalty* to keep company with nature.[41] With the Quarto's reflection "He childed as I fathered" (3.6.107), Edgar himself encourages us to notice his affinities with Lear. And Edgar's assumption of the royal pronoun "we" in the Folio's closing words of the play (5.3.322–25) both echoes Lear's kingly proclamations of the opening scene (e.g., 1.1.35–54, 1.1.169–79) and completes the transition from one reign to the next.[42]

Shoring up an "experimental philology" with a Renaissance version of Stoic philosophy, then, Shakespeare uses the terms *loyal* and *royal* with remarkable precision, returning, in fact, in one of his latest tragedies to a pairing that makes a poignant but passing appearance in one of his earliest when the wrongly imprisoned Clarence expostulates with the murderers sent by his own brother:

Clarence.	In God's name, what art thou?
2nd Murderer.	A man, as you are.
Clarence.	But not, as I am, *royal*.
2nd Murderer.	Nor you, as we are, *loyal*. (Richard III, 1.4.169–72)

In *Richard III*, Shakespeare deploys the jangling of this rhyme to drive home not only the deadly tensions between political and familial ties but also the collision between the rule of law and kingship. In *King Lear*, in contrast, he showcases the same two rhyming words in a much more subtle way, tethering them to a Stoicized worldview that broadens and deepens the stage on which both political and family drama is performed.

For the popular Stoicism of his day provides Shakespeare, as we have seen, with a framework for integrating two separate but similar stories into a tragedy about the extralegal exchange of giving, receiving, and returning favor. Under the jurisdiction of natural law, this exchange does more than just ensure human survival; it creates and sustains the conditions for all human bonding, for society itself. But the same popular Stoicism also provides Shakespeare with a narrative for the relation between law and kingship as competing sources of rule. *King Lear* dramatizes this narrative as the movement from the corruptible laws of the court to their deeper and more enduring prototypes in nature—a nature here identified with the true nobility of *royalty*. Vastly complicating his source material, then, Shakespeare stages the surrender of a shallow legality to a natural law that underwrites authentic kingship no less than community itself.[43]

NOTES

1. Throughout this essay, I am concerned, as stated in the text, with the popular reception of Stoicism in sixteenth-century England, and especially with a few key texts of Cicero and Seneca, and not with either the more rigorous arguments of the ancient Stoics or the complications of Cicero's philosophical allegiances. In light of this concern, I refer to the world of the play as "Stoicized" rather than Stoic. I am very grateful to Bradin Cormack, Martha Nussbaum, and Richard Strier for their critical readings of the essay in an earlier version.

2. On the sources, see Geoffrey Bullough, *Narrative and Dramatic Sources of Shakespeare* (London: Routledge and Kegan Paul, 1973), 7:269–420; and W. W. Greg, "The Date of *King Lear* and Shakespeare's Use of Earlier Versions of the Story," Library 20 (1940): 377–400.

3. On Stoic anger in *King Lear*, see Gordon Braden, *Renaissance Tragedy and the Senecan Tradition: Anger's Privilege* (New Haven, CT: Yale University Press, 1985), esp. 215–16; and Richard Strier, "Against the Rule of Reason: Praise of Passion from Petrarch to Luther to Shakespeare to Herbert," in *Reading the Early Modern Passions*, ed. Gail Kern Paster, Katherine Rowe, and Mary Floyd-Wilson (Philadelphia: University of Pennsylvania Press, 2004), 23–42, esp. 36–39; on the gods, see William R. Elton, *King Lear and the Gods* (San Marino, CA: Huntington Library, 1966). In addition, individual passages in the play rehearse Stoic assumptions and even echo Stoic texts. An illustration of the first is Gloucester's reflection on suicide at 4.6.61–64, discussed by Strier, "Against the Rule of Reason," 37–38. Illustrating the second are Lear's words at 3.2.59–60 ("I am a man / More sinned against than sinning"), which recall Seneca's formulation at *De beneficiis*, 5.17.1, referring to the republic (*non minus saepe peccaverit, quam in ipsam peccatum est*). Shortly thereafter (5.17.3), Seneca proclaims universal sinfulness and pardon, anticipating Lear's words in 4.6 and his own treatment of clemency, another extralegal transaction. On Seneca's *De clementia* and its impact on Renaissance political theory, see Peter Stacey, *Roman Monarchy and the Renaissance Prince* (Cambridge: Cambridge University Press, 2007).

On *King Lear* and the form of exchange appropriate to gifts, see Natalie Zemon Davis, *The Gift in Sixteenth-Century France* (Madison: University of Wisconsin Press, 2000), 71–72, where she reads the play as a dramatic example of gift-giving gone wrong. While the older *King Leir* (printed in Bullough) uses here and there the language of giving and receiving favor (ll. 803–6, 900–901, 2020, 2048, 2142), Shakespeare greatly intensifies this language, granting it thematic importance.

4. In *The Gift in France*, Davis refers to *De officiis* and *De beneficiis* as "those great Roman guidebooks on gifts . . . [that] were pouring off the printing presses" (8). On the availability of these two Roman works, including in such English translations as Nicholas Haward's *The Line of Liberalitie dulie directinge the wel bestowing of benefites and reprehending the commonly used vice of ingratitude* (1569) and Arthur Golding's *The Woorke of the Excellent Philosopher Lucius Annaeus Seneca concerning Benefyting* (1578), see E. Catherine Dunn, *The Concept of Ingratitude in Renaissance English Moral Philosophy* (n.p.: Folcraft Press, 1946; rpt., 1969), 9–10. Dunn, it is worth noting, considers "the Renaissance concept of ingratitude considerably more complex than the Senecan one" (10), in large part through the influence of feudalism, which she characterizes as "the continuous circle of benefits and thankfulness between lord and vassal" (45–69, esp. 56). On the Senecan influence on Elizabethan views of ingratitude, see Joseph William Hewitt, "Some Aspects of the Treatment of Ingratitude in Greek and English Literature," *Transactions of the American Philological Association* 48 (1917): 37–48.

On the centrality of Seneca's *De beneficiis* to two other Shakespearean tragedies, see two articles by John M. Wallace: "*Timon of Athens* and the Three Graces: Shakespeare's Senecan Study," *Modern Philology* 83 (1986): 349–63; and "The Senecan Context of *Coriolanus*," *Modern Philology* 90 (1993): 465–78.

5. On the *munus* of *communitas*, see, for instance, Emile Benveniste, *Indo-European Language and Society*, trans. Elizabeth Palmer (London: Faber, 1973), 79–80 and 149–50. For his philological discussion of gift-giving, see 53–83.

6. Seneca, *De beneficiis*, in *Moral Essays*, trans. John W. Basore (Cambridge, MA: Harvard University Press, 1935; rpt., 2001), vol. 3. All quotations of Seneca are from this edition. Compare Cicero, *De officiis* 1.45–56 and 2.61–72; and see Aristotle, *Nicomachean Ethics* 5.5, 1133a1–6.

7. All references to the play, indicated in the text, are from *King Lear*, ed. R. A. Foakes, Arden Shakespeare (Walton-on-Thames, UK: Nelson, 1997), italics added. For similar language in the older *King Leir*, see, for instance, ll. 796–97, 803–4, 2198. On the terms *officium* and *beneficium*, see J. Hellegouarc'h, *Le vocabulaire latin des relations et des partis politiques sous la République* (Paris: Les Belles Lettres, 1963), 152–69.

8. See Jonas A. Barish and Marshall Waingrow, "'Service' in *King Lear*," *Shakespeare Quarterly* 9 (1958): 349: "Lear, who finds such talk of duty legalistic and heartless, as he finds Kent's kind of loyalty mutinous, fails to perceive that the reciprocal nature of the bond supplies the guarantee that it is not merely mechanical, but dynamic and vital. It proves in fact sufficiently vital to withstand Lear's onslaught upon it: both Kent and Cordelia continue to regard it as binding even after Lear has cut it."

9. On Gloucester's disobedience to his masters in serving the king, as well as on

disobedience as an approved form of service in this play and elsewhere in early modern literature, see Richard Strier, *Resistant Structures: Particularity, Radicalism, and Renaissance Texts* (Berkeley: University of California Press, 1995), 165–202.

10. On this cluster of words, see Laurence Berns, "Gratitude, Nature, and Piety in *King Lear*," *Interpretation* 3 (1972): 27–51, esp. 28. And see Benveniste, *Indo-European Language*, 159–62.

11. On the etymological relation between *munus* as the root of *communitas* and the verb *munire*, repeated in this passage, through *moenia*, Latin for "fortification" or "walls" (Sanskrit root mû, bind), see *A Latin Dictionary*, ed. C. T. Lewis and C. Short (New York: Oxford University Press, 2002), S. V. *Munus*. On the singular importance of gratitude as a duty, see, in addition, *De officiis* 1.47. For an earlier version of this account of man's frailty in comparison to the other animals, see Plato, *Protagoras* 320c–323a, which is, not incidentally, about the earliest formation of political community.

12. On the relation between *charis* and *gratia*, see Benveniste, *Indo-European Language*, 159–61; and on that between *charis* and *caritas*, see Lewis and Short. Whereas Paul's choice of *agapē* echoes the Septuagint as well as other Hellenistic sources, the Vulgate's choice of *caritas* as the Latin equivalent tightens the connection between Paul's own Stoicism and the Stoicism of early Latin Christianity. On Pauline *agapē*, see Margaret M. Mitchell, *Paul and the Rhetoric of Reconciliation* (Tübingen, Germany: J.C.B Mohr, 1991), 165–71, 270–79. On Paul's Stoicism, see Abraham J. Malherbe, *Paul and the Popular Philosophers* (Minneapolis: Fortress Press, 1989); and Troels Engberg-Pedersen, *Paul and the Stoics* (Edinburgh, UK: Westminster John Knox Press, 2000). On Stoic *caritas*, see *De finibus* 3.62–64, 3.69, 4.65–67; and *De officiis* 1.54–55. Christian *caritas*, in other words, receives its Stoic coloring from several quarters; and Shakespeare's charity can draw simultaneously on Christian and Stoic foundations.

13. On this episode, see Strier, *Resistant Structures*, 190–93. Writing not long after the first productions of Shakespeare's play, Hobbes reminds the English reader of the association between *grace* and *charity* and their relation to the discourse of benefits: "When the transferring of right, is not mutual; but one of the parties transferreth, in hope to gain thereby friendship, or service from another, or from his friends; or in hope to gain the reputation of charity, or magnanimity; or to deliver his mind from the pain of compassion; or in hope of reward in heaven; this is not contract, but GIFT, FREE-GIFT, GRACE: which words signify one and the same thing." See Thomas Hobbes, *Leviathan*, ed. J. C. A. Gaskin (Oxford: Oxford University Press, 1996), 1.14.12. And see, in addition, 1.11.7 and 1.15.16: "As justice dependeth on antecedent covenant; so does GRATITUDE depend on antecedent grace; that is to say, antecedent free gift: and is the fourth law of nature; which may be conceived in this form, *that a man which receiveth benefit from another of mere grace, endeavour that he which giveth it, have no reasonable cause to repent him of his good will.*"

14. On the extralegal nature of gratitude, see Berns, "Gratitude, Nature, and Piety," 29. In the older *King Leir*, Mumford, servant to the Gallian King, sets in high relief the extralegal nature of ingratitude by jesting about an "action of unkindness" (ll. 1851–53 in Bullough, *Narrative and Dramatic Sources*, 7:382):

For promise is debt, & by this hand you promised it me.

Therefore you owe it me, and you shall pay it me,

Or ile sue you upon an action of unkindnesse.

15. On the commonplace recognition in this philosophical tradition of the instinct of even brute beasts to return kindnesses received, see Dunn, *The Concept of Ingratitude*, 17–20; and on the interchangeability in sixteenth-century English of "unkindness" and "ingratitude," see 13–16. Like Seneca, Montaigne, whom Seneca has influenced everywhere in the *Essais* and whose influence on Shakespeare has been well documented, stresses that the great virtue of a benefactor is that he expects no reciprocity: "It is here that gratitude shows in its proper luster. A benefit is less richly bestowed when there is reciprocity and return." *The Complete Essays of Michel de Montaigne*, trans. Donald Frame (Stanford, CA: Stanford University Press, 1957), III.9, p. 762. For some striking resonances between Montaigne's *Essais* and *King Lear*, see II.8, pp. 283–84; and see also Peter Mack, "Rhetoric, Ethics, and Reading in the Renaissance," *Renaissance Studies* 19 (2005): 1–21.

16. See, for example, A. G. Harmon, *Eternal Bonds, True Contracts: Law and Nature in Shakespeare's Problem Plays* (Albany: State University of New York Press, 2004), 159–61; Paul W. Kahn, *Law and Love: The Trials of "King Lear"* (New Haven, CT: Yale University Press, 2000); Mark A. McDonald, *Shakespeare's "King Lear" with "The Tempest": The Discovery of Nature and the Recovery of Classical Natural Right* (Lanham, MD: University Press of America, 2004); R. S. White, *Natural Law in English Renaissance Literature* (Cambridge: Cambridge University Press, 1996), 185–215.

17. Cicero, *On the Commonwealth and On the Laws*, trans. and ed. James E. G. Zetzel (Cambridge: Cambridge University Press, 1999), 2:8, 132. In his introduction, Zetzel explains,

> The exposition of the idea and implications of natural law in Book 1 [of *On the Laws*] is the fullest exposition of Stoic doctrine on the subject that survives, the idea of the *cosmopolis* or world city. In this account positive human law, if it is to be considered true law, must be in accord with the natural law: that is to say, it must embody the principles of reason as reflected in the order of the world. That is, in effect, precisely the argument that Cicero seems to have made in Books 3 and 4 of *On the Commonwealth*, but here it is expressed in general terms rather than with specific relevance to Roman institutions. (xxii)

18. Cicero, *On the Laws*, 1:42–43, 120–21. Marcus's brother Quintus is made to agree (2:11, 133): "What is right and true is also eternal and neither rises nor falls with the texts in which legislation is written."

19. On the long-standing alliance between natural law and equity, see John Locke, *Second Treatise of Government*, ed. C. B. Macpherson (Indianapolis: Hackett, 1980), 2:8: "In the transgressing the law of nature, the offender declares himself to live by another rule than that of reason and common equity, which is that measure God has set to the actions of men, for their mutual security; and so he becomes dangerous to mankind, the tye, which is to secure them from injury and violence, being slighted and broken by him." And see Mark Fortier, *The Culture of Equity in Early Modern England* (Aldershot, UK: Ashgate, 2005); White, *Natural Law*; and my *Poetic and Legal Fiction in the Aristotelian Tradi-*

tion (Princeton, NJ: Princeton University Press, 1986). For the contemporary conflicts between the common law and courts of equity under James I that occasioned the "mock trial" from the Folio, see B. J. Sokol and Mary Sokol, "Shakespeare and the English Equity Jurisdiction: *The Merchant of Venice* and the Two Texts of *King Lear*," *Review of English Studies* 50 (1999): 417–39.

20. On the relation between /l/ and /r/ in these languages, see Benveniste, *Indo-European Language*, 309–11, whose use of French for illustration foreshadows the argument that follows (310): "In French it is not permissible to confuse *roi* and *loi* ('king' and 'law'), for r and l are certainly two different phonemes, each of which has its place within the phonetic system." On Indo-Iranian, see Leonard R. Palmer, *Descriptive and Comparative Linguistics: A Critical Introduction* (London: Faber, 1972), 383–84. On the behavior of liquids in various languages, see Keren Rice, "Liquid Relationships," *Toronto Working Papers in Linguistics* 24 (2005): 31–44.

21. Bradin Cormack, "Tender Distance: Latinity and Desire in Shakespeare's Sonnets," in *A Companion to Shakespeare's Sonnets*, ed. Michael Schoenfeldt (London: Blackwell, 2007), 244–45.

22. So Viola in *Twelfth Night* writes "loyal cantons of contemnèd love" (1.5.289), and Lysander in *A Midsummer Night's Dream* vows to "end life when I end loyalty" (2.2.63). For the legal dimension of the language of affect, see my *The Renaissance Rediscovery of Intimacy* (Chicago: University of Chicago Press, 2012).

For the influence of French on the formation of English, see David Burnley, "Lexis and Semantics," in *The Cambridge History of the English Language*, ed. Norman Blake (Cambridge: Cambridge University Press, 1992), 2:423–33.

23. For the larger question of loyalty in the play and its manifestation under certain circumstances in disobedience, see Strier, *Resistant Structures*, 165–202.

24. At l. 2135, King Leir acknowledges Perillus's "loyal love" when the latter offers his own body to sustain the starving king (Bullough, *Narrative and Dramatic Sources*, 7:389), whereas Perillus, in soliloquy, complains (ll. 767–68), "Trust not alliance; but trust strangers rather, / Since daughters prove disloyall to the father" (7:356).

25. In "The Two Natures in *King Lear*," *Accent* 8 (1947): 51–59, Robert B. Heilman refers to this address as "punning praise" (54), but he does not gloss the pun; and the editor's note in the Arden edition (222) misses the point in ascribing both law and nature to the second term, "natural," leaving the first term, "loyal," unnoted. In *Law and Love*, on the other hand, Paul Kahn assumes, if he does not state outright, the relation between loyalty and legality (86): "Loyalty is only another way of expressing the claim of duty and law. Nature has quite literally given way to law. Edmund has become the father; he is the Earl of Gloucester."

In Sidney's *Arcadia*, the blind king, the model for Gloucester, reverses the Shakespearean pair of terms after recognizing his bastard son's treachery, by referring to him as "that unlawful and unnatural sonne of mine." Bullough, *Narrative and Dramatic Sources*, 7:405.

26. On the legality of the exchange between Edmund and Cornwall in 3.5, see McDonald, *"King Lear" with "The Tempest,"* 121–22. If Edmund is the only character described by either himself or others as "loyal," he is also, according to Jonas A. Barish and Mar-

shall Waingrow, "'Service' in *King Lear*," "the one with the word 'service' most often on his tongue" (350) in a play where the concept of service "does not wholly deny the reciprocal element in the relationship, but . . . makes the reciprocity contingent; it turns it into a legal transaction, a *quid pro quo*. . . . The bond becomes a document negotiable by a bond salesman, instead of a vital covenant expressive of mutual love and responsibility" (353). In *Resistant Structures*, Strier's subtle reading of the various kinds of service in the play virtually excludes Edmund, who, despite his numerous declarations to the contrary, actually serves no one but himself (198).

27. See, for instance, *3 Henry VI*, 4.7.44; *Richard III*, 3.3.3–4; *Henry V*, 1.2.127; *Henry VIII*, 3.2.180; *Macbeth*, 1.4.22; *Coriolanus*, 5.6.142.

28. See, for instance, *Richard III*, 1.2.7, 1.3.125, 4.4.211; *Titus Andronicus*, 5.1.49; *Richard II*, 1.1.58, 2.1.118; *King John*, 5.1.11; *Cymbeline*, 4.2.174. And see the *Oxford English Dictionary Online*, s.v. "royal," which gives "Of blood" as the first definition.

29. See, in addition, ll. 221 and 1170.

30. See, for instance, *Lateinisches Etymologisches Wörterbuch*, ed. A. Walde and J. B. Hofmann (Heidelberg, 1982); the *Oxford Latin Dictionary*, ed. P. G. W. Glare (New York: Oxford University Press, 1982); and the *Dictionnaire Etymologique de la Langue Latine*, ed. Jacques André (Paris, 1985). See also Mario Pei, *The Families of Words* (New York: Harper, 1962), 220–23; and Benveniste, *Indo-European Language*, 307–26.

31. See Benveniste, *Indo-European Language*, esp. 311–12, who concludes (312): "The Indo-European *rex* was much more a religious than a political figure. His mission was not to command, to exercise power but to draw up rules, to determine what was in the proper sense 'right' ('straight'). It follows that the *rex*, as thus defined, was more akin to a priest than a sovereign. It is this type of kingship which was preserved by the Celts and the Italic peoples on the one hand and the Indic on the other." On *regere finem*, see 307 and 311–12.

32. See Pei, *Families of Words*, 220–22; and Benveniste, *Indo-European Language*, 307–11.

33. For the etymology of Greek *nomos*, see *A Greek Dictionary*, 9th ed., ed. H. G. Liddell, R. Scott, H. S. Jones, and R. McKenzie (New York: Oxford University Press, 1996); Benveniste, *Indo-European Language*, 69–70; and Cicero, *On the Laws*, 1:19, 111–12, where he offers an alternative etymology for *lex*: "And therefore they think that law (*lex*) is judgment (*prudentiam*), the effect of which is such as to order people to behave rightly and forbid them to do wrong; they think that its name in Greek is derived from giving to each his own (*suum cuique tribuendo*), while I think that in Latin it is derived from choosing (*legendo*)."

34. Cicero, *On Duties*, trans. M. T. Griffin and E. M. Atkins (Cambridge: Cambridge University Press, 1991), 2:41–42.

35. Seneca, *Epistulae Morales*, trans. Richard M. Gummere, 3 vols. (1920; rpt., Cambridge, MA: Harvard University Press, 1970).

36. For Seneca's views of kingship, especially in *De clementia*, in opposition to Cicero's, see Stacey, *Roman Monarchy*, 23–72. On the reciprocity between *lex* and *rex* in the English legal tradition, see Henry of Bracton, *On the Laws and Customs of England*, ed. and

trans. Samuel E. Thorne (Cambridge, MA: Belknap Press of Harvard University Press, 1968), 2:33, who insists that "law makes the king. Let him therefore bestow upon the law what the law bestows upon him, namely rule and power. For there is no *rex* where will rules rather than *lex*." In "The State of Law in Richard II," *Shakespeare Quarterly* 34 (1983): 5–17, Donna B. Hamilton, in addition to citing this passage (11), notes its invocation by both Hooker and Bacon (n19).

37. On the dramatic pairing of the two invocations of Nature, see Berns, "Gratitude, Nature, and Piety," 39–40; John F. Danby, *Shakespeare's Doctrine of Nature: A Study of "King Lear"* (London: Faber, 1961), 31–43; Robert B. Heilman, *This Great Stage: Image and Structure in "King Lear"* (Baton Rouge: Louisiana State University Press, 1948), 115–30; and Heilman, "The Two Natures," 52–53 and 58. For the complementarity of Lear and Edmund based on their corresponding "love test," see Joseph Alulis, "The Education of the Prince in Shakespeare's *King Lear*," *Interpretation* 21 (1994): 373–90, esp. 386. For the skill of the bastard son of the source, like Edmund, at finding "the places whence arguments might grow," see Bullough, *Narrative and Dramatic Sources*, 7:407.

38. On the place of primogeniture in the play, see Ronald W. Cooley, "Kent and Primogeniture in *King Lear*," *Studies in English Literature* 48 (2008): 327–48.

39. In *Everybody's Shakespeare: Reflections Chiefly on the Tragedies* (Lincoln: University of Nebraska Press, 1993), Maynard Mack characterizes the "remorseless process" in *King Lear* as one that "begs us to seek the meaning of our human fate not in what becomes of us, but in what we become" (180). For a reading of the opening scene that acknowledges Lear as "the greatest of Shakespeare's kings" and argues for both the political savvy of Lear's original plan for dividing the kingdom and the undoing of such political planning, see Harry V. Jaffa, "The Limits of Politics: *King Lear*, Act I, Scene i," in *Shakespeare's Politics*, ed. Allan Bloom (New York: Basic Books, 1964), 113–45. While disagreeing with Jaffa's (and my own) judgment of Lear, Strier, following Jaffa, makes a compelling case in *Resistant Structures* (177–82) for the plan of division. See also Charles Spinosa, "'The name and all th' addition': King Lear's Opening Scene and the Common-Law Use," *Shakespeare Studies* 23 (1995): 146–86, esp. 160–64.

40. For readings of the play that take account of Lear's kingly nature, see, for instance, Roger Warren, "The Folio Omission of the Mock Trial: Motives and Consequences," in *The Division of the Kingdoms: Shakespeare's Two Versions of "King Lear*," ed. Gary Taylor and Michael Warren (Oxford: Oxford University Press, 1983), 45–57; and Danby, *Shakespeare's Doctrine of Nature*, who places *King Lear* in Shakespeare's final category of plays about kingship, where the "king in fact should be also a king in nature" (200).

41. Shakespeare presses the same point when he has the usurper Macbeth fear Banquo's "royalty of nature" (3.1.50). On nobility (*nobilitas*) as rooted in one's nature or one's character as opposed to one's pedigree and thus applicable to servants as well as masters, see Seneca, *De beneficiis*, 3.28.1–4. Book 3 also treats the benefits that children can provide to parents and servants to masters.

42. On this assumption of the royal plural, which Albany himself assumes for his authoritative act of passing on the right to rule (5.3.317), see the editor's note (392). On Edgar as Lear's counterpart, see Alulis, "The Education of the Prince," 373–77. Without

citing Albany's lines in recognition of Edgar's natural royalty, Alulis does argue for Edgar as the play's embodiment of "a good or royal character" (374) who is prepared for rule by the dramatic action (382).

On the differences between Edgar's role in Quarto and Folio, see two articles by Michael J. Warren: "Quarto and Folio *King Lear* and the Interpretation of Albany and Edgar," in *Shakespeare: Pattern of Excelling Nature*, ed. David Bevington and Jay L. Halio (Newark: University of Delaware Press, 1976), 95–107; and "The Diminution of Kent," in Taylor and Warren, *The Division of the Kingdoms*, 59–73, where Warren reads the changes in the Folio to play down Kent's role while emphasizing "Edgar's triumph" (70). In "Edgar: Once and Future King," in *Some Facets of King Lear: Essays in Prismatic Criticism*, ed. Rosalie L. Colie and F. T. Flahiff (Toronto: University of Toronto Press, 1974), 221–37, Flahiff makes a compelling case that Shakespeare's earliest audiences would have identified Edgar, who is referred to as Lear's godson, whom the King himself named (2.1.91–92), as the royal King Edgar who enjoyed "an extraordinary reputation in Tudor and Stuart England" (231) and who was "held up as a model for Elizabeth, for James I, and for Charles I" (232). Flahiff also reminds his reader that Edgar's "coming to power in the play is Shakespeare's innovation on his historical and dramatic sources" (227).

43. This surrender of a debased *lex* to an ennobled *rex* would, to say the least, have engaged the audience at the play's first recorded performance on December 26, 1606, at Whitehall, where the principal spectator was the king himself. On the king's attendance at this first recorded performance, see Bullough, *Narrative and Dramatic Sources*, 7:269; and Gary Taylor, "Monopolies, Show Trials, Disaster, and Invasion: *King Lear* and Censorship," in Taylor and Warren, *The Divisions of the Kingdoms*, 75–119, esp. 78, where he speculates that "it might have been" the play's première. On the topicality of the play's handling of kingship to James's reign and the direct interest he took in it, see Annabel Patterson, *Censorship and Interpretation: The Conditions of Writing and Reading in Early Modern England* (Madison: University of Wisconsin Press, 1984), 58–73. On James's controversial views on the relationship between kingship and law and his controversy with Coke, see Sokol and Sokol, "Shakespeare and the English Equity Jurisdiction," 428–39. And see also Nigel Smith, "Forms of Kingship in *King Lear*," in *Critical Essays on King Lear*, ed. Linda Cookson and Bryan Longhrey (Glasgow, UK: Longman, 1988), 31–41.

STANLEY CAVELL

SAYING IN *THE MERCHANT OF VENICE*

Invited to think whether I had something to contribute to a discussion of some aspect of Shakespeare in relation to law and perhaps to the argumentative or confrontational registers of everyday life, I was put in mind of several mostly unfruitful efforts of mine over the years to consider why Shakespeare presents trial-like exchanges in the context of the unending and endlessly intimate, not necessarily hate-filled, conversations between Christians and Jews. I had, for instance, sought to articulate my sense that in *The Merchant of Venice* Shakespeare is portraying his command of, or his service to, language as such—to the fact of speech as such, as ineluctably claiming or denying, or, say, establishing or modifying or rejecting, in every breath, the right to, the standing deserving of, human exchange. A way of specifying this observation is to say that understanding the point of offering and accepting excuses is preparation for understanding the point of the law of torts, that knowing the force of making and breaking promises measures the seriousness of entering and challenging contracts, that being subject to hope and to trust fashions the space of prayer. Most particularly, I want in what follows to continue my efforts to call attention to the familiar philosophical presentation of the so-called problem of knowing other minds as neglecting, or occluding, the problem of being known, say, acknowledged, by another.[1] *The Merchant of Venice*, most single-mindedly among Shakespeare's works, displays, to the point of caricature, the fact that the failure to be known (hence eventually to know another) is not fundamentally a matter of ignorance (an epistemological lack) but a gesture of rejection (a moral stance).

Can Shakespeare's judgment ever be wrong? I have never satisfied myself about the ending of *The Merchant of Venice*, reading it or attending it. Shylock's defeat has kept seeming to me to be abruptly pat and his thwarting and grief to go insufficiently expressed. I seem to recall, or recall the description of, a performance of Laurence Olivier's in which, after Shylock's expulsion at the end of act 4, he is heard to utter a long scream. But I am sufficiently convinced by Shylock's taking his departure on saying he is sick that I do not imagine him to have available energy enough to scream. I perceive him, with his penultimate words—"I am content" (4.1.391)—as spiritually disabled, without

221

recognizable emotion or comprehension, not even angry or contemptuous.[2] I do not regard this as a particularly contentious observation (it is probably not clear enough to be so), but I am concerned to understand what causes this perception and to ask how it might plausibly be played.

How do we get from endlessly expressed murderousness to a virtually immediate acceptance of a quibbling, at best, interpretation of "the law" that supposedly concerns the taking of "a pound of flesh" (a matter it is hard to understand as having any established precedent in law)? Even if a law existed in Venice using words such as taking or spilling or wishing to spill Christian blood (since Portia doesn't tell the unvarnished truth about almost anything else, why believe her implicitly here?), there is room for interpretation that makes these descriptions equivalent to killing or seeking to kill. But on that understanding, Shylock ought to be able to deny this as his motive for demanding his "bond."

What then suddenly, as if physically, deprives him of all protest or contest, reducing him, as it were, essentially to an all-suffering Jew, a creature without the right to speak? It was my impression of Shylock's overly swift reduction and acquiescence to silence and ruin and departure as suggesting a fatal sense of the loss of the right, hence of the power, of speech, in the general context of a legalistic process, prepared or backed by a scene of blind interpretations of the externals of three caskets, that set me thinking about this play as taking up the uniquely human fate, explicit since Aristotle, in being the animal possessed of language, fated to speak, that is, to converse, more controlled by words and their (other) speakers than controlling of them. And if responsible for speech, then responsible for silence, that is, for the refusal to speak, whose consequences equally famously interest Shakespeare (e.g., Cordelia and Lady Macbeth).

This was not the first time the right to speak has come up in my work. I have, for example, recurrently been moved to recognize, as I put the thought, that philosophy does not speak first.[3] (This is, I suppose, my version of Wittgenstein's perception that philosophy does not advance theses.[4] Or as I sometimes have urged the point: philosophy knows only what everyone knows.[5]) Perhaps once more, reading a play of Shakespeare's will help arrive at fresh tuitions for intuitions.[6] My first impulse was simply to check my impression that the word *say* occurs an unusually large number of times in *The Merchant of Venice*. My Shakespeare concordance shows the number to be large but not uniquely so. Then I considered further that my impression could have been formed by the occurrence in the play of other terms calling the fact of speech to attention. A not particularly rigorous search produces, beyond the words *say* and *speak*, the following terms: *talk, bid, exclaim, utter, presage, pray, tell, swear, promise, call, whisper, cite, praise, question, answer, inquire, urge, gossip, report, voice, pronounce,* and *eloquence*. I shall not undertake to compare this array of human possibilities of articulation with their notation in the rest of the Shakespearean corpus. I am immediately moved to express my surprised sense that the play precisely presents the fate of humans and their capacity for speech as incessantly demanding attention and calling for pertinent response from one another. As if we are the law for one another.

A perfectly decisive emphasis on word and sentence in the play is present in its climactic, mortal point turning on an interpretation of words, namely of the now too-familiar "pound of flesh." Or, it is rather more accurate to say that it turns not on interpreting the words but on literalizing or stressing them past the possibility of reference and verification. (This result uncannily to my mind resembles the philosopher's denial that we see a material object on considering that we do not really, or strictly, or literally see all of it.) "Pound" is said by Portia to mean one pound determined within the difference of a hair or a grain (what could measure the measurer?); and this quantity of "flesh," more famously, is taken explicitly to require cutting into a piece of living flesh without shedding blood—as likely as running without standing. Shylock's response is to accept without argument Portia's interpretations as faithful representations of what he calls "the law" and to proceed at once to commence bargaining—increasingly weakly—for the former, more normal, return on his loan.

This instant collapse is what I have had recurrent trouble in understanding. Are we seriously to understand this as his believing Portia's testimony and reasoning? And is this because he is so foreign to, or alienated from, his surrounding culture that nothing a Gentile says makes much sense in any case? But where has the daring gone that proposed his surrealistic bond of the notarized pound of flesh? I find I can only assume that he is not convinced by Portia's mock Talmudism but is, at a stroke, spiritually overborne, rendered helpless or hopeless to expect mere tolerance of his existence, let alone whatever is to be called justice. He is incapable of so much as questioning the forced, dubious meaningfulness of Portia's surrealist interpretations. But rendered helpless, overborne, by what?

I note first the possibility of envisioning and performing this reading. The concluding, retreating protests on Shylock's part against his destruction can all be imagined to be voiced by him in an increasing state of bewilderment or dream. Coming to earth in the everyday realm of principal and bond and forfeiture invokes his previous form of life as having become unreal in comparison with the fantasy of disfiguring a voluptuously hated enemy. Even when he arrives at Portia's demand to acknowledge his stripped state, he uses the words "I am content" (4.1.390), which are repeated from Antonio's previous speech (4.1.378), as if manifesting that even the possibility of originating words is past his invention. If nothing matters, there is no cause for speech.

But the sense of my claim is that the voiding of Shylock's hold on an entitlement to speech and existence is not gradual—only his manifestations of dissociation from the world are comparatively gradual—but is in calamitous effect with his first response to Portia's initial interpretation or dictation of the laws of Venice. He responds to her merely by forming the question "Is that the law?" (Call this the essential Jewish question—but now voiced not as the route to divine acceptance but as the edict of man's rejection.) If this sense of sudden inner collapse is accurate, there is something in Portia's words of interpretation that has caused it. What she has announced is

> This bond doth give thee here no jot of blood.
> The words expressly are "a pound of flesh."
> . . . But in the cutting it, if thou dost shed
> One drop of Christian blood, thy lands and goods
> Are by the laws of Venice confiscate. (4.1.303–8)

Am I alone in wondering why apparently it is not given to Shylock to contest this reading, say, to insist that everyone knows blood must be implied in the bond and not be understood as a separate element meant to make the bond effectively unachievable?[7]

I find my answer to be that this was not known and understood, or rather its imagination was unavailable, to Shylock, so that confronted with it, or opened to it, he is, let us say, appalled. How could he not have known and imagined this inevitable consequence of his demand, as if for the first time awakened to the horror of his wish? When Portia cautions Shylock to have a surgeon in attendance to prevent the possibility of Antonio's bleeding to death, Shylock asks whether the possibility is named in the bond, and discovers that it is not. This may be taken as drawing Shylock's attention to blood, but it may also be taken as showing his obliviousness to its existence unless it is officially "nominated." Portia agrees that it is not named expressly ("not so expressed") but adds that "'Twere good you do so much for charity" (4.1.256–58). That charity here is implied to be Christian (as moments earlier "the quality of mercy" was so taken, in explicit opposition to how the Jew thinks of justice) is an implication as clear as that blood is implied in cutting living flesh.

At this point, so I propose, with the knife in hand before Antonio's bosom laid bare, implying blood, Shylock perceives the madness in his fantastic fury;

he has no quarrel with this man. Disfiguring him, or perhaps anyone, is no recompense for the injustices Jews learn to live with and perhaps become disfigured by. I imagine the knife to fall, as Shylock's mind and body fall slack, going through now irrelevant and diminishing memories of motion and interest. He cannot, even if he had thought to say it, claim that blood was irrelevant to his invented bond, because he now sees that Christian blood is what he wanted.

This is, I am not unaware, bound to seem to some, to many, far-fetched, at least at first. So this may be a good time to go a step further in accounting for what I think of as Shylock's imagination of horror. I do not know the relevant Jewish law, but I know from my childhood the Jewish custom of cooking (typically boiling) meat until, explicitly, it is well enough done to be cut without showing blood. The step further is to suggest that in preparing to carve into the Christian's body, Shylock is imagining (not now, something I suggested in an earlier encounter with the play, carving the Christian into a—circumcised—Jew),[8] but now imagining feasting from that body, cannibalizing it (an act explicitly found worth forbidding, I believe, in Jewish law), in that way incorporating, internalizing, the Christian. This realm of reasonably horrible association is something I am helped to by the play's unexplained shift in specifying the place from which the pound of flesh may or must be taken.

When Shylock initially proposes his "merry bond" (1.3.172) at the end of act 1, he arranges with Antonio to meet at the notary's, where the condition expressed will be to

> let the forfeit
> Be nominated for an equal pound
> Of your fair flesh, to be cut off and taken
> In what part of your body pleaseth me. (1.3.147–50)

But when in act 4 Shylock's knife is out, and Portia, disguised as a judge, draws Shylock into pressing the claim that she will suddenly prove undoes him according to a Venetian law regulating behavior between Jews and Venetians, Portia declares to Antonio: "You must prepare your bosom for his knife" (4.1.242). Shylock soon leaps in for extra and indeed sterner emphasis:

> Ay, his breast.
> So says the bond, doth it not, noble judge?
> "Nearest his heart"—Those are the very words.

To which Portia responds: "It is so" (4.1.249–52). But again, we have only her word for this, out of her impersonation of authority and her capacity for invention.

Let us consider that this repeated, intensifying conjunction of the knife that is suddenly determined—as if from nowhere—to cut into the body in a place "nearest the heart" invokes, perhaps mocks, Saint Paul's idea of circumcising the heart.[9] The point of this invocation would be to bring to attention Paul's making explicit, in Romans, that the claim to being a Jew is not validated by noting an outward circumcision but amounts to the claim of inward circumcision, of possessing a circumcised heart, something the fact of outward circumcision most patently cannot assure the presence of and, Paul adds, the absence of outward circumcision cannot deny. (Not wholly unlike the relation between the outward appearance and the inward content of a casket.)

With Saint Paul's criterion in mind, if I ask myself who in *The Merchant of Venice* figures as a Jew (it is not unusual, I believe, to find people slipping into thinking the title designates Shylock), the only candidate to satisfy the idea is Antonio, who offers his life and body for his friend. Then the joke, if you like, of the play's title is that the merchant of Venice—or rather a merchant of Venice—designated in the play's Dramatis Personae to be Antonio—is, after all, or before all, according arguably to Paul (the Christian Apostle), the play's Jew. (It would not destroy the point—rather on the contrary—if one finds that this equally constitutes Antonio as the play's only true Christian.) I find this also, after countless exposures to the question, to give some access, more pertinent than any I have heard, to the lines with which Antonio opens the play:

> In sooth, I know not why I am so sad.
> It wearies me, you say it wearies you,
> But how I caught it, found it, or came by it,
> What stuff 'tis made of, whereof it is born,
> I am to learn;
> And such a want-wit sadness makes of me
> That I have much ado to know myself. (1.1.1–7)

The cause would understandably be hard to know in any of the ways Antonio lists, if his heart is circumcised. This is a condition, I suppose, since inherently unclaimable for oneself, unverifiable for oneself. And it seems to account for Antonio's combination of preoccupation and carelessness with himself, engrossed with and, so to speak, bored by his inescapable suffering, puzzled by some difference, undefined to himself, from his fellows. (I gather that a modern interpretation of Antonio's sadness relates it to indications of his homosexual attraction to Bassanio. Without denying the evidence for the attraction, I do not see how this is understood to create a feeling of pervasive and

226 STANLEY CAVELL

indecipherable sadness. Unrequited attraction may be a more plausible case, but that is surely no less easy to decipher in oneself.)

Then how are we to understand a play that features the interpretation of law, and ponders the difference between Christian and Jew, to permeate itself with terms for modes of speech? Salerio answers Antonio's opening expression of weary unease by observing, "Your mind is tossing on the ocean" (1.1.8), but Salerio can only imagine this unsettled condition as a concern about the fate of merchandise. Whereas the irreducible and perpetual promptings of the conversation of cities in the Western world demand our keeping afloat, beyond imagining the fate of moneys (the fortunes awaiting fortunes), in looking for settlements of so many strifes and injuries we inevitably cause each other as our paths and our decisions cross and we are entangled, within finite spaces, in one another's lives. More particularly, The Merchant of Venice stresses mysterious questions of publicly validating our choices in the exclusions of marriage and hence the exclusiveness of families and in the undying perplexities of the life and death of God shaped by the unholy and limitless crisis of Western civilization lodged in Christianity's birth out of Judaism.

It seems familiar by now to take up the question whether the play is anti-Semitic or whether it is about what it is to be anti-Semitic. The problem for me in understanding the play's conversation along this line is that it seems to take too much for granted that we are apt or deft in recognizing expressions of anti-Semitism and feeling confident in the justice, or perhaps the mercy, in our responding to it, or in resisting response to it, in its conventional or in novel forms. Over the years in writing my autobiography, recently brought to an end and published, I have included a range of such uneasy encounters over my eight decades of memory.[10] (I began the record imagining that I did not want to be alive when it came out. This thought pretty thoroughly vanished as I grew more and more interested in, fascinated by, the sheer facts of what survives in a life, and in what forms.) For a certain minimal concrete orientation here, I abbreviate from the autobiography two trivial but lucid expressions of the attitude coming my way from my high school years.

The immediate background is that my father and mother, during the Great Depression, had moved back and forth several times from Atlanta, Georgia, to Sacramento, California. My father had lost his reputedly swanky jewelry store, and the large and for me boisterously happy household of my mother's musical family was broken apart. An adventurous brother of my father who had sought his fortune out West and had established, of all things given this present exposition, the largest and busiest pawn shop in Sacramento, offered my father a job, which was gratefully if humiliatingly accepted. When I was fifteen years old, roughly two miserable years younger than my classmates because of the "reward" of being what was called "skipped" two grades (a more accurate description would have been "sent into exile"), I still bore the obviously Jewish name Goldstein, given to my father's family—when my father was himself something like fifteen years old—by immigration officers upon their arriving in New York from Bialystok, on the ground that the officers could not spell the family's actual name, Kavelierusky (or Kavelierisky—I have seen it both ways). The following year, turned sixteen, I in effect took back the stolen name by legally changing it to an Anglicization of the opening two syllables of the Russian name, whereupon I went down the road ninety miles to the university in Berkeley, as it were anonymously. Why my family acceded to this drastic early self-transformation (because of my age, they were legally required to approve it) is a considerable story.

The first of the encounters I have in mind is as follows. Friends of mine who played in the Sacramento high school dance band, of which I was the first and last student to become the leader (the faculty sponsor of the band had, without warning to us, been drafted into the army), proposed to nominate me for membership in their high school fraternity. This was, at this point in my life, perfectly irrelevant to me, but trying not to offend the friendly offices of my companions, I asked them not to go ahead with this, on the ground that while they might not think so, some one or other among the members of their group would in a secret vote cast a blackball against me, and this would cause embarrassment and unpredictable difficulty for us. They protested that this could not happen, that I was oversensitive and unjust to their comrades. So I relented and the blackball promptly came, along with embarrassments that proved to be permanent, sometimes it seemed because we did not have, and did not know how to acquire, the language in which to modify them. The second contretemps, rather more imaginative, concerns the moment at which, walking with a member of the band on a path across the high school's large playing field, as we approached a student I did not know, my companion called out to him not to fail to get tickets for the Senior Ball, where the Goldstein band would be playing. The boy's response was to touch together the five fingertips of one hand forming a kind of claw, and with it pull on his nose to lengthen it. My companion's baffled response was to baffle all three of us by introducing me to the fellow.

Of course I count such incidents to be common as dirt, certainly not lethal, hardly even consequential; yet they occur to me after some sixty-five summers. It is equally common, I believe, to take it that Shylock's extremities of response, his unforgiving giving of offense, is a caricature of being a Jew. One can hardly fail to see that his behavior is extreme, but I do not think of the violent passions his behavior encases as themselves caricatures. The clearest evidence I perceive as caricaturing and discounting his passions would be the inevitably quoted speeches (wrongly credited as fact, or remembered as dramatic fact) in which Salerio and Solanio are pleased to elaborate a report of Shylock hysterically juxtaposing the disappearance of his daughter and the theft of his ducats (2.8.13–24), always interpreted, so far as I know, as suggesting that Shylock vulgarly equates these losses. This is no doubt intended by those amused and engaged reporters, but it seems to me an imposition of caricature. The relation for Shylock of his daughter to his ducats is that she has stolen his ducats (as it were, her eventual dowry), thereby marking that he has lost not alone his daughter but his trust in his daughter's feeling for him, as she hurries away from him leaving behind her trust in him.

The inability to recognize and to acknowledge (which means, as I have elsewhere argued, to avoid) the unpleasant Shylock's incoherent grief is something I understand the play to offer as an image of the perpetual failure to recognize the unfathomable reach and spread of lethal radiation in racial distortion and fumbling. Shakespeare's play has struck me as unique in the fullness of this perception. This is how I answer my opening question about Shakespeare's judgment in his calibration of Shylock's decline in the scene of his exclusion or expulsion. I take it that we are to perceive Shylock's ending, his continued mere repetition of words he once upon a time could mean and could use to effect in confronting others, as showing him now working to cover the vanishing powers, or the increasing consciousness of the emptiness, the suffocation, of his possibility of speech; put otherwise, showing him becoming drained of the effort to continue assuming, to the extent he has ever assumed, participation in the human.

NOTES

1. See especially Stanley Cavell, "Knowing and Acknowledging" and "The Avoidance of Love: A Reading of *King Lear*," in *Must We Mean What We Say? A Book of Essays* (New York: Scribner's, 1969), 238–66, 267–353; and part 4 of Cavell, *The Claim of Reason: Wittgenstein, Skepticism, Morality, and Tragedy* (Oxford: Clarendon Press, 1979), 329–496.

2. All line citations to *The Merchant of Venice* are to William Shakespeare, *The Complete Works*, ed. Stanley Wells and Gary Taylor, 2nd ed. (Oxford: Clarendon Press, 2005).

3. See Stanley Cavell, *Cities of Words* (Cambridge, MA: Harvard University Press, 2004), 324.

4. Ludwig Wittgenstein, *Philosophical Investigations*, trans. G. E. M. Anscombe (New York: Macmillan, 1953), sections 127–28.

5. See Stanley Cavell, *Philosophical Passages: Wittgenstein, Emerson, Austin, Derrida* (Cambridge, MA: Blackwell, 1995), 23; also Cavell, *Emerson's Transcendental Etudes* (Stanford, CA: Stanford University Press, 2003), 3.

6. See Stanley Cavell, *Disowning Knowledge in Seven Plays of Shakespeare* (Cambridge: Cambridge University Press, 2003), 4–5.

7. On the role of blood in the contract, see the divergent views of Richard Posner and of Charles Fried in their essays in this volume [editors' note].

8. See Cavell, *The Claim of Reason*, 478–81.

9. On this possibility, see James Shapiro, *Shakespeare and the Jews* (New York: Columbia University Press, 1996), 113–30 [editors' note].

10. Stanley Cavell, *Little Did I Know: Excerpts from Memory* (Stanford, CA: Stanford University Press, 2010).

MARIE THERESA O'CONNOR

A BRITISH PEOPLE
CYMBELINE AND THE ANGLO-SCOTTISH
UNION ISSUE

When Shakespeare wrote *Cymbeline* (c. 1608–10),[1] King James VI and I's project to unite Scotland and England into Britain seemed politically dead, having come to a close with a general legislative defeat and one judicial victory. In brief, on James's accession to the English throne in 1603, he had been king of Scotland for nearly thirty-six years, and one of his foremost ambitions was the union of his two kingdoms. This ambition was thwarted in 1607 when the English House of Commons defeated the prospect of a legislative union.[2] James is generally regarded as having achieved one significant Union victory, which would have been anticipated or settled by the time of *Cymbeline*'s composition: Calvin's Case.[3] The case stemmed from James's contention that all Scots and Englishmen born after James's English accession, referred to as the "*post nati*," were automatically mutually naturalized. Calvin's Case, which was decided in 1608 by England's highest judicial authority, the Exchequer Chamber, and reported by England's famous common-law jurist Sir Edward Coke, affirmed that the Scottish *post nati* were naturalized in England.[4]

Some critics have interpreted *Cymbeline*'s protagonist, the suggestively named Posthumus, as allegorizing the Scottish *post nati*, in particular, as paying a compliment to James's success in the outcome of Calvin's Case. The play's action begins when Posthumus, a poor gentleman orphaned in infancy and taken in by King Cymbeline, is banished by Cymbeline for marrying Cymbeline's daughter, Imogen. The play concludes with Posthumus's return to court and Cymbeline's apparent acceptance of Posthumus and Imogen's marriage (5.5.453). In a detailed reading, Leah S. Marcus demonstrates how Posthumus evokes the Scottish *post nati* through the many correspondences between Posthumus's circumstances and the circumstances of Scots in England: Posthumus is a gentleman of Cymbeline's bedchamber, a position associated with the Scots during the Union issue and a cause of much jealousy among the English; Posthumus is poor, which was how anti-Unionists characterized the Scots; Posthumus's surname, Leonatus, links him to James, whose heraldry featured the lion; and Posthumus's marriage to Imogen, whose name recalls Innogen (the wife of Brutus, Britain's founder), may be seen as allegorizing the Union, as well as glancing at James's attempts to foster connectedness between the Scots and the English through intermarriage. Marcus further argues that Posthumus's name evokes the Scottish *post nati*'s quality of being "born after" James's English accession.[5] For Marcus, Posthumus's "alienation and restoration" over the course of the play parallels the Scottish *post nati*'s alienation from "their king and from the center of government when James assumed the English crown" and their restoration per Calvin's Case.[6] Constance Jordan agrees, figuring Posthumus as the Scottish *post nati* "about to be integrated into the English body politic."[7]

I follow these critics in seeing a rich connection between Posthumus and the Scottish *post nati*. I will, however, aim to show that the play should not necessarily be read as celebrating the restoration or integration of the Scottish *post nati*, because Calvin's Case was not necessarily a Union victory. More specifically, I will argue that there were two visions of Britain during the Union issue, a pro-Union vision that supported a legally and politically equal British citizenry and that was indebted to Roman citizenship ideology, and an anti-Union vision that supported English hegemony. Despite the seemingly pro-Union outcome of Calvin's Case, the reasoning of Coke's report actually advanced the anti-Union vision, contributing to, rather than resolving, the uncertainty of the *post nati*'s status following the Union's legislative defeat.

In this essay I key Posthumus's belatedness not, per Marcus, to the *post nati*'s quality of being born after James's accession but to their quality of being a people outliving the Union that allegedly created them.[8] The Union's legislative defeat, I contend, rendered the *post nati* a "posthumus" people—with the lingering potential to be seen as the embodiment of an equal British citizenry but the competing susceptibility, through focus on the Scottish *post nati*, to be recast as a vehicle for English imperialism. In claiming that *Cymbeline* explores this uncertain afterlife, I contest two critical tendencies in the scholarship on the play: (1) a tendency to see the play's engagement with the Union issue, which is generally agreed to be deep and pervasive, as a retrospective consideration of an issue whose consequences were already largely determined, as opposed to an imaginative intervention into an issue with continuing stakes, and (2) a tendency to interpret the play's engagement with the Union issue in terms of James's absolutist "Roman" imperialism and English parliamentary resistance thereto,[9] as opposed to interpreting it in terms of competing visions of "Britain." The essay's main point will be that the play's exploration of the status of the *post nati*—through not just Posthumus but also King Cymbeline's kidnapped sons (Guiderius and Arviragus)—cautions against the production of an English-dominated Britain and orients its audience instead toward a receding but still possible vision of a cosmopolitan Britain, one that the *post nati* might embody, namely Britain envisioned through a transnational Roman model with an equal citizenry.

Two Visions of Britain

This section will explore the competing visions of Britain during the Union issue, aiming to establish, on the one hand, the centrality of an idea of equal citizenship (indebted to the Roman tradition) in Union advocacy and, on the other hand, the imperial dimension of English nationalistic Union resistance. In his study showing the importance of classical humanism and republicanism to English political culture prior to the Civil War, Markku Peltonen observes that many Union advocates advanced an idea of British "citizenship" on the Roman model in advocating the mutual naturalization of the English and Scots.[10] Pro-Union treatises, written mostly in 1604 and 1605, presented such mutual naturalization and its attendant liberties as necessary for Britain's success. For example, David Hume, a Scottish Union advocate, argued that equality was crucial for the production of a British people: "The citizens and the people shall now be called British. The rights and duties of citizenship shall be the same in all respects for each and every citizen in such a way that it no longer matters to which of the two peoples an individual formerly belonged."[11] Union supporters envisioned such mutual naturalization as creating a common community in which origin, English or Scottish, was irrelevant. An anonymous treatise, "The Union of England and Scotland," proposed that "the mutuall commerce and entercourse of trafficke be enterteined amongst them, not as strangers but as naturall subjects of one lawfull sovereigne prince, members of one commonwealth and breathers of the common aire of one native soille."[12] John Russell specified that the Scots and the English would be equally eligible for benefits and offices and have the right to land and title and to the movement of goods among themselves.[13] The Scottish Union advocate Sir Thomas Craig observed "that union must either be founded on equality in everything, honours, dignities, official and general employments . . . or it could not be expected to last for long."[14] Likewise, John Thornborough warned: "But whosoever entendeth truely the common good, let him remember, that Solon said: the only way to keepe Subjects in unitie, is to maintaine an equalitie for al."[15] Union supporters thus focused on the importance of all the *post nati* having the same rights, privileges, and liberties with respect to office and economic opportunities, and they envisioned that such equality would produce a lasting integrated political economy.

Some contemporary writers made a point of stating that this equality was not intended to alter social status.[16] Yet, there are hints in Union supporters' writings that the equality of the Union would generate greater social as well as geographical mobility within Britain. For example, Craig wrote: "It must also be permitted to every man born in the island to live where he likes, and to enjoy the rights and privileges of citizenship, to pursue whatever trade and livelihood he pleases, just as though his parents had been born and brought up there. It ought to be open to all to better their position and means, to acquire real property, personalty, landed property, in the country and in the towns."[17] Craig was addressing the equality of the English and the Scots, but his notion of British citizenship as entailing a right to mobility and choice of livelihood hints at a broader equality. Similarly, John Skinner, in describing Britain as a new "Rome," argued that the equal merit of England and Scotland might warrant greater equality in the distribution of resources between them: "Yet since the men on both sides are serviceable, make their conditions as agreeing amongst themselves; so fit for the Common-Wealth: let the one injoy more, the other covet lesse; so shall both encrease apace, and *Rome* be well served."[18] Skinner's concern is with leveling the English-Scottish distinction; his logic is that men who are equally "serviceable" (meaning willing, active, diligent)[19] should have like conditions.

Like Skinner, many Union supporters invoked Rome as a model for an equal citizenship. John Hayward used the Roman example to explain why equality was necessary, arguing that the Roman empire enjoyed stability "because the people did so easily impart the libertie of their citie almost unto all" and warning that no people would accept unequal conditions for longer than necessary.[20] "The Union of England and Scotland" invoked Rome as a model for how "uniformitie of name, language and habilites or freedoms of a naturall subject" could coexist with independent laws, which England and Scotland would retain under the Union.[21] Francis Bacon, the well-known philosopher and statesman who also represented James's interests in the English Parliament during the Union issue, similarly observed that mutual naturalization might produce *communis patria* even if "ancient forms" remained intact.[22] Even Craig, who viewed Rome as a corrupting influence on ancient Britain, still invoked Rome to exemplify the need for equal privileges and liberties within an empire.[23]

Union opponents also advanced a vision of "Britain," but one in which England was dominant. These anti-Union Members of Parliament (MPs) were keen to establish that the Scottish *post nati*, whom they sometimes described simply as the *post nati*, had not been naturalized by James's accession and, furthermore, that such naturalization was not desirable. In particular, they argued that the Scottish *post nati* should be subordinate to the English, not equal. Henry Yelverton opposed naturalization because "if the Post-Nati be naturalls wee cannot restraine them, for then are they Northerne Englishmen."[24] Similarly, a Commons committee debated whether the term *naturalization* should even apply to the Scots, since naturalization "maketh a Man Inheritable unto Magna Charta, and then not limitted, nor to be restrained."[25] Union opponents contested Union supporters' vision of Rome, pointing out that the Romans did not give their privileges and immunities to every nation they annexed but rather apportioned such privileges as they saw fit.[26]

During the 1606–7 parliamentary session, Sir Edwin Sandys, one of the most prominent anti-Union MPs in the Commons, put forth an idea of what he called a "perfect union."[27] He described this as to be crafted by the English Parliament and motivated by the desire "that the Scottish Nation be ruled by Our Lawes."[28] This "perfect union" appears to have become a rallying point among anti-Union MPs.[29] With it, anti-Union MPs effectively displaced the idea of an equal union and its equal citizenry with that of English hegemony—not to mention displacing James's overriding power with the overriding power of English law. In effect, these MPs sought to convert James's project to create an equal Union and a new British culture into an opportunity to assert England's power over Scotland. In an anti-Union speech recorded by Sir Thomas Craig, the English MP Christopher Pigott echoed the ideology of the "perfect union," though more crudely and sensationally, when he remarked that "the only possible relation between the two countries would be that of judge and thief, the one decreeing, the other undergoing the penalty."[30]

In an ironic twist, Union opponents' attempts in 1606–7 to defeat the equal Union and subordinate the Scots elicited support from an unlikely corner: King James himself. Already at the start of the session, James seems to have sensed the possibility of the Union's legislative defeat, for he showed a sudden willingness to sacrifice the equality of the Union for the accomplishment of it. In particular, James made several statements indicating his openness to seeing the Union as, in some sense, an English conquest of Scotland. In his opening speech in November 1606, he responded to objections that Scotland was too poor to enter into a union by stating "that it was not his Purpose to deprive *England* of its Laws, nor of Goods, nor of Lands; but to lay *Scotland* subject to the Laws."[31] In March 1607, James told the English MPs: "*London* must be the Seat of your King, and *Scotland* joined to this Kingdom by a golden Conquest, but cemented with Love."[32] Implicitly, James asserted that an unequal union could be a strong and loving one, a stance antithetical to pro-Union claims that the Union could not last without equality. If James's turnabout seems surprising, it should be remembered that he was facing the prospect of the Union's defeat by the Commons, which would constitute an offense against his divinely granted power.[33]

Coke's Britain

In 1608, a case was brought before the judiciary that seemed to offer James an opportunity to save face more satisfactorily. Calvin's Case was designed to challenge the English Parliament's 1607 refusal to acknowledge the Scottish *post nati* as naturalized. In the case, Robert Calvin, an infant Scot born after James's English accession, was alleged to have been denied a freehold in England.[34] In his report of the case, Sir Edward Coke described the case as the "weightiest for the consequent, both for the present, and for all posterity."[35]

Some critics view Francis Bacon (the solicitor-general) and Coke as holding the same or very similar positions with regard to Calvin's Case, despite the oddness of agreement between Bacon, who represented the king's interests, and Coke, whose commitment to the power of the English common law is well known.[36] Other critics, however, argue that, while ruling for James, Coke's account of the reciprocal nature of allegiance worked to limit sovereign power and protect the English common law.[37] A close reading of Bacon's legal argument and Coke's report reveals that the latter not only protected the English common law but also subversively and subtly advanced the English nationalism and imperial ambitions driving the "perfect union."[38] Far from being a victory for James's Union, Coke's report advanced the anti-Union vision of Britain. Instead of affirming a mutual and equal relationship with the English, the report rendered the Scottish *post nati*—and the Union itself—subject to definition by English jurists and by English law.

Bacon based his argument for Calvin on the power of James's person to transcend his kingdoms and their laws and command allegiance directly. Thus the English and the Scots were equal and, fundamentally, the same under him. Bacon located the king's power in nature and God, as opposed to the law. Monarchies, he argued, are not "creatures of law" like other forms of government, but the shadow of "the government of God himself over the world." According to Bacon, "allegiance cannot be applied to the law or kingdom, but to the person of the king, because the allegiance of the subject is more large and spacious, and hath a greater latitude and comprehension than the law or the kingdom."[39] James thus stood above his two kingdoms and was capable of defining, in this case merging, the status of their inhabitants. He had a relationship with his subjects superior to the kingdoms and their laws.

Coke's report was antithetical to Bacon's argument, although on the face of it the report looks pro-Union. Coke held that the Scottish *post nati* are not aliens in England. Moreover, he held that James's English accession had indeed formed a union between England and Scotland. But Coke identified the force behind this union as the English common law, not the king's superior power over all his subjects. Coke gave the English common law this stature by entwining it—as Bacon had the king's power—with natural law: the "law of nature is part of the laws of England" (*State Trials*, 613). He decided the case on the grounds of natural law after having folded it into the authority of the English common law (629). Coke identified his method of figuring out natural law as "demonstrative reason" (630–32). He thereby found, in keeping with James and his supporters, that allegiance is owed to the king's person, thus making Calvin not an alien. But, crucially, he rendered this decision into a function of his understanding of the scope of the common law.[40]

The significance of the authority that Coke gave to the English common law in deciding the case is evident in the sweeping scope of the report. Coke did not limit himself to the legal question posed by the case but went on to determine the nature and extent of the union that had formed between England and Scotland. Coke carefully specified what that union did and did not entail, stating, "The law hath wrought four unions, so the law doth still make four separations." The four unions were (1) "both kingdoms under one natural liege sovereign king"; (2) "ligeance and obedience of the subjects of both kingdoms, due by the law of nature to their sovereign: and this union doth suffice to rule and over-rule the case in question; and this in substance is but a uniting of the hearts of the subjects of both kingdoms one to another, under one head and sovereign"; (3) "protection of both kingdoms"; and (4) "the three lions of England and that one of Scotland united and quartered in one escutcheon" (*State Trials*, 633). The four separations are that England and Scotland will remain separate kingdoms with separate laws, parliaments, and nobilities (633–34). Simply put, in Coke's formulation, "Britain" implies a common king, a common defense, a common allegiance, and a common but, notably, unequal "escutcheon" (shield bearing the coat of arms).

Coke's description of the escutcheon injected inequality, a three-to-one ratio, into the union. He also restricted the extent to which the English and the Scots could be integrated. Coke determined that title was a matter of state—"by the king's creation, and not of nature"—and did not cross the border, thus protecting English offices from the Scots and barring any merging of the two aristocracies (*State Trials*, 634–36). He narrowly defined the common allegiance as granting the *post nati* the right to own property in the other realm and as giving the king certain reserve rights over all his subjects. An example of such a reserve right is that the king could make an exception to a law passed by the English Parliament providing that no one could be sheriff of a county for more than one year, because the king had the right to his subjects' service (631–32).

Coke's rhetoric emphasized Calvin's foreignness and the assertiveness of English law in relation to him. It anthropomorphized the encounter between the case and English law: "I find a mere stranger in this case, such a one as the eye of the law, our books and book-cases, never saw . . . such a one, as the stomach of the law, our exquisite and perfect records of pleadings, entries, and judgments, that make equal and true distribution of all cases in question, never digested" (*State Trials*, 613). The bodily imagery figures English law as large and pressing. The common law eyes "the stranger"—and looks to ingest him. Coke's stress on the infallible operations of the common law and the "mere" strangeness of Calvin's plea implies both the ease and the justice with which the former will impose definition on the latter. Coke suggests a relationship between England and the Scottish *post nati* that is forged through an English interrogation and assessment of the Scots, not integration and mutuality with them.

Coke's report advanced the same combination of English protectionism and outward-aimed aggression that was articulated in the 1606–7 English Commons. The ruling was nationalistic in the sense that it conflated natural law and the English common law. But it also had an imperial dimension. It made the English common law a tool for defining England's relationship with others. Coke thus paved the way for an English-dominated "British" imperialism grounded in the English common law.[41] Consequently, the time of *Cymbeline*'s composition should not necessarily be seen as a moment when the energy of the Union proposal was already spent. The nature of Britain was still open to dramatically different conceptions depending on how one viewed the status of the *post nati*, whether per Bacon (and James's other supporters) or per Coke. Did the *post nati* embody a vision of an equal "Roman" Britain, notwithstanding the Union's political failure? Or were they merely a category of persons available for redefinition and thus control? These were still live questions.

The Posthumus *Post Nati*

Cymbeline's action is driven by the deterioration of Posthumus's character from virtuous to insecure and rashly murderous, a deterioration that corresponds to a macropolitical shift in the play from a Roman Britain to the insular yet outwardly aggressive nationalism of King Cymbeline's wicked Queen and her repugnant son Cloten. Posthumus's banishment at the start of the play's action is associated with the rise of new powers at court. The Queen (Cymbeline's second wife) and Cloten (whose ambition is to marry Imogen himself) lie behind both Posthumus's banishment and the larger coterminous event: Cymbeline's break from Rome. Consequently, there is a likeness between the start of *Cymbeline*'s plot and the late years of the Union issue: an idea of a Roman Britain has given way to an idea of Britain grounded in indigenous ancient laws, with the king swaying, under pressure, from the former to the latter.

As discussed earlier, scholars of the play have been intrigued by the possibility that Posthumus evokes the *post nati*. Yet, despite this critical attention, no satisfying account has been given for why Shakespeare would allegorize the *post nati* as "posthumus." Marcus, as mentioned, proposes that Posthumus be understood as "born after" because he is exiled, just as she sees the Scottish *post nati* as having been exiled from James upon his English accession.[42] However, at Shakespeare's time (as now), "posthumus" specifically meant born after the death of that which has given life, a central meaning that Marcus's reading does not address. "Posthumus" as a name was given to a posthumous child.[43]

I would suggest that Posthumus's evocation of the "*post nati*" may have registered as a political joke, but one with serious significance. The 1607 political defeat of the Union made the *post nati* uncannily like posthumous children. They lived on, and more of them were born, after that defeat. In allegorizing the status of the *post nati*, especially the Scottish *post nati*, as "posthumous" at this moment when the possibility of the Union's being realized legislatively had been extinguished and the king's power and political will further to pursue the Union had waned, the play explores both the vulnerability and the potential of this "posthumous" people.

In the remainder of this essay, I aim to make four points about the play. First, the play's representation of a conflict between Roman (cosmopolitan) and nationalistic imperialism maps onto values associated with each side in the Union issue. Second, the play's "*post nati*"—Posthumus and King Cymbeline's kidnapped sons (Guiderius and Arviragus)—embody, respectively, the vulnerability of the Scottish *post nati* to be subordinated following the Union's political defeat and the latent potential of all the *post nati* to constitute an equal British citizenry on the Roman model. Third, while the play associates Posthumus and the kidnapped brothers with the *post nati*, it also broadens their social identities, revealing the potentially leveling effects of the pro-Union stance if widened beyond the Scoto-Anglo context. Finally, the play jostles the somewhat ironic alignment of Roman citizenship ideology and absolutism within pro-Union thought by sympathetically anticipating a Roman "British" future while subtly disentangling that future from absolutism.[44]

Like the Roman Britain envisioned by Union advocates, Rome in the play represents a model of empire that puts little value in origin, is highly fluid, and enables a sense of community that transcends national borders. Roman culture, as represented in the play, questions the role of origin in determining office and identity and focuses instead on upbringing and service. The importance of upbringing in establishing identity is evident in Cymbeline's relationship with Caesar. Cymbeline hints at a Roman political economy based on educating and cultivating another entity, and on the bonds of obligation thereby created, which Cymbeline replicates in his own rearing of Posthumus. Cymbeline tells Lucius, who is Caesar's ambassador as well as, later in the play, head of the Roman army:

> Thy Caesar knighted me; my youth I spent
> Much under him; of him I gather'd honour,
> Which he to seek of me again, perforce,
> Behoves me keep at utterance. (3.1.70–73)

Cymbeline charges Caesar with violating the honors that Caesar brought him up to expect. He contends that it is an answerable breach to take honors away once they have been bestowed through upbringing and that he will defend them "at utterance," meaning to the utmost extremity.[45] Cymbeline's view of his relationship to Caesar imbues his dishonor of Posthumus with irony, since Posthumus's upbringing should similarly entitle him.

A Roman de-emphasis on origin is also evident in the play's envisioning of complex overlapping alliances, which are associated with Rome as an alternate jurisdiction. Both Posthumus and Imogen step easily into and out of the Roman world. Posthumus becomes part of the Roman army, then assumes the garb of a poor British soldier, and then, after the battle, resumes his Roman affiliation. Neither Posthumus's uncertain origins nor his Britishness seems to have bearing on his place among the gentry in the Roman forces. Imogen, in disguise as Fidele, enters the service of Lucius. She gains place through her perceived virtue rather than through origin or degree. Specifically, she becomes Lucius's servant through her manifest devotion to the supposedly dead Posthumus, whom she has presented as her master.

Lucius's encounter with Imogen in the Welsh woods, and Cloten's parallel encounter with Guiderius, strike a contrast between Rome's internationalism and the Queen's and Cloten's aggressive nationalism. Upon meeting Guiderius, Cloten immediately perceives him through the lens of self and other. Cloten apprehends an exotic inferior, a "rustic mountaineer" (4.2.100). Lucius, by contrast, registers no self-other divide upon encountering Imogen in the same woods, even though she self-identifies as "other." Imogen tells Lucius that her supposedly fallen master was a "very valiant Briton" (4.2.369), identifying her and her master as Lucius's enemy, since the Romans are in the process of invading Britain. Yet Lucius's judgment of Imogen and his decision to invite her to enter his service takes no account of her Britishness, only of the perceived quality of her service to her dead master.

Posthumus as an allegory for the Scottish *post nati* embodies the success of the pro-Union "Roman" position. His origin is irrelevant with respect to his advancement; merit and serviceability are instead what matter. The play opens with two Gentlemen talking about Posthumus and Imogen's marriage. The First Gentlemen gives an account of Posthumus. Of Posthumus's origin, he says: "I cannot delve him to the root" (1.1.28). Posthumus's stature is based instead on his upbringing, and on how he flourished through it:

> The king he takes the babe
> To his protection, calls him Posthumus Leonatus,
> Breeds him, and makes him of his bed-chamber,
> Puts to him all the learnings that his time
> Could make him the receiver of, which he took,
> As we do air, fast as 'twas minister'd,
> And in's spring became a harvest: liv'd in court
> (Which rare it is to do) most prais'd, most lov'd. (1.1.40–47)

The glory of Posthumus's father is similarly predicated on merit over birth. His father acquired his Roman name (Leonatus) and status through service (1.1.28–33). Yet Posthumus also broadens the Union's challenge to origin. Despite the many ways in which Posthumus allegorizes the Scottish *post nati*, the play does not displace origin with merit and serviceability specifically with respect to the Scots. The First Gentleman's suggestion that Posthumus's origins are in some sense ultimately unfathomable works to generalize his identity. Posthumus's simultaneous links to the Scottish *post nati* and to "everyman" suggest how the pro-Union position's devaluation of origin and its promotion of equal access could embolden broader challenges to social distinctions, a possibility gestured to in Craig's vision of a British people enjoying mobility and a choice of livelihood across Britain. The play represents Roman Britain as a culture in which a person of sufficient merit might become the husband of the king's daughter.

The Queen and Cloten's idea of Britain, by contrast, bears an unflattering resemblance to the anti-Union grounding of English imperialism in English nationalism. Specifically, their insular sense of national identity goes hand in hand with an aggressive drive to dominate others within Britain. The Queen and Cloten attack the values associated with a Roman Britain, in particular its de-emphasis on origin. Cloten figures birth as the key measure of a person, telling Imogen that her marriage to Posthumus is voided by Posthumus's low birth:

> You sin against
> Obedience, which you owe your father; for
> The contract you pretend with that base wretch,
> One bred of alms, and foster'd with cold dishes,
> With scraps o' th' court, it is no contract, none. (2.3.110–14)

Cloten's arguments against the marriage evoke anti-Union arguments. His allusion to Posthumus's poverty echoes anti-Union MPs' allusions to Scottish poverty, since anti-Union writers railed against the Union as little more than charity to Scotland.[46] Cloten also argues that Imogen has sinned against obedience, presumably by not obtaining consent for the marriage and because the marriage is not an equal one. These arguments parallel anti-Union claims that the Union could not have been formed without Parliament and that an equal Union was intolerable because the Scots were not equal to the English. Likewise, the Queen dismisses the fluidity of identity across realms associated with Rome. She urges Pisanio to abandon loyalty to his master Posthumus on the grounds that Posthumus in exile has become no one:

> His fortunes all lie speechless, and his name
> Is at last gasp. Return he cannot, nor
> Continue where he is. (1.6.52–54)

In being exiled, Posthumus has lost all the markers by which others could recognize and respect him. The Queen's argument puts great weight on origin and national identity and implies a dismissal of the fluid internationalism that the play associates with Rome.

The Queen's nationalism, in persuading Cymbeline to resist Rome, echoes the insular and aggressive nationalism of the English Commons. She emphasizes the British isle's martial heritage, self-containment, and self-sufficiency:

> The natural bravery of your isle, which stands
> As Neptune's park, ribb'd and pal'd in
> With rocks unscaleable and roaring waters. (3.1.19–21)

Critics have noted the likenesses between the Queen's speech and John of Gaunt's "sceptered isle" speech in *Richard II*:

This other Eden, demi-paradise,
This fortress built by Nature for herself
Against infection and the hand of war,
This happy breed of men, this little world,
This precious stone set in the silver sea,
Which serves it in the office of a wall
Or as a moat defensive to a house
Against the envy of less happier lands,
This blessed plot, this earth, this realm, this England,
This nurse, this teeming womb of royal kings,
Feared by their breed and famous by their birth.[47]

As the Queen does, Gaunt figures the British island as both a garden and a fortress. She has spoken of how Cassibelan's victory "Made Lud's town with rejoicing-fires bright, / And Britons strut with courage" (3.1.33–34). He too harks to a line of martial kings, and he too conveys the idea of the island as self-contained and self-sufficient. Shakespeare—whether unconsciously or by design—encourages his audience to identify the Queen's brand of nationalism with Gaunt's. In the context of the late stages of the Union issue, such identification would have given the Queen's speech an Anglocentric bent, already suggested by her stress on Lud as Britain's center. Gaunt's speech conflates England and Britain. In describing England as the whole island, he imaginatively assumes English dominion over the whole. When *Richard II* was written (c. 1595), such conflation would have been an unremarkable assertion of English hegemony over Britain. James's vision of the Union had, however, deconflated England and Britain. The idea of Britain as coterminous with England was no longer a commonplace but rather a politically charged, anti-Union position. By importing Gaunt's English-dominated British nationalism into *Cymbeline* and putting it in the mouth of the evil Queen, Shakespeare shows the political meaning that Gaunt's vision of the island had acquired.

The basic conflict between the two visions of Britain is encapsulated in the issue of Britain's tribute to Rome. The Queen and Cloten interpret the tribute as submission to Roman domination. As Cloten puts it, "Britain's a world by itself, and we will nothing pay for wearing our own noses" (3.1.13–14). Cymbeline, at the play's end, however, reinterprets the tribute as a mechanism for achieving parity, peace, and integration with Rome:

Although the victor, we submit to Caesar,
And to the Roman empire; promising
To pay our wonted tribute. (5.5.461–63)

Cymbeline, moreover, aligns this peace with a complex account of sovereignty:

> Set we forward: let
> A Roman, and a British ensign wave
> Friendly together. (5.5.480–82)

Cymbeline suggests that the payment of the tribute will lay the foundation for a Roman British community—the antithesis of Cloten's image of Britain as a world by itself. Cymbeline's idea that both British and Roman flags may be flown—so that Britain is still Britain but also part of Rome—supports the possibility of multiple overlapping identities and jurisdictions that was so crucial to James's idea of Union. Anti-Union MPs argued that the Union would destroy England precisely because English sovereignty could not coexist with British sovereignty. James, by contrast, argued that English and Scottish integrity, as defined by their ancient customs and laws, would continue within the Union, making Britain into an overarching culture and jurisdiction. Cymbeline's new accord shatters the Queen and Cloten's paradigm of self and other, in which boundary breaches entail anxiety and anger. Britain may be British and Roman at once, and this very fluidity and confluence will breed peace.

There is a great difference between what the audience hears of Posthumus prior to the play's action and what the audience sees of him over the course of the play's events. The Posthumus of report is virtuous; the Posthumus the audience sees is increasingly base. Over the course of the play's action, Posthumus rashly comes to doubt Imogen, seeks to murder her, and becomes, as Heather James observes, indistinguishable from Cloten.[48] Ann Thompson has argued that the play's action reveals Posthumus's true nature. She sees Posthumus's degeneration as evidence that he was unworthy all along and, hence, that Imogen overvalued Posthumus when she married him.[49] The play's action, though, shows Posthumus not as having an absolute value, which is alternately hidden and revealed, but rather as having a value that is generated differently within two competing cultures. In the context of Roman Britain or Roman culture, Posthumus was treated as if he were Imogen's equal and by all report acted accordingly. In the context of the aggressive yet insular nationalism associated with the Queen, Cloten, and Iachimo, Posthumus deteriorates.

The scene that depicts Posthumus's degradation encapsulates a shift from a fluid Roman culture to a nationalistic one in an uncanny overlay of the latter over the former. When Posthumus arrives at Philario's house, the expected Roman world dissolves into a competitive nationalistic early modern one. In embarking for exile, Posthumus at first appears poised to enter a transnational Roman community formed through the bonds of friendship. In heading for

Rome and the home of one of his father's soldier friends, Posthumus relies on the internationalism of the empire and on a community of friendships that span it. Yet the context that Posthumus enters on arriving at Philario's house suggests early modern Europe. Philario is entertaining Iachimo and a Frenchman, a Dutchman, and a Spaniard, and awaiting "the Briton" (1.5.26). There is no reason for the Dutchman or the Spaniard to be part of the scene, as they do not speak. Rather the point seems to be that the room is filled with persons who are primarily identified by nationality. There is a temporal collapse of the Roman world into an early modern one, and indeed part of the drama of the scene might have been the moment when the audience realizes that the scene is not located in ancient Rome but in early modern Italy among jostling national identities.

Posthumus's deterioration is keyed to his embrace of nationalism. His wager on Imogen is sparked by a comparison among the men of their respective "country mistresses" (1.5.54–55) as to whose is, among other things, more virtuous and chaste. The wager parallels Cloten's earlier challenge to Rome in seeing identity and value as contingent. Posthumus says of Imogen (to Iachimo): "if you make your voyage upon her, and give me directly to understand you have prevail'd, I am no further your enemy; she is not worth our debate" (1.5.154–57). Cloten presents Britain's identity similarly: "you shall find us in our salt-water girdle: if you beat us out of it, it is yours" (3.1.80–82). Imogen and Britain are both made the basis of a blend of insular protectiveness and aggressive nationalism, a blend reminiscent of anti-Union thought. Posthumus's and Cloten's speeches, however, reveal the instability of this mentality—in particular how readily it may turn against what supposedly sustains it. Posthumus and Cloten are shown not to be attached to a particular object (Britain or Imogen) but to fantasies about it of purity and containment. Their mentality is further shown to breed violence but not strength. Posthumus's embrace of competitive nationalism generates a fear of inferiority and of others' contempt and, with it, violence.

Despite the play's broad engagement with the Union issue, critics have tended to focus on Posthumus when they consider the play's interest in the *post nati*. The play may, however, be seen as more deeply immersed in the issue of the *post nati*, exploring the vulnerabilities and potential of the *post nati*'s status through multiple characters. Cymbeline's kidnapped sons Guiderius and Arviragus, raised in the mountains of Wales, may be seen as "*post nati*" as well, yet if they are seen thus, they offer a contrast to Posthumus.[50] After waking from his dream of Jupiter, Posthumus finds a prophecy attached to him, which describes the two kidnapped brothers as "lopp'd branches, which, being dead many years, shall after revive, be jointed to the old stock, and freshly grow" (5.5.439–41). The prophecy implies that the brothers are, while living on the periphery, like the living dead. Posthumus and the brothers are thus shown in chiastic relation. Posthumus lives on after the death of what created him; the brothers are "dead" but will return to life. More specifically, Posthumus embodies the vulnerability and potential for the degradation of the *post nati* after the death of a "Roman" Britain. By contrast, the brothers, sequestered in an alternate jurisdiction, embody the continuing political possibility of a Roman Britain as a "dead" yet still imaginable alternative.

The brothers raise the issue of British as distinct from English identity. Geographically they are Welsh. Belarius's cave is located in a remote, rural part of Wales. The strategy of their defense of Britain, though, associates them with Scotland. Their deeds mirror those of the Scottish heroes from Holinshed's *Historie of Scotland*, the sons of Haie, who fought off the Romans at a pass.[51] This conflation of Welsh and Scottish identities in the context of a play so concerned with the Union issue may have queried the distinction between Scotland and Wales in relation to England. James (before his capitulations in the 1606–7 session) and his supporters envisioned a very different union from England's earlier incorporation of Wales, namely an equal one. Some English writers, however, invoked the Welsh example as precedent. For example, in a 1598 treatise that anticipated the possibility of an Anglo-Scottish union, Peter Wentworth posed the rhetorical question: "Is not this the way to subordinate (if not to subdue) to us, that people by policie, whome wee coulde not by force?" and then likens union with Scotland to union with Wales.[52] Cloten's attempt, on arriving in the Welsh woods, to subordinate the brothers by extending the law over them raises the question of whether the Scots had become like the people of Wales, incorporated as opposed to fully equal.

Specifically, Cloten's encounter with Guiderius stages a conflict between the pro-Union idea of an equal British people and the anti-Union pursuit of an imperialistic extension of ancient laws, where the center controls the periphery. Cloten disparages the brothers as "villain mountaineers" (4.2.71), and Guiderius reports that Cloten called him "traitor, mountaineer," as if the two words were coterminous (4.2.120). Cloten thus implies that he does not consider ancient British laws to protect this part of Britain but to seek to control it. The people of the Welsh countryside, despite being in Britain, are—as villains and traitors—living in violation of its law. Cloten's conflation of traitor and mountaineer could be seen as a disparaging allusion to Scottish highlanders. His view of the law extending over Britain as a controlling force evokes the anti-Union MPs' "perfect union," as well evoking Coke's more subtle use of the

English common law to define Britain. Cloten's attitude toward the brothers exposes what is implicit in his and the Queen's nationalism, namely that the ancient British laws do not emerge from all of Britain but rather are imposed from London.

Guiderius's response to Cloten in turn evokes pro-Union arguments that laws should also apply equally over all of Britain, though with a twist that suggests that such equality should apply to all distinctions among men. Guiderius queries: "What art thou? Have not I / An arm as big as thine? a heart as big?" (4.2.76–77). On a register of degree, as far as both men know, Cloten, as a member of court and the Queen's son, is Guiderius's clear superior. On a register of merit, Guiderius knows he is Cloten's superior, since shortly after the exchange he describes Cloten as a fool. Yet, in the line quoted above, Guiderius asserts abstract equality between them, implying the existence of a register on which both men are equals. Imogen echoes this idea of an abstract equality when she is introduced to Guiderius and his brother's cave, and exclaims:

> Gods, what lies I have heard!
> Our courtiers say all's savage but at court;
> Experience, O, thou disprov'st report!
> Th' emperious seas breed monsters; for the dish
> Poor tributary rivers as sweet fish. (4.2.32–36)

Brian Lockey interprets this quote as establishing that "Poor tributary rivers" are more civil than Roman imperial seas.[53] But Cloten is the voice of the courtier in the play, and it is he who insists that those outside the court are savage. What Imogen is critiquing is not Rome's imperialism but London's. Imogen's speech is, moreover, notable for what it does not do. She expresses disgust at the courtiers of the court and admiration for the inhabitants of the cave. Yet she does not simply reverse center and periphery in a pastoral gesture that would raise the countryside over the court. Rather she introduces parity; the tributary rivers produce "*as* sweet fish." As in Guiderius's exchange with Cloten, Imogen suggests registers on which the court may be inferior. It has produced "monsters." Nevertheless, also like Guiderius, Imogen insists on a relationship of equality.

After Guiderius kills Cloten, he defends himself on the grounds that he is entitled to equal protection of the law and, moreover, that its denial authorized his resistance:

> The law
> Protects not us, then why should we be tender,

To let an arrogant piece of flesh threat us,
Play judge, and executioner, all himself,
For we do fear the law? (4.2.125–29)

Guiderius rhetorically conflates Cloten with law. The "arrogant piece of flesh" is "the law." Guiderius's defense is not grounded on a counterargument within law, such as a right to self-defense, but on a right to dismiss "the law" altogether if does not offer equal protection. Guiderius's contention that the unequal application of the law authorizes violence echoes pro-Union arguments for why the Union must be equal. John Hayward asserted the need for the equal protection of law across "Britain": "That as the Sunne riseth and shineth to all alike, so the law should comprehend all in one equall and unpartiall equite."[54] Union advocates further linked equality with peace and inequality with violence. Sir Thomas Craig argued that an unequal union would produce contempt and, ultimately, violence. Quoting Dio Cassius, Craig observed: "Where there is equality on both sides, there friendship reigns. But if one excel the other, arrogance and contempt will dominate the one, jealousy the other, and hatred, resentment, war and strife will follow."[55] Craig thus imported the high standard of equality propounded by classical friendship theory into the context of the Union issue. Hume attributed violence between the Scots and the English to English contempt, claiming it would continue "As long as the Englishman despises the Scot and holds him in contempt; likewise, as long as the Scot believes himself to be an object of contempt, and gives as good as he gets."[56]

Guiderius's justification for killing Cloten pushes these arguments a step further to apply to inequality grounded on degree. Guiderius claims that Cloten's unequal treatment of and contempt for him justified killing him, notwithstanding Cloten's (at least apparently) higher degree. For Guiderius, if the law does not apply equally, violence is authorized, even against social superiors. When Cymbeline later insists that there is no justification for killing a prince (namely Cloten) and that even Guiderius's heroism will not mitigate his crime, Guiderius responds by denying the relevance of Cloten's degree:

The wrongs he did me
Were nothing prince-like; for he did provoke me
With language that would make me spurn the sea. (5.5.292–94)

What counts for Guiderius is not degree but conduct. A prince must be prince-like in behavior in order to be protected by his degree. He argues that sufficient provocation by Cloten—which was in fact no more than treating Guiderius as an inferior—warranted spurning all other considerations.

The play's coupling of Guiderius's rejection of Lud's law with his decision shortly thereafter to risk his life for Britain raises the topical question of to what the *post nati* owe their allegiance. Posthumus derisively observes that the heroic stand that he, Guiderius, Arviragus, and Belarius take against the Romans might easily be put into the service of unthinking, jingoistic patriotism: "Two boys, an old man twice a boy, a lane, / Preserv'd the Britons, was the Romans' bane" (5.3.57–58). But Guiderius gives a reason for his defense of Britain that is antithetical to such patriotism, specifically self-interest:

> This way, the Romans
> Must or for Britons slay us or receive us
> For barbarous and unnatural revolts
> During their use, and slay us after. (4.4.4–7)

Guiderius's actions have the effect of bringing Britain together, although they are motivated by self-preservation. Moreover, the audience's awareness of this fact does not seem meant to undermine Guiderius's heroism. If anything, Posthumus's scornful ditty encourages the audience to appreciate the actual motives behind Britain's salvation. Guiderius's pragmatism dramatizes a key tenet of pro-Union thought, namely an insistence that one's interest should make one support Britain and the British common good.[57] Yet, Guiderius may be seen as taking this line of thinking to a more extreme conclusion. Guiderius's Britishness is seemingly exclusively rooted in his interest—and unmediated by either law or king. King Cymbeline is absent from Guiderius's embrace of British identity, an absence emphasized in the prophecy at the play's close.

Whereas in the political arena the status of the *post nati* was entwined with James's power, in the play their status is rendered distinct from the king's power. The play's presentation of a king who turns away from a Roman idea of Britain to one grounded on indigenous ancient laws, and in doing so turns his back on Posthumus, could be interpreted as satirizing James's politically expedient abandonment of the idea of an equal *post nati* during the 1606–7 parliamentary session. This interpretation would give insight into the otherwise perplexing issue of why a play that seems unmistakably at its close to celebrate James's Roman Britain, and thus to allegorize James in Cymbeline, shows the king throughout its action as overshadowed and irresolute.[58] The play's emphasis on the king's turnabout with respect to Posthumus—and thus on James's turnabout with respect to the *post nati*—further makes it possible to consider the *post nati*'s status without immediately translating such consideration into support for or opposition to James.

The "Roman" microworld of Belarius's cave similarly disengages royalism and "Roman" Britain—at least in the pro-Union sense of valuing upbringing and merit over origin. Belarius's strict humanist education of the two brothers, who are of course disguised princes, may have alluded to that of James by George Buchanan. Buchanan, who was James's childhood tutor, sought to teach James to accept that a king's power is inherently limited, a lesson James rejected as a king.[59] Belarius's education of the two brothers is similarly concerned with the problem of tyranny. Like Buchanan, Belarius suggests that monarchs should be restrained. Belarius tells the brothers:

> Stoop, boys: this gate
> Instructs you how t' adore the heavens; and bows you
> To a morning's holy office. The gates of monarchs
> Are arch'd so high that giants may jet through
> And keep their impious turbans on. (3.3.2–6)

Belarius conveys a startling association here between monarchy and impiety. Monarchy's gates are constructed for giants with "impious turbans," an image that associates monarchs with impiety and, through the image of the turban, with opposition to Christianity. It attributes such impiety to monarchs' scorn of restrictions on their power, specifically their building of gates so high that they need never bend their head. Belarius envisions the monarch's gate being replaced by another "gate," one to which the boys (princes, albeit unknowingly) must bow their heads. The instructive gate renders the princes' relationship to God neither unimpeded nor unfettered, as the gate functions as both tutor and obstacle. Belarius figures piety as learning to submit to limits. Belarius thus suggests how education and upbringing may healthfully trump origin. He instructs the two princes how to be virtuous—how to bow their heads—in spite of the impious leanings of their actual degree.

Much then rests on how the princes' education under Belarius is represented. Is the princes' virtue dependent on this education? Or is the princes' virtue inherent, ready to manifest itself at the appropriate time? The play allows either interpretation. Belarius himself marvels at how the brothers seem unknowingly to intuit their degree. Yet the play's representation of the culture of the cave insistently locates the princes' virtue in its context. The political economy of the cave is based on the day's accomplishment, functioning as a kind of game and adjustable meritocracy rather than according to any notion of fixed hierarchy. Office is in celebratory fashion distributed by merit. The best hunter of the day is allowed to be the "master of the feast" (3.7.2), while the other two cook and serve. Moreover, the cave culture embraces the two ideals prominently associated with the Union: peace and prosperity.[60] Belarius and the two brothers expand their community through an open-handed distribution of resources. They scorn the notion that Imogen should pay for what she has taken, but they encourage her to stay, and they sweep him/her quickly into their group. This representation of redistribution as part of community building supports pro-Union arguments that some redistribution across Britain, especially toward the Scots, was necessary for the peace and prosperity of the new British community.[61] The play lingers over the details of the cave community—how food is obtained, cooked, shared—and how a balance is achieved among its members. There is an idyllic aspect to the harmony of the cave culture that is linked to an attendance to needs and to distribution.

Finally, the prophecy, which is read at court at the play's end, subtly disentangles the importance of the *post nati* to Britain from royalism. The prophecy reads: "When as a lion's whelp shall, to himself unknown, without seeking find, and be embrac'd by a piece of tender air: and when from a stately cedar shall be lopp'd branches, which, being dead many years, shall after revive, be jointed to the old stock, and freshly grow, then shall Posthumus end his miseries, Britain be fortunate, and flourish in peace and plenty" (5.5.436–43). The prophecy envisions Britain much as did the pro-Union writers discussed earlier—with an emphasis on its benefit, specifically a general flourishing that values peace and material comfort. Conversely, Britain's happiness is conspicuously not tied to the person we might expect: Cymbeline. The prophecy's slighting of Cymbeline may be gleaned from Cymbeline's somewhat brusque response, which returns attention to him: "Well, My peace we will begin" (5.5.459–60). It might also be gleaned from comparison to the well-known Welsh prophecy that purportedly foretold James's union of Scotland and England. William Morris, a Welsh MP, recited the prophecy for the 1604 English Commons: "A kinge of Brittyshe Bloud in Cradle Crowned with lyones Marke shall Joyne all brittyshe ground, restore the Crose and make this Ile Renowned."[62] Whereas the Welsh prophecy celebrates James, the prophecy in the play keys Britain's future to the validation and happiness of the play's various "*post nati*"—to Posthumus (the "lion's whelp") and the brothers (the "lopp'd branches"). Furthermore, the prophecy offers a political creativity for Britain's future that is antithetical to the idea of the state as grounded in ancient laws. In the prophecy, the tree, the image of continuity and rootedness, becomes instead an image of discontinuity and the possibility of newness (lopped branches revived). Allegorically, the prophecy locates the long-term British "peace and plenty" (a phrase coterminous with the Union) in the future of the *post nati*, that is, in a British people.

Cymbeline, I have argued, imagines a British future entwined with the welfare of the *post nati* and indebted to a pro-Union "Roman" Britain, though at the same time disentangled from absolutism. It shows the degrading effects of insular yet aggressive nationalism on Posthumus and sympathetically renders Guiderius's British yet non-English bid for equality. Perhaps most provocatively, the play broadens the pro-Union challenge to the value of origin and social status beyond the Scottish-English context to "everyman," a broadening that may be associated with pro-Union treatises that envisioned a British people enjoying equal liberties and equal access to opportunity.

NOTES

1. For discussion on dating the play, see J. M. Nosworthy, introduction to *Cymbeline*, by William Shakespeare, ed. J. M. Nosworthy (1955; rpt., London: The Arden Shakespeare, 2000), xiv–xvii. All references to the play are to this edition.

2. Specifically, the English House of Commons refused to ratify the "Instrument of Union," which had been negotiated in 1604 by a large joint English and Scottish Union Commission. For a detailed account of the Union Commission, see Bruce Galloway, *The Union of England and Scotland, 1603–1608* (Edinburgh, UK: John Donald, 1986), 58–78.

3. As Leah S. Marcus observes, the outcome of Calvin's Case was generally expected. *Puzzling Shakespeare: Local Reading and Its Discontents* (Berkeley: University of California Press, 1988), 125.

4. Coke is the only judge who published a report of the case, although Lord Chancellor Ellesmere published his views separately. *Cobbett's Complete Collection of State Trials . . .*, vol. 2 (London, 1809), 561, 612, hereafter abbreviated *State Trials* in text and notes.

5. Marcus, *Puzzling Shakespeare*, 122–23, 125.

6. Ibid., 106–36, esp. 125. Marcus, though, complicates this reading by proposing that the play's attention to acts of interpretation may enable critique of James, 137–48.

7. Constance Jordan, *Shakespeare's Monarchies: Ruler and Subject in the Romances* (Ithaca, NY: Cornell University Press, 1997), 75.

8. John Kerrigan points toward continuing ambiguity about the status of the *post nati* after the Union's legislative defeat, as well as the play's interest in such ambiguity, when he observes that the play's concern with "the relationship between natives and strangers, is part of a scenario that deals with alienation within Britain itself," as evidenced by Scotsmen's continuing to be designated "aliens" in England as late as the 1620s. See Kerrigan, *Archipelagic English: Literature, History, and Politics, 1603–1707* (Oxford: Oxford University Press, 2008), 133.

9. See Marcus, *Puzzling Shakespeare*, 126–28; Heather James, *Shakespeare's Troy: Drama, Politics, and the Translation of Empire* (Cambridge: Cambridge University Press, 1997), 151–88, esp. 155; Willy Maley, *Nation, State, and Empire in English Renaissance Literature: Shakespeare to Milton* (Houndmills, UK: Palgrave Macmillan, 2003), 31–44, esp. 32–33.

10. Markku Peltonen, *Classical Humanism and Republicanism in English Political Thought, 1570–1640* (Cambridge: Cambridge University Press, 1995), 214–16.

11. David Hume, *The British Union: A Critical Edition and Translation of David Hume of*

Godscroft's "De Unione Insulae Britannicae," ed. Paul J. McGinnis and Arthur H. Williamson (Aldershot, UK: Ashgate, 2002), 155.

12. "A Treatise about the Union of England and Scotland," in *The Jacobean Union: Six Tracts of 1604*, ed. Bruce R. Galloway and Brian P. Levack (Edinburgh: Clark Constable, 1985), 61.

13. John Russell. "A Treatise of the Happie and Blissed Unioun," in Galloway and Levack, *The Jacobean Union*, 125–27.

14. Sir Thomas Craig, *De Unione Regnorum Britanniae Tractatus*, ed. and trans. C. Sanford Terry (Edinburgh: Scottish History Society, 1909), 354.

15. John Thornborough, *The Joiefull and Blessed Reuniting the Two Mighty and Famous Kingdomes, England and Scotland into their Ancient Name of Great Brittaine* (Oxford, 1604), 61.

16. See Samuel Daniel, *A Panegyrike Congratulatorie to the Kings Majestie, Also Certaine Epistles* (London, 1603), sig. A5v; "A Treatise about the Union," 61.

17. Craig, *De Unione*, 467.

18. John Skinner, *Rapta Tatio: The Mirrour of his Majesties Present Government, Tending to the Union of his Whole Iland of Brittonie Martiall* (London, 1604), sig. G4r.

19. *The Oxford English Dictionary*, s.v. "Serviceable."

20. I. H. [John Hayward], *A Treatise of Union of the Two Realmes of England and Scotland* (London, 1604), 20.

21. "A Treatise about the Union," 44.

22. Francis Bacon, *A Briefe Discourse, touching the Happie Union of the Kingdomes of England, and Scotland* (London, 1603), sigs. B4v–B6v.

23. Craig, *De Unione*, 381, 441–42.

24. *The Parliamentary Diary of Robert Bowyer, 1606–1607*, ed. David Harris Willson (Minneapolis: University of Minnesota Press, 1931), 283.

25. Ibid., 219.

26. Sir Henry Spelman, "Of the Union," in Galloway and Levack, *The Jacobean Union*, 182.

27. Bowyer, *Parliamentary Diary*, 219–20.

28. Ibid., 218–25.

29. See ibid., 243–44, 263–66, 269–71, 276–77.

30. Craig, *De Unione*, 356.

31. *The Journals of the House of Commons*, vol. 1 (London, [1742]), 315, hereafter abbreviated C. J.

32. Ibid., 363.

33. In a letter to the English Commons in May 1604, James told the MPs that a refusal to implement the Union would be "to spitte and blaspheme" in God's face. C. J., 194.

34. "The Case of the POSTNATI, or of the Union of the Realm of Scotland with England," in *State Trials*, 607–9.

35. *State Trials*, 612.

36. Conrad Russell sees Calvin's Case as confirming English MPs' fears that the Union might empower the king at the expense of English law and associates the case

with the beginnings of parliamentary distrust of the judiciary. *The Causes of the English Civil War* (Oxford: Clarendon Press, 1990), 40, 157–58. See also Keechang Kim, "Calvin's Case (1608) and the Law of Alien Status," *Journal of Legal History* 17, no. 2 (1996): 158–59.

37. Harvey Wheeler, "Calvin's Case (1608) and the McIlwain-Schuyler Debate," *American Historical Review* 61, no. 3 (1956): 589–91. Polly J. Price claims that "Coke's resolution of the case essentially followed that suggested by Bacon," but also that Coke aimed to limit sovereign power through the reciprocal relationship between subject and sovereign. Price, "Natural Law and Birthright Citizenship in *Calvin's Case* (1608)," *Yale Journal of Law and the Humanities* 73 (1997): 114, 120–21.

38. Daniel J. Hulsebosch has also identified sympathy for the anti-Union position in Coke's report, specifically in Coke's claim that the king "could make no new law in an inherited land except with the 'consent of parliament,'" which, he argues, protected the English common law from the king and spoke to anti-Union MPs' fears that the Union would destroy English sovereignty. See Hulsebosch, "The Ancient Constitution and the Expanding Empire: Sir Edward Coke's British Jurisprudence," *Law and History Review* 21, no. 3 (2003): 463–65.

39. Francis Bacon, "The Argument of Sir Francis Bacon, Knight, His Majesty's Solicitor-General, in the Case of the Post-Nati of Scotland, in the Exchequer Chamber," in *The Works of Francis Bacon*, ed. James Spedding, Robert Leslie Ellis, and Douglas Denon Heath, vol. 7, part 2 (London: Longmans, 1879), 645.

40. Price notes that the case empowered the judiciary by making it responsible for determining citizenship. "Natural Law," 74–75.

41. For differing stances on whether Coke extended any English common-law rights to subjects living outside of England, see Price, "Natural Law," 73–74; and Hulsebosch, "The Ancient Constitution," 445–46; 467–69. However sympathetic (or not) Coke may be seen toward extending such rights, he relies on the idea that the common law properly defines England's relationship with non-English subjects. Coke's very ambiguity over whether such rights are thereby created only emphasizes the report's legalization of a peripheral status for non-English subjects.

42. Marcus, *Puzzling Shakespeare*, 125.

43. For example, the younger brother of the anti-Union MP Sir Edward Hoby was named Thomas Posthumous Hoby. See entry for Sir Edward Hoby in the *Oxford Dictionary of National Biography*.

44. Pro-Union discourse should not be viewed as mere propaganda or flattery. It bore a complex relationship to James's absolutism, with some Union supporters embedding a notion of consent into their Union advocacy. For example, see Hayward, "A Treatise of Union," 8–9, 17; "Treatise about the Union," 56.

45. *Oxford English Dictionary*, s.v. "Utterance."

46. For example, see Spelman, "Of the Union," 174–75.

47. William Shakespeare, *King Richard II*, ed. Charles R. Forker (London: Arden, 2002), 2.1.42–52. For a discussion of this likeness and the interpretive problems it raises, see G. Wilson Knight, *The Crown of Life: Essays in Interpretation of Shakespeare's Final Plays* (Oxford: London, 1947), 134–36.

48. James, *Shakespeare's Troy*, 160.

49. Ann Thompson, "Person and Office: The Case of Imogen, Princess of Britain," *Literature and Nationalism*, ed. Vincent Newey and Ann Thompson (Liverpool, UK: Liverpool University Press, 1991), 81.

50. Bradin Cormack also sees a relationship between the king's sons and the status of the *post nati*, although his focus is more on a relationship between Guiderius and the *ante nati* (subjects born before James's English accession). See Cormack, *A Power to Do Justice: Jurisdiction, English Literature, and the Rise of Common Law, 1509–1625* (Chicago: University of Chicago Press, 2007), 251–53.

51. As critics have noted, this allusion would have readily linked the brothers to Scotland, since the ancestor of these heroes, the Scottish Lord Hay, was serving in James's court. See Appendix A in the 2000 reprint of the 1955 Nosworthy edition of *Cymbeline*.

52. Peter Wentworth, *A Pithie Exhortation to her Majestie for Establishing her Successor to the Crowne* ([Edinburgh], 1598), 77–79.

53. Brian C. Lockey, *Law and Empire in English Renaissance Literature* (Cambridge: Cambridge University Press, 2006), 177–78.

54. Hayward, *A Treatise of Union*, 19.

55. Craig, *De Unione*, 462.

56. Hume, *The British Union*, 113.

57. As Hume put it, "Let all men think their own private interest is involved in this; if it be beneficial for the island, then it is good for them." Ibid., 71.

58. Heather James observes that critics generally see Cymbeline as "the play's vacant center." See *Shakespeare's Troy*, 154.

59. See George Buchanan, *A Dialogue on the Law of Kingship among the Scots: A Critical Edition and Translation of George Buchanan's "De Iure Regni Apud Scotos Dialogus,"* ed. Roger A. Mason and Martin S. Smith (Aldershot, UK: Ashgate, 2004). For a discussion of James's relationship to Buchanan, see David Harris Willson's *King James VI and I* (New York: Oxford University Press, 1956), 25.

60. For example, see James VI and I, *Political Writings*, ed. J. P. Sommerville (Cambridge: Cambridge University Press, 1994), 133–37; "A Treatise about the Union," 47; Hume, *The British Union*, 77–81.

61. For example, see earlier discussion of Skinner, as well as "A Treatise about the Union," 52–53.

62. Simon Healy, ed., "Debates in the House of Commons, 1604–1607," in *Parliament, Politics, and Elections, 1604–1648*, ed. Chris R. Kyle, Camden fifth series. vol. 17 (London: Cambridge University Press for the Royal Historical Society, 2001), 49.

MARTHA C. NUSSBAUM

"ROMANS, COUNTRYMEN, AND LOVERS"

POLITICAL LOVE AND THE RULE OF LAW

IN JULIUS CAESAR

> For the weight of his character, and the fact that he did not yield easily
> to anyone who asked him for a favor, but instead acted on the basis of
> reasoning and the deliberate selection of noble principles, brought it about
> that, wherever he turned his efforts, they were strong and effective.
> —Plutarch, *Brutus* 6.8–9

> 'Tis well—here lies my hope: let but a sense,
> A manly sense of injured freedom wake them,
> The day's half won. The cold inactive spirit
> That slumbers in its chains—at this I tremble.
> Oh! patriots rouse.
> —"Brutus," in Mercy Otis Warren, *The Adulateur* (Boston, 1773),
> shortly before the Boston Tea Party

> Yet it is not necessary to praise political success or to idealize the men who
> win wealth and honors through civil war.
> —Sir Ronald Syme, *The Roman Revolution*, 1939

Love of Institutions, Love of a Father

Julius Caesar shows us two different kinds of political love, in tragic
opposition. Brutus is principled, but he is not cold. He loves the institutions of
the Roman Republic, and he tells us that this abstract love has driven out his
personal love of Caesar, as fire drives out fire. He appeals to the emotions he
believes all Romans have for their threatened republican form of government.
Addressing them as "countrymen and lovers" (3.2.13), he summons them to
love of country and hatred of oppression.[1] Suspicious of any particularistic attachment, Brutus prefers emotions resolutely fixed on an abstract object, which
reason can justify and commend. He expects all Romans to be like him: deliberative citizens, who value liberty with both their judgment and their hearts.

Brutus's antitype is Antony, who can understand no kind of love other than
the personal, who cannot refrain from calling the dead man "Julius" even in
the presence of the conspirators, and whose "Oh, pardon me, thou bleeding

256

piece of earth" spills out over this world of philosophically moralized emotion like a red stain (3.1.206, 256). Antony knows how to manipulate the people's desire for a beneficent father, and he plays on that love of the individual, that desire to be cared for as a parent cares for a child, in a way that rapidly subverts the people's love of institutions and laws. The play's verdict would appear to be that love of laws was never strong enough in the people to sustain a stable republic. The people's hearts are touched by the particular, and the government they get is what their hearts crave.

The play thus poses one of the darkest questions of political life: can Brutus's type of love ever motivate masses of people or determine the course of events? And if it cannot, what lies in store for freedom and the rule of law? Must the rule of law, if it is to endure at all, be undergirded by emotions more particular, more quasi-erotic, than those that Brutus favors? And if a successful love of country must be particularistic, must it take the form that Antony favors—the dependent child's gratitude for its parent's strength? If indeed infantile love of the father is the only love strong enough to secure political stability, then republicanism must be sustained by a type of love more suited to monarchy, if not tyranny. Perhaps, however, Brutus and Antony do not exhaust the terrain of political emotion. Perhaps there is a type of patriotic love more particularistic than Brutus's abstract emotion that still supports the institutions that Brutus favors.

The question posed by the play tracks a debate that began in antiquity, in the reflections of Roman republicans about the foundations of republican self-government. It continues today, as some defenders of liberal republican values (John Rawls, Jürgen Habermas) insist that patriotism ought to take the abstract form favored by Brutus and as defenders of a more romantic type of nationalism insist on the need for a more particularistic type of love, focused on symbols of ethnic belonging. There is also what one might call a "third way": some thinkers (I am one of them) believe that good laws and institutions need to be supported by emotions that are particularistic and not simply abstract, but they believe it is possible to create and sustain a particular love that reinforces and deepens the love of principles and institutions based on equal respect for the dignity of all human beings.[2] My plan is to investigate this debate,[3] using Shakespeare's play and its historical sources as my guide.

I begin with the debate over tyranny and the rule of law that spurred on the real-life assassins of Julius Caesar, showing how Shakespeare's sources portray the issues at stake and the emotional postures of the participants. I then turn to Shakespeare, arguing that he adheres rather closely to his sources but changes significantly their account of how the common people react to appeals of various sorts. He thus presents a far more monarchy-friendly and (for republicans) pessimistic picture than do the Roman sources. Brutus certainly lost, but the ancient sources do not agree with Shakespeare that the fickleness of the populace was the main reason for his defeat.

I turn next to a modern example in which Brutus's type of love seems to have prevailed, with Brutus as its paradigm: the American Revolution, in which images of Brutus served to propel people to an idealistic love of freedom that self-consciously rejected the trappings of paternal and monarchical power. But then, in a more general meditation on patriotic emotion, I suggest that this sort of success for abstract philosophical love is unstable. Even in the United States, Brutus's success, so to speak, was due at least in part to the fact that the patriots' abhorrence of all particularistic symbols was quickly relaxed, as myths of the nation's founding acquired a narrative form that mobilized emotion more stably than the bare announcement of resistance to tyranny. Fortunately for the future of constitutional self-government, the nation had leaders who understood how to mobilize patriotic symbols in a way that supported the love of a regime of equal political rights. I then argue, more generally, that a love of abstract principles and institutions needs to be undergirded by a deliberate construction of patriotic emotion as a love of the nation's history and struggles, where these are seen as linked to a love of political liberty and the impartial rule of law. To the American example I add the case of Indian independence in 1947, where Gandhi and Nehru's shrewd use of symbols provided good principles and laws with vital energy.

"Not Even Gentle Despots": Roman Republicanism and Its Downfall

The period of the so-called Roman Revolution is one of those relatively unusual periods in Western political history in which abstract philosophical ideals played a central role in defining the terms of the political debate. Such periods, when they do occur, are more common in times of revolutionary change. In this case, political leaders of great skill and dedication articulated their goals in terms of large-scale ideals familiar from philosophical texts. Although some were undoubtedly insincere, at least some really meant what they said. As the situation was seen by Brutus, Cicero, and many other Romans of the senatorial class, what was at stake in resisting Julius Caesar was nothing less than the republican form of government itself and, with it, the cherished ideal of liberty as nondomination.

According to these Roman republicans—and the modern "civic republicans" whom their writings have inspired[4]—liberty is not absence of government or absence of legal interference. Instead, the essence of liberty is nondomination, or the absence of arbitrary power within a polity.[5] Thus liberty is compatible with, and indeed requires, the rule of law: only law protects people from being at the mercy of arbitrary power. Of course the laws in question also have to be good laws, carefully crafted to protect people from arbitrary power; and the laws must establish stable republican institutions. The condition to be feared is the condition of the slave, or of the slavish follower of a demagogue—someone who can be pushed around by someone else's whim. Good laws prevent us from living in that condition, by setting up barriers between each person and the arbitrary will of another. Such laws (and institutions) respect people as free beings and prevent them from being pushed around like slaves. Protective laws are good laws only if they respect the equality of citizens, refusing to set up any orders and ranks among them. The brand of republicanism I am developing here is opposed to all caste-like hierarchies as forms of arbitrary domination; anticaste republicans, in the modern debate, are strong supporters of antidiscrimination laws. They understand the ideas of "due process" and "equal protection" to rule out hierarchies of all sorts, racial, gender-based, and so forth, that affect the opportunities of citizens for effective political agency.[6]

The Roman Republic was hardly a perfect instance of the political program of modern republicans, given the roles played in it by birth, wealth, and, of course, gender. Nonetheless, republicans, both at the time of the American founding and today, have not implausibly seen in its values—liberty, the absence of despotism, and effective opportunities for political agency—an inspiring source of their own political program.

To people who believe in this republican ideal, as articulated by Brutus, Cicero, and many others, the good character and gentle temperament of a despot make no difference at all. "Our forefathers," wrote Brutus in a letter, "could not endure even gentle despots."[7] Republicans objected to Julius Caesar's portrayal of himself as a kindly paternal benefactor of the people, because they saw this as irrelevant to the issue of lawless domination. (Antony later erected a statue of Julius, inscribed, "To Father and Benefactor" [parenti optime merito]—a step that Cicero viewed with utter contempt, saying that the liberators were now going to be condemned not only as assassins but also as parricides.)[8] To the republicans, a kindly parent is just a polite name for a tyrant, because the issue is one of arbitrary power. Fathers have the power of life and death over their children,[9] and so their children are not free, however nice the father is. So too, an absolute monarch may be ever so benign, but the extent of his power, if unlimited by appropriate laws, makes slaves of his people. Freedom requires laws that protect all alike from both malign and benign parental interference, where that involves unlimited monarchical or despotic power, power not checked by the rule of law. Repeatedly, Brutus insisted that the rule of law (in a sense focused on the protection of all from arbitrary domination) was his primary goal.[10]

But Rome was, and long had been, in a state of civil strife, and the ascendancy of a single man promised to end strife, whereas the assassination of Caesar threatened to (and really did) unleash full-scale civil war. When Brutus tested the conspirators, therefore, he posed to them a question from political philosophy: Which is better, a lawless monarchy, or civil war?[11] Platonists like Brutus said the latter; Stoics said the former.[12] Brutus chose only people who were willing to risk civil war in order to remove arbitrary power.

The ancient sources consistently represent Brutus as a person who was very effective at motivating people of all sorts. The fact that he used arguments rather than manipulation made people trust him and listen to him and made his efforts, says Plutarch, "powerful and efficacious" (*Brutus* 6.8). People longed for him passionately, after he departed from Rome (21.3). Cassius, Plutarch tells us, was feared rather than loved, but "Brutus was loved by the populace (*phileisthai*) because of his virtues, loved passionately (*erasthai*) by his friends, wondered at by the upper classes, and not hated even by his enemies, for he was an exceedingly gentle and large-minded man, unswayed by any anger or pleasure or greed, who kept his judgment straight and unbending in defense of what was noble and just" (29.3). Cicero's letters, too, provide ample evidence of the intensity with which Brutus was loved. Cicero himself wrote to his son-in-law Dolabella that he had always loved Brutus, but "the Ides of March increased my love so much that I am amazed that there was room for increase, since I had thought I was already full to overflowing."[13]

So Brutus was neither cold nor unlovable. Indeed, he was intensely loved. Still, he lost. As Cicero says, despairingly, the tyrant was removed, but tyranny remained.[14] Why did Brutus and liberty lose? One of the twentieth century's great works of historiography, Sir Ronald Syme's *The Roman Revolution*, notes that this question is all too rarely asked, because people have tended to assume that Augustus and the era he inaugurated were wonderful, peaceful, and hence self-justifying:

> Heaven and the verdict of history conspire to load the scales against the vanquished. Brutus and Cassius lie damned to this day by the futility of their noble deed and by the failure of their armies at Philippi. . . . The rule of Augustus brought manifold blessings to Rome, Italy and the provinces. Yet the new dispensation, or "novus status," was the work of fraud and

bloodshed, based upon the seizure of power and redistribution of property by a revolutionary leader. The happy outcome of the Principate might be held to justify, or at least to palliate, the horrors of the Roman Revolution: hence the danger of an indulgent estimate of the person and acts of Augustus.[15]

Syme's great book, written amid the fascist takeover of much of Europe, at a time when the survival of an independent Britain hung in the balance, is "pessimistic and truculent" in tone, as he announces at its start. And yet, as he notes, "it is not necessary to praise political success or to idealize the men who win wealth and honors through civil war."[16] Following Tacitus and other ancient writers closely in both style and darkness of outlook, Syme tells the story of a ruling class worn out by civil strife, who allowed themselves to be hoodwinked by the manipulations, based on carefully cultivated personal relationships, of a masterful and utterly unprincipled politician. Augustus played the cards of political philosophy when it suited him, pretending that he had committed a few necessary illegalities on the way to establishing a constitutional government that would protect old rule-of-law values. But it was all a fraud, and people more vigilant and less exhausted would have seen through it immediately. When the pressure was off, Augustus showed that domination was his real game. By then, however, people had bought peace at the price of their souls: "In the beginning kings ruled at Rome, and in the end, as was fated, it came round to monarchy again. Monarchy brought concord. During the Civil Wars every party and every leader professed to be defending the cause of liberty and of peace. Those ideals were incompatible. When peace came, it was the peace of despotism. '*Cum domino pax ista venit.*'"[17]

Writing with fierce passion about his own time, as well as about ancient Rome, Syme makes it clear that Brutus and Cassius were correct and that they might have won—but for the exhaustion, spinelessness, and sheer laziness of the ruling classes, as well as institutional weaknesses in the structure of the Roman constitution. "[A]s it was fated" is written with heavy irony: people like to think that domination is fated, because it excuses their lack of struggle. In Europe, similarly, Syme suggests, fascism came to power not because of fate, or the nature of the common people, or any lack of devotion they might have had to republican ideals of self-rule, but rather because (against the background of Germany's humiliation after World War I) political leaders made too many concessions for too long a time, fearful of conflict and hoodwinked by a supposed friend's promises of peace. What happened at Rome (the book's implicit argument goes) could happen in Britain—and almost did with Neville

Chamberlain's shameful concessions to Hitler. Syme's book antedates Winston Churchill's prime-ministership by a year. In 1939 it did seem plausible to think that Britain would soon go the way Rome had gone. Shortly after that, Syme apparently began to work under cover for British intelligence in Turkey, risking his life for republican ideals.[18]

Syme's book and his subsequent conduct argue that capitulation need not happen—if people care enough about liberty to endure a lengthy and difficult conflict. In 1939 the future was dark. Brutus and Cassius might win, or they might lose. But the fate of republican values was not sealed. Their future depends, Syme suggests, on whether enough people, and especially leaders, will care enough to fight for them long and hard enough, disdaining rest and safety. Or, as Churchill would indelibly say in May, 1940: "I have nothing to offer but blood, toil, tears, and sweat. We have before us an ordeal of the most grievous kind."

The brilliance of Syme's book lies both in its passionate rhetoric and in its unconventional method, which came to be known as "prosopography," that is, focusing on the individual alliances and family connections of leaders of the state, and the ways in which Augustus cannily manipulated them, in a void created by institutional weaknesses. What is crucial for our purposes—and it is Syme's central idea—is that people are perfectly capable of loving republican ideals, and these ideals can prevail, in the presence of the right leadership. In this case, it was a combination of exhaustion and laziness on the part of leaders that sold the people out. Even then, had Augustus not been a consummate master of deception, leading figures like Cicero would never have joined his cause. And even then, Brutus and Cassius might have prevailed—with a little more military luck, or a stronger institutional structure, or a slightly less ruthless and brilliant adversary.

Now we turn to Shakespeare. As we shall see, his story of the downfall of Brutus and Cassius is very different and is distinctly promonarchical: the common people, in their very nature, cannot deal with self-government and need a kindly father to establish order.

Brutus, Antony, the People

Throughout *Julius Caesar*, Shakespeare focuses on the people's emotional reactions to the speeches of a variety of leaders. In his famous speech after the assassination, Brutus appeals to the people to love the abstract political institutions of the Republic. He addresses them as "Romans, countrymen, and lovers" (3.2.13), summoning them to a rather abstract love of country and hatred of oppression. Argument is supposed to be enough for people. (Were

Antony Caesar's son, he says earlier, compelling moral arguments should satisfy him.) Shakespeare gives him prose, not poetry, at this crucial moment.

Brutus's speech is not rhetorically artless: in many ways it is a fine speech, careful in its use of rhythm and balanced syntax. It is, however, exceedingly abstract and dry. "Who is here so base, that would be a bondman? . . . Who is here so rude that would not be a Roman? . . . Who is here so vile that will not love his country?" (3.2.29–33). Here Brutus puts forward the key values of liberty and nondomination, but he joins them to no story of the nation, no particular symbols or memories around which people's passions might crystallize. He doesn't even mention his own famous ancestor, who overthrew the kings and established republican *libertas*. Without such elements, the speech is a shade too pat, its antitheses too obvious. Even though he speaks of love, the love is not made real to the audience but remains a remote abstraction.

Antony, of course, is different from the start. In soliloquy, he reveals himself as a lover of individuals: With "Oh, pardon me, thou bleeding piece of earth" (3.1.256) he pours out his apparently genuine passion for the fallen leader, seen not as an abstraction but as a unique embodied individual. He addresses particular features of Caesar's corpse with passionate, almost erotic love, speaking of the "ruby lips" of Caesar's bloody wounds as imploring his own "tongue" to speak (3.1.262–63). His words spill out over this world of philosophically moralized emotion. For him, the Servant gives proof that his "heart is big" only by being dumbstruck at the sight of Caesar's corpse (3.1.284–87). A monarchist from the bottom of his heart, Antony seems unable to understand Brutus's type of principle-based love. He is brilliant at inspiring the more usual, particular-directed type of passion. The brilliant rhetoric of his famous oration proves riveting for the way in which it appeals to a very physical love of the dead leader. He tells them how Caesar cared for them, like a kindly father, and then he predicts that they will "dip their napkins in his sacred blood, / Yea, beg a hair of him for memory" (3.2.135–36), thus invoking a fetishistic worship of the allegedly divine ruler that has sustained many monarchies in many times and places. The idea of the ruler's body as having magical properties (an idea that derives further resonance from Catholic fetishism of the relics of Christ and the saints) is of course a major threat to republican institutions, since those require people to prefer self-government to any sort of rescue by a single powerful figure.[19]

The two speeches, appealing to different types of political love, also construct two different conceptions of self and of self-love: in Brutus's speech, the self-love of the free citizen, participant in free and law-governed institutions; in Antony's, the warmer, cozier self-love of a child of a beneficent father.

So Shakespeare neatly captures the basic issues at stake in the Roman conflict, as both his sources and other sources known to us depict them. If we now look more closely at his relationship with those sources, however, we find that he diverges from them in one crucial respect.

Shakespeare follows his Roman materials closely up to a point, portraying the struggle as one between republican self-rule through law and the rule of arbitrary power; he portrays the emotions cultivated by Brutus and Antony as diverging around just that contrast. So closely does he follow the sources that many remarks are just slight reworkings of Plutarch (to take just two examples, Caesar's complaint that Cassius is too thin, and the entire scene in which Portia wounds herself to show her courage). Like the sources, he shows how Caesar, through his generosity and his clemency to rivals and foes, was able to make arbitrary power look beneficent. Indeed, one of his key alterations of the historical record sharpens up this contrast between the principled and the personal. For while he keeps a version of Caesar's dying remark of reproach to Brutus, he does not quote it as Suetonius gives it, thus directing attention away from a possible personal motive for Brutus's actions. In Shakespeare, Caesar says, "Et tu, Brute," "You too, Brutus" (3.1.78). In Suetonius's Latin text, Caesar speaks in Greek, saying "kai su, teknon," "You too, child." So Shakespeare has retained the fact of a dying reproach and retained, as well, the fact that Caesar spoke in a language not everyone around him could understand.[20] He leaves out, however, the key issue: Brutus was widely believed to be an illegitimate son of Caesar, so Suetonius is validating that story and giving Caesar words that impute to Brutus a motive of personal resentment. Shakespeare also omits the story that Brutus stabbed Caesar in the groin.[21] So nothing about love/hate of fathers confuses the picture. Shakespeare's Brutus is a man of republican principle, through and through.

The primary alteration Shakespeare makes in the sources, however, is his systematic rewriting of the behavior of the people. Throughout, the common people are fickle, volatile, and venal in a way that corresponds to nothing in Plutarch and Suetonius. From the beginning, it is the people who are inclined, as Brutus puts it, to "choose Caesar for their king" (1.2.80). First, the Lupercalia story. According to Plutarch, the idea of offering Caesar a crown on the Lupercalia was cooked up between Caesar and Antony in the expectation that the common people would applaud the offer of the crown. When the expected cheering did not materialize, the plan was rethought, and Caesar refused, seeing that "the experiment had failed" (*Caesar* 51.4). The people's behavior seems both dignified and shrewd. In Shakespeare, by contrast, there is no mention of the existence of a plot, no mention of the dead silence from the people that greeted the offer or of Caesar's reaction to that silence. Instead, as Casca tells the story, Caesar refuses three times without attending to the people at all, and then the people start to cheer in a mindless way: "the rabblement hooted, and clapped their chopped hands, and threw up their sweaty nightcaps, and uttered such a deal of stinking breath because Caesar refused the crown that it had almost choked Caesar" (1.2.242–46). Plutarch has nothing corresponding to this depiction of smell and dirtiness.

A similar, though more subtle, rewriting takes place in the key scene in which the two address the people after Caesar's death. Plutarch, in both *Brutus* and *Caesar*, emphasizes that the people listen to Brutus's speech both respectfully and enthusiastically. *Caesar* mentions their respectful silence (57.4); *Caesar* elaborates: "At sight of him the multitude, although it was a mixed crowd and prepared to raise a disturbance, was awestruck, and waited to hear him speak with orderly silence" (*kosmôi kai siôpêi*). They cheer after he speaks. Nothing is said to indicate that they want him to be king or misunderstand the republican values for which he has taken this huge risk. More generally, Plutarch emphasizes throughout that Brutus is an extremely popular speaker, and popular on account of the republican values for which he stands.

In Shakespeare, by contrast, the people have no interest in republican values. In this scene they misunderstand from the beginning: "Bring him with triumph home unto his house"; "Give him a statue with his ancestors"; "Let him be Caesar" (3.2.49–51). From the start, they just want a king, a god, a father. Brutus's goose is cooked before Antony even begins to speak. They are simply incapable of caring about republican liberty.

Shakespeare's subsequent account of Antony's speech agrees far more closely with the sources: Plutarch tells us that Antony did brilliantly manipulate the crowd, producing an outbreak of disorder. The mention of Caesar's will is, as in Shakespeare, a key turning point, and the sight of Caesar's wounds inspires extreme emotion in the crowd. However, according to Plutarch this needn't have happened, and it happens only on account of Antony's brilliant demagoguery: had he been killed along with Caesar, things would have turned out very differently. Moreover, the outcome is unclear even then; it becomes clear only when Octavian/Augustus comes upon the scene, manipulating the senatorial leadership for his own ends. Plutarch, like Syme, makes it perfectly clear that Antony's success could have been transient: the real political force was Augustus, pulling the strings behind the scenes. Like Syme, Plutarch is unsparing in his indictment of the fraudulence, rapacity, and utter amorality of Augustus, who convinced the upright Cicero to go along with his project to restore the republic and who all the while was plotting to murder Cicero and his brother.

Shakespeare's portrait of the people has, then, no basis in the sources, which show Augustus's manipulative brilliance but do not portray the people as particularly gullible. In Shakespeare people are too dumb, venal, and, really, bestial to have the slightest attachment to republican liberty. In any time and any place, people will prove unable to be republican citizens. They will have to be ruled by a king, so we should hope for one who is kindly and upright (as Antony clearly is not). In Plutarch, Cicero, and other sources, people can be manipulated by a brilliant despot in a time of upheaval and general stress, but that does not mean that they cannot think or cannot feel for the values of the Republic. (Indeed, Shakespeare himself presents a far more complex and respectful picture of the thinking of the common people in *Coriolanus*, a much later play.)

Finally, there is the depiction of Augustus. The ancient sources, read closely, tell the story Syme has made definitive: of a consummate hypocrite, ravenous for absolute power, who used the rhetoric of republicanism when it suited him and discarded it when it constrained his choices, a person who believed in nothing but himself and who played upon the exhaustion of both elites and masses in order to snatch from them the liberty they were no longer able to defend. Shakespeare's Octavian, by contrast, is a monarchist's Octavian: the benign leader who restores order and good government to a people racked by civil war. Syme's legitimate complaint against prevailing historiographical traditions in his own time—they are indulgent to Augustus because they see that he put an end to civil war—is also a legitimate charge against the Shakespeare of *Julius Caesar*, who certainly sells the losers short and flatters the winner. People need a kindly father; Augustus is that father; so people get what they really need and all is apparently well.

According to Roman sources, however, the Roman people had sustained republican institutions for six hundred years, a period of unparalleled length in human history—and they might have continued to do so. A particular crisis brought a despot to the fore. As Syme says, we know that this side did not win, but that was not how it looked at the time, from the point of view of people involved in the struggle. According to Shakespeare, by contrast, monarchical domination is natural, because people are incapable of republican self-government.

Brutus as Victor: *Julius Caesar* and the American Revolution

Need Brutus always lose? The Roman story suggests a negative answer: he might have succeeded but for the combination of general turmoil with the machinations of two extremely unprincipled and politically brilliant tyrants (Julius and Augustus). The people, and especially their leaders, yielded to the force of arms and, finally, to exhaustion, but they never lost the love of freedom. Indeed, it was Augustus's ability to pretend to be restoring the republic and the rule of law—while actually seizing absolute power and destroying the republic—that gave him a success that eluded Julius. Trust in his paternal stewardship crept in so gradually that nobody was even surprised when, at his death, he was divinized as a god.

Brutus remained throughout European history a symbol of resistance to tyranny, and sometimes his friends prevailed. They did prevail in the Second World War—because Syme himself, and many like him, following Winston Churchill's leadership, refused to acquiesce in domination and were prepared to give their lives for freedom. Sometimes people do passionately love abstract ideals, and that love propels them into painful conflict.

Sometimes, indeed, people use abstract ideals not simply to fight for a liberty they already have, but to acquire a liberty they have never had. If there was any political upheaval in history that was Brutus-like in its inspiration and execution, it was the American Revolution, in which patriots endlessly talked about Roman Republican ideals of nondomination and nonslavery, casting various British officials in the role of the arbitrary tyrant. Brutus, as one might expect, was the hero of the hour. Shortly before the Boston Tea Party—an act of popular symbolic resistance that showed a "mob" acting in quite a principled and law-oriented manner—Mercy Otis Warren, one of the literary giants of the Revolution and its first historian, published in Boston a drama called *The Adulateur* in which she mocked those who fawned on British power and invoked the name of Brutus to urge her fellow citizens on to defiance for the sake of liberty.[22] The play is set in a fictional "Upper Servia," which means "Upper Slaveland." Servia is "the once famed mistress of the north, / The sweet retreat of freedom," now terrorized by the "sullen ghost of bondage." Her foreign governor, Rapatio, is contemptuous of the inhabitants' liberty, both political and economic. But Brutus and Cassius remember their noble Roman ancestors, who fought and died for freedom. They resolve to rise up against the tyrant and to perish, if necessary, in a way worthy of "a free man."

Warren had read her Cicero and Plutarch well. As historians of the period have frequently noted, the idea of liberty as freedom from domination was taken over from Roman republican texts as the hallmark of the Revolution.[23] Brutus urges restraint and a dignified demeanor in misfortune, hoping to attain freedom by persuasion. Shortly, however, the murders of several of his fellow citizens cause the leaders to resolve to throw off the yoke of tyranny. They do so, however, not by assassination but through the rule of law, as the British rulers are convicted of various crimes before a patriot court. As Rapatio and his minions scheme to get their revenge, suppressing liberty yet more completely, Brutus and his supporters predict, though with reluctance, that bloodshed on both sides will soon follow. Ultimately, the land will become a free nation.

The most interesting aspect of the play, for our purposes, is its very anti-Shakespearean depiction of the American people. Although Rapatio scorns them as "some half-formed peasants, / Unmeaning dull machines," Brutus knows better. They can be motivated, he predicts, by "a manly sense of injured freedom." When one among them urges indiscriminate violence, Brutus successfully preaches restraint:

> Let us not sully by unmeaning actions
> The cause of injured freedom: this demands
> A cool, sedate and yet determined spirit.

And when he makes his big speech—the American analogue of "Romans, countrymen, and lovers"—the stage directions tell us that he is "interrupted with a universal shout, which Brutus welcomes, making it clear that it is a strong expression of passion:

> Oh! what a burst of joy was that—there broke
> The warm effusion of a heart that feels
> In virtue's cause. What a throb of pleasure!

Not only are the people passionate about liberty and virtue; they also absolutely refuse the lure of royalist symbolism. When Hazlerod, another leading British official, enters, the stage directions mention that the scene "opens with a procession of coaches, chariots, etc.," and that the whole scene, together with Hazlerod's paean to the charms of monarchy and Caesar, is "highly pleasing to creatures of arbitrary power, and equally disgusting to every man of virtue."

And of course the play was part of the incitement to the Revolution of which it speaks. It really did move people, and the evidence is that people at that time really did find freedom itself profoundly alluring and the signs of monarchy disgusting.[24] Not only did people not give way to a longing for a beneficent father, as in Shakespeare; they were also too smart and savvy to allow themselves to be tricked by an Octavian, as happened at Rome—although it must be admitted that the British were so unprepared and inept that any comparison to one of history's great evil-doers is inappropriate.

Patriotism and the Rule of Law

Can a republic sustain itself that way over time, through intense passion for abstract ideals? As the new nation formed itself, many patriots were alarmed at the whole institution of the presidency, surrounded, as it was, with what many saw as quasi-monarchical symbols. Very soon, in addition to accepting that very person-centered institution, the new nation was suffused with narratives of past struggles, stories we've all heard as children before we had any clear notion of republican virtue. As a child, like so many American children, I was taken to Valley Forge, where (so we were told) the patriots lived in frigid cabins and walked with bloody feet through the snow. To Trenton, where Washington boldly crossed the Delaware, catching by surprise the sleeping British command and those drunken Hessian soldiers. To Gettysburg, where other soldiers, four score and seven years later, "gave their lives that that nation might live." Not until I became an adult was the narrative of Martin Luther King Jr. added to that sequence, but now the soaring rhetoric and symbolism of his "I Have a Dream" speech is part of the conception of the nation that American schoolchildren form.[25] Now we here in Chicago live in the middle of yet another narrative, as the journalists of the world come to us for stories of the youth of the nation's first African American president.

John Rawls and Jürgen Habermas have argued that the Shakespearean Brutus's sort of emotion is all the nations of the world need: a "constitutional patriotism" whose emotions take as their object the institutions and principles of the good society.[26] Shakespeare, as I've suggested, seems to take the other extreme course: people are too fickle, too inconstant, to have any real devotion to abstract ideals, and they will always prefer kings to republican institutions, because people are essentially infantile, and kings satisfy their longing for a kindly father.

But history shows, I believe, that the truth lies somewhere in the middle: a nation with good principles and institutions will do well to call symbol, story, and rhetoric to its aid, because particularistic emotions and emotionally stirring rhetoric are essential to the stability of such institutions. As Ernst Renan famously argued, a nation exists in people's minds not primarily as an abstract blueprint, but as a narrative of past struggles and future hopes.[27] Unless a nation can tap into the love of particulars with Antony's psychological shrewdness, it will have a hard time withstanding the challenge of corrupt political entrepreneurs who can do the same with enormous skill. (Think of the collapse of the Weimar Republic in the face of Hitler's masterful use of symbolism and appeals to the love of the father. Think, on the other side, of the emotional power of Churchill's speeches in stiffening the resolve of the British people.)

Why do our minds work this way, needing to connect ideals to concrete historical particulars? No doubt the answer lies partly in our innate equipment. I believe it lies, as well, in the way we learn abstract values as children, from parents who connect them to stories, both personal and historical. My parents nicely provided me with *Stories of Famous Women*, where I read about courage and defiance through the stories of Volumnia and Cornelia.[28] My father offered his own variant of the bloody-feet-at-Valley-Forge story when he told me with great pleasure that he was too poor to own shoes until he went to college. Such stories shape our growing allegiance to abstract principles, and so we look for similar particularity when we form a conception of our nation.

Political rhetoric is an important part of this job of emotion-construction, but so too is the shrewd selection of a nation's visual symbols: architecture, photography, the design of public parks; all these and others play their role in creating a story of the nation and its people.[29]

What is crucial is to find symbols and stories that reinforce and strengthen, rather than subvert, the attachment people have to good institutions and the ideals that embody them. The stories of the American Revolution that I heard as a child do just that: for the bloody feet at Valley Forge are signs of the courage and determination of the patriots in the cause of freedom, and those drunken Hessians taken by surprise at Trenton are symbols of monarchical corruption outflanked, as it always must be (the story goes) by patriot shrewdness and resourcefulness. Washington is there in the front of the boat, but the story is carefully told as a patriot story, a liberty story, not a story in which the common people remain passively dependent on the care of a fatherly ruler. And although the institution of the American presidency always risks tipping over into monarchical exaltation of a beneficent father-figure, somehow or other this danger has for the most part been avoided (more at some times than at others, certainly), because of the way in which successful presidents, from Washington to Obama, have portrayed the president as one who asks all Americans to join in active support for the nation's core principles and values.

The career of George Washington provides, in fact, a fine example of delicate negotiation between an excess of monarchical paternalism and an excess of unemotional routine. It is now clear, thanks to Ron Chernow's pathbreaking (and Pulitzer Prize–winning) biography, that Washington thought about these issues with unusual subtlety.[30] Mercy Otis Warren and her fellow anti-Federalists probably would not have been happy with any choices made by Washington in his role as president, but we can now appreciate the shrewdness of his choices.[31] Already as commander he made a point of emphasizing the vulnerable humanity he shared with his soldiers: a famous story describes him suddenly putting on reading glasses during a speech and commenting, "I have grown gray in your service and now find myself growing blind." He astonished foreign visitors by the simplicity of his dress: "an old blue coat faced with buff, waistcoat and britches . . . seemingly of the same age and without any lace upon them composed his dress."[32] When he was subsequently elected as the nation's first president, he acknowledged the difficulty of crafting this new office and the importance of his judgment for the nation's future: "I should consider myself as entering upon an unexplored field, enveloped on every side with clouds and darkness."[33]

One of the greatest dangers, as anti-Federalists saw it, was that the presidency would become hereditary. Already upset at Washington's membership in the Society of the Cincinnati, where membership initially was hereditary, they were somewhat assuaged by the fact that Washington himself strongly opposed hereditary membership and soon got others to end it. Best of all, however, was something that Washington did not choose: he and Martha were childless. Washington was well aware that this otherwise unhappy situation made him uniquely suited to be the first president, and this fact may have influenced his decision to allow his name to go forward.[34]

When the time came to craft the first presidential inauguration, Washington's taste for a combination of dignity and simplicity was strongly in evidence. He made a major decision when he refused to wear a military uniform at the inauguration—or ever after that (although he did wear a sword on formal ceremonial occasions). Instead, he decked himself out with patriotic symbols. To encourage American industry, he choose "a double-breasted brown suit made from broadcloth woven at the Woolen Manufactory of Hartford, Connecticut. The suit had gilt buttons with an eagle insignia on them." Washington remarked that Americans ought to imitate their president and favor domestic industries. During the entire period surrounding the inauguration, although always imposing by his good looks and six-foot stature, and although he continued to favor white horses whose coats had been treated with a shiny substance, he also took care to walk around in the streets of New York like an ordinary citizen, greeting people affably. As one antimonarchical correspondent observed, "It has given me much pleasure to hear every part of your conduct spoke of with high approbation, and particularly your dispensing with ceremony occasionally and walking the streets, while Adams is never seen but in his carriage and six."[35] Washington has long been thought of as a heroic leader rather than a thinker. It is clear by now, however, that he exercised judgment superbly, both in isolated gestures (the glasses) and in overall patterns of conduct (his walks, his style of dress), knowing that his heroic attributes were helpful in the nation's first leader but that they also had to be balanced and to some degree undercut by gestures of a more egalitarian sort, if fears of a monarchical presidency were to be proven groundless. The symbols Washington favored (the eagle, native woolens, the eyeglasses) united people and cemented devotion, and they led the mind toward, rather than away from, the central ideals of the nation.

It is entirely appropriate, and a sign that he communicated his ideas about public symbolism effectively, that the Washington Monument is not the portrait of an individual, far less a shrine inviting the worship of an individual. It is, instead, an abstract symbol, an obelisk—alluding to Washington's Masonic connections. At the same time, it is not a monolith, like classical obelisks, but is composed of separate blocks: at its dedication this design was said to symbolize the unity of the states and, with its graceful ascent, the high goals of the nation.[36]

In general, then, what does the creator of a decent patriotism for a new nation need to guard against? Above all, Shakespeare suggests, the new republic needs to guard against the desire to relax into the sheltering care of a kindly father. The image of the leader as father must be replaced by the image of the president as one among other citizens, defender of citizen freedoms. Washington clearly understood this well.

Another danger, mentioned in 1792 by the German philosopher Johann Gottfried Herder, is a fixation on images of aggressive masculinity that can lead people to attach too much of their self-image to warlike exploits and the idea of heroic glory.[37] So good symbols, if they use war at all, will portray war as a necessary struggle for liberty and peace against tyranny and oppression. The bloody feet in the snow tell us that freedom is worth pain and risk; they do not glorify irresponsible cowboy antics, as some other symbols might do and on some occasions have done. (Churchill's "blood, sweat, and tears" speech is another fine example.) The danger of seeking a father and the danger of overvaluing warlike exploits are connected, clearly, since a fixation on aggressive war-making easily leads to imputing heroic properties to the leader.

Another danger that pervades all patriotic symbol construction is ethnic polarization and the construction of subordinate groups. Republicanism asks us to see all citizens as free and equal. But if a nation's narrative is identified with language, or with ethnocultural or religious homogeneity, then immigrant groups and other local minorities can easily be excluded, made to seem like not full Americans or even like subversives. Good symbols therefore need to avoid basing national identity on ethnicity, race, or religion and need to find ways to include all the diverse elements that a nation contains. An important set of debates about this question has surrounded the jurisprudence of the U.S. Establishment Clause, as applied to symbolic public displays. Justice Sandra Day O'Connor influentially proposed an "endorsement test," grounded in the thought of James Madison, which tests the constitutionality of a display by asking whether an "objective observer," acquainted with relevant facts about both history and context, would view the display in question as one that made a statement of exclusion, creating an in-group and out-groups.[38] This is exactly the right sort of question for a society committed to equal respect to be asking.

Finally, good symbols need to bring people back down to earth, reminding them that leaders are not gods—as Augustus soon claimed to be—that they are extremely human and flawed. Washington's pointed reference to his need for reading glasses did not become famous merely by accident: for it came as a welcome reminder that the president, though a man of imposing stature and achievements, was made of the same flesh and blood as his troops and was not a species apart.

Such symbols, I would argue, can complement abstract republican ideals and render them more stable. People can love those ideals for their own sake, but they will do so more effectively and continuously if the ideas are bolstered, in turn, with symbolism of the right sort.

Let me conclude with one further example of patriotic symbolism at the dawn of a new nation. Like the American example, it shows Brutus triumphant, but not without the help of passions that are warmer and more particularistic than his. This is the case of India in 1947. Like the United States, India achieved independence from Britain through a revolution in which much attention was paid to the principles of liberty and nondomination. As in the case of the United States, those abstract ideals really moved people. So too, however, did Gandhi's theater of civil resistance and his use of his own body as a symbol of solidarity with the poor and the lower castes. A brilliant theatrical director and actor, Gandhi arranged mass events (the great salt march, the protest at the salt-works during which the British repeatedly clubbed down rows of disciplined and nonviolent Indian patriots) that displayed the dignity and self-government of the Indian people, contrasted with the thuggishness of the British, who could never resist the bait that Gandhi offered. He thus showed the world that the nation was ready for self-government—more ready, indeed, than the Raj, which, pretending to govern India, could not even govern its own aggressiveness. At the same time, Gandhi's theatrical self-dramatization (his own dress, the tasks he asked his followers to perform) demonstrated repeatedly that class and caste were irrelevant to citizenship in the new nation. He proclaimed that even religion, potentially the most divisive factor of all, was no barrier, as he accepted from Maulana Azad the orange juice with which he broke his fast unto death, a violation of all traditional ideas of Hindu ritual purity.

When the time came to choose a flag for the new nation, the choice was significant: the saffron of courage, the white of purity and dedication, the green of fertility—and, at the center of the flag, the wheel, a Buddhist symbol of the rule of law associated with the emperor Ashoka, a great favorite of Nehru's. Because Ashoka, a convert from Hinduism to Buddhism in the second century B.C., famously stood for religious toleration and mutual respect, the wheel is also a symbol of religious inclusion and equality. All citizens, no matter what their religious or ethnic origin, are equals under the law.[39]

As for the national anthem, the founders turned to "Jana Gana Mana," words and music by Rabindranath Tagore, who famously supported the removal of caste, gender, and religion as barriers to human equality. The anthem is beautiful and sensuous. Its first stanza mentions many geographical regions of India from which her people come and thus deepens love of India's geography. But it states that all these people from all these regions owe allegiance to law—thus deepening attachment to ideal principles at the same time. The second stanza does the same thing with religion: India's citizens belong to all the major religions, and all alike give reverence to morality and law. Once again, the rule of law is made appealing and sensuous by being embedded in beautiful stirring symbols.

At each point, these symbolic choices were contested by symbols more exclusionary and, at times, more monarchical, put forward by the Hindu Right. The Hindu Right attacked Gandhi's nonviolence and defended an aggressive style of manly self-assertion. They attacked "Jana Gana Mana," preferring a song that showed the patriot as exclusively Hindu, offering deferential worship to a variety of Hindu deities—before going to war aggressively against India's enemies. They attacked the flag and its symbolism of law, preferring the pure saffron banner associated with an eighteenth-century Hindu emperor who rose up against the Muslims—but with no particular interest in the rule of law. The values attached to the symbols connect aggressiveness to unquestioning obedience: the daily pledge of members of the RSS (Rashtriya Swayamsevak Sangh), the leading Hindu Right social group (as they raise the saffron banner) is, "I take the oath that I will always protect the purity of Hindu religion, and the purity of Hindu culture, for the supreme progress of the Hindu nation. I have become a component of the RSS. I will do the work of the RSS with utmost sincerity and unselfishness and with all my body, soul, and resources. And I will keep this vow for as long as I live. Victory to Mother India." We are in Antony country here, and Hindu Right groups (*shakhas*) teach young boys to love fatherly leaders and to do their bidding without question.[40]

What pledge, by contrast, did India's Brutus ask her people to take? Jawaharlal Nehru's famous "tryst with destiny" speech is a fitting comparison piece to Brutus's "Romans, countrymen, and lovers," for it asks all Indians to dedicate themselves to ideals. It has great poetry, however, and it soars above Brutus in its indelible images of past struggle and future commitment:

> Long years ago we made a tryst with destiny, and now the time comes when we shall redeem our pledge, not wholly or in full measure, but very substantially. At the stroke of the midnight hour, when the world sleeps, India will awake to life and freedom. . . . It is fitting that at this solemn moment, we take the pledge of dedication to the service of India and her people and to the still larger cause of humanity. . . .
>
> . . . Before the birth of freedom, we have endured all the pains of labour and our hearts are heavy with the memory of this sorrow. Some of those pains continue even now. Nevertheless, the past is over and it is the future that beckons us now.
>
> That future is not one of ease or resting but of incessant striving so that we may fulfill the pledges we have so often taken and the one we shall take today. The service of India means, the service of the millions who suffer. It means the ending of poverty and ignorance and disease and inequality of opportunity. The ambition of the greatest man of our generation has been to wipe every tear from every eye. That may be beyond us, but as long as there are tears and suffering, so long our work will not be over.
>
> And so we have to labour and to work, and to work hard, to give reality to our dreams. Those dreams are for India, but they are also for the world, for all the nations and peoples are too closely knit together today for any one of them to imagine that it can live apart. Peace is said to be indivisible, so is freedom, so is prosperity now, and also is disaster in this one world that can no longer be split into isolated fragments.
>
> To the people of India, whose representatives we are, we make an appeal to join us with faith and confidence in this great adventure. This is no time for petty and destructive criticism, no time for ill will or blaming others. We have to build the noble mansion of free India where all her children may dwell.

The fame of this speech, both at the time and afterward, testifies to its success in communicating a vision of independent India to a large public. While it is somewhat closer to Brutus's abstract political rhetoric than is the visionary poetry of Martin Luther King Jr., Nehru's speech is nonetheless very powerful, emotionally and rhetorically. Its unforgettable image of the midnight liberation of a new nation (though of course literal truth as well as symbol) has come to stand for the idea that India's activity and vigilance took charge while British complacency and empire slept—rather like, then, the image of Washington crossing the Delaware at night and taking those sleeping Hessian soldiers by surprise. Even before Salman Rushdie wrote *Midnight's Children*, the idea of the midnight birth of a freeborn generation grabbed the imaginations of people all over the world.

Particularly significant, perhaps, is Nehru's narrative of the nation as one born in struggle and pain, with a commitment to a future of striving. This is a powerful narrative, and by asking people to join in the project outlined in the speech, Nehru constructs an active citizenry, determined to move forward in a life of service.

The speech refers prominently to a particular individual: for all know that Gandhi is "the greatest man of our generation." And Gandhi, like Antony's Caesar, is depicted as wanting to help the people, ending their poverty and suffering. How different, however, is everything else. Caesar was a beneficent despot giving out handouts. Gandhi is a "great soul" among citizen equals, dressed in the clothes of the poorest and humblest, asking all citizens to join in the shared project of ending inequality of opportunity, a project to be pursued under free democratic self-government and the rule of law. Freedom is just as indivisible as peace, says Nehru; and he positions himself and his fellow founders, humbly, as the representatives of the people of India, thus gesturing toward a future of law-governed democracy.

The rule of law, as Shakespeare's Brutus depicted it, seemed abstract and remote; it could not sufficiently hold the attention of the populace. Nehru's portrait of the rule of law, by contrast, connects it to a narrative of the nation's successful, albeit extremely painful, struggle against the Raj: it is a birth of freedom and of self-governed striving, which Nehru connects to a moving vision of opportunity for all. Moreover, Nehru is at pains to show why India's particular version of the rule of law is admirable: because it is built on an idea of the equal worth of all citizens and an effort to secure decent life conditions for all. Brutus, we might say, forgot who he was: for the history of his ancestor, who rose up against the kings, would have given republican antimonarchical ideals a narrative to hang on to, a narrative that might have energized the passions even of the fickle populace Shakespeare depicts. Such a narrative would also have shown what sort of law Brutus takes to be admirable, and why it should be admired. Nehru has the advantage of immediacy: for nobody who heard his speech could forget the pain of the independence struggle and the atrocities committed by the British monarchists in order to preserve their empire. The speech contains no explicit mention of the Amritsar massacre, no mention of the years of civil resistance and brutal opposition to that resistance, no mention of the years Nehru himself spent in British jails, because any member of his audience, hearing the words "the pains of labour" and "the memory of this sorrow" would know exactly what was meant and would see Nehru—standing there in his simple clothing—as the living embodiment of sacrifice.

Many new republican nations are born, and only some of them survive. Perhaps one might see Mohammed Ali Jinnah as Pakistan's Augustus, a wily manipulator who used republican language while aiming at personal power. The people of Pakistan—after all, the very same people as the people of India so far as education and history go—proved unable to keep a republic alive, unlike the people of India. This failure shows us that republican values are vulnerable and that their success depends on many factors. Gandhi and Nehru did many things well, and the careful political structure that they created for the new republic is surely one large factor accounting for its success and vitality.[41] Another large factor is their personal honesty and integrity. Yet another is their unswerving dedication to and solidarity with the whole nation, rather than to personal power. But narrative, symbol, and the emotions these generate matter too, and in Nehru's speech they go to work in a way that does Brutus's job better than Brutus did, constructing a joy mixed with civic responsibility, a hope grounded in a commitment to service, and a compassion expressing a willingness to sacrifice for the common good—emotions that are particularistic because linked to a narrative of struggle and to the vision of an outstanding servant of the people, but that are also general, because they take as their object, and usher in, an era in which representation and the rule of law will take over from monarchical domination. Moreover, they transcend the values of Britain and Europe, which pursued nondomination internally, within each nation, but aggressively pursued domination of other nations and peoples. Nehru, by contrast, announces that his dreams are not just for India but for the entire world: the birth of India means not just a republic in India, but the death-knell of colonialism.

Shakespeare's *Julius Caesar* is a misleading, even a dangerous work. It tells the countless people who read it that republican values cannot succeed, because people simply need to be taken care of. It accomplishes this goal, in part, by representing the common people as bestial and herdlike. This part of Shakespeare's design is relatively easy to spot and to criticize. Another, more insidious part of the play's strategy, however, is its representation of the republicans as unwilling or unable to use emotive symbolic materials—which may not always be necessary for the successful defense of liberty but are surely a great help. We should take issue with Shakespeare here too: Brutus need not be cold (and apparently was not so in real life), nor need Antony use his rhetorical genius for monarchical ends. A passionate republicanism is possible, and we all know what it looks like.

NOTES

1. All references to the play are to William Shakespeare, *The Complete Works of Shakespeare*, ed. David Bevington, 6th ed. (New York: Pearson Education, 2009).

2. Obviously, not all varieties of republicanism emphasize equal human dignity. Some verge on aristocracy, by focusing on the contributions of a virtuous elite. In what follows, I accept an understanding of the American Revolution according to which its form of civic republicanism, and its understanding of Rome in this connection, is profoundly egalitarian (as argued, for example, by Gordon Wood; see discussion below); the founding of India is indisputably based on ideas of human equality, as is my own normative political theory. For the latter, see especially my *Frontiers of Justice: Disability, Nationality, Species Membership* (Cambridge, MA: Harvard University Press, 2006); and *Creating Capabilities: The Human Development Approach* (Cambridge, MA: Harvard University Press, 2011). Philip Pettit's normative view of republicanism is also very egalitarian, given its strong commitment to nondomination in all areas of society (see discussion and references below).

3. Or rather, to continue my investigation of it, since I have addressed the question already in two papers: "Radical Evil in the Lockean State: The Neglect of the Political Emotions," *Journal of Moral Philosophy* 3 (2006): 159–78, of which a longer version, "Radical Evil in Liberal Democracies," appears in *Democracy and the New Religious Pluralism*, ed. Thomas Banchoff (New York: Oxford University Press, 2007), 171–202; and "Toward a Globally Sensitive Patriotism," *Daedalus* (Summer 2008): 78–93. These articles were preparations for a book, *Political Emotions: Why Love Matters for Justice* (Cambridge, MA: Harvard University Press, forthcoming 2013).

4. See Philip Pettit, *Republicanism: A Theory of Freedom and Government* (Oxford: Clarendon Press, 1997); Cass R. Sunstein, "Beyond the Republican Revival," *Yale Law Journal* 97 (1988): 1539–90; Sunstein, *The Partial Constitution* (Cambridge, MA: Harvard University Press, 1993); and others. Significant, too, is the real-life adoption of these principles in Zapatero's Spain, which made Pettit a key adviser to the government: see Pettit and José Luis Martí, *A Political Philosophy in Public Life: Civic Republicanism in Zapatero's Spain* (Princeton, NJ: Princeton University Press, 2010).

5. Accepting nondomination as a key value within a polity does not entail being

committed to not dominating other nations and peoples, as the history of the British Empire shows. Nonetheless, if one takes the key idea to be that morally irrelevant distinctions such as caste, race, and gender should not be turned into systematic sources of social hierarchy (Sunstein's conception, for example), then it does appear difficult to justify empire, and most empire-builders have simply ducked the issue of providing a coherent philosophical defense of their goals.

6. Pettit, for example, strongly and successfully argued that nondomination where Spain was concerned required an absence of hierarchy along lines of sexual orientation; hence the remarkable fact that Spain has endorsed same-sex marriage. Here and throughout, in speaking of "citizens," I do not mean to imply that noncitizens have no rights in a decent society. Since, however, noncitizen residents are of many types, and since the questions their presence poses are not relevant to my argument, I leave them to one side.

7. Quoted in Plutarch, *Brutus*, 22.4–5, but also in the collection of letters between Cicero and Brutus. D. Shackleton Bailey has cast doubt on the authenticity of Brutus's letter because of its negative portrayal of Cicero, but these sentiments, at any rate, are clearly the sort of thing Brutus consistently stood for.

8. Cicero, letter to Cassius, October 2, 44, *Ad Fam.* no. 345 in Shackleton Bailey's numbering.

9. Under Roman law, this power was utterly unqualified; see Richard Saller, *Patriarchy, Property, and Death in the Roman Family* (Cambridge: Cambridge University Press, 1994).

10. See Plutarch, *Brutus* 14.7: "Caesar does not and will not prevent me from acting according to the laws." See also 8.5–6: Cassius hated the ruler, but Brutus the idea of rule.

11. See Plutarch, *Brutus* 12.3–4: *monarchia paranomos* versus *polemos emphulios*.

12. For this and other evidence that Brutus was a Platonist, see David N. Sedley, "The Ethics of Brutus and Cassius," *Journal of Roman Studies* 87 (1997): 41–53.

13. Cicero, *Ad Fam.* no. 326 Shackleton Bailey.

14. Cicero, *Ad Att.* 14.14; *Ad Fam.* 327, 344.

15. Sir Ronald Syme, *The Roman Revolution* (Oxford: Clarendon Press, 1939), 2, 4. Syme (1903–1989), born in New Zealand, spent most of his life in England. For an authoritative appreciation of Syme's career, see Glen W. Bowersock, "Ronald Syme (March 11, 1903–September 4, 1989)," *Proceedings of the American Philosophical Society* 135 (1991): 118–22; he describes Syme as "the greatest historian of ancient Rome since Theodor Mommsen and the most brilliant exponent of the history of the Roman Empire since Edward Gibbon. Syme's authority far transcended that of most scholars." It is worth adding that Syme was a fan of the American Revolution: Bowersock mentions the pride he always took in his honorary membership in the American Philosophical Society, which he referred to affectionately as "the B. Franklin gang" (121).

16. Syme, *The Roman Revolution*, viii.

17. Ibid., 9. The first sentence translates the opening sentence of Tacitus's *Annals*, "Urbem Roman a principio reges habuere," which is followed in Tacitus by the state-

ment that Brutus (the ancestor) "introduced liberty and the consulship." The last sentence is a quote from Lucan's *Pharsalia*, an epic poem about the civil wars that espouses republican values. (Lucan, himself a republican, died in a failed conspiracy against the emperor Nero, along with his cousin the philosopher Seneca.)

18. During the war (and right after the publication of *The Roman Revolution*), he worked as a press attaché at the British embassy in Belgrade. Because he refused to discuss his work during this period, it is generally believed that he was working for British intelligence in Turkey. Bowersock concludes, "One may suspect that his contribution to the intelligence network of the Allies was substantial, perhaps even reflected in the Order of Merit that he received long afterward." "Ronald Syme," 120.

19. Shakespeare's connection of Antony to Catholic notions that would have seemed sinister to much of his audience is significant, and it shows (if we needed anything further to show this) that Shakespeare wanted his audience to be highly skeptical of Antony. Octavian, not Antony, is the solution to the problem posed by the people's weakness.

20. That, at least, seems to be the way it comes across in the play. At Rome, though, Greek was widely understood by educated people, and so I am inclined to think Cicero used Greek for the remark not to conceal its meaning but to express a kind of friendly intimacy that often characterizes the use of Greek in Cicero's correspondence.

21. Plutarch, *Caesar* 66. Given the presence of the Jove-Saturn castration myth in the treatment of Hal and Falstaff (noted by Richard Strier in his essay in this volume, Shakespeare's omission of it here seems significant, a sign of his interest in representing Brutus as principled and impartial).

22. Mercy Otis Warren, *The Adulateur* (Boston, 1773). Warren (1728–1814) was a prominent intellectual figure throughout the Revolution and until her death. She corresponded with John Adams and other leaders and produced the first book-length history of the Revolution.

23. See Gordon S. Wood, *The Radicalism of the American Revolution* (New York: Vintage, 1991); and Pettit, *Republicanism*.

24. Of course they found it disgusting only when it involved the enslavement of white males and notoriously failed to reject it when it concerned men of African descent, notwithstanding the strong antislavery views of many among them. Nor, again notoriously, did they even debate the subordination of women.

25. I discuss King in "Radical Evil" and "Toward a Globally Sensitive Patriotism"; I discuss Lincoln in "Toward a Globally Sensitive Patriotism."

26. John Rawls, *A Theory of Justice* (Cambridge, MA: Harvard University Press, 1971), 479–504; Jürgen Habermas, "Citizenship and National Identity: Some Reflections on the Future of Europe," *Praxis International* 12 (1992–93): 1–19; see my discussion of their views in "Toward a Globally Sensitive Patriotism."

27. Ernst Renan, "What Is a Nation?" delivered at the Sorbonne on March 11, 1882, translated by Martin Thom in *Nation and Narration*, ed. Homi Bhabha (Oxford: Routledge, 1990), 8–22. Renan remarked that "suffering in common unifies more than joy does" (19). One could also think of Edmund Burke's earlier and highly influential views of particular attachment.

28. I remember the book as primarily Rome-focused; perhaps Greek models like Sappho and Aspasia were too unsavory, and they certainly did not include some very famous Roman women, such as Agrippina and Messalina.

29. In "Radical Evil" I discuss FDR's use of photography during the Depression and Chicago's construction of Millennium Park. Many more such examples are investigated in *Political Emotions*.

30. Ron Chernow, *Washington: A Life* (New York: Penguin Press, 2010).

31. In 1788 Warren published *Observations on the New Constitution* (Boston, 1788), which developed a sharp anti-Federalist argument.

32. Chernow, *Washington*, 435–36.

33. Ibid., 549.

34. Ibid.

35. Ibid., 566, 584–85.

36. See Charles Griswold, "The Vietnam Veterans Memorial and the Washington Mall: Philosophical Reflections on Political Iconography," *Critical Inquiry* 12 (1986): 688–719; at the dedication, Robert Winthrop's oration mentioned both the theme of unity in diversity and the absence of "vainglorious" symbols (716n9).

37. I discuss Herder's ideas in "Toward a Globally Sensitive Patriotism." See Johann Gottfried Herder, "Letters on the Advancement of Humanity," in *Herder: Philosophical Writings*, ed. and trans. Michael N. Forster (Cambridge: Cambridge University Press, 2002), 374–410.

38. See *Lynch v. Donnelly*, 465 U.S. 668 (1984), citing Madison's 1785 "Memorial and Remonstrance"; and *County of Allegheny v. ACLU*, 492 U.S. 573 (1989). I discuss these cases and the concept of endorsement in Nussbaum, *Liberty of Conscience* (New York: Basic Books, 2008), chap. 6.

39. For discussion of both flag and anthem, and the alternative proposals of the Hindu Right, with references, see Nussbaum, *The Clash Within: Democracy, Religious Violence, and India's Future* (Cambridge, MA: Harvard University Press, 2007), chap. 5.

40. See the study of these organizations and their symbols, ibid.

41. Ibid., chap. 4.

DIANE P. WOOD

A LESSON FROM SHAKESPEARE TO THE MODERN JUDGE ON LAW, DISOBEDIENCE, JUSTIFICATION, AND MERCY

One of the oldest tensions in law is the one between adherence to consistent and objective rules applicable to all and recognition of individual variations that justify differing levels of culpability. On the one hand, there is the classic image of Lady Justice, blindfolded and heedless of the wealth, rank, or influence of the people who come before her to be measured in her balance. On the other hand, the law itself at times seems to be the villain. One thinks, for example, of Jean Valjean in *Les Misérables*. Valjean was pursued relentlessly by the unforgiving Inspector Javert for the simple offense of stealing bread and then later stealing a coin from a boy. Victor Hugo's message is clear: it is Javert who is in the wrong, in his blind insistence on enforcing the law to the letter despite the minor nature of Valjean's crimes, their moral setting, and Valjean's transformation into a near-saintly figure.

Both themes—strict adherence to the letter of the law and the willingness to bend when circumstances demand—are woven through Anglo-American law. To a significant degree, this explains why the English developed two parallel institutions for the resolution of civil disputes: the common-law courts and the courts of equity. Over the centuries, the common-law courts came to apply the law in an ever-more-inflexible way. This led to the growth of the chancellor's court of equity, which eventually became a place where executive discretion was at its zenith—both for better and for worse.[1] When the English colonists migrated across the Atlantic Ocean, along with their legal system, these two concepts came along with them. Even today, in some states law and equity continue to be administered in separate courts. The Circuit Court of Cook County, Illinois, for example, has a Chancery Division and a Law Division. In other states and in the federal courts, law and equity have been merged as a formal matter. But the substance of each tradition lives on.

Legal scholars continue to debate whether it is preferable to follow a strict, rule-bound regime or to tailor findings of guilt or responsibility to the particular characteristics of the individual before the court. One prominent modern area in which anyone can watch that debate unfold is sentencing policy. For approximately twenty years before *United States v. Booker* (2005) was decided,[2] criminal sentencing in the United States was governed by strict rules from which deviations were rarely accepted. Now that *Booker* has established that the federal Sentencing Guidelines merely recommend the length of imprisonment, there has been some loss in uniformity of sentencing but an equally predictable gain in the power of judges to make the punishment fit the crime.

What is the responsible judge to do in the face of these competing imperatives? It is easy enough to see that neither blind adherence to inflexible rules nor unfettered discretion is optimal, or even acceptable, in a society that prizes not only adherence to the rule of law but a broader concept of justice. Rigid laws that admit no exceptions can end up condemning people who ought to be excused or punishing them in a disproportionately severe way. But too much equity is no better—at the extreme, discretion would mean the loss of the rule of law itself, and society would be governed by the proverbial chancellor's foot.[3] The trick is how to find the right middle ground. It is here that literature can help a conscientious judge. Literature provides distance from ordinary times and problems; it is free to engage in dramatic exaggeration; and at the same time it can focus on the essential problem and distill what matters from a complex mass of facts. And once one is open to the insights that literature can offer, it is an easy step to turn to Shakespeare.

I

In a number of plays, Shakespeare confronts questions about the law that are as timely today as when he was writing: Are there legitimate ways to avoid the harsh result of a law without undermining its status altogether? What devices do people use to push back against laws that are either too strict or too mushy? Are the solutions that Shakespeare describes still available in principle, or did those possibilities fade from the scene along with Elizabethan styles of dress?

The short answer is that the more things have changed, the more they have stayed the same. It is helpful to begin by looking at devices that judges today use to reach the right balance between adherence to the letter of the law and applications tailored to a particular situation. Three such tools come to mind: prosecutorial discretion, the clemency power, and jury nullification. Each of these finds its counterpart in one or more of Shakespeare's plays. In addition, judges enjoy some interpretive leeway: faced with an ambiguous contract or statute, they strive to avoid absurdities, to implement the intent of the drafters (to the extent that this can be discerned), and to respect broader norms of public policy.

The first-line defense against foolish or inappropriate application of law, as any modern judge knows, is prosecutorial discretion. Prosecutors exercise substantial judgment over whether and how laws are enforced against individuals. They do so for several good reasons. First, pragmatically, no prosecutor's office will ever have the resources needed to pursue every violation of every law; second, even assuming no resource constraints, a prosecutor will not always be able to assemble the evidence needed to convict, and only the prosecutor will know whether her case can be supported; third, as a formal legal matter, courts would be infringing the powers of the executive branch if they micromanaged which cases were brought and how they were pursued.

This is not to say that prosecutorial discretion is absolutely unfettered; it is just to say that judicial review of its exercise is strictly limited. Without a doubt, there have been instances in U.S. history in which prosecutors have based their decisions on impermissible factors, such as race or national origin. One thinks of the prosecutors in early California who enforced laws governing laundries only against Chinese nationals;[4] or racially motivated prosecutions in the old South. The Supreme Court recognized in *United States v. Batchelder* (1979)[5] that a prosecutor's discretion is constrained by the Constitution. Prosecutorial discretion, properly exercised, can counteract unjust laws in numerous ways. Sarah Cox has identified five characteristics of criminal codes that might induce a prosecutor to refrain from bringing charges:[6] overcriminalization (think of how some state prosecutors handle medicinal marijuana use); duplication (coordination about who should punish an offense regularly occurs between state's attorneys and federal prosecutors); moral extremism (think of the almost complete lack of enforcement, prior to *Lawrence v. Texas* [2003],[7] of laws prohibiting adults from engaging in consensual same-sex intimate behavior, or the current lack of enforcement of laws prohibiting adultery); social control (for example, Prohibition or teen curfew laws); and finally, antiquated laws. These are constraints with which judges today are familiar, and they appear regularly in the worlds that Shakespeare created.

A second mechanism by which equity, or individualized justice, intervenes to ameliorate the effect of a law that is either too harsh in general or falls too heavily on a particular person is also within the purview of the executive branch of government. This is the power of executive clemency, which modern U.S. presidents and governors have inherited from the English monarchs. The premise of executive clemency is that leniency or mercy is appropriate in some circumstances. Someone whose sentence has been commuted or whose crime has been pardoned altogether has not been fully vindicated. He has, however, been exempted to a greater or lesser degree from the usual consequences that attend his behavior.[8] Although some scholars date the practice of clemency in England to the 1700s,[9] others attribute the practice to Queen Elizabeth I.[10] One might add that Elizabeth Tudor's vision of clemency appears in some instances to have been considerably stingier than a modern executive's would be—in a grand treason case, "mercy" to her meant that criminals should be permitted to "[h]ang till they were quite dead, before they were cut down and bowelled," rather than suffering dismemberment first.[11] Over time, however, clemency came to include pardoning criminals who were suspected or convicted of a crime.

A different institution is responsible for a third way in which modern American law tempers the harshness of criminal statutes. Once again, however, this institution does not directly involve judicial power. It is the jury—a group of laypersons gathered together to decide one case, and one case only. Juries are the sole deciders of the facts of a case, and their deliberations are entirely secret.[12] Nullification occurs when a jury acquits a defendant because it thinks that it would be unjust to convict even though the evidence indicates that the law has been violated. (This would violate the judge's instructions to the jury; those instructions would tell the jury to acquit only if it concludes that the prosecution failed to present enough evidence to demonstrate beyond a reasonable doubt that the law was violated.) The presiding judge is forbidden to look behind the jury's reasons for the outcome it chose, and so it is normally not possible to say for certain whether a particular jury decided to acquit because it found the evidence insufficient or because it concluded that it would be intolerable to apply the law to that particular defendant. Even if members of the jury reveal after the case is decided that the latter explanation is the correct one, a verdict of acquittal cannot be disturbed.[13] This, too, is a doctrine with a long pedigree. It reached maturity in the late seventeenth century in *Bushnell's Case* (1670).[14] There, the jurors refused to find William Penn or William Mead guilty for disturbing the peace by preaching a Quaker sermon. Dissatisfied with the prospect of an acquittal, the judge tried to force the jurors to return a guilty verdict by leaving them for three days without "meat, drink, fire and tobacco." Later, the jurors were actually imprisoned. In the end, one of the four jurors was granted a writ of habeas corpus. The Court of Common Pleas held that jurors could not be punished for returning a verdict with which the judge disagreed.

American juries have used nullification from the start. They do so even though most judges refrain from telling them that they have this power. Courts do, however, attempt in various ways to restrain the jury's power to nullify. Thus, for example, in the Massachusetts case of *United States v. Luisi*, the court dismissed from the case a juror who was trying to nullify. In contrast, in *United States v. Polizzi*,[15] the district court for the Eastern District of New York upheld the right of juries to nullify (in an opinion running 179 pages!).

II

The problems with which modern courts struggle are not new, nor are they unique to any particular legal system. Shakespeare was acquainted with them, too, and wrote about them in his plays. For a modern judge, the plays thus offer much more than a pleasant excursion into rich language, human passions, and resolution. They present usable lessons about justice and judging. A look at several plays, on their own terms and in light of modern issues, demonstrates where some of those lessons may be found.

THE COMEDY OF ERRORS

The Comedy of Errors opens with a discussion of a draconian law that immediately sets the audience on edge. Solinus, the Duke of Ephesus, tells Egeon, a merchant of Syracuse, in act 1, scene 1, that the law requires that Egeon must die, because he was seen at the Ephesian "marts and fairs" (1.1.16–19).[16] The Duke adds, underscoring the seriousness of the infraction, that he is "not partial to infringe our laws" (1.1.4). He does tell Egeon that if Egeon raises a one-thousand-mark ransom by the end of the day—an alternative to death recognized by the law—his life will be saved, but Egeon does nothing to pursue this option (1.1.18–22, 149–55). This is no surprise to the Duke; he has already remarked to Egeon,

> Thy substance, valued at the highest rate,
> Cannot amount unto a hundred marks;
> Therefore by law thou art condemned to die. (1.1.23–25)

As the play unfolds, the audience is introduced to twin brothers, each named Antipholus, and to their twin servants, each called Dromio. One Antipholus-Dromio pair is from Syracuse, and the other from Ephesus. This sets up all the fun, as the two Antipholuses and Dromios become increasingly mixed up. Much of the play allows the audience to enjoy the confusion.

At last, when in act 5 the audience meets the Lady Abbess, things finally get sorted out. Antipholus of Syracuse and his Dromio have gone into the priory. Adriana, wife of Antipholus of Ephesus, comes and demands to see her husband, but the Abbess refuses, believing that the person who has taken refuge is the one Adriana seeks. Next, Egeon, without the necessary money and resigned to his imminent execution, shows up with the Duke and a headsman. Before proceeding to the execution, however, Adriana asks the Duke to help her persuade the Abbess to send her Antipholus out. The Duke, acknowledging the service that Adriana's husband once gave him, takes charge and promises to "determine this before I stir" (5.1.167). At that moment, Antipholus and Dromio of Ephesus enter from another direction, to everyone's amazement. Egeon recognizes Antipholus as his son and Dromio as his son's long-lost companion. The Abbess returns with the Syracusan Antipholus and Dromio, and we learn that she is actually Emilia, Egeon's wife.

Happy as all these events are, any judge worth her salt would note that none of them affects in the slightest the fact that Egeon was unlawfully near the Ephesian "marts and fairs." Nor has anything in the play suggested that the prohibition against "any Syracusian born / Com[ing] to the bay of Ephesus" (1.1.18–19) is limited to Syracusans who are trying to break the Ephesian monopoly rather than to aged fathers searching for their sons. A modern judge inclined to take into account the purpose of the law before her would realize that the Ephesian law is designed to prevent competition and that this might suggest a narrower interpretation of the phrase than meets the eye. Why else would a monetary fine be a satisfactory substitute for execution? If the fine is high enough, it will deter enterprising Syracusans almost as effectively as death. It appears, therefore, that if the case had come before a court disinclined to exercise any interpretive flexibility, Egeon would be doomed: no money, no life.

Fortunately for Egeon, the Duke decides to exercise executive clemency and exempt Egeon entirely from the force of the law—he neither has to pay the one thousand marks nor be put to death. Antipholus of Ephesus says, "These ducats pawn I for my father here," but the Duke makes it clear that Egeon is fully pardoned, saying, "It shall not need. Thy father hath his life" (5.1.390–91). By taking this step, the Duke has effectively thwarted an application of the law that was never intended by its drafters.

THE TWO GENTLEMEN OF VERONA

The theme of executive clemency also appears in another early comedy, The Two Gentlemen of Verona. In that play, the Duke of Milan banishes one of the "gentlemen" (Valentine) mentioned in the title because the Duke learns that Valentine is about to elope with Silvia, the Duke's daughter (3.1.135–69). The Duke wants Silvia to marry Sir Thurio (whom Silvia finds boring and unattractive). Banishment is no small matter for Valentine (or anyone else). Once banished, if he is later found and taken within the territory, he must die.

In act 4, scene 1, Valentine meets some outlaws on the frontiers of Mantua. In an effort to appear tough, he maintains that he was banished because he

killed a man, whose death I much repent,
But yet I slew him manfully in fight,
Without false vantage or base treachery. (4.1.27–29)

After the others tell him why they were banished, one of the outlaws unaccountably invites Valentine to join the group and

be the captain of us all.
We'll do thee homage and be ruled by thee,
Love thee as our commander and our king. (4.1.65–67)

(This is an offer Valentine could not refuse; another of the outlaws follows the invitation up with the comment, "But if thou scorn our courtesy, thou diest" [4.1.68]). Not surprisingly, Valentine agrees to be their captain.

All is resolved in act 5, scene 4. In the forest Valentine still yearns for Silvia. His friend Proteus (the other "gentleman") approaches and has with him both Silvia and another woman, Julia, who has loved Proteus for some time. Proteus makes an advance on Silvia, who reprimands him for his infidelity to Julia and for making oaths that "Descended into perjury" (5.4.49). Proteus decides to use force on Silvia; Valentine then interposes, and Proteus quickly apologizes for his "Uncivil" behavior (5.4.60). Valentine accepts the apology (Silvia is silent), the lovers are all reconciled, and then the outlaws show up with the Duke and Thurio. Thurio announces that he no longer cares for Silvia—and a lucky thing that is, because the Duke has lost all respect for Thurio and has come to "applaud" Valentine's "spirit" (5.4.140). The Duke then lifts the sentence of banishment that he had pronounced: "Know then, I here forget all former griefs, / Cancel all grudge, repeal thee home again" (5.4.142–43). Valentine pleads for clemency for the rest of the outlaws, and the Duke, underscoring his newfound respect for Valentine, replies, "Thou hast prevailed. I pardon them and thee. / Dispose of them as thou know'st their deserts" (5.4.158–59). It is worth noting that, however deserving Valentine might have been of clemency, there is no reason to think that the rest of the outlaws were equally so. Nevertheless, no one questions the Duke's power to take this action, nor his prerogative to allow Valentine to "dispose of them" as he saw fit. (Similarly, no one questioned President Gerald Ford's power to pardon former president Richard Nixon, or President Bill Clinton's power to pardon Marc Rich, even though both acts were quite controversial.)

It is hard to imagine a modern counterpart to the immediate situation in *The Two Gentlemen of Verona*: after all, in the United States arranged marriages are largely a thing of the past and banishment as a punishment for crime does not exist. But stepping back a pace, it turns out that U.S. courts frequently see a cousin to banishment. This occurs in immigration cases, where a noncitizen of the United States faces removal from the country if she or he has overstayed a limited visa, or has committed certain crimes, or fails to persuade the authorities that asylum is warranted. Interestingly, this is an area in which the statutes confer great discretion on the executive authorities (the attorney general and the secretary of homeland security),[17] and so even if the noncitizen failed to demonstrate an entitlement to stay within the country, the executive authorities are entitled to show mercy and permit her or him to stay. Whom to prosecute for these offenses, how many resources to devote to this area as opposed to others (drugs, violent crime, financial fraud, and so on), and how harsh the terms of removal should be are all issues determined by executive discretion.

A MIDSUMMER NIGHT'S DREAM

A Midsummer Night's Dream is another play set in motion when someone is faced with the grim choice between death and a form of banishment, this time to a nunnery. As the play opens, Hermia is in love with Lysander, but her father Egeus, exerting his patriarchal prerogative, wants her to marry Demetrius, who now apparently wishes to marry Hermia, although he earlier loved Helena (1.1.242–43) (it is not evident, in any case, how important his preferences are in the proposed match with Hermia). Hermia's view, however, is clear: she is firmly opposed to her father's wishes. She asks Theseus, Duke of Athens, to tell her "[t]he worst that may befall me in this case / If I refuse to wed Demetrius." Theseus responds, "Either to die the death or to abjure / Forever the society of men" (1.1.63–66). Exercising her residual right to refuse consent, she proclaims that she will become a nun rather than wed Demetrius (1.1.79–82). She and Lysander then plot to flee Athens and go to a place where they will be permitted to marry. (It is apparently understood that Athens will have no extraterritorial jurisdiction over the lovers once they cross beyond its borders.) Hermia reveals this plan to Helena, who, as Hermia knows, is in love with Demetrius. Helena decides to tell Demetrius about Hermia's elopement, hoping that her revelation will make Demetrius look favorably on her once again, and this sets up the famous night in the forest.

For present purposes, the details of that night do not matter. It is enough to recall that harmony prevails in the end. In the morning, Theseus and Egeus (along with Hippolyta, who is betrothed to Theseus) find the two pairs of lovers about to wake up. Theseus reminds Egeus that this is the day when Hermia must make her choice (4.1.134–35). Lysander confesses that he and Hermia were fleeing "to be gone from Athens, where we might, / Without the peril of the Athenian law," marry. (Laws about marriage still vary from state to state and country to country, and so Lysander and Hermia were on solid ground when they assumed that their status would probably be different once they escaped Athens.) Egeus is unmoved; he asks Theseus for "the law, the law, upon his head," because Lysander and Hermia were trying to thwart him and Demetrius (4.1.151–54). But Demetrius surprises Egeus by saying that although he knew about the elopement plot and followed the lovers, planning to thwart them—miracle of miracles!—sometime during that bewitching night he realized that he no longer loved Hermia; now he loves only his former beloved, Helena (4.1.159–75). After hearing all this, Theseus assumes jurisdiction. Telling Egeus that he "will overbear your will" (4.1.178), Theseus decrees that the two couples shall marry as they wish.

Putting this moment in modern terms, it suggests several things. First, political hierarchy matters. Egeus's "natural" right as a father to dictate his daughter's marriage can be overborne by Theseus's political right as duke. Egeus raises no objection, either because he knows his place or perhaps because he has been influenced by Demetrius's change of heart. Modern law is also full of hierarchy: trial courts must defer to the interpretations of intermediate appellate courts; appellate courts are subordinate to the Supreme Court. Written texts are also unequal: the Constitution sits at the top of the heap, while statutes, treaties, regulations, and interpretive statements trail behind. What we do not know is whether things could have been happily resolved if Theseus had been indifferent to the problem.

THE MERCHANT OF VENICE

The Merchant of Venice illustrates a more legalistic way—which is to say, one more within a judge's control—out of a draconian rule. The pivotal scene occurs in a formal courtroom, and it is legal argument, not executive clemency, that turns the tide. This may not be surprising if one sees the play as a simple tale about a spendthrift who has borrowed too much, a kind friend who overestimates the security of his own assets, and onerous collateral demanded by a lender. The newspapers in recent years have been full of stories of despairing debtors—although they face only financial ruin, not death.

Our spendthrift is Bassanio, a friend of Antonio, the eponymous Merchant of Venice. Bassanio loves Portia, who is identified only as a rich heiress, from "Belmont," with quite a few suitors. Unfortunately, however, Bassanio's profligate ways have caught up with him; he tells Antonio that his "chief care" is to get rid of his debts (1.1.127–28). Antonio is not only his friend but also his biggest creditor. Rather than offering to set up a payment schedule, however,

Bassanio asks Antonio to loan him even more money. This is a good risk, Bassanio suggests, because with those funds he will be able to woo and win Portia (1.1.174–76). Antonio is willing to take the risk; in fact, it is a double risk, because repayment is uncertain and Antonio lacks the immediate funds to loan to Bassanio. Even though all his "fortunes are at sea," he agrees to help Bassanio secure the necessary funds (1.1.177).

Bassanio and Antonio go to the Jewish moneylender Shylock, who agrees to loan Bassanio three thousand ducats for three months, with Antonio as surety. Now comes Shylock's infamous bargain, in which he demands a sealed, notarized bond providing that if Antonio fails to live up to his surety, "the forfeit" will be "an equal pound / Of your fair flesh, to be cut off and taken / In what part of your body pleaseth me" (1.3.142–50). Antonio accepts the deal at face value (1.3.151–52), but Bassanio, fearing a trap, warns Antonio to reject the deal and assures him that he'll manage without the funds (1.3.153–54). Confident that his ships will return with ample treasure, Antonio dismisses Bassanio's fears and seals the bond. At the end of the scene, Bassanio foresees trouble: "I like not fair terms and a villain's mind" (1.3.178).

In Belmont, Bassanio has won Portia's hand, but another friend arrives from Venice and reports that Shylock is insisting on literal enforcement of the bond (3.2.277). Jessica, Shylock's daughter, who has eloped with a Christian and some of Shylock's money and possessions, reports that she heard her father say that

> he would rather have Antonio's flesh
> Than twenty times the value of the sum
> That he did owe him. (3.2.286–88)

Portia offers to pay whatever it takes—double, twelve-fold, twenty times face value—to retire the bond. First, however, Portia agrees that, after she and Bassanio marry, Bassanio should "away to Venice to your friend" (3.2.304). However, Shylock is in no mood to bargain. Whatever Shylock meant when he initially set up the bond of flesh, he is now ready to enforce the promise to the letter. He has arranged for Antonio to be brought to jail, where he calls on the jailer to "look to" this "fool that lent out money gratis" (3.3.1–3). Left with his friend Solanio, Antonio acknowledges that his life is at stake. Solanio cannot believe that the Duke would enforce such a bond, but Antonio indicates that he expects that the Duke is more likely to see the virtue of strict enforcement of the letter of the law, given the importance of commerce to Venice (3.3.24–31).[18]

In the courtroom, the Duke tells Antonio that he is sorry for him and that Shylock is behaving as a "stony adversary, an inhuman wretch," but he gives no hint that this is any reason to override the law (4.1.3–6). Antonio appears resigned to the fact that he is doomed and that "no lawful means can carry me/Out of [Shylock's] envy's reach" (4.1.8–10). (Like litigants today who let their emotions get the better of them, Shylock has rejected all reasonable efforts at settlement—a move that he will come to regret, again like his modern counterparts.) The Duke tries to flatter Shylock by telling him that everyone thinks that he will be merciful at the last minute, but Shylock is unmoved (4.1.36–39). He admits that he has no reason apart from his loathing of Antonio for insisting on strict enforcement, but, he argues, the law cannot bend—a contract is a contract. When Bassanio offers six thousand ducats for the three thousand, Shylock rejects the offer, taking the position that he is under no compulsion to accept late payment. (This answer is not particularly compelling; Shylock was obviously not obligated to accept a late payment, but he nonetheless might well have been willing to accept a 100% return on his money as compensation for the delay.) Still reluctant to refuse publicly to enforce the contract, the Duke tries once more: "How shalt thou hope for mercy, rendering none?" Shylock replies, "What judgment shall I dread, doing no wrong?" (4.1.88–89). He accuses the Venetians of comparable hard-heartedness, speaking of their "purchased slave[s]" and concluding, "I stand for judgment. Answer: shall I have it?" (4.1.90–103). The Duke parries with a procedural move that might help Antonio: he announces that he may "dismiss this court" unless "Bellario, a learnèd doctor, . . . Come here today" (4.1.104–7).

This is when the young Balthasar—Portia in disguise—enters and is allowed to stand in for Bellario. She gives her famous speech urging that the letter of the law be tempered with mercy (4.1.182–203). Notably, the plea is a flop and has no effect on Shylock. The Duke (who may not be as much a scholar of contract law as he should be) believes that he is left with only two options: first, he might adjourn the court and continue to wait for Bellario himself (thus buying some time), or second, he might rule for Shylock. Shylock urges immediate action, crying out, "I crave the law, / The penalty and forfeit of my bond" (4.1.204–5). Bassanio offers again to pay twice, even ten times the sum, and pleads with the Duke to "do a great right, do a little wrong, And curb this cruel devil of his will" (4.1.212–15). The disguised Portia, meanwhile, insists that the law is immutable and that, once ignored, "many an error by the same example will rush into the state" (4.1.218–20). Shylock is thrilled—"a Daniel!" he exults (4.1.221). Then Portia makes her move: she lays a trap for Shylock by insisting even more vehemently than he that the "plain language" of the contract must be honored. She begins to show her hand when she tells Shylock to have a surgeon nearby to stop the bleeding. Finally Portia turns the tables on him and notes that if he sheds so much as a drop of blood—to which the bond did not entitle him—while taking his pound of flesh, then his

> lands and goods
> Are by the laws of Venice confiscate
> Unto the state of Venice. (4.1.307–9)

Now it is Gratiano who praises her wisdom. Shylock, dismayed, asks: "Is that the law?" And Portia replies, "as thou urgest justice, be assured / thou shalt have justice, more than thou desir'st" (4.1.310–14).

At last, too late, Shylock backtracks and tries to accept Bassanio's settlement offer. Bassanio is amenable, but Portia is not. "He hath refused it in open court," she insists (conveniently forgetting her earlier appeal to mercy), and so "he shall have merely justice and his bond" (4.1.336–37). Portia by now will not even allow Shylock to settle for return of the principal. In modern terms, she argues that only the bond is due as a matter of law (that is, the bond has fully substituted for payment of the debt), but that performance on the bond is legally impossible. Her argument depends entirely on an interpretation of the word "flesh" in the bond as meaning only muscle and skin, not the associated blood vessels. A modern court intent on a practical interpretation of words that gave full effect to the intent of the parties—a standard practice in today's contract law—might reject that understanding of the key word.[19] Shylock soon gives up on getting the principal back, but Portia is not finished. She tells him that the laws of Venice provide that if an alien (which Shylock is, since he is a Jew) makes an attempt on the life of any citizen (as Shylock did in trying to enforce the bond against Antonio), the penalty is loss of all of his property, one-half to the victim and one-half to the state, and "the offender's life lies in the mercy / Of the Duke only" (4.1.353–54). Now it is Shylock's turn to need mercy (he protests but does not plead), but he gets precious little. The Duke spares his life but imposes the two forfeitures. Antonio then offers to forgo his half and give it to Lorenzo and Jessica. Rubbing salt in the wound (recall Antonio's happy acknowledgment of regularly spitting on Shylock [1.3.125–26]), he also demands that Shylock convert to Christianity and agree to bequeath his possessions at his death to Jessica and Lorenzo.

In the end, Shylock failed to enforce his bond because he was not as adept a player at the game of hyperstrict contract interpretation as Portia. This simple action to enforce a bond ballooned into something far more complex; modern procedural rules would probably have stood in the way of such a fundamental shift. Whether the final result was a just one for Shylock is a question to which the Elizabethan audience might have had a different answer than a modern one. Matters could have been worse: the Duke might have decided that his life was forfeit. On the other hand, the Duke might have simply sent Shylock home empty-handed based on a finding that the contract was unenforceable; or the Duke might have permitted him to settle for late payment of the three thousand ducats by Bassanio. Portia escalated matters by moving from contract to punishment for attempted murder.

Those engaged in the debate today over the appropriateness of "strict construction" of statutes or documents would do well to study this play. Merchants, like other people, often do not expect that the words they use will be limited to the strictest literal meaning found in a dictionary. Portia's seeming acceptance of Shylock's understanding of his rights under the bond only sets the stage. All right, she seems to say, if we are going to be literal, then there are several additional steps that must be taken. As she pursues this line, the mercy for which she called earlier disappears from consideration. In the end, the only person displaying any sign of mercy is the Duke, who does leave Shylock with his life. The law is shown to be incapable of adjusting to the unusual facts of this case. A city like Venice, built on commerce, must maintain a reputation for strict enforcement of contracts. This external constraint, more than anything, is what prevents even the Duke from adjudicating the case as he might have wanted to.

MEASURE FOR MEASURE

The last and perhaps best example of a play whose plot turns on the injustice that can result from enforcing laws too harshly is *Measure for Measure*. In it, Shakespeare enriches the debate by suggesting that problems lurk on both sides: law can be neither too strict nor too lax. The latter issue is at the fore as the play opens. Duke Vincentio has ruled in Vienna for many years, but he decides to absent himself from the city for while, leaving Angelo in charge. In act 1, scene 3, the Duke admits to Friar Thomas that he has failed to enforce the city's "strict statutes and most biting laws" for some fourteen years, and the result is said to have been a loss of social order (1.3.19–23). The Friar notes that the Duke himself would be better suited than Angelo to fix the problem, but the Duke is set on carrying out his plan. Recognizing that there is some risk, however, the Duke reveals that, disguised as another friar, he will monitor Angelo's actions.

Meanwhile, some of the locals find out that the young man Claudio has been taken to prison and will be beheaded in three days, because he violated the law forbidding lechery and impregnated his fiancée, Juliet. Claudio explains to Lucio that he and Juliet have done no wrong, because the two were betrothed; they lacked only the final formalities of marriage (1.2.142–52). Understandably, he complains that Angelo is enforcing the laws unexpectedly (because they had been ignored for so long) and too rigidly; he speculates that Angelo is trying to build his reputation at Claudio's expense (1.2.162–68). He asks Lucio to go to the cloister and find Claudio's sister Isabella, so that she can plead with Angelo for mercy. He would like her to persuade Angelo that this is not one of the laws that should be revived after years of neglect; instead, he urges that the lechery laws have lost the community's support.

Lucio goes to see Isabella, who, while at the nunnery, is as yet "unsworn" and so may speak to him (1.4.9). He explains the situation—both the substitution of Angelo for the Duke and Claudio's problem (1.4.62–68). Angelo, in short, is planning to make an example of Claudio, for an offense that at most violated the letter of the law but not its spirit (or as judges today might put it, the legislative intent). Lucio asks Isabella to intervene with Angelo, and she agrees to do so.

Isabella arrives with Lucio and pleads for mercy, but Angelo is adamant. Isabella then appeals to religious principles, asking Angelo how it would be if Christ behaved so. Angelo replies, "It is the law, not I, condemn your brother" (2.2.85). She then appeals to equity, wondering whether anyone else has died for Claudio's particular offense—sexual intercourse with someone to whom he is all but married. Angelo is still unmoved; he argues, "The law hath not been dead, though it hath slept/ . . . I show [pity] most of all when I show justice" (2.2.95, 105). His meaning is unclear. Perhaps he is suggesting that he is acting for the good of the greater community when he shows justice, even though the result in Claudio's individual case may seem harsh. Perhaps he means only that he has no personal quarrel with Claudio. Either way, by the end of this scene it appears that Isabella is beginning to make progress, because Angelo tells her to return tomorrow. After she leaves, he confesses to himself that he desires her. When she returns, he offers to spare Claudio, but only on terms that she is bound to abhor: she must give herself to him (and thus violate the same law forbidding lechery that Angelo is so eager to enforce against Claudio).

Angelo's moral weakness is becoming ever more evident. The disguised Duke tells Isabella about Mariana, Angelo's former betrothed, and reveals that Angelo broke his vows to her because of the loss of her dowry and then "pretend[ed] in her discoveries of dishonour" (3.1.228–29). Nonetheless, Angelo continues to present himself as Justice incarnate; there will be no mercy for Claudio. The Duke responds, "If his [Angelo's] own life answer the straitness of his proceeding, it shall become him well; wherein if he chance to fail, he hath sentenced himself" (3.2.249–51). At this point, the Duke arranges to test everyone. He has Isabella pretend that she will keep an assignation with Angelo; in fact, the jilted Mariana will take Isabella's place and seal her own marriage with Angelo. In the fifth act, after some ploys that seem to make the situation worse, leaving Isabella crying for "justice, justice, justice, justice" (5.1.26), the Duke sheds his disguise and returns with Isabella to set matters straight: Claudio escapes execution; Angelo is brought to marry Mariana; and the Duke restores normal political order.

So what lesson can a modern judge take from all of this? There are several. The first is that clemency—here exercised by the Duke—is perhaps the most effective antidote to the unjust law. In addition, the play makes a good case for the idea that literalism can be the enemy of sensible interpretation of the law (this is a somewhat different lesson about literalism than the one found in *The Merchant of Venice*, but it is interesting that the theme reappears). Imagine how much better things would have gone if Angelo had simply refrained from arresting Claudio, given how different his relationship with Juliet was from that of the local whores with their customers. The laws of Vienna forbidding fornication were not addressed to people who behaved like Claudio and Juliet. *Measure for Measure* also illustrates the disruption that can occur as a result of uneven or arbitrary enforcement of the laws. The Duke had let things slide too badly for too long, to the point that, supposedly, people no longer acted as if there were any prohibition at all. And then the pendulum swung abruptly in the opposite direction when Angelo took over. There is no rule of law if legal norms can shift randomly at the whim of the prosecutor. Finally, although this is a point better addressed to legislators than to judges, *Measure for Measure* offers a strong argument against laws that run against human nature. In Lucio's words, "what a ruthless thing is this, . . . for the rebellion of a codpiece to take away the life of a man!" (3.2.111–12). History has not dealt kindly with such laws, whether they be laws prohibiting the consumption of alcoholic beverages, laws attempting to dictate sexual preference, or laws attempting to confine people to certain stations in life.

III

In all these plays, Shakespeare turns a spotlight on the law, and in particular the problem of either a law that is inherently unjust or a law that is susceptible to being applied in an unjust way. This happens more often than one might expect, for the simple reason that fallible human beings cannot foresee the ways in which the words they write might be understood in the future, nor do they have a crystal ball that will reveal new fact patterns. At the time the Fourth Amendment to the Constitution was written, people thought that a "search" involved a direct action—patting down a person, entering a building, or the like. But has a "search" taken place when an airplane is flown over a piece of property?[20] What if the police aim a thermal imaging unit at a house where they believe marijuana is being grown illegally?[21] On a more prosaic level, what is a court to do with a statute that says that "a court of appeals may accept an appeal from an order of a district court [in connection with a remand of a class action to state court] if the application is made . . . not *less than* 7 days after entry of the order."[22] Virtually every court to look at this law realized that Congress did not mean to exclude appeals for seven days and then to permit them forever thereafter. But that is what the law said. Judges had to step back and think about what the law was trying to accomplish, as well as how other laws bore on the subject.

Shakespeare helps the judge in at least two ways. The first is to show how, within the judge's proper sphere, interpretation of a text might proceed. The second is the reminder that once the judge's task is done and the law has been applied, there is one more chance for an appeal to the kind of mercy or clemency that can be dispensed only by the executive authority. Each of the plays discussed here shows that tensions can arise when unanticipated situations are presented, when societies are changing faster than the laws, or when people lose sight of the broader principles undergirding particular laws. Across the centuries, and even jumping from autocracy (or monarchy) to democracy, the problems of legal interpretation have remained startlingly similar. Shakespeare reminds us that literalism offers at best false certainty, often at the price of dictating an unjust result. Sometimes that outcome can be avoided through a broader look at the law in question—a look that takes into account the problem it was designed to solve and the context in which it was meant to operate. Perhaps more often in Shakespeare's time than in ours, that outcome could be avoided only by the action of a wise ruler. The message is, however, that even well-meaning laws can sometimes have unintended or perverse consequences. The task of avoiding such results, while at the same time upholding the rule of law, is not an easy one, but if Shakespeare's dukes could succeed at it, why can't we?

NOTES

1. See George B. Adams, "The Origin of English Equity," *Columbia Law Review* 16, no. 2 (1916): 87–98, at 87, 96–97, who notes that as the common law became rigid, "a new field must be found for the action of the royal prerogative in securing general justice not specially provided for in the ordinary way, for this duty and this function still remained to the king." The chancellor's broad powers, however, were subject to few

constraints and thus were susceptible to arbitrary exercise. This occurred most notably during the chancellorship of Cardinal Wolsey during the early reign of Henry VIII. See W. H. Bryson, ed., *Cases concerning Equity and the Courts of Equity 1550–1660*, vol. 1 (London: Selden Society, 2001), xlii; J. H. Baker, *An Introduction to English Legal History*, 4th ed. (London: Butterworths, 2002), 106–7.

2. *United States v. Booker*, 543 U.S. 220 (2005).

3. See John Selden, *Table Talk of John Selden*, ed. Fredrick Pollock (London: Selden Society, 1927), 43.

4. See *Yick Wo v. Hopkins*, 118 U.S. 356 (1886).

5. *United States v. Batchelder*, 442 U.S. 114 (1979).

6. Sarah J. Cox, "Prosecutorial Discretion: An Overview," *American Criminal Law Review* 13 (1976): 383, 387–89.

7. *Lawrence v. Texas*, 539 U.S. 558, 569–74 (2003).

8. While executive clemency does not necessarily implicate moral blameworthiness, it may from time to time. Consider the case of Arthur Baird, convicted in Indiana for murdering his pregnant wife, his mother, and his father. See *Baird v. Davis*, 388 F.3d 1110 (7th Cir. 2004). Although all of Baird's legal appeals failed, Governor Mitchell E. Daniels Jr. of Indiana commuted his sentence from death to life in prison without parole two days before his scheduled execution. Daniels's reason was straightforward: the record was replete with evidence that Baird was seriously delusional and committed these acts for bizarre reasons. In other words, Baird, though certainly guilty of the murders, was not morally responsible in the same way that a normal person would have been.

9. See, e.g., *Hererra v. Collins*, 506 U.S. 390, 412 (1993), citing W. H. Humbert, *The Pardoning Power of the President* (Washington, DC: American Council on Public Affairs, 1941), 9.

10. Daniel Defoe, *A History of the Clemency of our English Monarchs, from the Reformation down to the Present Time with Some Comparisons* (London, 1717), 3.

11. William Camden, *History of Queen Elizabeth* (London, 1630), 80.

12. Indeed, Federal Rule of Evidence 606(b) provides that "[u]pon an inquiry into the validity of a verdict or indictment, a juror may not testify as to any matter or statement occurring during the course of the jury's deliberations or to the effect of anything upon that or any other juror's mind or emotions as influencing the juror to assent to or dissent from the verdict or indictment or concerning the juror's mental processes in connection therewith." Jurors may testify only about extraneous prejudicial information, improper outside influences, or mistakes on the verdict form. See Fed. R. Evid. 606(b).

13. See U.S. Const. amend. V (Double Jeopardy Clause), which applies not only to federal prosecutions but also to state prosecutions. *Benton v. Maryland*, 395 U.S. 784, 794 (1969).

14. 124 *English Reports*, 1006 (C.P.).

15. *United States v. Luisi*, 568 F.Supp. 2d 106 (D. Mass. 2008); *United States v. Polizzi*, 549 F.Supp. 2d 308 (E.D.N.Y. 2008).

16. All citations to Shakespeare's plays are to *The Compete Works of Shakespeare*, ed. David Bevington, 6th ed. (New York: Longman, 2009).

17. See, e.g., 8 U.S.C. § 1252(a)(2) (barring judicial review of certain decisions made by executive authorities).

18. On strict enforcement in the play, see Charles Fried's essay in this volume.

19. See the remarks of Judge Richard Posner in his essay in this volume.

20. The answer is no. See *Dow Chemical Co. v. United States*, 476 U.S. 227 (1986).

21. The answer is yes. See *Kyllo v. United States*, 533 U.S. 27 (2001).

22. 28 U.S.C. § 1453(a) (2008); later amended by Pub. L. No. 111–16, § 6(2), May 7, 2009, to say "not more than 10 days."

PART V Roundtable

SHAKESPEARE'S LAWS

A JUSTICE, A JUDGE, A PHILOSOPHER, AND AN ENGLISH PROFESSOR

University of Chicago Law School, May 2009

Professor Martha Nussbaum: This conference originated in a seminar on Shakespeare and the law that Richard Posner and I have taught for the past two years, along with Richard Strier of the English Department. We began thinking that the law-and-literature movement had not done anything new lately and seemed in need of a boost. At the same time, Judge Posner's *Law and Literature* is now appearing in a third edition. So we thought it would be good to coordinate this with the conference. We were very lucky to be able to convince Justice Stephen Breyer to be our honored guest, and he selected the three plays from which we performed scenes: *Hamlet*, *Measure for Measure*, and *As You Like It*.

Justice Breyer will say a few words about why he chose those plays and about the origins of his interest in Shakespeare. Then each of us will take a few minutes saying something about our own interest in the plays and how we might connect the plays to law, in the following order: Strier, Posner, Nussbaum, and Breyer. Then we're going to open it to questions from the floor.

So, tell us, why did you choose these three plays?

Justice Stephen Breyer: I liked them. (Laughter.) I'm not an expert on law and literature. I chose *As You Like It* because I love this play. It's about love, and I love Rosalind. When I think about my daughters, I realize that the play embodies a problem that intelligent women have had forever. I happened to see *Siegfried*, the opera, not too long ago; in it there's a wonderful duet between Brünnhilde and Siegfried in which she expresses a problem. The problem is, she says (approximately), "I'm peaceful, I'm happy, leave me alone, but my God there's passion, and I'm going to have to get married." It used to be particularly difficult, for an intelligent woman in particular. "I mean what do I do here, he's going to run my life, oh, but he's so good looking." (Laughter.) But in Shakespeare we have Beatrice and we have Rosalind, and Rosalind hits on the solution. She'll teach the guy. She'll teach him; and I'm a teacher, so I like that. What does it remind me of? *Groundhog Day.* (Laughter.) That's it. You'll do it until you get it right. That is the solution for the intelligent woman.

All right. Now, *Measure for Measure.* Probably it came into my mind because it seems to be about law, but then I'm not certain it's about law because when I read it actually I read the word "measure" as not "measure for measure" but proportion, and all these people are out of proportion. It's a mess. Nobody's doing the right thing. I mean the Duke is leaving, the whole city is poor, they're all running off to brothels, nobody gets married anymore, there are these little illegitimate children running all over. Instead of getting married, Isabella goes to a convent, and, my goodness, the Duke picks somebody who is really just terrible to run this city—Angelo, who can't control himself or anything else. Can law help here? No, not really, but moderation can and proportion can. So I thought there could be a discussion about that.

Why *Hamlet?* Well, why *Hamlet,* that's an absurd question. (Laughter.) But I think you see things differently as you get older and you reread things; each time something appears to you differently. This time I thought that the play was really about two things—and I can say it's "really about" because it isn't my profession to be interpreting Shakespeare, whereas anyone who is in that field as a profession wouldn't dare say what it's "really about." But since I'm an amateur, I can say anything. So I think that what it's about in large part is a certain progression—the progression from "To be or not to be" to "Readiness is all." This reminds me of the progression in Aeschylus's *Oresteia* from the law of revenge to the establishment of formal justice, all of which is dramatized in the story. To return to *Hamlet,* what struck me is at the very end. What does Hamlet want there? He wants Horatio to tell his story. He wants the story. Why? To justify himself? Not necessarily. Maybe to tell what has happened to him, spiritually, in the course of what we have seen in this play. And he says, when Fortinbras comes in, Please, please you tell this story too, for you will repeat it. He says it in much better writing; and then he says silence. (Laughter.) Yeah.

So we know, there is everything in Shakespeare, even law, but those were the reasons that I picked these three plays.

Nussbaum: Okay. Thanks very much. Now, we'll each just say something about the themes in those plays that interested us most. Richard?

Professor Richard Strier: Well, I'm happy to say as, I suppose, the professional in this field, that I think the plays are really about things also. (Laughter.) And I think it's good to think the plays are really about things, because I think that Shakespeare was interested in issues. I mean we have to imagine Shakespeare in composition. Well, what do we know about his means of composition? Every play, with the exception of two, has a narrative or dramatic source for its plot. So here's this guy, he's reading and reading and reading and reading, looking for material. His sources are all sorts of things: classical histories, little trashy novels, other plays, etc. He has to produce two plays a year for a while, and then eventually a little less than one play a year, but he's constantly got to come up with new plays, got to produce scripts, dramatic poems to be performed. So he's reading, reading, reading.

One of the reasons I find the very charming movie *Shakespeare in Love* rather silly is that it shows Shakespeare doing absolutely everything except the one thing we know he did, aside from acting in plays, writing plays, and being involved in lawsuits involving property: reading books. So we have to imagine Shakespeare as reading, reading, reading. Presumably he read more books than he used as sources. So how does he decide, I'm going to write a play on the basis of a little Italian novel and it's going to be *Othello*; or I'm going to write a play on a familiar story like *King Lear* or *Hamlet*; or I'm going to redo some stories about English history? Well, as he was reading promiscuously, I think something caught his attention in the sense that it made him intellectually interested. I think that issues caught his mind, and that he constantly asked himself, What can I see in this story. Obviously he's interested in characters, but he's interested in characters within situations. So this seems to me a good way to approach each of the plays: to ask "What are the issues that interested Shakespeare in this particular story?"

For instance, in *As You Like It*, one of the things that helped me in thinking about how the play might be relevant to this kind of occasion, a conference on Shakespeare and the law, was the little scene that we performed (act 2, scene 7), where the issue of potential violence toward a community that you assume is very alien to you is raised. This scene seems to offer quite an important lesson in not assuming that the unexpected and unofficial is uncivilized. Part of the interest of a scene like this is that the armed and potentially violent interloper is accused not of wickedness but of "incivility."

Here they are, miles from "civilization," in the middle of a forest, and the guy's accused of incivility. The key words and values here are civility, gentleness. It seems to me there's some kind of serious thought here about how social values can appear in places where you might not expect them. I think this has relevance to colonial situations and to all sorts of situations, and I think it's not a stretch to see Shakespeare as interested in it.

Now I want to say something about *Hamlet*, something that again seems relevant to this particular gathering. It seems to me that *Hamlet* is a play very interested in issues of evidence and justification, with the questions of on what basis you can know something and on what basis you are justified in taking a major action on something that you think you know. It seems to me that one of the things that's extremely interesting in the play is that while we know that Hamlet actually gets something right, namely that Claudius did, in fact, kill Hamlet Senior, Hamlet himself never has any good evidence for this (true) belief. He's told about it by an apparition—repeatedly called a "thing"—that claims to be the ghost of his father released from Purgatory. Well, England was a dominantly Protestant country, and Protestants didn't (and don't) believe in Purgatory. So (let's say) two-thirds of the audience was going to be absolutely suspicious, and was going to think this can't be a figure from Purgatory, since there's no such place. Rather, it's a devil—which, of course, Horatio says, and Hamlet comes to consider. Moreover, even if you were a Catholic and believed in Purgatory, people mostly don't come back from Purgatory; they stay there. (Laughter.) And in stories where they do come back, there's only one thing they say. They say "Pray for me so I can get out of here," because Purgatory got more and more hell-like as the Middle Ages progressed. (Laughter.) So if someone's going to come back from Purgatory, they're going to say "Pray for me," not "Go kill somebody." (Laughter.) So Hamlet gets this dubious advice from this dubious "thing." Then, to gather evidence, to check up on the thing, he decides to rely on the bizarre idea, which only somebody who is a humanistically trained scholar would believe, that somehow literature is more powerful than life. He thinks that his uncle, who was perfectly happy to commit a murder, to kill his brother, etc., is somehow or other going to be so moved by a play . . . (Laughter) . . . that because of what he sees in a play, he's going to cough up his guilt. It's completely ridiculous, and the only context in which such a claim appears is Defenses of Literature. (Laughter.)

So Hamlet's been reading Sidney's *Defense of Poetry*, where there's a story about this, and Hamlet believed it. Critics often think this bizarre plan worked—Claudius got upset at the play. But at a crucial point during the play-within-the-play, Hamlet makes a disastrous slip of the tongue and describes the murderer in the play as the nephew rather than the brother of the King. He thereby absolutely confused the experiment, because now we can't know what Claudius has responded to. He might be responding to Hamlet, his nephew, saying he's planning to kill him. So just at the point where Hamlet thinks he's got conclusive evidence, we, as people watching the play, know (or should know) that he doesn't, even though we know that he's right since in the next scene Claudius confesses his guilt—but of course, in a soliloquy, which nobody hears but God and us. So the whole question of evidence and justification is wonderfully rich and vexed in *Hamlet*.

Now, to *Measure for Measure*. It's obviously a play very interested in issues about law and regulation and such. The one piece of it that I want to point to, which is in the scene that we performed, is when Angelo says to Escalus, "What knows the laws / That thieves do pass on thieves?" This is a perfectly intelligible bit of legal formalism: it doesn't matter who's in the jury as long as the court operates properly. It's the system that has to operate. That's all that matters.

I think Shakespeare was very troubled by this view, and while my dear friend Judge Posner thinks that the Sermon on the Mount is one of the silliest utterances ever produced, and only relevant to its immediate apocalyptic context—which in a way, I think, is true—nonetheless that document is something that had an enormous effect on Western culture from the time of its original production onward. It said "Judge not, that ye be not judged." This issue of the corrupt judge, even in the face of a perfectly intelligible legal formalism, really troubled Shakespeare and was, I think, part of the motive for this play. So I'll stop there.

Judge Richard Posner: Actually the comment about the Sermon on the Mount is from one of my favorite nineteenth-century English judges, James Fitzjames Stephen, the uncle of Virginia Woolf. What he said was that the Sermon on the Mount is a pathetic overstatement of duties. That's exactly right. (Laughter.) It's beautiful nonsense, right? It makes sense if you actually think the world is going to end before your next mortgage payment is due. Otherwise not. (Laughter.)

I do want to emphasize one point about the law-and-literature movement, which is that it's a lot more than what we've been doing today and will be doing tomorrow. Here we're focusing on works of literature that have law as their theme, maybe incidental theme, but somehow touch on law, but there are other really interesting aspects of the movement. One is the use of literature and the techniques of literary analysis and criticism to help lawyers and judges do their jobs better. There are very interesting discussions in modern literary criticism of narrative techniques, and that's something that lawyers and judges can, I think, really learn from. There's a very interesting opinion by Justice Souter in a case called *Old Chief*, in which he actually uses—I don't know whether deliberately or not—narrative theory to reach an interesting and, I think, correct result having to do with the laws of evidence.

In addition, there have been attempts—I don't find them terribly convincing, but I think they're very interesting—to use notions of literary interpretation to help in the interpretation of statutes and constitutional provisions. Also there have been efforts to use works of literature which really aren't about law as such to provide a kind of background understanding to problems that lawyers and judges encounter. A very interesting example of this is a novel, probably largely forgotten, by Erich Maria Remarque called *Arch of Triumph*. It's about a German refugee in France on the eve of World War II. I happened to reread it a few months ago, and thought it illuminated the plight of the paperless refugee in a way relevant to the asylum cases that have become a major area of adjudication in my court and the other federal courts of appeal.

Of course, the heaviest emphasis of the law-and-literature movement has been on what we've been doing in this conference, which is exploring legal themes in literary works. I understand why law is such a common theme in literature. It's a ubiquitous institution in societies ancient as well as modern, and trials are dramatic, so they lend themselves to presentation in literature. There is a wide variety of works of literature that have law as their theme, and many wonderful ones. I'll just mention a couple of really good modern books. One is an early novel by Joyce Carol Oates called *Do with Me What You Will*. Another is a novel by William Gaddis called *A Frolic of His Own*. These are terrific books that you might not know. Many others you do know: Stendhal and Kafka and, of course, the Greek tragedies (although I don't really think law is the most interesting aspect of any of these works).

The authors of these works are using law as a foil, as a background; they're playing with the law, changing the law, making up the law—as in a play like *The Merchant of Venice*. I don't think you learn much about the law from such works. What I find more interesting about works of literature about law is that they provide insights into jurisprudence, as distinct from law at the practical level. *Measure for Measure* deals with the perennial problem of the balance between rules, strict rules, and a looser notion of standards, and of concepts of equity that bend strict rules. Angelo, in his speech that you heard a little while ago, articulates a kind of legal formalism, which is quite interesting and actually makes a lot of sense. When he says that he shows pity most of all to persons he doesn't know when he applies strict rules, what he's saying is that there's always a danger that the judge is going to be so moved by the plight of a particular party before him that he'll depart from the rule—a departure that may actually have bad consequences for more people, but since they're people who aren't before the court, they're less salient in his thinking. So even though Angelo's a wicked guy—one of the great things about Shakespeare is that he always gives villains really good lines—you have to say Yeah, to a number of Angelo's sallies. And take the great speech by the bastard Edmund, in *King Lear*. Edmund is a real devil, but when he talks about bastards and aren't they as good as people who aren't, and about the stale bed of a married couple in a society of arranged marriages for aristocrats, he makes great points, though he's still very, very villainous.

In *Hamlet*, the jurisprudential interest—I'm touching on issues that Justice Breyer and Professor Strier were discussing—focuses on revenge, which is a stage in the evolution of law and actually remains important even today. If you ask why victims of crime will cooperate with the police and prosecutors, even though in most cases they have no financial stake in cooperation, revenge is a factor. The support of the death penalty is, I think, mainly motivated by a feeling of revenge, which is very deep in people, really with genetic roots.

In *Hamlet* you have a critique of revenge, and I'm using "critique" in a precise sense. It's not just critical; it's an effort to look at both sides of the problem. I disagree with Professor Strier and I'll explain why. I think Hamlet has two incompatible beliefs. I think he takes the ghost seriously. You have to take a ghost seriously. And it really is the ghost of Hamlet's father, rather than a devil as Hamlet initially fears. I mean just look at him [pointing to Justice Breyer, who played the part of the Ghost in the scene that was performed]. (Laughter.) So there's a duty of revenge laid on him by his father, and that's very understandable because Hamlet can't appeal to the law. Claudius controls the laws of Denmark, and it's when the legal system is ineffectual that the pressure for revenge is really strong. So Hamlet's under a heavy duty. On the other hand, we read in the New Testament that "Vengeance is mine . . . saith the Lord." Now, what exactly that means—whether you can have delegation of the divine vengeance monopoly to human beings—that's a big issue.

The deeper problem with revenge is that it's a self-help system. The victim, or his family, has a duty of revenge, and yet these people are not necessarily well equipped by temperament or experience or skills to be law enforcers, and you see that in *Hamlet*. You have three major revengers. (There's a minor one in the recitation by the players before the play, Pyrrhus, but let's forget Pyrrhus.) You have Hamlet, Laertes, and Fortinbras, and they're very nicely contrasted. Hamlet is too hesitant, too cool, to be a really effective revenger. Laertes is too hot, too impulsive, so he's no good as a revenger either. The mean, the golden mean, is Fortinbras, who is perfectly cast to be a revenger, but the problem is that he is perfectly cast because of his extraordinarily exalted notion of honor, which leads him in the fourth act to be willing to sacrifice an army to capture a few acres of worthless ground. So we see deep problems with both honor as motivation and revenge as implementation.

Although I think *Hamlet* is interesting as a critique of revenge, I don't think that's the greatest interest of the play, which in my opinion is by far Shakespeare's best—and since I'm not a professional literary critic, I'm not required to admire all of Shakespeare's plays. (Laughter.) I think actually they vary a lot in quality. (Laughter.) But *Hamlet* to me is the very best. What makes it great is not the revenge motif, but that it's a great play about relationships, about personality and character, about styles of being in the world. It's about a profoundly dysfunctional family and it also has the great theme of maturation. In a famous essay many years ago, Maynard Mack pointed out that Hamlet undergoes a mysterious but decisive change between the first three acts, which precede his aborted voyage to England, and the last two acts. He's impulsive, immature, in the first three acts, occasionally violent; in the last two acts he seems to be a different personality, fatalistic in a way, accepting of the lack of control that people have over their fates. It's really fantastic.

One of the things I particularly like about *Hamlet*, and this is true in many of Shakespeare's plays, is that it has an almost musical structure; you have the three revenge plots in counterpoint, and for a playwright to be able to handle the three parallel plots without repetition or tedium and somehow intertwine them is remarkable. The plot is full of parallels and ingenious touches and has great dramatic variety. It has the play within the play, it has—what?—seven killings, I think, it has a ghost, it's got everything. As you saw about an hour ago I was killed by stabbing. [Judge Posner played the part of Polonius in the scene that was performed (act 3, scene 4).] And that's foreshadowed in a curious way by what seems a completely idle remark earlier in the play by Polonius, about how he had acted Julius Caesar. It's a funny reference (the rare case in which an actor tells the audience in effect, "This is just a play") to another recently composed play by Shakespeare; but the fact is that Julius Caesar was stabbed to death, and that's what's going to happen to Polonius. That's the kind of ingenious touch that makes *Hamlet* such a charming play.

Let me just explain very, very briefly why I do not agree that there's any doubt about the authenticity of the ghost. I don't think an Elizabethan audience would be bothered by encountering Purgatory, because the play is set in medieval Denmark before the Reformation, so whatever strange religious customs are encountered should not have troubled Shakespeare's audience. But I acknowledge the different take on this issue in William Empson's famous essay on *Hamlet*.

I should say here that I experienced a kind of arrested development in literary appreciation. I was an undergraduate of Yale, an English major in the 50s, when the New Criticism, as it was called, was the dominant style of literary criticism in—well not everywhere (not Chicago) but certainly at Yale. Yale was the hotbed of the New Criticism, and Cleanth Brooks, perhaps the most famous New Critic, was my senior thesis adviser. The basic premise of the New Criticism was that a work of literature should be interpreted in such a way as to make it the best aesthetic object that it can be. It wasn't to be looked to as a source of ideas, a source of ethics, or a source of history. It wasn't to be judged by any of those external criteria. It was to be judged the way you might judge a work of music or an abstract painting. There's a famous crack by T. S. Eliot about Henry James's having had a mind so fine that it could not be violated by an idea. What he meant was that the task of a writer, of an artist, is not making ideas, it's not analysis. If an artist uses ideas, they are tools to make a work of art, and the accuracy, the historicity, the consistency of the ideas is really secondary—unless we're talking about strongly didactic works of literature, which I don't regard Shakespeare as having produced.

It seems to me that if the ghost of Hamlet's father is a fake, a devil, it makes the play rather pointless. It makes Hamlet a terrible dupe. It says, Well, look, this guy Hamlet, he didn't realize there's no Purgatory, so the ghost has to be a devil, and so Hamlet kills, and he dies at the end, all because of a mistake he made. I think it diminishes the play to think of it in those terms, and I use aesthetic rather than historical criteria to evaluate works of literature.

Nussbaum: As a philosopher, I work a lot on the emotions, and I have been working a lot on the role of emotions such as anger, fear, compassion, and disgust in the law. So of course, that's a very good reason to turn to works of literature, because you find very complicated and nuanced and deep explorations of human emotions and how they work. So that is what I'm going to talk about now. I think there are so many other things that are of interest in these plays, but I think *Measure for Measure* and *Hamlet*, which were probably written pretty close to each other in Shakespeare's career, have a similar focus on sexuality as fearful and disgusting, and as a danger to good order and political authority.

In *Measure for Measure*, which was written around the time of a plague in London that actually led to the closing of the theaters for a while in 1603, we see that there's thought to be a link between the sex trade and disease, and between the closing of the sex businesses and the reestablishment of public health and public order. So successful is the fictional regime depicted in the play in making that link, that Claudio—whose crime was to have had intercourse with his own fiancée to whom he would have been married but for some problem about dowry—even he thinks of his own and his fiancée's mutually consensual sexual acts as both dangerous and disgusting. He describes people's sexual desires, including his own, as making them like "rats that raven down their proper bane, / A thirsty evil, and when we drink, we die." Now, that's very striking and it's a classic image of the disgusting.

Now, I think the play—I mean who knows what we can say about Shakespeare's attitude?—but at any rate the play lets us see that the disgust with which people view sexuality is profoundly irrational, and there's no greater risk of getting a disease in the brothel than there is of getting it in the theater. That comparison would have been on people's minds at the time, but unfortunately most people in most times and places, including the present, do not think of risk rationally and weigh costs and benefits. The sex businesses, the bathhouses in New York, and other sex clubs in various places have been closed down with equally flimsy arguments about so-called alleged public health nuisances. If you really were to look at it and ask where is the risk and is it really a bigger risk than some other dangerous things that people engage in, you probably would get a negative answer, but people allow their phobic reactions to sexuality to determine what the law ought to be, and so I think that's a very significant issue for law.

In *Hamlet*, it's the sexual relationship between Gertrude and Claudius that has apparently led to murder and the toppling of legitimate political authority. As numerous critics have remarked about the play, we don't learn much about Gertrude from her own point of view, so to speak. As I thought of playing it as an actress [Professor Nussbaum played the part of Gertrude in act 3, scene 4], I thought that Gertrude is probably not so bad. She probably doesn't know about the murder of her former husband, and she really is enjoying her newfound sexuality with her new husband. She wants to have some fun in life. But of course, that's not the way Hamlet sees her, and I think the scene we played, the "closet" scene, is about Hamlet's view of his mother and of his mother's sexuality.

His view of life in general throughout the play is suffused with images of disgust at the female body in general and, of course, at his mother's body in particular. Janet Adelman in her book on Shakespeare's plays entitled *Suffocating Mothers* has written brilliantly about this, and I recommend that chapter of her book to anyone who wants to follow this theme further. Hamlet finds his mother's sexuality filthy; he uses images of sticky, slimy things and so on, and he feels himself contaminated by the fact that he has been born of such a body. Remember that he tells Ophelia to go to a nunnery so that she won't be a breeder of sinners. Well, this theme interests me a lot, because there has been a long tradition of talking about an allegedly good role for disgust in law. Lord Devlin in the 1950s, and, quite recently, our own University of Chicago colleague Leon Kass, when he was head of the President's Council for Bioethics, have both said that the disgust of an average person is a sufficient reason to make something illegal, even if it causes no harm to others. But by now there's a large psychological literature, an experimental literature on disgust, which really does corroborate what *Hamlet* suggests—namely that people's disgust is quite irrational, and that it often tracks an anxiety that people feel about their own animal nature, their own bodies. And sexuality, women's sexuality in particular, is very often the focus of that anxiety. I think we are given, in the play, reasons—which modern psychology corroborates—to view such disgust with great skepticism, and to think that the disgust of an average person might actually not be a good reason at all to make something illegal.

Of course, people find various themes in the plays, and there are critics who see *Measure for Measure* as a play that focuses on quite different topics, such as Christian mercy, equity, and so on. Those are certainly themes in the play, but I think that the theme of political control over human sexuality is a very important one. In law, I think we can now, in our post-Millean age, articulate—perhaps better than Mill himself did—some reasons why we do not have to follow the tradition of Fitzjames Stephen, who really began this tradition, and of Devlin and Kass, who have continued it. If we understand how disgust operates, and how it is linked with misogyny and also with racism and the subordination of various other groups who are found disgusting, we would probably have some good reasons to mistrust disgust as a guide to law.

Now a word about *As You Like It*. I think it is a very different play from *Measure for Measure*, as Justice Breyer has very nicely brought out. *As You Like It* is a play, interestingly, where the women are free and are not viewed as disgusting by anyone. Adelman remarks on the fact that this only happens when we're outside the city and women somehow transform themselves into boys. It's only then that their bodies escape from the gaze of disgust. But in any case it's a very different play, and the characters are forced outside the legal realm and they're forced to improvise. I think, as they do that, we see a new form of reciprocity emerging. Here, I'll get back to Richard Strier's remarks about civility. The characters discover some important things about how people should treat each other, about common human vulnerability and the importance of responding to basic bodily need—which is a major theme in *King Lear*.

Certainly there was much discussion of basic human need in Elizabethan England, surrounding the poor laws and various other proposals to relieve hunger and misery. So the theme of hunger and the mandate to be gentle and gracious to people who are in need is very nicely treated in the play, and I would see in it the thought that we all have our experiences of need and unhappiness, and we therefore should use that experience to be gentle and compassionate. That's a kind of proto-Rousseauian reflection if you will, on the role that an awareness of our common vulnerability can have; and it is linked to thinking—at least beginning to think—about what laws in the area of distribution and redistribution ought to be. Now, I'll turn it over to Justice Breyer for anything that he wants to say. (Laughter.)

Breyer: Well, as the ghost, I can assure you I was authentic. There was a ghost. (Laughter.) I basically agree with Dick [Posner]—in particular, with what he said about literary works as aesthetic objects. That's why we read them. We can clearly have all kinds of interesting discussions about them, but basically that's what I think of them too. But where I somewhat disagree is that I don't think that to say literary works are "aesthetic objects" means that they don't have ideas; and it doesn't mean that philosophy is irrelevant to them. I like Camus, and one of the reasons why I think Camus is a great novelist is because he speaks to me probingly about morality—and in that sense, he is a moralist. Maybe Conrad is too, though Conrad thinks that he is primarily writing aesthetically. So there: I don't separate morality from aesthetics. In some works, ideas and thought play a larger role than in others, and the morality enters in much more. A Jane Austen novel might be another good example.

[Interpolated here is a relevant comment by Robert Henry, a university president and former federal appellate chief judge, who was not present at the roundtable but sent us a response to Judge Posner's remarks.]

Robert Henry: I think I part company with Judge Posner on his view that "Hamlet is a criticism, but not a rejection, of revenge." He thinks that just to ask the question—"Should this be taken to be Shakespeare's 'position' on revenge?"—is to make a number of mistakes, especially that of projecting the implied moral values in a work of literature onto the author, and that of wanting literature to be edifying or didactic. I don't see that simply asking the question makes any mistakes. Shakespeare certainly had moral values, and he may have wanted to convey them. The fact that he may have offered several views about revenge doesn't make it improper to question whether he is advocating any of them. And, wanting literature to be edifying or didactic doesn't make it so, but neither does denying literature's edifications extinguish them. Putting my point differently (however inelegantly), I doubt that all, or even most storytelling in literature is done for the sake of storytelling. The fact that a philosopher might have a more transparent didactic purpose than a dramatist does not entail the nondidacticism of literature.

Judge Posner also believes that reading *The Merchant of Venice* without preconceptions leaves no doubt that Shylock is a villain. He notes, correctly I believe, that the poet's "detached perspective" is what strikes the modern reader. But perhaps such detachment strikes me harder than it does Judge Posner. I doubt that Shylock is a villain (or at least the only one). It seems to me that he is pushed to his legalistic rage by a remarkable series of events orchestrated mostly by Antonio. The business rivalry is probably fair, but Shylock is spat upon and kicked; his two greatest loves, his daughter and his fortune, are stolen from him while he is leaving his home to meet with Antonio; and one of his most valued possessions, his deceased wife's turquoise ring, is bartered for a monkey. As he leaves the stage, he is denied the mercy Portia urged him to give and, especially when played by a great actor, leaves a tragic and broken figure.

[Here we return to Justice Breyer.]

Breyer: Do I have other disagreements or differences in emphasis with Judge Posner? He says that if the ghost is a fake, then Hamlet is a dupe. I don't think the point was primarily that the ghost is a fake. I think the point is that Hamlet isn't sure; and I think there's very good reason for his not being sure. That's why I claimed once to my wife's nephew, who teaches philosophy, that I've finally found out who Hamlet really is, and he said, "Who?" I said, "Hamlet is a judge." He said, "No, no, Hamlet is a philosophy professor." (Laughter.) I said, "No, I think now he's a law professor." Why? because he's looking for truth. He's looking for truth, and by the time he's pretty sure what the truth is, it doesn't really matter that much any more. And now I see he is a judge. (Laughter.) There we are.

Then the only other thing I could find that I might want to disagree with is Judge Posner's "Goldilocks and the Three Bears" theory of revenge. Do you remember that? He said it's either too hot, too cold or just right. (Laughter.) I don't think I buy into Goldilocks and the three bears, because I do think the three theories of revenge are there, but I think that . . . Well, Fortinbras, who knows? Fortinbras isn't there that much, and maybe it is true that he does try to get revenge. Maybe he was going to conquer all of Denmark; we're not certain. I wouldn't give him permission to enter my kingdom. I wouldn't be sure whether he would keep going or not. And Laertes is rather pathetic and does, in fact, get revenge. Hamlet is not after revenge at the end really, because he's ready. Readiness is everything or, as he says, all.

So I basically agree more than I disagree, and I think the other revengers are there as a counterpoint, but not mathematically. But really I think the interesting thing is, Are the plays speaking to us as judges? No. Well . . . No. (Laughter.) But Dick pointed out the very same thing that I noticed in the scene from *Measure for Measure* that was performed, a thing that was emphasized on the stage by having the law book there. Angelo says of pity in relation to his role as a judge that "I show it most of all when I show justice, / For then I pity those I do not know." As Supreme Court justices, we're speaking to the 300 million Americans who aren't in our courtroom. Wow, how often I've used that line of reasoning, and how often I've justified all kinds of things by it! And there it is, right there in *Measure for Measure*. So now Shakespeare has spoken to me as a judge. But of course, when I read it, I'm not sure Shakespeare knows what to do about this issue any more than I do, because in fact, Angelo, a villain, is the one who said it, so he must be wrong in relying on it. Yes he is correct there; but after all, in the particular case, Claudio didn't do anything wrong. Moreover, in the end, Angelo himself is pardoned; he didn't kill anybody and he didn't even sleep with the wrong person. It was even right not to punish Lucio harshly, since what he did wasn't even slander, so he didn't commit a crime.

The easy cases come out right in *Measure for Measure*, but now let's look at a hard case. What do we do with the brothels? Shakespeare does not seem quite prepared to say, in a world where there are lots of illegitimate children, that brothels should be legalized. But he is prepared to say, Let's not overdo punishment. That's it—let's not overdo it; but legalize, I'm not sure. What happens to Pompey, the bawd? He gets off, but with a warning, Don't come back. So I say yes, the sentiment of a judge is there, in Angelo's speech and in the play, and we don't quite know what to do about that. Don't rely too heavily upon awareness of the 300 million people not in the room, but don't give it up either.

So I say, Thank you, Shakespeare; you have reinforced my instinct as a judge. Where am I overall with Shakespeare? I read George Lyman Kittredge [a literary scholar and editor of Shakespeare] years ago, and I've never gotten beyond him. Kittredge said of Shakespeare, and I can't, unfortunately, quote it exactly, and say it as beautifully as he did, that here is a man who knows every human being, every kind of human being, every different kind of character. He knows what they want, he knows how they think, he knows how they behave; and he expresses every one of those characteristic thoughts, methods of behavior, intuitions, and understandings in ways that they, themselves, couldn't do, though it is them. And he does it all in great poetry.

Nussbaum: Okay. Now, we have probably about fifteen or maybe even twenty minutes for questions.

Strier: Can I just say a word about the dupe business?

Nussbaum: Yes, you can respond, yes.

Strier: Well, first of all, there's no doubt the supernatural "thing" is there, so it's not an illusion, certainly not in the first act, since everyone sees it, including a skeptic. "The spirit that I have seen / May be a devil"—this is Hamlet talking. This is not something that's being made up by the credulous. The question is what does it mean if, let's say, there is at least the possibility, or even maybe a certainty, that "the thing" is a demon, and that, despite the apparent success of "The Mousetrap," Hamlet is acting without sufficient evidence, even though he's right?

It seems to me this is part of what makes the play a tragedy. I agree with Dick that criticism should try to see the maximal possible aesthetic value in a work of art. In my view, with regard to *Hamlet*, adding the element of uncertainty and of the demonic, perhaps even adding the element of mistakenness, intensifies the tragedy and is part of what makes it such a deeply, deeply sad and moving play. Anyhow, I think that the view that I'm suggesting doesn't necessarily harm the aesthetic appreciation of the play.

Posner: That's not my conception of tragedy. (Laughter.) My conception of tragedy . . . (Laughter) . . . is that it deals with insoluble dilemmas, not with some mistake someone makes.

Nussbaum: Okay. A speaker is waiting.

From the floor: Where do you think that Angelo went wrong? Was it his fault that he experiences an overwhelming desire for Isabella?

Posner: I think he had an exaggerated sense of the need to adhere to absolutely strict rules, and the fact that he turns out to be so brittle is his undoing. It's interesting that at the very beginning of the play he doesn't want to be put in charge when the Duke is taking his little vacation. Angelo knows he's a natural number two guy. He doesn't like to make decisions. That's why he retreats behind "the law made me do it" idea. He doesn't want to exercise discretion. You know, what the Duke does is taken right out of Machiavelli's *The Prince*, where Machiavelli recommends that if you want to do something that will be unpopular, you should delegate it to an underling. The underling does the deed; it makes him very unpopular. Then you kill him. (Laughter.)

Nussbaum: I think there are several different places where Angelo goes wrong. Constance Jordan showed very successfully that there was a lot of talk in Shakespeare's period about how you read laws. One position appealed to Aristotle to say that you should read laws in the light of what can rationally be imagined to be what the lawgiver would say about this case if the lawgiver were present. One of the things Angelo does is to read the law so strictly that the case of Claudio falls within it, whereas if the lawgiver were present, he might reasonably be presumed to have read it to make an exception for that case. The second thing is the severity of the sentence, which is, I think, a separate issue. Isabella says, Look, even if he's guilty, you shouldn't punish it with death; you should be more merciful. And then of course, stepping one step back, which is what I wanted to do here, I think there is reason to call into question the whole idea that there should be laws against fornication. The play shows that this is inspired by some sort of fear and by bogus arguments about contagion and so on. Why on earth should a person be punished for sleeping with an adult woman who consents? I think at that level there are issues too.

Okay, other questions? I hope the participants will join in at this point and other faculty. Kenji?

Professor Kenji Yoshino [of New York University]: I have a question inspired by what Justice Breyer said about Rosalind, about loving Rosalind. I want to ask all the panelists which of the characters of the plays you identify with, and why. (Laughter.)

Strier: I will answer this on behalf of Dick. It seemed to me he played the right role in *As You Like It* [Judge Posner played Jaques in act 2, scene 7]. Jaques is acerbic; he's highly intelligent; he knows a lot of what goes on; he's interested in everything; and instead of going back to the court, what's really interesting to him is a man who is living in a cave and has had a sudden conversion. And that, by the way, happens to be Judge Posner's next book. It's about cave people. (Laughter.)

Nussbaum: [To Posner] Do you want to answer this for yourself?

Posner: No. (Laughter.)

Nussbaum: [To Justice Breyer] I liked your example, at the beginning of this discussion, of Rosalind. I've always liked the women in comedies who manage to defy the rules in a successful way. Rosalind has always been one that I've enjoyed. I found Gertrude extremely difficult to play in the closet scene because she gives up everything so quickly, and she kind of breaks down in such a brief time. So the question I had to ask myself is, Why would she do that. I think when somebody you really love says terrible things to you, that's quite different from hearing them from a stranger, so that's how I tried to play it. But I do think that Shakespeare's stronger women are much more appealing.

Posner: I think Martha's sexy Gertrude was very well performed. (Laughter.) But I don't see Gertrude that way. I see Gertrude as maternal, and I think Hamlet's problem was that at the beginning of the play he is a young man who admired his father greatly. His father was the kind of guy that a boy admires greatly. What Hamlet was too young to realize is that his father was not necessarily a delightful husband. He was probably very stiff, and he was always off fighting. On the other hand, we know that Claudius is uxorious. He really loves Gertrude and we know that he's politic and smooth; and he's very much a civilian. He's not going to go off fighting, so he's more satisfactory as a husband. But obviously Hamlet can't understand this, especially since he regards Claudius as a murderer.

This is what I think gets Hamlet so terribly upset about his mother. His mother is a middle-aged woman. Now, it doesn't matter in terms of the sixteenth century whether she's forty or fifty; she's middle-aged from that prospective. Hamlet can't understand why this middle-aged woman is clinging to Claudius and having sex with Claudius. Probably at his age Hamlet thinks that middle-aged women don't have sex unless there's something wrong with them. When he says the heyday in the blood is tame, it's humble, it waits upon the judgment, he's saying, Mom, what are you doing sleeping with this toad. That, I think, is what horrifies him—inappropriate sexual activity by his own mother. It's disturbing and turns him against women in general. I don't think it's the sexual act as such that disgusts him; it's who performs it. It's his mother having sex with his uncle, who is physically loathsome (to Hamlet), and a murderer.

Nussbaum: Does Richard want to answer the identification question?

Strier: One of the things that immediately came into my mind was T. S. Eliot's great, early poem, "The Love Song of J. Alfred Prufrock," in which we have the lines, "No I'm not Prince Hamlet, nor was meant to be." I think there's a kind of egomania in thinking that any of us are likely to be reasonable facsimiles of Hamlet or Rosalind or any of these astonishing, brilliant creatures that Shakespeare created for his leads. My sense would be that maybe I could aspire to Horatio. (Laughter.) He seems like an honorable man. One of the things that Shakespeare does is to give his major characters an astonishing eloquence and also, in some cases (as in that of Hamlet), astonishing other capabilities. This is why Tom Stoppard's play *Rosencrantz and Guildenstern Are Dead* is important. It reminds us that other works of literature find a place for ordinary people, for, that is, people who are just ordinarily eloquent and ordinarily intelligent and ordinarily courageous, ordinarily loyal, but are not Kent or Hamlet or Rosalind. This seems to me quite important. And so, again, Horatio seems to me a rather high goal. But it seems to me that at my best I could perhaps hope to be a loyal friend, to maintain a fairly calm head in a situation which after all is not mine, and could perhaps be persuaded not to commit suicide with my friend and to tell his story, which, as Justice Breyer said, is so extremely important at the end of that play. I guess I think that recognizing how extraordinary the central characters are is important to getting a reasonable sense of ourselves in ordinary human life.

Nussbaum: Okay. We have time for a few more questions.

From the floor: It seems to me that part of the disgust thing, which is also relevant to Hamlet and his mother, involves seeing his mother as on a level with everyone else. And this has to do, in a sense, with class as well, where it seems that the lower classes are seen as base, as not refined. They're more bodily; so Hamlet is very disgusted at seeing his mother as someone "common," rather than as someone particular and defined, and I think Gertrude invites that contrast. In the scene with Isabella and Angelo, what's interesting to me is Shakespeare kind of turns this theme around by having a very refined and uncommon person move Angelo to come to see himself within the universal, as like others in having criminal tendencies. So I wonder what the law is meant to do in relation to the individual. Is it to see that there's a uniqueness about the individual, or is it to see the individual as like everyone else?

Nussbaum: Well, let me just answer about the women. I think Adelman is right that Hamlet's disgust with his mother is the starting point, and that he can't get away from the idea that there's something quite disgusting about having a mother who is sexual. Because of that, he then projects all these disgusting properties onto Ophelia, who is, as far as we know, a perfectly properly behaved young woman. But Hamlet says these terrible things to her about what women are like and what she's like, and I think that's all inspired by the view of his mother and what he really wants. I think Adelman is right about this. If he can make his mother pure again, then he, himself, can be free from the stain that comes of being born of woman. That's what he's trying to do at the end of the closet scene where Hamlet wants Gertrude to just refuse sex with her husband and become a chaste woman again. So I don't know how that fits with your overall question about where we start, but I guess, in terms of my interests, I think that the way that disgust is often irrational is that it often starts from some anxiety that's extremely personal and then projects itself in a global form onto all people of a certain type in a quite irrational way.

Strier: Well, I agree with Professor Nussbaum's general point about how disgust is projected, but I want to say something in mitigation of Hamlet's behavior in the "Get thee to a nunnery" scene. Let's think a bit about the background to this. First of all, Hamlet loved Ophelia, wrote letters to her, and spent time with her. Then Ophelia tells everything about their relationship to her brother, who warns her against Hamlet, and her father, who commands her to stay away from him. So this woman Hamlet loves has been keeping away from him—we don't know for quite how long, but it could have been weeks. Then, the first time he sees her after this hiatus, she says I'm giving you back all the letters you've ever written me, and she does so. Then, the next time he gets to interact with her (when she is pretending to meet him by accident and pretending to read a book of devotion), Hamlet looks up and sees Ophelia's father spying on them and realizes that she has been sent to trap him. And in those circumstances, where he wants his uncle to believe that he (Hamlet) is going insane, he starts to rant. Now, he does show disgust with Ophelia, with sexuality, and with women. But he does have some reason to feel disgusted by Ophelia's behavior and perhaps that of his mother (who does note that her marriage to Claudius has been "overhasty").

From the floor: Could you say more about Hamlet's madness? Other characters in the play note this transformation as well, so I wonder if it's something we're meant to believe. How does this affect our assessment of the Ghost?

Strier: Well, I think it's a fair question. But I think that Shakespeare goes out of his way to make it clear that the "thing" is not an illusion. Horatio, my current hero, is brought in as the skeptic, as someone who says oh, pish-tush, and is completely skeptical, as many Elizabethans were, about ghosts. And he is then completely convinced that the sentinels have indeed seen something. I think we are meant to take the "thing" literally (if not at its word). This is a very different dramatic situation than what we get in *A Midsummer Night's Dream*, where it seems to me that Shakespeare signals to us to allegorize, not to take literally, what we see on stage. I mean the joke about Bottom turning into an ass is like, gee, that's not much of a transformation, the guy was an ass to start with; and the magic potion is from a plant called "Love in Idleness"—hint, hint; and then you get jokes about people being "wood within the wood,"—being mad. Shakespeare is telling us to allegorize, and how. I think that the plays, in cases like this, tell us how to read apparently nonnatural phenomena, and I think that we've got to be alert to how each play is telling us how it wants us to read such.

Breyer: Ah—you've just made me think who I'd like to be. I think I would like to be Owen Glendower, and my reason is that he can summon spirits from the vasty deep. Now, I'm often in dissent and maybe that would help. (Laughter, Applause.)

Strier: The panel of experts said you can summon them, but will they come? (Laughter.)

Posner: That's his problem. (Laughter.)

Breyer: Yes, that's the problem, absolutely.

Posner: But Richard, I don't think you should settle for Horatio. (Laughter.)

Strier: I aspire to Horatio. (Laughter.)

Posner: No, you shouldn't, and the reason you shouldn't is that Horatio's role is to be the straight man. He's Abbott to Hamlet's Costello, and Horatio is *so* straight, he's so dull, a loyal retainer type, a yes man. He highlights by contrast Hamlet's extraordinary personality—his effervescence, his uncontrolled imagination, his wildness. Hamlet would be less vivid if he didn't have this square attending him and trying to keep him a little bit under control.

Nussbaum: Okay, last question.

From the floor: I have a question about a theme that is not too far from what this panel has addressed so far, and that is the theme of music. A couple of months ago I read in the *New York Times* about the appearance of musical lyrics in judicial opinions. More recently, in this panel discussion, I heard Judge Posner referring to a "musical pattern," and Justice Breyer mentions the term "score," and someone else spoke of the "great hits" of the law. So I wanted to ask the panel to address the topic of musical themes in your work, including what you make of Shakespeare's use of music.

Nussbaum: [To Justice Breyer] Would you like to comment on that?

Breyer: Yes. Learned Hand used that image, and I use it quite often. He said that a judge interpreting statutes is like a performer interpreting a musical score. He said that you want to stay true to the statute, and that staying true to the statute is something that can't easily be reduced to a formula, and here I couldn't agree with him more. It can't easily be reduced to a formula any more than being true to the composer's intent can be reduced to a formula for a good performance. So Learned Hand made that analogy, and I've thought of it from time to time. Another more theoretical work that I've found useful on the theme you cite is by Claude Lévi-Strauss, a French anthropologist who has written a lot about the stories of the South American Indian tribes, and who dedicates one of his books to music, because he thinks, as probably the Romans did (I mean in the rhetoric schools), that the form of a cultural production matters a lot. Lévi-Strauss calls one chapter Rondo, and he alludes to the sonata form. I have thought of that awareness of form from time to time. People used to be taught that when they were in law school, and I'm glad I have a passing familiarity with Cicero's account of rhetoric, even though in Latin class I would sometimes read the pony (but don't tell anyone). (Laughter.) But I mean forms, abstract forms, matter a lot. Cicero, you know, says start with an introduction, and then state your theme, and then have an elaboration—just like the sonata—and then the counterargument, and then return to the summation. And yes, I think such awareness helps.

Nussbaum: I'm very interested in the theme of emotional expression in music, and I think it has long been a puzzle for philosophers who work on it, because they think, Well, emotions seem to have some sort of cognitive content, but how can music have cognitive content? But actually, why should we think that it's only language that can have an intelligent structure and expressive power? So that's the issue that interests me: how to think about that issue of the expression of emotion in music and how to track that down in particular musical works.

Strier: One thing that occurs to me to say in general about Shakespeare and music is that music is one of the very few things I can think of that seems to be invariably positive in Shakespeare's plays. I can't think of any negative associations with music. One of my learned colleagues might come up with a case that I haven't thought of, but music does tend to play a very positive symbolic role in the plays.

Nussbaum: Before we adjourn, does any of the panelists have any last remarks?

Posner: Yes. (Laughter.) I've got to get Professor Strier off the Horatio line. (Laughter.) So I'm going to quote a great essay by W. H. Auden in which he summarizes the characters in Hamlet in a couple of sentences. He says Laertes likes to be a dashing man of the world who visits all houses, but don't you touch my sister. Rosencrantz and Guildenstern are yes men; and Horatio is not too bright, though he has read a lot and can repeat it. (Laughter.)

Nussbaum: [To Strier] Do you want to have a last word? (Laughter.)

Strier: My last word is that we're going to come back to our never-ending argument about the "thing" in Hamlet. Horatio speaks out boldly in act 1, scene 4, and tries to stop Hamlet from going to see the thing. He's the one who says "What if it tempts you toward the flood, my lord, / Or to the dreadful summit of the cliff?" He's worried that the thing is demonic and is going to tempt Hamlet to suicide, so in that case he's not a yes man, and he believes the thing might be a demon. (Laughter.)

Nussbaum: I'm going to give the last word to Justice Breyer.

Breyer: My last words would be to say, Thank you for inviting me here, and for this afternoon, and to ask whether, after we have spent time reading these plays of Shakespeare and spent an afternoon discussing them, will it really help us to be better law students or better judges? And I think, well, it just might, it just might. So thank you very much.

(Applause.)

The audio file on which this edited text is based was a production of the University of Chicago Law School (www.law.uchicago.edu).

CONTRIBUTORS

DAVID BEVINGTON is the Phyllis Fay Horton Distinguished Service Professor Emeritus in the Humanities at the University of Chicago. His books include *From "Mankind" to Marlowe* (1962), *Tudor Drama and Politics* (1968), *Action Is Eloquence* (1985), *Shakespeare: The Seven Ages of Human Experience* (2005), *This Wide and Universal Theater: Shakespeare in Performance, Then and Now* (2007), *Shakespeare's Ideas* (2008), *Shakespeare and Biography* (2010), and *Murder Most Foul: Hamlet through the Ages* (2011). He is the editor of *Medieval Drama* (1975), *The Bantam Shakespeare*, and *The Complete Works of Shakespeare* (6th edition, 2009). He is a senior editor of the Revels Student Editions, the Revels Plays, *The Norton Anthology of Renaissance Drama*, and the Cambridge edition of the works of Ben Jonson (2012).

STEPHEN J. BREYER has been an Associate Justice of the Supreme Court of the United States since 1994. He has taught at Harvard Law School and the Kennedy School of Government at Harvard University. His books include *Administrative Law and Regulatory Policy* (with Richard Stewart, 1979; 3rd edition, 1992), *Regulation and Its Reform* (1982), *Breaking the Vicious Circle: Toward Effective Risk Regulation* (1993), *Active Liberty: Interpreting Our Democratic Constitution* (2005), and *Making Our Democracy Work: A Judge's View* (2010). He is also coeditor, with Robert Badinter, of *Judges in Contemporary Democracy: An International Conversation* (2004).

DANIEL BRUDNEY is Professor of Philosophy at the University of Chicago and Associate Faculty at the Divinity School and at the University of Chicago Hospitals' MacLean Center for Clinical Medical Ethics. He writes and teaches in political philosophy, philosophy and literature, bioethics, and philosophy of religion. He is the author of *Marx's Attempt to Leave Philosophy* (Harvard, 1998). His recent work includes "Styles of Self-Absorption," in *The Blackwell Companion to Philosophy of Literature* (2010), "Producing for Others," in *The Philosophy of Recognition* (2010), "Agency and Authenticity: Which Value Grounds Patient Choice?" in *Theoretical Medicine and Bioethics* (2011), and "Nineteenth Century Ideals: Self-Culture and the Religion of Humanity," in *The Cambridge History of 19th Century Philosophy* (2012).

STANLEY CAVELL is the Walter M. Cabot Professor of Aesthetics and the General Theory of Value, emeritus, at Harvard. His work focuses on the intersection of the analytical tradition (Austin and Wittgenstein) with the Continental tradition (Heidegger and Nietzsche), with American philosophy (Emerson and Thoreau), with the arts (Shakespeare, film, opera), and with psychoanalysis. His autobiography, *Little Did I Know*, was published in 2010. His other books include *Must We Mean What We Say?* (1969), *The Senses of Walden* (1972), *The Claim of Reason* (1979), *Pursuits of Happiness* (1981), *Conditions Handsome and Unhandsome* (1990), *A Pitch of Philosophy* (1994), *Contesting Tears* (1996), *Emerson's Transcendental Etudes* (2003), *Disowning Knowledge: In Seven Plays of Shakespeare* (2003), *Cities of Words* (2004), and *Philosophy the Day after Tomorrow* (2005).

BRADIN CORMACK is Professor of English at the University of Chicago and Director of the Nicholson Center for British Studies. He is the author of *A Power to Do Justice: Jurisdiction, English Literature, and the Rise of Common Law, 1509–1625* (2007), coauthor (with Carla Mazzio) of *Book Use, Book Theory* (2005), and coeditor (with Leonard Barkan and Sean Keilen) of *The Forms of Renaissance Thought* (2008). He is working on two books, on Shakespeare and law and on Shakespeare's sonnets and Aristotelian philosophy.

KATHY EDEN is Chavkin Family Professor of English and Professor of Classics at Columbia University. She is the author of *Poetic and Legal Fiction in the Aristotelian Tradition* (1986), *Hermeneutics and the Rhetorical Tradition: Chapters in the Ancient Legacy and Its Humanist Reception* (1997), *Friends Hold All Things in Common: Tradition, Intellectual Property, and the "Adages" of Erasmus* (2001), and *The Renaissance Rediscovery of Intimacy* (2012).

CHARLES FRIED is the Beneficial Professor of Law at Harvard Law School, where he has taught public and private law courses since 1961. His books include *Right and Wrong* (1978), *Contract as Promise: A Theory of Contractual Obligation* (1981), *Saying What the Law Is: The Constitution in the Supreme Court* (2004), *Modern Liberty and the Limits of Government* (2007), and (with Gregory Fried) *Because It Is Wrong: Torture, Privacy, and Presidential Power in the Age of Terror* (2010). He served as Solicitor General of the United States during the second Reagan administration and as an associate justice on the Supreme Judicial Court of Massachusetts from 1995 to 1999.

ROBERT HENRY is President, CEO, and Professor of the Humanities at Oklahoma City University. He has served as Chief Judge of the U.S. Court of Appeals for the Tenth Circuit, Attorney General of Oklahoma, and Dean and Professor of Law at OCU. He chaired the International Judicial Relations Committee of the Judicial Conference of the United States, is a lifetime member of the Uniform Law Commission, and is a member of the American Law Institute and the Council on Foreign Relations. He has published widely on subjects ranging from legislation to literature. Recent law review articles include "A Decent Respect to the Opinions of Mankind Sometimes Requires a Second Look" (*SMU Law Review*, 2009), "Do Judges Think" (*Duke Law Journal*, 2009), and "Overcoming Advocacy" (*Kansas Law Review*, 2009). He is completing a book on Senator Thomas Gore of Oklahoma.

LORNA HUTSON is Berry Professor of English Literature at the University of St. Andrews. Her publications on early modern English literature and law include *Rhetoric and Law in Early Modern Europe*, edited with Victoria Kahn (2001) and *The Invention of Suspicion: Law and Mimesis in Shakespeare and Renaissance Drama* (2007). She is also the author of *The Usurer's Daughter: Male Friendship and Fictions of Women in Sixteenth-Century England* (1994).

CONSTANCE JORDAN, Professor Emeritus of English at Claremont Graduate University, has published widely on topics in Renaissance literature and culture. She is the author of *Renaissance Feminism: Literary Texts and Political Models* (1990) and *Shakespeare's Monarchies: Ruler and Subject in the Romances* (1997). She is coeditor of *The Longman Anthology of British Literature* (1999; 3rd edition, 2006) and, with Karen Cunningham, of

The Law in Shakespeare (2007). Her *Reason and Imagination: The Selected Correspondence of Learned Hand* is published by Oxford University Press (2012).

RICHARD H. MCADAMS is the Bernard D. Meltzer Professor at the University of Chicago Law School. While getting his B.A. in economics from the University of North Carolina at Chapel Hill, he studied Shakespeare under Alan C. Dessen. He has served on the boards of the Annual Review of Law and Social Science and the American Law and Economics Association. His scholarship uses economics to examine a variety of topics, including criminal law. He has published major articles on the entrapment defense, racially selective prosecution, hate crime and hate speech, the economics of status competition and race discrimination, and the interaction of law and social norms. He is currently working on a book entitled "The Expressive Power of Law: Theories and Limits."

MARTHA C. NUSSBAUM is Ernst Freund Distinguished Service Professor of Law and Ethics at the University of Chicago, with appointments in the Law School, the Philosophy Department, and the Divinity School. Her most recent books are *Not for Profit: Why Democracy Needs the Humanities* (2010), *Creating Capabilities: The Human Development Approach* (2011), and *The New Religious Intolerance* (2012).

MARIE THERESA O'CONNOR received her Ph.D. from the English Department at the University of Chicago in 2009. She has taught at Cambridge University and is currently a Lecturer in the English Department at Johns Hopkins University. She is working on a study of how the political and economic discourse generated by King James VI and I's project to unite Scotland and England entered into the plays that Shakespeare composed during the period of the Union debates.

RICHARD A. POSNER is a graduate of Yale College, where he studied English Literature (with Cleanth Brooks, among others), and of Harvard Law School. He is a judge on the U.S. Court of Appeals for the Seventh Circuit and a Senior Lecturer at the University of Chicago Law School, where, until his appointment to the court in 1981, he was a professor specializing in the application of economics to law. He is the author of books on a variety of topics, including *Economic Analysis of Law* (8th edition, 2011), *The Crisis of Capitalist Democracy* (2010), and *Law and Literature* (3rd edition, 2009). *The Quotable Judge Posner: Selections from Twenty-five Years of Judicial Opinions* appeared in 2010.

RICHARD STRIER is the Frank L. Sulzberger Distinguished Service Professor in the English Department and the College at the University of Chicago and associate faculty at the Divinity School. He is the author of *Love Known: Theology and Experience in George Herbert's Poetry* (1983), *Resistant Structures: Particularity, Radicalism, and Renaissance Texts* (1995), and *The Unrepentant Renaissance from Petrarch to Shakespeare to Milton* (2011). His coedited collections include *Religion, Literature, and Politics in Post-Reformation England, 1540–1688* (with Donna B. Hamilton, 1996) and *Writing and Political Engagement in Seventeenth-Century England* (with Derek Hirst, 1999).

DIANE P. WOOD has been a judge on the U.S. Court of Appeals for the Seventh Circuit since 1995. She is also a Senior Lecturer at the University of Chicago Law School, where she was a professor from 1981 until 1995 and Associate Dean from 1989 through 1992. In 1990 she was appointed to the Harold J. and Marion F. Green Professorship in International Legal Studies, the first woman to hold a chair at the Law School. She served as Deputy Assistant Attorney General in the Antitrust Division of the U.S. Department of Justice from 1993 until her court appointment in 1995. She has published widely in journals and law reviews, especially on antitrust law and regulation, and she is coauthor of *Trade Regulation* (6th edition, 2010). She is a Fellow of the American Academy of Arts & Sciences and is on the Council of the American Law Institute.

INDEX